THE WAY
OF RIGHTEOUSNESS

A REVEALING HISTORY &
RECONCILIATION OF JUDAISM,
CHRISTIANITY,
AND ISLAM

WILLIAM JOHN COX

Copyright © 2020 William John Cox

All Rights Reserved.

No part of this publication can be reproduced or transmitted in any form or by any means, electronic or mechanical, without permission in writing from William John Cox, who asserts his moral right to be identified as the author of this work.

Unless otherwise indicated, All quotations from the Gnostic Gospels are from *The Nag Hammadi Library in English*, edited by James M. Robinson; all quotations from the Dead Sea Scrolls are from *The Dead Sea Scrolls in English*, translated by Giza Vermes; all quotations from the Noble Quran are from *The Koran*, translated by N. J. Daywood and edited by Betty Radice; and all quotations from the Holy Bible are from the Revised Standard Version.

Cover painting by Helen Werner Cox

Mindkind Publications
Mindkind.info

By William John Cox

You're Not Stupid! Get the Truth:
A Brief on the Bush Presidency

Mitt Romney and the Mormon Church: Questions

Target Iran:
Drawing Red Lines in the Sand

The Holocaust Case: Defeat of Denial

Transforming America:
A Voters' Bill of Rights

Sam: A Political Philosophy

An Essential History of China:
Why it Matters to Americans

Millennial Math & Physics

The Gift of Mind Series

A Message of Mind:
Hello, We Speak the Truth

The Book of Mindkind:
A Philosophy for the New Millennium

Mind & Its Languages of Reason

Mind: Before & After The Way of Righteousness

The Choices of Mind: Extinction or Evolution?

Table of Contents

Prologue 1
Origin of the Way of Righteousness 21
   Palestine-Israel The Land Bridge Between Africa and Asia 23
   The People of the Land and Those Who Passed Through 27
      An Overview of the People of Palestine-Israel........................28
      Halfway Between The Great Ancient Civilizations of Egypt and Iraq ...29
      Invaders From Syria and Iraq Occupy Israel and Conquer Egypt 31
      The Egyptians Drive Out the Invaders and Israel Becomes an Egyptian Province 32
      David and His Band of Horse Thieves Establish the Little Kingdom of Judah 35
      The Magnificent Kingdom of Israel Outshines Poor Judah 38
      Conquest of the Northern Kingdom of Israel by the Iraqis.................39
      Judah Cooperates With Iraq and Prospers From Israelite Immigration...41
      The Religious Reforms of King Hezekiah of Judah 42
      Judah Rebels and is Crushed by the Iraqis..44
      The Religion of The People...45
      King Josiah, Jeremiah, and a Skilled Staff of Editors Create the Bible ...47
      The Babylonians Destroy the Temple and Deport the People to Iraq....51
      In Exile, Ezekiel Created a Novel Theory of Sin and Redemption 53
      Learning About the Good and Evil of Zoroastrianism From the Iranians 54
      The Iranians Rescue the Jews and Fund the Rebuilding of Their Temple 56
      Ezra, the Priest, Revises the Bible and Seizes Power Over the People ...57

   The Books of the People..60
      The Masoretic Text of the Torah and the Septuagint Greek Translation 61
      The Historical Writings of Josephus Based on the Book of Maccabees...62
      The Dead Sea Scrolls of The Way 63
      The Gnostic Gospels of Mary Magdalene 67
      The Authors and Editors of the New Testament 69
      The Books That Were Not Included in the Old or New Testament 70

The Growth of the Way of Righteousness..................................73

The Hasideans and Zaddiks 75

The Pious Hasideans Oppose the Corrupt High Priests 75
The Greek Syrians Conquer Judah-Israel and Force Hellenization on the People 77
The Righteous Priests of the People Oppose the Corrupt Priesthood....77
The Zaddik and Their Teacher of Righteousness Create the Way of His Heart 78
Daniel Imagined The Angels and Resurrected the Dead.....................81

The Maccabean Revolution Frees the People From the Syrians ...83

Restoration of the Temple by Judas Maccabaeus...............................84
The Hasideans Split Into the Pharisee Party and the Essene (Osim) Congregation..85
Development of a Jewish Missionary Movement Beyond the Land 86

The Priest Kings of the Hasmonean Dynasty 88

Jonathan Establishes the Congregation of Israel 88
Simeon's Covenant With the People...90
The Regrettable Conquest and Forced Conversion of Idumea to Judaism..92
The Growing Political Power of the Pharisee Party as Roman Collaborators 93
The Romans Conquer Judah and Install Antipater the Idumean Over the People...95

The Osim: Followers of the Way of Righteousness 99

Herod Becomes King and Marries Into the Hasmonean Dynasty 109

The Pharisees Extend Their Collaboration With the Romans to Herod....111
Herod Builds Magnificent Palaces and Remodels the Temple............114

The Way Flees Into Jordan and Makes a New Covenant With God 117

How Did the Way Organize its Community?...................................118
What Did the Covenant Believe? 119
Who Were the Opponents of the Congregation?..............................119
How Many Messiahs Did the Way Expect? 120

Gnosis and Sophia (Wisdom)..126

The Bloody Legacy of Herod, Who Murdered His Wives and Children..129

The Way Was the Spiritual Leader of the Zealots 135

Perfecting the Way of Righteousness 137

Setting the Stage for Jesus 139

Jesus and His Nazarite Family 143

The Education and Maturity of Jesus 147

Just Who on Earth Did Jesus Think He Was? 149

John Baptized for the Way 154

Searching for the Truth in the New Testament 159

The Gospel of Yeshua 166

The Crucifixion and Resurrection of Jesus 175

The Salvation of Jesus 182

The Remnant of the Way of Righteousness 185

Jesus's Brother, James the Just, Was the Priestly Messiah 187

James Becomes Bishop of Jesus's Jerusalem Congregation of the Poor 188
Jesus's Congregation of the Poor Followed the Way 189
Paul Throws James Down the Temple Steps Breaking his Legs—James Forgives Him 191
James Was The Righteous Teacher and Priestly Messiah of the Way 193
The Way of Righteous Was the Predominate Practice of Judaism at the Time of Jesus 194
The Judicial Murder of James by the High Priests, the Pharisees, and Herodians 197
Who Was The Wicked Priest and the Spouter of Lies of the Scrolls? ... 201
The Righteous Legacy of James Preserved the Essential Message of Jesus's Gospel 204
Another Brother, Simeon, Succeeds James as Bishop of Jesus's Congregation 206

The War of the Sons of Light Against the Sons of Darkness 209

The Zealot Revolution and the Roman Destruction of the Temple 211

The Revolt of the Last Zealot, Simeon Bar Kochba, is Crushed by the Romans 215

The Righteous Remnant Clings to Jerusalem 217

Hiding the Scrolls of the Way in the Caves by the Dead Sea ...218

The Parting of the Way of Righteousness 221

The Gnostic Way of Mary Magdalene..223

Mary Magdalene, Jesus's Favorite Disciple, Was the Apostle
to the Apostles 224
The Mission of Mary Magdalene 227
Sophia's Spirit of Wisdom is the True Holy Spirit................................229
Gnosticism is the Heart of the Nag Hammadi Codices 231
Jesus's Resurrection: Spirit or Physical Body?......................................235
What If Jesus's God Was a Mother?...237
Is God Really Jealous, or is That Just Another Fable?..........................238
The Roman Christians Gain Political Power and Destroy Gnosticism....240
The Legacy of Gnosticism..241
Saving the Gnostic Codices by Burying Them in a Large Sealed Jar ...242

Jesus Sent His Brother, Joseph, as the Messenger to the Gentiles.....244

Joseph Was a Righteous Lay Minister of the Way in the
Order of Melchizedek 245
The Legacy of Joseph 248

Paul, the Pharisee, Goes Off the Path and Creates His Own Religion...249

Who Was Saul, The Man Who Became Known as Paul?....................249
Paul Sees the Light and Converts to the Way 252
Paul, the Wayward Missionary 255
James Sends Paul on a Mission to His Hometown to Teach
the Gospel of Jesus..255
Paul, Supervised by Jesus's Younger Brother, Joseph, Gets an
Expanded Territory 256
Paul Splits With Joseph and Goes Off on His Own Path 258
The Core of Truth in the Convoluted, Confusing, and
Conflicted Gospel of Paul 265
Was Paul Influenced by Gnosticism? 267
Paul, the Pharisee, Creates the Quick and Easy Justification by Faith...267
Paul, Who Never Met Jesus in Person, Creates the Theory of
a Physical Resurrection to Justify His Apostleship 269
Was Jesus the Son of God, or Was His a Spiritual Ascension?............271
Paul, Who Missed Out on The Last Supper, Creates The
Blood Covenant of the Eucharist 272

Paul's Baptism of the Holy Spirit Eliminates the Wisdom of
Sophia From His Religion 273
Paul's Dispute With James Created Christian Anti-Semitism 274
Paul's Unique Theory of Salvation and Forgiveness of Sin
Eases Access into Heaven 275
What Ever Happened to Paul? 275
The Paulines "Fix the Books" and Create the Gospels 280
Creation of the Roman Catholic Church in the Name of
Peter and Paul 285
The Destruction of Heresy by the Murderous Inquisitions 293
The Repeated Failure of the Christian Crusades Against the
People of Palestine 298
The Pauline Protestant Reformation of the Pauline Catholic Church 301
Fundamentalism is Driving Pauline Christianity Even
Further From The Way 304
Christian Terrorism is as Deadly as Islamic Terrorism 306
The Fraudulent Legacy of Paul 308

The Way of Rabbinic Judaism 310

Escape From Jerusalem and Accommodation With the Romans 312
The Pharisees Write Down Their Oral Torah and Create
Rabbinic Judaism 313
The Golden Age of Judaism Under Islam 315
Maimonides Restores Gnosticism to Judaism 316
The Kabbalah, Spinoza, Luria, and Mendelssohn Rationalize Judaism ... 317
Jewish Accommodation Failed to Prevent Pogroms, Ghettos,
and Political Oppression 320
The Spiritual and Joyous Revival of Hasidic Judaism 322
Reformation, Liberalization, and Reconstruction of Rabbinic Judaism ... 324
Zionism, Nationalism, the Holocaust, and the Palestine Settlement ... 327
Jewish Terrorism Creates the State of Israel 330
The Legacy of Rabbinic Judaism 331

The Righteous Way of Islam 335

Judas Thomas Was the Messenger of the Way to the East 337

Jesus's Twin Brother, Judas Thomas, Was the Third Messiah
of the Way 337
Judas's Message to the East Was the Only Branch of the Way
That Survived 340
Jesus's Congregation of the Poor and The Way Leave Judea-Israel 342
The Way of Righteousness That Judas Thomas Showed to
the Middle East 344
The Kingdoms of The Way in Syria, Ethiopia, and Arabia 347

The Land, People, and Religion of Seventh Century Arabia ...350

Muhammad, the Reluctant Messenger of God 355
    Muhammad Learned About The Way of Righteousness
    From His Relatives...357
    Muhammad Kept His First Gnostic Experience a Secret,
    Except From His Wife 358
    The Spiritual Insights of Muhammad 361
    The First Muslim Converts Surrender to Allah 363
    Suppression by the Authorities and Banning of the Umma 365

Muhammad, the Righteous Reformer 368
    Driven Out of Mecca, Muhammad Removes His
    Congregation to Medina..370
    Muhammad's Respect for the Way of Righteousness and Its Books ...372
    Jihad: Violently Creating a Just and Peaceful Society........................374
    Muhammad and His Muslims Become Desert Pirates to Survive 374
    Muhammad's Victorious Return to Mecca 377

Muhammad's Death and Succession................................. 381
    The Sunni and Shia Split Apart Over Succession—Never to Reunite...382

Islamic Mysticism, The Mahdi, Sufism, and the Druze 387
    Muslims Expect the Imminent Return of the Mahdi (Guide)............389
    Sufism, the Soul of Islam 390
    The Independent and Unitarian Druze 392

Islam, Today and Tomorrow 393
    Political Islam 393
    Islamic Fundamentalism 395
    The Radicalization of Islam and the Terror it Has Produced 397
    Islamic Reformation...402
    Imposition of an Islamic System 403
    Human Rights 404
    The Quran as the Eternal Word of God 406
    The Reformers 408
    The Legacy of Islam 409
    The Miracle of Islam..411

Reconciliation of the Way 413

One God, One Way, One Future 415
    One and the Same God 416
    Free Will..416

| The Manifestation of Mind and its Reach 417
| Agreeing on the True Nature of God 418
| The Soul is Pure Energy Seeking a Place to Rest 422
| Identifying the Nature of Sin and Overcoming Its Stigma.................422
| The Universal Rights of Liberty 423
| When's the Apocalypse? 425
| The Nature of Evil 428
| The Nature of Humans..428

The Way Forward...429

The Children of Salvation 431

A New Children's Crusade 431
The Way to Good Government 432

Epilogue...437

After The Way of Righteousness Was Written........................439

A Year of Political Insanity 439
The Internet and Social Media..442
Defining the Rights of Liberty and Reservation of Consent
to be Governed 443
Publishing Mind & Its Languages of Reason......................................444
Images of the Libraries and Graves of Jesus and His Family,
and the Ruins of Empire 444
The Library and Grave of Jesus 453
The Forgotten Children of Palestine and Israel 454
The Children of the Holocaust 455
The Children of the Nakba 455
The State of Israel 456
The Covenants of A Children's Constitution.....................................456
Choices for the Future 457

Summations 459

A True Story About an Amazing Family 461

The Osim and Their Way of Righteousness 462
The Children of Mary..464
Mary Magdalene, the Companion 466
The Revelation of the Books 467

A Summary Petition to the United Nations..........................469

The Nature of an Abiding Mind 470

Mind 470

- An Abiding Mind 471
- The Moment of Mind 471
- The Death of Life, and The Evolution of Mind 472
- History, Truth, and Lies 473
- War is an Evil Word, Best Forgotten 473
- Self-Awareness..474
- An Unavoidable Warning of Grave Danger 474
- A Strategy For Survival..475
- Creating Happy Tomorrows..476
- The Delicate Balance 476
- What Will Become of the Moments of Our Minds?........................477

The Origin and Power of Mind 479

Sources and Attributions 485

Minnie Irene Oswalt Cox
At age 19
1899-1946

For my Mother,
who has walked with me,
every step of the way.

PROLOGUE

BEFORE
THE WAY OF RIGHTEOUSNESS
WAS WRITTEN

My mother went to the hospital for "female" surgery in January 1946, the month before my fifth birthday. On the day my father left to bring her home, he told my older sisters to clean the house, and they told me to take a nap. When my father returned, I could hear him through the closed door telling my sisters that our mother had died that morning. As I listened to their wails of grief, I began to search through my mind for the sense of what I was hearing. Living on a farm, I had seen death, but it was difficult to comprehend the *meaning* of the fact that my mother was *never* coming home.

I pretended to sleep for the remainder of the day and that night as I lay—alone—seeking answers to my questions. Self-awareness arose within me on that long and sad day, and, although I have now become old and wrinkled, that lost and lonely little boy named Billy Jack remains inside of me, looking out, thinking about the world and we who inhabit it, and telling stories.

My father took me—the youngest of his eight children—to his bed to sleep. He would often read dime western novels at night, and when I became bored with looking at the book covers, he taught me to read.

Cotton farming had been profitable during the war, and electricity had just been extended to the farm supplanting the kerosene lamps we used for lighting. Indoor plumbing was being installed, and our work horses were replaced with a gasoline tractor. Each day, I stood beside my father on the tractor axle clinging to the seat as he plowed the fields of our Texas Panhandle dry land farm, and I washed the red dirt off his feet each evening in a pan of water beside the bed.

My father told me to take a bath one evening, as the principal of our country school was coming to visit. As I lay in the bathtub, I fell asleep listening to them conspire in the next room to enroll me in the first grade that fall—using my father's August birthday instead of my own. Even though I was a year younger than the other students in my class, I already knew how to read and quickly worked my way through the school's small collection of books.

Before *The Way of Righteousness* Was Written

A lonely child, I read everything I could to escape the bleakness of rural life on the semiarid Great Staked Plains, including my father's secret Masonic texts. Following his death and that of my last remaining grandparent when I was ten, I withdrew even further into books and read the Bible several times—searching for a description of God and a purpose for my lonely existence.[1] I found comfort in our small Methodist Church, and I was baptized under the large painting of Jesus praying in the Garden of Gethsemane. I thought about becoming a minister.

Living with my married brothers and sisters, I turned away from the church toward the open road and became a habitual runaway. After stealing my brother-in-law's car and heading for the hill country of Central Texas, I was arrested and declared a ward of the court. Following military school—where I was sent as a condition of probation—I joined the Navy when I was seventeen to see the world. Instead, I served out my enlistment as a medical corpsman at the San Diego Naval Hospital.

I was married, fathered three children, became a police officer, completed community college, and ended my marriage amid a deep emotional depression. My career in the police profession continued as I transferred to the Los Angeles Police Department. Needing a birth certificate for the first time, I discovered my name had never been filled in. I named myself William John.

I attended law school while I wrote the policies and philosophy of the LAPD and the role of the police in America for President Nixon's National Advisory Commission on Criminal Justice Standards and Goals. Following a year in Washington, DC working for the Justice Department implementing national criminal justice standards, I returned to Los Angeles to serve as a Deputy District Attorney.

---

[1] I became the reader in me, who has read thousands of books, but who cannot write. Instead, the reader tells stories about what I see and read. I also became the writer in me, who cannot read, but who listens to the stories told by the reader. Using a very basic vocabulary and limited writing skills, the writer outlines the story told by the reader. The writer prints the paper, and the reader, seeing it all as new, and using a much more expansive reader's vocabulary, adds detail, commentary, and corrections to the outline, which the writer then enters and prints as another revision. The reader reads and corrects the paper, which the writer revises, for as many times as it takes for the two to agree, or for the editor in me, to stop typing, and hit the save button.

Prologue

Living at the beach for several years and enjoying all the freedoms offered by the Seventies, I spent a long, lazy summer considering the direction of my life. As I reflected on everything I had read in the Bible and compared it to what I had learned about life, I regained a belief in the historical Jesus and his essential message—which I had earlier lost.

At about this same time, I began to reread the journals I had kept over the years and realized I had not always been honest with myself. I resolved to discard the evasions and to retain the truth—much of which had been written as poetry. I published the remnants in *A Message of Mind: Hello, We Speak the Truth*, which was my earliest attempt to examine and express the consciousness I experience within my own mind. It is divided into three parts, When, Now, and Then:

To be what you thought,

And I wished I was,

Would be to be,

What I'm not,

Because,

I am what I am,

And not what I'm not,

But,

That's no reason

I can't be what I want.

For,

Not is now,

And then is when,

I will myself change,

Now and then,

Not to be what I'm not,

But to be what I want.

Before *The Way of Righteousness* Was Written

Differentiating between a belief in an historical Jesus, who was loving and forgiving, and the existence of an all-powerful, judgmental God, the book also included this little poem:

> I dreamed of a God in the sky
> One night.
> He was a schoolboy who had
> Erected an experiment
> We call the universe
> On his bedroom desk.
> He was occasionally chastised
> By his father
> For failing to better care for that
> He'd created.
> But, most of the time
> He neither noticed
> Nor remembered.
> I awoke from my dream
> And found
> That I could never again
> Believe in a
> God in the sky.

In writing about Jesus in *A Message of Mind*, I made what I later concluded to be the one error I would have avoided had I greater knowledge at the time. I said, "If only Jesus had learned to write, there wouldn't have been others to confuse his might." I am now convinced that Jesus could not only write, but that he was probably literate in multiple languages.

I considered returning to school to become a minister, but upon further reflection, I was moved to use my professional legal training to act as a lawyer for Jesus. Uncomfortable with a new assignment of having to prosecute juveniles accused of crimes, I made the decision to open a public-interest law practice primarily devoted to the representation of young people and other social, legal, and political matters.

Acting on one such issue, the Christmas holidays of 1979 found me in a small West Jerusalem hotel, where I had a prophetic dream about the children of the Holocaust. I awoke, dressed, and walked in the predawn hours into the Jaffa Gate, along the narrow cobblestone streets of the old city, and out the eastern gate into the Kidron Valley. I walked to where Jesus had spent his last night praying in the Garden of Gethsemane and climbed up the Mount of Olives. There, I sat on a large stone as the sun rose over the hill behind me to shine down on the ancient walled city.

As the sunlight was reflected from the roofs of the synagogues, churches, and mosques in Jerusalem, this powerful thought occurred to me: Just as the same sun shines on all of the roofs, those within all worship the same God, and there are no footnotes, asterisks, or exceptions to the Ten Commandments. (See Photo #1)

I did not immediately understand all my experiences in Jerusalem, but the following year my dream became clear when I undertook legal representation of a child of the Holocaust—Mel Mermelstein, a Jewish survivor of Auschwitz. Having committed myself to defending the interests of Jesus—I did not feel I had a choice when given the task of prosecuting those who denied the murder of so many of his family's children, trashed their memory, and harmed survivors by forcing them to relive their terror.

I filed a civil lawsuit against those who denied that the Nazi genocide of European Jewry ever took place, and I spent the next year exposing the dark side of America's radical rightwing politics. The lead defendant was the powerful figure described by the *New York Times* as "a reclusive behind-the-scenes wizard of the far-right fringe of American politics who used lobbying and publishing to denigrate Jews and other minorities."

The case was resolved favorably in October 1981, when the judge took judicial notice of the fact that "Jews were gassed to death at Auschwitz concentration camp in the summer of 1944." The decision was widely reported, and the case became the subject of the motion picture, *Never Forget*.

Shortly after the verdict, I returned to Israel to investigate some unresolved issues. While there, I was invited to share morning tea with Prime Minister Menachem Begin, who vowed that "never again would Jews be led like sheep to the slaughter."

In comprehending the mindboggling deaths of as many as 80 million people during World War II, the suffering of the little children sometimes gets lost in the magnitude of the horror. In a letter, I attempted to explain why I had undertaken the Holocaust Case; it concluded:

> Recently, I was out at Mel's and he had just received several boxes of artifacts from Auschwitz. As we stood together and looked at the pile of rusty and melted scissors, spoons and forks, and other items taken from the victims and later burned, I saw a small rectangular flat piece of metal which I asked for and he gave me as a gift. It is the musical note bar of a harmonica. The rest of the instrument has been burned away and we will never know whose lips were upon it or the songs it played, but I will forever choose to hear in my mind the happy sounds of singing children, too innocent for such death, rather than the screams of their final agony.

During a trip associated with my prosecution of the Holocaust Case, I visited a bookstore on Fifth Avenue in New York City and purchased a copy of *The Gnostic Gospels* by Elaine Pagels. Dr. Pagels was a member of the team of biblical scholars that produced the English translation of the Nag Hammadi Codices (Gnostic Gospels). I read her book during my late-night flight back to Los Angeles and was excited by the discovery of books about the ministry of Jesus I had been unaware of.

Reading whatever I could find on the subject in bookstores and public libraries, I began to search for other historical information about the ministry of Jesus. *The Messianic Legacy,* by a team of popular writers, mentioned Dr. Robert Eisenman, the Director of the Institute for the Study of Judeo-Christian Origins at the California State University in Long Beach near my home. A scholar of Middle East religions, Dr. Eisenman proposed some interesting, alternative views about the origins of Christianity based upon his study of the Dead Sea Scrolls.

I telephoned Dr. Eisenman and he agreed to meet. It turned out he was aware of my *pro bono* work on The Holocaust Case and asked if I might be interested in a legal matter concerning the Dead Sea Scrolls. He told a remarkable story.

The major scrolls recovered from the first cave at the Dead Sea were quickly published shortly after their discovery in November 1946, but thousands of scroll fragments subsequently discovered had never been published. These were primarily sifted from a thick layer of dust on the floor of Cave Four (that had served as a major library) and were the remains of more than 900 books. Considered by many scholars to be the greatest manuscript find of all times, the suppression of these documents was called "the academic scandal of the twentieth century" by Dr. Géza Vermes.

I was as intrigued by the Dead Sea Scrolls—as I had been about the Gnostic Gospels—and by how these newly discovered ancient documents could help answer questions concerning the true mission of Jesus. I resolved to do everything I could to bring the remaining scrolls to publication and set about to learn all I could about them.

The unpublished fragmentary scrolls were primarily purchased with funds provided by the Jordanian government and were stored at the Rockefeller Museum in East Jerusalem. They had come under the control of Catholic Dominican priests associated with the École Biblique et Archeáologique Francaise de Jérusalem—established in 1890 under the Pontifical Biblical Commission to defend the Catholic faith against the threat posed by developments in historical and archaeological research. The head of the Commission was Cardinal Joseph Ratzinger (later Pope Benedict), who was also the head of the Congregation for the Doctrine of the Faith—previously known

Before *The Way of Righteousness* Was Written

as the Holy Inquisition. Members of the École Biblique operated under the injunction that "At all times the interpreter must cherish a spirit of ready obedience to the Church's teaching authority."

Following the Six Day War in 1967 and the conquest of East Jerusalem (where the Rockefeller Museum is located) by the Israelis, *de facto* ownership of the scroll fragments was claimed by the State of Israel, but the Catholic priests of the École Biblique continued to maintain day-to-day control.

By 1991, the unpublished scroll fragments had remained unavailable to biblical scholars for almost 50 years. As I researched a legal basis for a lawsuit to compel their publication, it was apparent the potential defendants were very powerful—the Vatican, the Israeli government, and the Rockefeller Foundation.

Photographic negatives of the scroll fragments had been deposited for safe keeping at the Hebrew Union College in Cincinnati and the Oxford Centre for Postgraduate Hebrew Studies in England. These photographs were sequestered, and access was denied to scholars. With funds provided by Mrs. Elizabeth Hay Bechtel and a grant from the National Endowment for the Humanities, noted manuscript photographer Robert Schlosser of the Huntington Library in San Marino, California was commissioned and authorized to photograph the scroll fragments in Jerusalem. Upon completion, the new set of almost 1,800 photographs was lodged at the Huntington Library; however, they too were embargoed.

Dr. Eisenman had been active in seeking the release of the suppressed photographs, and he and Dr. James M. Robinson, Chair of the Religion Faculty, Claremont Graduate School, had attempted to publish an unauthorized microfiche set of the Huntington photographs in April 1991 by the scholarly publisher, E.J. Brill in Leiden, the Netherlands. The publisher, however, apparently alarmed about legal threats made by representatives of the Israeli government, cancelled the agreement.

These were the facts I considered as I sought a solution to the problem. There were photographic copies of the suppressed scrolls; however, people were too afraid of litigation to publish them.

One day, as I was driving along the ocean on my way to visit my granddaughter in San Diego, I imagined a way to resolve the dilemma. Under still secret circumstances, I arranged to obtain legal possession of a set of the Huntington Library photographs. Then, acting on behalf of an undisclosed client—whose identity I have never revealed—I signed a contract with the Biblical Archaeology Society (BAS) to publish the images. Under the agreement, Professors Robinson and Eisenman—neither of whom was my client—prepared an index of the photographs and wrote an introduction.

Prior to publication, it was learned that Hershel Shanks, the president of BAS, intended to include a Publisher's Foreword documenting his publicity campaign to "Free the Scrolls." He also planned to attach a 120-line Hebrew-language transcription of a scroll fragment known as 4QMMT, which had been worked on by Elisha Qimron, an Israeli professor. An earlier attempt by a Polish scholar to distribute the same transcription was blocked by the Israel Antiquities Authority under a threat of litigation. It was that risk which had caused Brill to cancel the microfiche edition. Believing that the Foreword was too journalistic for the academic purpose of the proposed book, Robinson, Eisenman, and I objected to its publication; however, Shanks, as the publisher, had the last word, and his Foreword was included.

A Facsimile Edition of the Dead Sea Scrolls in two folio-sized volumes was published in November of 1991. With that publication and the contemporary access to the photographic archive granted by the Huntington Library, the monopoly over the scrolls was broken, and biblical scholars around the world could finally study them.

Alleging that the publication of 4QMMT by Hershel Shanks had caused him a loss of earnings and mental distress, Professor Qimron filed a lawsuit in the Israeli courts in 1992 against the Biblical Archaeology Society and Shanks. As editors, Robinson and Eisenman were also named as defendants. The trial was held in the first week of February 1993 in the District Court of Jerusalem. Attorney Amos Hausner—the son of Gideon Hausner, the prosecutor of Adolph Eichmann—represented Dr. Eisenman.

Amos Hausner wanted me to testify that Professors Eisenman and Robinson had both objected to inclusion of the Publisher's Foreword. Dr. Eisenman provided an airline ticket, and I traveled to Jerusalem and checked into the guest house at Christ Church within the Old City.

It was late in the evening on the final day of the trial, and I was the concluding witness in the case called on behalf of Professors Robinson and Eisenman. The last question to me on cross examination was the identity of my client. I declined to answer. Although I had been testifying in English, the judge and attorneys lapsed into Hebrew—as Professor Qimron's counsel urged the judge to compel me to answer, or to be imprisoned for contempt of court. I was relieved when Judge Dalia Dorner said that the hour was late, and she didn't believe the answer was all that relevant.

Inasmuch as I had just admitted, judicially, that I had contracted for the publication of the *Facsimile Edition*—and since I could be easily served as a defendant as long as I remained in Israel—we decided that it would be best if I caught the next airplane flight out of the country. As can be seen from the footnote, I later returned.[2]

Ultimately, Hershel Shanks and the BAS were forced to pay $40,000 in damages, $60,000 for court costs, plus Qimron's attorney fees.

During the year following the trial—as a matter of personal interest—I researched and wrote a 1,000-page brief on the history of monotheism generally, and the ministry of Jesus specifically. My goal was to access and combine, in one file, the most up-to-date information provided by the Gnostic Gospels, Dead Sea Scrolls, and other ancient manuscripts, along with the latest discoveries in biblical archaeology, to ascertain the basic facts as best they could be determined at the time. I concluded that the Scrolls we published were probably the remains of the library where Jesus actually studied to prepare for his ministry.

The title of the brief, *Mary: Mother of Israel's Messiahs,* was based on an expectation of three different messiahs by the group known as the Way of Righteousness. The conclusion was that Jesus was most likely the Suffering Son of Man Messiah, his brother, James the Just, had been the Priestly Messiah, and his twin brother Judas Thomas—who established a spiritual dynasty of the Way in the Middle East—was the Davidic Leader Messiah. In addition to the roles played by Jesus and his brothers, the brief explored the Gnostic ministry of Mary Magdalene, in identifying her presentation of the Spirit of Wisdom as the true Holy Spirit.

Intriguing as these findings were, I had to get on with my life, so I printed out the brief and placed it on a bookshelf in my study, where it gathered dust.

---

[2] There was a rare and beautiful snowstorm in Jerusalem during the trial, and I resolved to return someday to where I had stayed. On Valentine's Day, February 14, 2000, my wife, Helen and I were married in Christ Church across from the Citadel within the walls of the Old City. She is my best friend, my editor of last resort, the helpmate of my existence, and my spiritual companion in all that awaits us. There is no better place to think and write than in her garden. Helen, a truly gifted artist, says, "Those who can create do not destroy."

Before *The Way of Righteousness* Was Written

A number of books about the Gnostic Gospels, the Dead Sea Scrolls, and new discoveries in biblical archaeology have been written in the 26 years that have now passed, and I have followed these developments with great interest, searching always for the most logical interpretation of the documentary and archaeological evidence.

Historian Neil Asher Silberman published *The Hidden Scrolls: Christianity, Judaism, and the War for the Dead Sea Scrolls* in 1994. In his book, Silberman detailed our efforts to publish the suppressed scrolls and presented a well-balanced interpretation of the community believed to have written the scrolls. In 1996, Dr. Eisenman published *James the Brother of Jesus: The Key to Unlocking the Secrets of Early Christianity and the Dead Sea Scrolls* to both public acclaim and the professional derision of orthodox biblical scholars—whose fundamentalist views he challenged.

Following near death from full body sepsis several years ago, I resolved to bring to publication my writings about the various matters that have occupied my thinking over the years. My memoir, *The Holocaust Case: Defeat of Denial* came out in July 2015, and later that year, I published *The Book of Mindkind* and four other philosophical and political policy books.

In February 2016, I decided to condense my original research manuscript into a book that tells—as accurately and simply as possible—the true story about the original Way of Righteousness and how it inspired Christianity, Rabbinic Judaism, and Islam.

The Way of Righteousness is divided into these parts:

- The Origin of the Way is an essential background about the land of Palestine-Israel, its people, their religion, and the books they produced.

- The Growth of the Way reviews the historical narrative commencing two hundred years before the life of Jesus and examines the social, political, and religious conditions of Palestine-Israel in the period preceding the birth and ministry of Jesus.

- Perfecting the Way examines the essence of Jesus's mission, particularly its Gnostic and Eastern elements, and presents the Gospel of Yeshua.

- The Remnant of the Way documents the aftermath of Jesus's execution and the leadership of the Way by his brothers, James the Just, Simeon, and Joseph.

- The Parting of the Way summarizes the evolution of Jesus's mission into the Gnostic ministry of Mary Magdalene, the Roman Christian church established by Paul, and the creation of Rabbinic Judaism.

- The Righteous Way of Islam examines the origin of Islam and its relationship to the mission of Jesus's twin brother, Judas Thomas, to the East.

- The Reconciliation of the Way reviews what has gone awry during the past 2,000 years—as these interrelated religions have become increasingly fundamentalist and have sought to destroy and eliminate each other. The last chapter identifies the commonality of these religions and searches for the true nature of their shared God, in order to reconcile their beliefs and to reunite their believers.

- The Way Forward describes how the young people of the world can save their future.

- Following the Epilogue are the Summations. These three papers were written after the Epilogue was completed: A True Story About an Amazing Family; A Petition to the United Nations General Assembly, on behalf of the Children of Palestine and Israel; and The Nature of an Abiding Mind.

The Way organizes about 200 brief papers and stories, the titles of which were devised to be read as a summary of the book in the Table of Contents. The Prologue and the Epilogue tell the story about the author, and how *The Way* came to be told.

Now, almost 40 years after first watching the morning sun rise over the Mount of Olives and shine down upon the ancient walled city of Jerusalem, I believe I finally understand the thought that occurred to me as I looked at the rooftops. All those who worship therein believe in the same God, and, upon careful reflection, they should not expect justification for hating, oppressing, or harming others for having a different interpretation of their common belief.

Irrespective of the strength of our own faith, none of us can possibly know for certain whether our own religious belief is valid, until after the light of our physical existence has been extinguished and we can finally see for ourselves if the expectations of our faith are realized.

In all I have done ever since that long summer at the beach during which I resolved to use my legal training to act as Jesus would want me to, including this present work, I have striven to analyze and present the facts I uncovered to the best of my abilities and as fairly as possible. Much like a legal brief, I have tried to let the quoted texts and other evidence speak for themselves, and I have limited my own observations.

It has been a remarkable and interesting journey along the Way, and what is most amazing is what is yet to come. If it could be that I am granted twenty more years in which to live my life to its fullest, then I shall depart from here just before my century expires—well satisfied with the experience, and filled with the love and joy of those with whom I have shared my time in life.

You are one of the 7.5 billion people living in the world today, and *The Way of Righteousness* was written for you—for each one of you. It may not be lengthy enough or include adequate arguments to convince those who are unable to reconsider their religious convictions, but it may give the fair-minded faithful some pause for reflection. *The Way* should have a greater appeal for those—of every faith, or none—who have a genuine curiosity about the past and a thirst for knowledge. The truth is always far more interesting than fiction, no matter how well written or based on the best lies ever told. What one believes, even most earnestly, must always be subject to the test of reality, else the way forward is obstructed by the lies and distortions of the past and present.

The Way was primarily written for Jews, Christians, and Muslims, to help each better understand their own religion and that of the others who seem to be competing—like insecure siblings—for the attention and favor of their common progenitor God. The most rigorous fundamentalists in each of these faiths may reject out of hand, and refuse to read, anything said here that threatens their deeply held beliefs and convictions about God, the origin of the universe, and life here on Earth. Others, however, may find comfort in an understanding of the theological foundation of the religions they practice—that is not in contradiction to the knowledge and science that illuminates the reality of the world we all live in today.

A belief in a caring and nurturing collective consciousness has occupied the thinkers in each of these religions, as they too contemplated the books and science of their times and imagined a spiritual and comforting God of mind. They referred to it by many names in their efforts to describe a peace that comes from an acceptance of reality—no matter how torturous and threatening the times might be—to find the freedom of mind and time to think about how it might be, in an alternative future of peace, harmony, justice, and joy.

An Abiding Mind—an understanding of which is a goal of all who seek self-awareness in life—provides an ethical basis by which to live our daily lives. It encourages us to work for a future in which our children soar through the stars, instead of dying out, with most of other life on Earth, in a great extinction. As a practical matter, this ethical standard can be experienced by simply living a peaceful life of tolerant righteousness—the essence of the Way.

It is not the intent of this book to attack or diminish any religion or practice—it is offered solely to help the believers of every religion to better understand and appreciate their own faith, and to respect that of others. There is value in having a spiritual life in the understanding and acceptance of the perils of life, but there is no justification in denying the essential right of others to practice their own faith in a different manner.

At the core of all religions is the quest for peace and justice to ensure the wellbeing and survival of our children. No other logical or spiritual lesson can be derived—if we look at the essence of our religions, rather than at the exceptions that have been created to justify the horrible crimes, violence, and wars committed and justified for the sake of their God, however defined.

The value in spiritualism is that it helps us to cope with that we seek to comprehend but have not yet the means or knowledge to see and understand. At that point, our faith takes over and helps us to imagine what and who most *reasonably* awaits us over the horizon *and* through the unseen adjoining dimensions that exist side-by-side with, and within us. On a more personal level, a spiritual belief allows us to imagine what, if anything, remains, when we reach the end of our physical lives and discover for ourselves what lies beyond the grave. A sense of spiritualism also helps us to accept our inability to comprehend the unimaginable power of an Abiding Mind—that has been continually learning, expanding, and creating since before time and eternity were first imagined by mind.

Our children are our fount of knowledge—for it is the children, always, everywhere, who learn new things we did not know. The fruit of wisdom is creativity, and its harvest is an Abiding Mind—which is the guide of our consciousness. Gnostics refer to the inner voice as the Spirit of Wisdom, which came to be known in Pauline Christianity as the Holy Spirit.

Especially for young people who are coming of age in this new millennium, *The Way* provides a vision with which to view our accelerating and ever-expanding universe of light, and to see beyond its boundaries, in the endless energy of eternity. Never in human history has there ever been a generation so challenged, as the one being born today, and the millennials, who are now coming of age to confront the realities of this time of common peril. These generations will either lead our society outward to the stars, or else the children of these generations will be among the last to die in the flames of war and atmospheric warming.

It is into the capable hands and intelligent minds of these generations that we are now placing the most terrible weapons of war—which have the power to instantly and totally destroy the vast and wonderful store of human creativity accumulated over tens of thousands of years—or we can empower our young people to travel through the stars searching for warm water planets with large yellow moons to churn their oceans—the cradles of Mindkind and the Way of Righteousness, watched over by an Abiding Mind, speaking as the Spirit of Wisdom.

There are few tomorrows left remaining for this choice to be made. Evolution or Extinction? The moment is upon us.

Before *The Way of Righteousness* Was Written

Abiding Mind,
Surveyor of the Universe,
Timekeeper of Eternity,
Curator of Creativity,
Witness our Works,
Hear our Thoughts,
and
Illuminate our Way
to Knowledge, Wisdom, Justice, Peace, and Joy.

Origin of the Way of Righteousness

Without a basic knowledge of the geophysical nature of the ancient Land of Israel, the people who occupied it, their society and religions, and their books, one cannot possibly understand the foundation of Judaism, the essential message Jesus taught, the prophecies of Muhammad, and how they are all related.

PALESTINE-ISRAEL
THE LAND BRIDGE BETWEEN
AFRICA AND ASIA

Floating on the molten mantle of the earth, the continents slowly drift about the surface on rocky plates that are constantly splitting apart and colliding with each other. The African plate has been creeping along at about two centimeters a year in a northeasterly direction for the past 100 million years, as it slowly slides (subducts) under the Eurasian plate. This movement has caused a separation along the eastern side of the African plate, as the Nubian plate and the Somalian plate break apart—which appears on the surface as the Great Rift Valley. The crack in the earth continues in a northeasterly direction through the Red Sea, up through the Dead Sea (the lowest point on Earth) and the Jordan River Valley through the land we know as Palestine-Israel.

In the same manner that the Red Sea has been formed between Africa and Saudi Arabia, and the Mediterranean Sea between Europe, Asia, and Africa, the Great Rift Valley will be submerged someday under the ocean.

Five million years ago, the Mediterranean was a great, wide valley, which must have been very congenial to life. A breech occurred in the retaining wall at the Strait of Gibraltar allowing the Atlantic Ocean to violently fill the valley. A similar breech occurred on the northeastern end of the Mediterranean Sea at the Bosporus Strait about 7,600 years ago, flooding and expanding the Black Sea—which may be the geophysical basis of the Biblical Great Flood.

Subduction of the African plate has caused the uplift creating the European Alps and the volcanoes of Etna, Stromboli, and Vesuvius in Italy, and the Santorini in Greece. Tectonic activity also pushed up the north-south range of low mountains between the Jordan Valley and the Mediterranean Sea. This highland range includes Mount Carmel, on the northwest adjacent to the Sea, and extends south—beyond where Jerusalem is sited on top of the ridge—into the Negev desert. Along the northeastern side of the mountain range is the Plain of Megiddo (Armageddon), which is located at the western end of the pass through the hills into the Jezreel Valley.

The lower and upper Galilee are to the north of the Jezreel Valley, with another range of highlands separating the coastal plain and the Jordan Valley.

The Jordan River—with its headwaters located near the intersection of Syria, Israel, and Lebanon—flows through the Sea of Galilee, past the ancient city of Jericho, and empties into the Dead Sea. Abundant water flows from springs at Jericho have attracted human habitation for more than 12,000 years.

The deltas of the Nile river and the Tigris-Euphrates rivers are located on approximately the same latitude, and travel between the ancient cultures established at these fertile locations led through the Jordan Valley. One international route was northeast along the coast from Egypt through Gaza up to Megiddo, east through the Jezreel Valley into the Jordan valley, and north past the Sea of Galilee through Hazor towards Anatolia and Mesopotamia. The other, so-called King's Highway was an ancient trade route that extended east from Egypt across the Sinai Peninsula to Aqaba, where it turned north through Petra across the Transjordan plateau to Damascus and on to the Euphrates River.

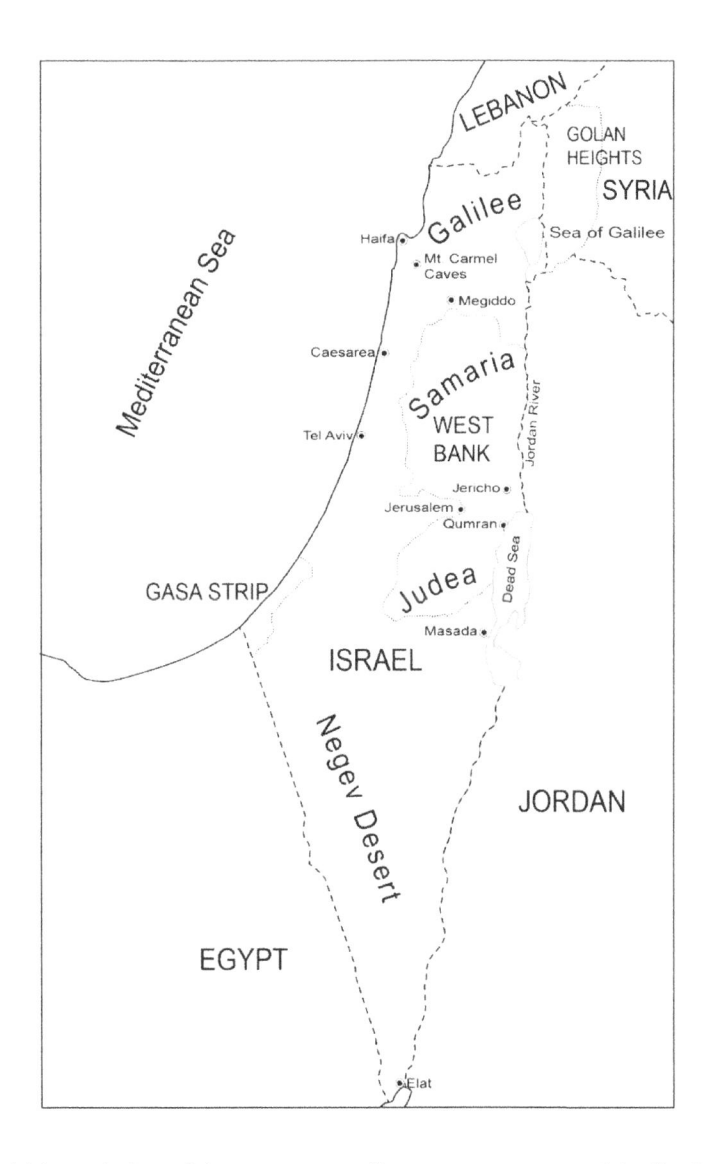

Although Israel is a very small country, geographically, it has areas of significant differences in climate and growing conditions. The southern highland (Judah)—where Jerusalem and Hebron are located—is rocky and surrounded on three sides by rugged terrain, including the Judean and Negev deserts, and suffers from low rainfall. All this isolated Judah from the main trade routes. The highlands open to the north beyond Jerusalem toward Samaria and the Galilee, where greater rainfall and broad valleys allowed the cultivation of olives, grapes, and grain crops.

The modern nation of Israel lies in the historical area of Canaan-Palestine between the Mediterranean Sea and the Jordan River. It is shaped like an arrowhead, with its pointed tip in the south at Elat on the Gulf of Aqaba and extending north 263 miles through the occupied West Bank to the occupied Golan Heights. Consisting of only 8,000 square miles, Israel is slightly larger than the small American state of New Jersey. Excluding the mostly unoccupied Negev desert, Israel is approximately the size of California's Los Angeles County and has a smaller population—by two million people.

THE PEOPLE OF THE LAND AND THOSE WHO PASSED THROUGH

Over millions of years, as the continental plates slowly rubbed together and constantly reformed the surface of the earth, human life arose in Africa. Significant paleoanthropological finds in the Great Rift Valley over the last century and associated scientific dating processes have established a basic outline of human evolution.

Millions of years ago, the progenitor of the Hominidae lineage of apes—gorillas, chimpanzees, bonobos, and humans—evolved in Africa. Around six to seven million years ago, the earth experienced a period of climate change that resulted in East Africa evolving from forests to grassland. One group of apes adapted to the change by developing the ability to walk upright on two legs and to use their arms and hands for carrying food and for making and using stone tools.[3] For several millions of years, undergoing several evolutions as hominids, they successfully spread throughout Africa.

Another climate change around two million years ago caused one lineage of hominids to migrate out of Africa. The Mediterranean Sea had filled by this time, and emigration from Africa was funneled through the Palestine-Israel corridor. Known as *Homo erectus* (upright man), the species migrated into Eurasia. The earliest fossils are dated almost two million years ago, and the species went extinct between 70,000 and 140,000 years ago. *Homo erectus* survived for more than a million years, making good use of hand axes to spread as far east as China and Java and north to Georgia. Evidence of symbolic language, including an elephant tibia inscribed with a series of straight lines and a mussel shell with zigzag lines, is as old as 450,000 years.

Some of the oldest *Homo erectus* sites outside of Africa have been found in the Jordan Rift Valley, which would have served as a life-sustaining gateway into Eurasia and beyond. It remains unclear whether *Homo erectus* is directly ancestral to modern humans; however, there are two additional ancient hominid species—Denisovans and

---

[3] A compelling minority view which holds that humans are descended from aquatic apes was documented by Elaine Morgan in *The Aquatic Ape: A theory of Human Evolution*, (Stein and Day, 1982).

Neanderthals—who do share a common ancestor with modern humans (*Homo sapiens*) and the genes of whom are found in human DNA. The migration of these two species out of Africa appear to have occurred earlier than that of humans. Denisovan remains are found mostly in the East, as far as China and Java, and Neanderthal finds are primarily located in Europe. There is DNA and paleoanthropological evidence that *Homo sapiens*, Denisovans, and Neanderthals coexisted in Siberia.

Anatomically resembling modern humans, *Homo sapiens* first emerged on the scene in Africa sometime between 400,000 and 200,000 years ago. DNA evidence has proven we are all related to a single African woman and her family, and that we migrated out of Africa to occupy all the earth.

Four caves located on the west face of the Mount Carmel range have provided protection during a 500,000-year period of human evolution. The caves are unique in demonstrating the coexistence of Neanderthals and anatomically modern humans between 100,000 and 40,000 years ago. (See Photo #2)

With the eventual extinction of Neanderthals just before and during the last glacial epoch—26,000 to 13,300 years ago—humans were engaged in exploring their earthly garden. The oceans were lower, and the seashores were not those of today—there was much more land and were far more islands. What we see as deserts today were then lush forests and grasslands which nourished great animals—one of which could feed a family for a winter—and gentle creatures such as goats and sheep that could be tamed and herded.

An Overview of the People of Palestine-Israel

Let us once again rise into the sky to look down on this crossroad, as it settled into its current geological configuration, and view the people who came to populate the land from time to time. At first, the people mostly passed through, but there were areas where springs and lush valleys invited longer stays.

As humans began to grow crops and herd animals, they settled the most fruitful places, rather than in the most defensible locations. These settlements continue to be discovered, and at the lowest levels of archeological digs, there is little evidence of warfare and burning. It is only later that defensive walls are found—the oldest discovered thus far having been built around 9400 BCE (Before Common Era) at Jericho in the Jordan Valley. (See Photo #3)

Who are the people of Israel? They are a combination of all those who came and went over the millennia since Jericho was first settled. The blood of those who live there today and call themselves Jews, is mostly Iraqi and Syrian, with Egyptian mixed in, as it was these civilizations that first settled in the land in real numbers, and it was they who primarily dominated the land and those who clung to it through thousands of years of conquest and occupation.

Who are the Jews who live in Israel today? They are an admixture of all the cultures where they have lived and survived during the last 2,000 years—after most were killed or enslaved by the Romans in the wars that immediately followed the lifetime of Jesus. The Israeli blood contains that ancient remnant, but it has become comingled with those in Eastern Europe who converted to Judaism, and with Gentiles who married Jewish people.

A DNA analysis done today shows that the Palestinian people—those who remained after most were slaughtered by the Romans—are much closer to the returning Israelis, than to their Arab neighbors on every side. Of anyone, it is probably true that the Palestinians and Samaritans are the people most closely connected to the ancient land of Israel.

Halfway Between The Great Ancient Civilizations of Egypt and Iraq

The land of Palestine-Israel lies at the intersection between two of the most ancient advanced civilizations on earth—Egypt and Iraq—both of which emerged at about the same time. The society that evolved in the land of Israel between the Mediterranean Sea and the Jordan River is inextricably connected with both civilizations.

A Neolithic culture originated in the Nile Valley around 6000 BCE, and the earliest evidence of the Egyptian hieroglyphic language has been found on pottery dated about 3200 BCE. Upper and lower Egypt were unified around 3150 BCE, and the kingdom was ruled by a series of dynasties for the next 3,000 years. The monumental pyramids at Giza were constructed during the Old Kingdom, which lasted between 2686 and 2181 BCE.

The Egyptian civilization reached the greatest extent of its geographical and political dominance during the New Kingdom between 1549 and 1069 BCE. It was during this later period that Egypt was ruled by Akhenaten (who sought to impose a new monotheistic religion on his kingdom) and the Nineteenth Dynasty founded by Rameses, which contended with the Hittite Empire for control of the Middle East. The Hittites came out of the Anatolian area of Turkey driving chariots and wielding iron weapons.

In the East, settlements along the Tigris and Euphrates Rivers evolved as farmers perfected irrigation agriculture as early as 5300 BCE. Products and commodities were traded, advanced city-states developed along the rivers, and dynastic rule was established around 2900 BCE. The earliest written records, known as cuneiform—consisting of impressions made in clay tablets with a stylus—evolved at about the same time, and syllabic writing commenced around 2700 BCE.

One of the first extensions of the Iraqi empire took place between 2047 and 1940 BCE. The empire was centered on Ur in southern Mesopotamia, and it was during this period that the Great Ziggurat of Ur was constructed. As invasions and migrations continued to take place, the primary language of Iraq became Semitic.

Named for Noah's son, Shem[4], derivatives of the Semitic language, including Arabic and Hebrew, are presently spoken in Iraq, Syria, Palestine-Israel, Saudi Arabia, Yemen, and Somalia. A key to their translation was discovered in 1835 when identical inscriptions in three languages—Old Persian, Elamite, and Akkadian—were found high on a cliff in Persia. Since Akkadian is a Semitic language, it was possible to decipher a Hebrew translation of the other languages.

---

[4] Starting a family when he was already 500 years old, according to the Biblical fable, Noah fathered three sons, the middle of whom was named Shem—which means "name." Shem was the father of the Sons of Eber, which is the root word for "Hebrew." Shem was blessed by his father over his brothers and supposedly lived for 600 years. The biblical patriarch Abraham descended from Shem. (Genesis 7-14)

Invaders From Syria and Iraq Occupy Israel and Conquer Egypt

The Old Testament story tells how the patriarch Abraham wandered from Ur (Iraq), through Syria into Canaan (Palestine-Israel), which is the earliest recorded historical name for the land between the Mediterranean Sea and the Jordan River. Egyptian records refer to the area as *Ka-na-na*.

According to Genesis (14:16-20), when Abraham sought sanctuary in the area of Jerusalem, following his raid into Canaan to rescue his nephew, Abraham was welcomed by the King of Salem (Jerusalem), Melchizedek (My King is Righteousness), who was a priest of "God Most High."

Melchizedek blessed Abraham, who gave the king a tenth of the goods he had seized during the raid. Abraham then experienced a vision in which God appeared and predicted that his descendants would be as many as the stars. Abraham believed God, "and he reckoned it to him as *righteousness*." (Emphasis added.)

God then made a covenant with Abraham giving his descendants the land of Israel (15:18-21). When Abraham was 99 years old, God appeared to him and named him the "father of a multitude of nations" (17:3), and, in a later appearance, God confirmed that Abraham shall "become a great and mighty nation," but commanded that Abraham "charge his children and his household after him to *keep the way of the* LORD *by doing righteousness and justice....*" (Emphasis added) (18:18-19).

Here it all begins. The biblical covenant of Abraham, as he sought to sojourn in the ancient Land of Israel, was and is conditional upon Abraham, and his descendants, following the Way of Righteousness. This is the essence of our shared spiritual heritage.

From history, we know that at some point in time Semitic people from the areas of Iraq and Syria migrated into Canaan. The exact place of their origin is unknown, but in addition to the advanced civilizations of Iraq, there were competing high civilizations in Syria dating back to 3000 BCE. A royal palace discovered at Elba[5]

---

[5] Tell Mardikh, the location of ancient Elba is located 34 miles southwest of modern Aleppo, Syria.

by archeologists in the 1970s included a vast library of cuneiform tablets documenting an advanced kingdom that was ruled by a series of merchant kings, who each served for seven years. The civilization reached its peak around 2250 BCE. It is highly unlikely that the merchant kings of Elba would have failed to cross into and through Canaan to trade with Egypt.

Evidence of the extension of Semitic migration from Canaan into Egypt has been uncovered in the eastern area of the Nile River delta—which formerly split into as many as seven tributaries, as the river flowed to the Mediterranean Sea. Arriving as traders and/or fleeing famine, the Canaanites gradually established a large community at Avaris in this area of Egypt between 1800 BCE and 1650 BCE.

The Egyptians referred to these Semitic immigrant-invaders as the Hyksos, which has been translated as both "shepherd kings" and "rulers of foreign lands." A horse culture, the Hyksos introduced the powerful composite bow, metal helmets, improved battle axes, and horse-drawn chariots into warfare, as they became strong enough to confront and conquer Lower (northern) Egypt and, for a few years, Upper (southern) Egypt.

The Hyksos were finally defeated and driven out of Egypt after several campaigns by the Pharaoh Ahmose of Upper Egypt—who adopted the Hyksos horse and chariot—around 1440 BCE. Archaeological excavations at the site of Avaris in eastern Egypt demonstrate that it was abandoned at about that time. Hyksos, as a name for the invaders from Canaan, Syria, and beyond to Iraq, continued to be mentioned in Egyptian writings at various times and locations in Egypt for hundreds of years.

The Egyptians Drive Out the Invaders and Israel Becomes an Egyptian Province

Exodus in the Bible tells us that the Israelites, led by Joshua, invaded the land we now call Israel and conquered its walled cities. Extensive archaeological excavations at the various sites mentioned in the Bible relating to the biblical invasion of Canaan by the Israelites following their Exodus from Egypt, however, have failed to reveal any physical evidence of such invasion. This absence is particularly true during the unified rule of the Rameses dynasty, under which the Israelites reportedly suffered according to the Bible. The first Egyptian mention of Israel is found in the records of the Pharaoh Merneptah, the son of Rameses II, who invaded Canaan around 1207 BC. He recorded that the people—not the nation—"Israel has been wiped out . . . its seed is no more."

Canaan was a province of Egypt during this time. A series of forts along the Mediterranean coast were prepositioned with supplies and fresh water, which facilitated the rapid movement of military forces into Canaan. The Egyptian occupation was headquartered at Gaza, and military and administrative outposts were established at strategic locations throughout the land.

There were no walled cities in Canaan as described in the Bible. Modern archeological digs determined that the visible walls of Jericho had fallen long before the time of Joshua. Egypt was primarily confronted by the Hittite Empire, with which it shared a border in Syria. The two nations fought a great battle at Kadish in 1274 BCE, which resulted in a stalemate and compromise.

Several hundred years earlier, in approximately 1590 BCE, an event took place on the Mediterranean island of Santorini (Thera) that may have had delayed consequences for both the Hittites and Egyptians, and for every other culture that touched upon the eastern Mediterranean Sea. The eruption of the Santorini volcano was one of the largest, most destructive volcanic eruptions in human history. It destroyed the Minoan maritime civilization on Crete—which was the most advanced and dominant culture in the Mediterranean at the time. Its environmental effects, including a 40-foot tsunami and massive ash cloud, were felt throughout the Middle East and Asia. This disaster is almost certainly the historical basis of Plato's story about Atlantis and probably resulted in the subsequent emergence of the Greek city-states. The eruption may also have contributed to the rise of the Sea People, who were first recorded as allies of the Hittites in the battle of Kadish.

Believed to have originated from the Aegean or Western Anatolia, Egyptian sources recorded the onslaught of their migratory invasions—as the Sea People ultimately defeated and destroyed the Hittite Empire around 1175 BCE and then seriously threatened Egypt. One inscription from the reign of Rameses III says, "the lands were removed and scattered to the fray. No land could stand before their arms, . . ." Several attacks against Egyptian strongholds were repulsed: "Those who reached my frontier, their seed is not, their heart and their soul are finished forever and ever." The weakened Egyptians did, however, allow the Sea People to settle along coastal Canaan, where they became known as the Palistin, or Philistines. They gave the land its name of Palestine.[6]

At about the same time, the central hill country of Palestine, south of the Jezreel valley, was being occupied by the early Israelites, with whom the Philistines would later come into conflict. Comprehensive modern surveys by the Israelis since the 1967 war have revealed about 250 hilltop villages as the first archaeological evidence of the presence of an Israelite people. The settlements are characterized by easy access to local fields and pastures and continual occupation over long periods. The villages were small, built of field stone, and most probably contained about 100 people. Life was difficult, without refinements, and there is no evidence of literacy. There were no fortifications or evidence of warfare.

One interesting discovery was that the villages were laid out in an oval shape, open in the center, the way pastoral nomads contain their goats and sheep within a circle of tents. Contrary to all other surrounding cultures, no pig bones were discovered in the villages. In this manner—if in no other—this small population of about 40,000 people were united and set apart by this common dietary practice. Economically based on small-scale animal husbandry and the cultivation of grain, grapes, and olives, the Israelite community expanded to more than 500 villages, including market centers and small cities, by the eighth century BCE.

From the best evidence available, it appears that the central highland came to be occupied by local pastoral nomads, who settled on hilltops near pastures and took up farming. While they may have shared a racial memory of the earlier defeat and expulsion of the Hyksos by the Egyptians, nothing has been found to support the

---

[6] According to the biblical fable, it was the giant Philistine, Goliath, that David, the shepherd boy, killed with a single rock from his slingshot.

myth of a mass exodus from Egypt under the leadership of Moses at the time of the Rameses dynasty, or a violent invasion and occupation of Canaan by Joshua and the Israelites.

It was this remnant of all those who had come and gone over the centuries—those who settled in the most fruitful areas of what we now call Palestine-Israel—who came to be called the Israelites. They were a peaceful people who settled on and worked the land; however, to the south, in the rugged land called Judah, a group of more violent nomadic raiders and horse thieves made a permanent home in the tiny walled city of Jerusalem.

David and His Band of Horse Thieves Establish the Little Kingdom of Judah

Egyptian records do provide some information about how the rugged southern portion of the central highlands surrounding Jerusalem evolved to become the tiny and isolated kingdom of Judah. During the brief period when the heretic monotheistic pharaoh Akhenaten (c. 1336 BCE) established the city of Amarna some 365 miles south of Cairo, administrative correspondence took place with the various petty kings of the Egyptian province of Canaan. Among them are cuneiform tablets written by Abdi-Heba, the vassal king of "Urusalim." His kingdom was a small, unpopulated and unproductive area of approximately 900 square miles—consisting of less than ten settlements around the small walled city of Jerusalem—extending from Hebron in the south to Bethel in the north.

Egyptian sources contain clues about how David, described in the Bible as an outlaw, conquered the small stronghold of Jerusalem and became the King of Judah. As early as 1420 BCE, there were written Egyptian complaints about Apiru horse thieves, and around 1300 BCE, pharaoh Seti I recorded that he had to send troops into Canaan in response to an attack by the Apiru. An alternative spelling is Habiru and these mounted armed bandits ranged far and wide through the Middle East and were also mentioned in records found in Syria and Iraq.

Nearer in time to the establishment of a Hebrew city-state in Jerusalem, the letters of Abdi-Heba specifically complain about the Apiru, a disorganized group of outlaws, renegades, horse thieves,

The People of the Land and Those Who Passed Through

and mercenaries, who roamed through the hills of Hebron and the Judean desert. The last known reference in Egyptian documents was around 1150 BCE, when Rameses IV sent 800 captive Apiru to work in the stone quarries—an event that may have contributed to a racial memory of enslavement in Egypt.

The Bible describes Jerusalem as occupied by an entrenched tribe of Jebusites and how the city was finally conquered by David (undoubtedly an Apiru raider). David allegedly led a sneak attack through a secret water shaft leading from a spring outside the city walls, which provided a route inside the wall. Such a tunnel was discovered by Charles Warren, a British engineer in 1867, and further archaeological support of the biblical story was found by Dame Kathleen Kenyon in 1961. She determined that the original city wall existed between the spring and the shaft's entrance within the city.

There is also some physical evidence that David occupied a town on a twelve-acre site on the ridge of the Ophel Hill—the original Mount Zion. There is, however, no proof that his "kingdom" ever extended much beyond that which he originally captured at Jerusalem. The Bible claims that David conquered the coastline between the Plain of Sharon north to Mount Carmel, defeated the nations east of the Jordan river, and annexed parts of their territories. He allegedly extended the boundaries of his unified empire from the border of Egypt to the headwaters of the Jordan River in Syria. This fable is entirely unsupported in the archaeological record and is probably a superimposition of the separate and contemporary northern Israelite kingdom that did achieve those borders. The prevailing view is that David's kingdom was a tiny city-state consisting of Jerusalem and its immediate surrounding territory, an area that came to be known as Judah.

The existence of a Davidic lineage was, however, proven by the discovery of an Aramean victory stele in 1993 at Tel Dan (in the far north of modern Israel), which was dated to 850-835 BCE. It referred to the "House of David." The Mesha Stele[7] from the same period was discovered east of the Dead Sea in Jordan and may contain the name of "David."

---

[7] The Stele is a large stone containing approximately 1,000 carved words and documents the battles between the Moab in the area of modern Jordan and the people of Palestine-Israel. It was discovered intact in 1868 but was smashed in a dispute over ownership. It was reconstructed and displayed by the Louvre Museum in Paris.

Most curious is the absolute absence of any physical or written evidence of the reign of David's famous son, the biblical Solomon. Nothing can be found about his widespread trade, dominance of surrounding countries, or construction of a temple to Yahweh in Jerusalem. While it may not have been as magnificent as described in the Bible, there is some circumstantial evidence of the temple's existence through the records of other nations about its subsequent looting, destruction, and rebuilding. Every other construction once attributed to Solomon has now been proven to have been built later in time by the more powerful northern kingdom of Israel.

The Bible also claims that David combined Judah and Israel in a unified monarchy, which he bequeathed to Solomon. As the story goes, the unified kingdom dissolved following the death of Solomon when his son misruled Israel.[8] Although the biblical fable says the northern ten tribes rebelled and became the separate Kingdom of Israel, the truth appears to be that Israel—consisting of the peaceful farmers who occupied the hills and fertile valleys in the north—independently established a far more powerful and independent kingdom around 932 BCE.

Judah and Israel were never united under David and Solomon, but Egyptian records do establish that southern Judah was easily defeated in 926 BCE by the Egyptian Pharaoh Shishak. Its Davidic king surrendered without resistance and handed over all the temple treasures as tribute. The destruction of Jerusalem may have been avoided by the surrender of its treasure and agreement to become a vassal.

Northern Canaan did not escape the destructive invasion by Shishak, and a history of his campaign on the walls of the Karnak temple in Upper Egypt documents the villages and towns he destroyed, including Megiddo. The invasion was also confirmed by a victory stele bearing Shishak's name found in the ruins of Megiddo.[9]

---

[8] This lineage of David's descendants (allegedly through Solomon) are known as the Davidic kings of southern Judah. The Davidic kings never ruled or controlled the much larger northern area known as Israel.

[9] It is entirely possible that David's son—the infamous and allegedly wise King Solomon, who had many wives and reigned over a vast kingdom—is yet another biblical fable created by religious writers in Judah to compensate for their own insecurities regarding their more powerful and cultured northern neighbors, the original Israelites. Every single construction once attributed to King Solomon, including the gates of Megiddo, have now been proven to have been built by the northern Israelites.

The Magnificent Kingdom of Israel Outshines Poor Judah

Taking advantage of the Egyptian destruction of the lowland cities of Megiddo, Gezer, and Hazor, the highland Kingdom of Israel prospered and expanded across the Jezreel Valley into lower and upper Galilee. The kingdom ultimately approached the approximate northern and eastern limits claimed in the Bible for David.

The boundaries of the two separate kingdoms, of Judah in the south and Israel in the north, are important to remember, as the extent of these kingdoms has influenced the military-political events that have taken place in the region ever since. The continued military occupation of the "Golan Heights" of Syria, the "West Bank" of Jordan, and the "Gaza Strip" of Egypt by the State of Israel for the past 50 years is in violation of international law.

Governing from its capital city in Samaria, the kingdom of Israel existed for approximately two centuries between 930 and 720 BCE. Israel was primarily based on the highlands south and north of the Jezreel valley. The separate, seagoing Phoenicians controlled the area of Lebanon to the north of Mount Carmel, while the iron-producing Philistines continued to occupy small city states, including Gaza, along the southern coast, as vassals of Egypt.

Establishment of the eastern boundary of Israel beyond the Jordan river was documented by the discovery of a stele in Jordan which refers to the domination of the area by "Omri King of Israel." The kingdom's northern border in the vicinity of Damascus was drawn by a peace treaty with the Syrians and the king of Israel's marriage to the Phoenician princess, known in history as Jezebel. The Bible complains that the Israelites allowed the introduction of foreign gods, including the worship of golden calves at Bethel (Beth-El), just north of Jerusalem, and at Dan in the far north near the headwaters of the Jordan river.

Fueled by an economy based on the breeding and export of war horses and the cultivation and export of grapes, wine, and olives, the Israelites engaged in a massive construction program. They build a magnificent capital in Samaria and major administrative centers at Megiddo, Hazor, Gezer, and Dan in the north, and at Jahaz and Ataroth east of the Jordan river. Once believed to have been built by Solomon, these administrative centers followed a similar building plan that established defensive walls and gates. Megiddo is the biblical Armageddon in the Book of Revelation, where the final battle is supposed to be fought between human governments and God. (See Photos #4 and 5)

As Israel's population grew to approximately 350,000, it became one of the strongest powers in the region. This brought it into conflict with the kingdom of Damascus in Syria and the Assyrian empire in Iraq. The Assyrians had defeated and replaced the Hittites as the dominant power in region. Around this time, the king of Damascus probably recaptured the city of Dan. He erected a victory stele that complained about an invasion by the King of Israel into "my father's land." The stele also acknowledges the "House of David" as an ally of the king of Israel. Thus, it appears that while the kingdoms of Israel and Judah were politically separated, they were at times allied against the same enemies.

Israel resolved its differences with Damascus and other neighbors to become the strongest member of an alliance to oppose an Iraqi invasion in 853 BCE. The coalition was defeated during a battle in western Syria documented by a "Monolith Inscription" discovered in 1861 at the Assyrian site of Nimrud in Turkey. The Iraqi king recorded that "Ahab, the Israelite" deployed 10,000 foot soldiers and 2,000 chariots in his losing battle. The "Arabs" are also listed as allies of the Israelites.

Conquest of the Northern Kingdom of Israel by the Iraqis

The Omri dynasty of Israel ended around 842 BCE and was succeeded by the House of Jehu. An Iraqi "black obelisk" shows Jehu bowing and offering tribute. The power and borders of Israel were reduced—it became a vassal of Iraq and had to pay tribute to avoid destruction. Nonetheless, Israel continued to prosper.

Around 738 BCE, an upstart Iraqi king decided he was no longer content with tribute. In a sweeping invasion, the Iraqis defeated Damascus and conquered several lowland Israelite towns and cities and the highlands of Galilee, annexing them to the Iraqi empire. The Kingdom of Israel was reduced to the Samarian highland north of

Jerusalem. The Iraqi king erected a monument on which he bragged he had defeated Israel, "all [of whose] cities I leveled [to the ground] . . . I plundered its livestock, and I spared only [isolated] Samaria."

In a last-ditch effort to avoid being completely overrun, Israel once again allied itself with Damascus and some of the remaining Philistine cities to oppose the Iraqi invasions. The alliance failed, and Iraq destroyed many, if not most of the remaining Israelite cities and deported many of the inhabitants to Iraq. Sargon II of Iraq recorded the following:

> The inhabitants of Samaria, who agreed and plotted with a king hostile to me not to endure servitude and not to bring tribute to Assur [a city in Iraq] and who did battle, I fought against them with the power of the great gods, my lords. I counted as spoil 27,280 people, together with their chariots, and gods, in which they trusted. I formed a unit with 200 of their chariots for my royal force.

Although the Bible relates that Israel was "removed" from the sight of God and handed over to the "spoilers," the "ten lost tribes of Israel" were not dispersed. From an original population of around 350,000, the Iraq records reveal that approximately 40,000 people were deported. These were primarily from the leadership and others whose skills were useful to the Iraqis—such as the charioteers—but most Israelites remained where they lived and continued to produce revenue for Iraq.

Judah Cooperates With Iraq and Prospers From Israelite Immigration

For several centuries, Israel and Judah had shared little more than a common border, an occasional military alliance, and the Hebrew language. Contrary to the biblical story, it appears the two countries also shared a common religion that was not particularly monotheistic. The people of both nations worshipped Yahweh, as well as other gods, including Yahweh's wife, Asherah. Inscriptions confirming a belief that Yahweh was married have been found in archaeological digs associated with both Israel and Judea. Circumstantial evidence is also provided by the condemnation of such worship in both nations by a series of prophets, including Ezekiel, who describes the abominations practiced in the inner court of the temple in Jerusalem.

Recent archaeological digs in Jerusalem have identified a tripling of the city's size at the end of the eighth century BCE from the small area of the City of David on Mount Zion to include all the western hill. The timing corresponds to the conquest of Israel by Iraq and is probably attributable to a migration into Judea by northerners displaced by the violence. Surrounding towns and villages also grew as Judah's population quickly expanded to 120,000.

For the first time, the archaeological record demonstrates that Judah was developing as a larger nation, instead of a tiny city-state. The accoutrements of a bureaucracy begin to appear, along with monumental architecture and elite burials. Judah accommodated to and cooperated with the Iraqi empire—as Judah evolved to play a more active economic and diplomatic role in regional affairs. With the influx of the more sophisticated and better educated northerners, Judah became a more literate society, and we are getting closer to the point where the written Bible appears in history.

The House of David continued to rule southern Judah; however, it accepted Iraqi protection and became a vassal of Iraq. For this, the king was berated by biblical writers for apostasy—for recognizing the gods of his masters in Iraq.

We are now at a time when the social-religious-political grouping that came to be known as the Jewish people can be identified as a related group. It was earlier shown that the biblical story about the invasion of Palestine by the twelve tribes of Israel never took place. What is most likely is that the various tribes indigenous to the land came to be united by their worship of the same God.

The biblical stories confuse the true situation, but what is most likely is that the tribes of Judah and Israel were converted to the same religion by the landless tribe of priestly Levites led by the legendary Moses, who may have immigrated from Egypt at some point in the past. We saw that the people avoided eating pork, which may have been influenced by their shared Mosaic priesthood. The priests told stories of the ancient past and its conflicts, and they introduced ritual cleanliness and a respect for all life by taking over the slaughter of animals as a sacrifice to God. The priests received a portion of the sacrifice and the harvest as a tithe for themselves and their families. Most importantly—for this history—the Levites, who created the Moses sermons and his Ten Commandments, learned to write and to reduce their stories to writing.

The Yahweh cult established by the Levites served to unite the tribes, first in the kingdoms of Judah and Israel, then—after the Iraqi conquest of Israel—by being forced to live together in Judah.

The Religious Reforms of King Hezekiah of Judah

Around 715 BCE, King Hezekiah succeeded to the throne of Judah. Hezekiah was to have a profound effect on the security of the nation, its practice of religion, and the future of monotheism. While maintaining an outward submissiveness towards the Iraqis, he set about quietly building up the internal strength of his kingdom physically and the spirit of the people morally. He built a new and greatly expanded perimeter wall and constructed the Siloam tunnel to bring a safe water supply into the city.

King Hezekiah separated a special group of "Aaronite" priests from the other Levites in the tribe of Moses. The Aaronid priesthood was opposed by the ordinary Levites—who saw the prophet Moses, and not his brother Aaron, as their model. The most powerful symbol of Moses's strength was his bronze serpent, which was smashed by King Hezekiah "because the children of Israel were burning incense to it in those days." According to the biblical tale, King Solomon had earlier promoted the Aaronid priesthood by giving the entire authority in his Temple to an Aaronid priest named Zadok.

These events are important to keep in mind, as this is the first of several subsequent schisms within the religions that followed, based on the succession of leaders—from Moses to Mohammad. Zadok becomes memorable, as we will later see another lineage of priests emerge who will be called the Sadducees, and yet another political-religious movement known as the Zaddik, all of which are derived from the same Hebrew root word, which means righteous. This is perhaps the key word in this entire history.

The Bible also relates that King Hezekiah launched a major religious reformation to destroy paganism and strengthen the central Temple cult: "He removed the high places, and broke the images, and cut down the groves . . . ." His reforms included the elimination of any forms of religious practice other than the sanctioned worship in the temple in Jerusalem.

In addition to the Temple, there had been traditional "high places" throughout the land where people could go to sacrifice to Yahweh. Hezekiah eliminated them. He centralized the Yahweh cult at the Jerusalem temple. This meant that if people wanted to eat lamb, they could not sacrifice their sheep at home, or at a local sanctuary. People had to bring their sheep to the priests at the Temple altar in Jerusalem. This also resulted in a sizable gathering of Levite priests at Jerusalem—which was now the only sanctioned location where they could conduct the sacrifices and receive their tithes.

More importantly, the reform also conferred considerable distinction and power upon the High Priest in Jerusalem and for his priestly (Aaronid-Zadok) family. This idea of centralizing religion around one temple and one altar was an important step in the development of Judah's religion and the subsequent formulation of the Bible as we know it. Moreover, this concentration was another manifestation of the growing power of the Yahweh priesthood *vis-à-vis* the secular leadership of the Davidic kings.

It was around this time that the necessary levels of literacy arose allowing the development of a religious literature in the Hebrew language. According to a report in the Proceedings of the National Academy of Sciences, recent excavations of a trove of pottery shards with ink inscriptions in the Hebrew language — found at an ancient military fortress in southern Israel—have been dated to the late seventh century BCE. Inscriptions were identified as having been written by six different hands, which indicates a high level of literacy.

The prophet Isaiah of Jerusalem lived at this time and prophesized for more than 60 years, although some of that attributed to him in the Bible was subsequently written by others. He proclaimed that Jerusalem would be punished and cleansed of evil; however, a righteous remnant would be purified and redeemed by God and would return to Judah. His prophecies would have a profound and lasting effect on monotheism, including being used as a prophecy for the messiahship of Jesus.

Hezekiah's building program envisioned a rebellion against Iraq, an attempt to extend Judah's control over areas that had once been a part of the kingdom of Israel and capturing the remaining Philistine cities along the coast. Coexistent with these religious reforms was a wave of nationalism. Judah flirted with open rebellion against Iraq, and Isaiah condemned all foreign alliances in favor of a reliance on God.

Judah Rebels and is Crushed by the Iraqis

Initially, the Iraqi king left Judah alone; however, when he was killed, his successor moved his capital to a new city to consolidate his holdings. Taking advantage of the disruption, Hezekiah rebelled against the Iraqis. The Bible tells us that three years later (in 701 BCE), the Iraqis "came down like the wolf on the fold and his cohorts were gleaming in purple and gold."

The Iraqis recorded, "As to Hezekiah the Jew, he did not submit to my yoke, I laid siege to 46 of his strong cities, walled forts, and to countless small villages in their vicinity, and conquered by means of well-stamped ramps, and battering-rams brought near, by attacks of foot soldiers, mines, breeches as well as sapper work . . . . Himself I made a prisoner in Jerusalem, his royal residence, like a bird in a cage." Sennacherib said he kept Hezekiah locked up until he provided tribute in the amount of 30 talents of gold and 800 of silver.[10]

The Iraqi conqueror of Judah was succeeded by Ashurbanipal, who founded a great library "in order that he might have that which to read." The 1853 discovery of Ashurbanipal's library in Iraq near the present city of Mosul provided a key to the understanding of the entire Iraqi civilization. The king assembled most of the library consisting of cuneiform writing on clay tablets by making copies of originals. In addition to works on magic, there was an extensive poetic literature—including the original great flood myth of Gilgamesh—

---

[10] A talent weighed between 75 and 110 pounds.

and more practical works on medicine, philosophy, astronomy, and mathematics. The authors of the Bible undoubtedly plagiarized some of these stories to create the fables of Noah and Moses.

Ashurbanipal went on to conquer Egypt, and in doing so, he stretched his empire to its maximum extent. He was to be the last great Iraqi king; however, the Aramaic language of his empire and library became the common language of the Middle East, including Judah, for many centuries thereafter and continues to be the basis of the languages spoken in the region today.

Following Ashurbanipal's death, Babylon began to emerge as a growing power. Iraqi forces returned to Judah during the reign of Hezekiah's son Manasseh—who was imprisoned for a while in Babylon. Upon his return, Manasseh, and his son Amon, reintroduced pagan worship in Judah. They allowed pagan statues in the Temple and the rebuilding of high places outside of Jerusalem.

The Bible accuses Amon of having done "that which was evil in the sight of Yahweh," for which he was assassinated. Amon was succeeded by his eight-year-old son, Josiah, who, as we will see later, created the monotheistic religion of Judaism and the biblical stories we continue to read.

The Religion of The People

The Bible tells us that the children of Israel were forced to work as slaves in building Egyptian cities. According to the fable, the Pharaoh became concerned about the prolific birth rate of the slaves, and he commanded that all male children be cast into the Nile. A man and woman from the tribe of Levi had a male child, which the mother hid in a basket among the reeds of the river. The boy was found by the Pharaoh's daughter, who named him Moses and raised him as her son. Moses is an Egyptian name, which is simply the suffix attached to the end of many names which means "son of."

The story of Moses is undoubtedly derived from cuneiform tablets recording the birth legend of Sargon the Great, who ruled in Iraq as early as 2270 BCE: "Sargon the mighty king, King of Akkad, am I. My mother was a changeling, my father I knew not . . . My changeling mother conceived me; in secret she bore me. She set me in a basket of rushes, with bitumen she sealed my lid. She cast me in the river which rose not over me . . . Akki, the drawer of water, took me as his son and reared me." The biblical fable plagiarizes almost verbatim, "she took for him a basket made of bulrushes and daubed it with bitumen and pitch."

Moses was the first prophet in the religion of Israel—in that God—who had previously been called El in the areas of Iraq and Syria—revealed his name to Moses as Yahweh. The Levites probably came from Egypt—for it is only among the Levites we find people with Egyptian names, such as Moses, Hophni, and Phinehas. The tribe may have emigrated from Egypt following the reign of Akhenaten, the Egyptian Pharaoh who briefly introduced the monotheistic worship of the single god known as Aten. Shortly after his death, all mention of Akhenaten was erased from Egyptian history, and his existence only became known as the result of modern archeology. If there were any residual Canaanites left in Egypt who may have been associated in some way with Akhenaten's reforms, their expulsion might explain their appearance in Judah and Israel.

The Israelites and Judahites shared traditions about the god El, his wife Asherah, and their son, Baal, which were current throughout the Middle East. The Bible tells us that the last words of Moses, just before he climbed to the top of Mount Nebo to die, concern the apportionment of the nations by God.

> When the Most High gave to the nations their inheritance, when he separated the sons of men, he fixed the bounds of the peoples according to the number of the sons of God. For the LORD's portion is his people, Jacob his allotted heritage.

The Hebrew Bible (Masoretic) says the allotment was as to the number of the "sons of Israel." The passage has been found on a fragment from the Dead Sea Scrolls as the "sons of God." Thus, at this point in the evolution of monotheism, while Yahweh may have become the God of the Israelites, he was considered by them to be just one of the sons of El. Yahweh chose Israel as his own portion, implying that each of the other deities—the other sons of God—also received a nation to rule over.

The biblical story tells us that the Levites did not receive property in the promised land like the other tribes. The Levites lived among the people and served as their priests, receiving a tithe of ten percent of all sacrifices and first fruits of the land. Levite priests descended through the families of the Tribe of Levi. These family offices were hereditary, and the included the duty to perform sacrifices for others.

The rite of sacrifice did not originate with killing animals to compensate for sinful behavior or to win favor with God; rather, the ritual comes from God's covenant with Noah.[11] The sacrifice honors the spirit of animals, particularly those domesticated for the purpose, who give their lives that others may live. The act of taking a life was sacred and had to be performed on an altar by a priest. The rites were performed by Levite priests throughout the towns and villages of Judah and Israel—before the priests and the practice were concentrated in Jerusalem by King Hezekiah and his great-grandson Josiah.

King Josiah, Jeremiah, and a Skilled Staff of Editors Create the Bible

People who read the Bible—particularly the first five books supposedly written by Moses—often find there are multiple versions of such matters as the creation of the world, the great flood, God's covenant with Abraham, the naming of his son Isaac, his claiming his wife Sarah to be his sister, Jacob's trip to Mesopotamia in search of a wife, God's revelation to Jacob at Bethel, the changing of Jacob's name to Israel, Moses getting water from a rock, and so forth.

During the 200 years of separate existence, the nations of Israel and Judah apparently developed their own independent versions of the history and worship of God. This fact was determined by scholarly analysis of the first five books of the Bible known as the Pentateuch. Scholars today recognize at least four basic versions. These are commonly identified as J (Yahweh/Jehovah), E (God/Elohim), D (Deuteronomy), and P (Priestly).

---

[11] God's promise that there "shall never again become a flood to destroy all flesh" was a covenant between "God and every living creature of all flesh that is upon the earth." (Genesis 9:15-16)

J and E appear to be the oldest versions of the biblical stories, for they do not discuss matters that are treated in the other documents. D came later than J and E, for it covers events that occurred later in history. P, the priestly version of the story, may have been written later than E and J, and perhaps earlier than D, for it refers to matters, such as the books of the early prophets, that are not in E and J.

The J stories come from the cities and territory of Judah, while the E stories concern the cities and territory of Israel. In E, Moses's faithful assistant is Joshua; however, Joshua plays no role in J—perhaps because Joshua was a northern hero. There are many similarities between J and E, and both may have derived from an even older source, or one may have been first and was copied by the other.

Both J and E were written before the Iraqis destroyed the Kingdom of Israel and deported its population. Many Israelites fled south to Judah at that time as refugees, and northern Levites may have brought the E text with them to Judah.

The priestly P version was most likely written by the Aaronid priesthood as it emphasizes the centralization of religion. Aaronids are the priests in authority in the temple—not the other Levites—as only those who are descended from Aaron could attend the altar. D speaks of priests generally as "the Levite priests," but P always refers to the Aaronid priests and the Levites as two distinct groups.

Another alternative has presented itself as biblical scholars have continued to scrutinize the ancient scriptures. Analysis of the elements and usage of the Hebrew language, and matters such as style and interests, have led several different scholars to the same conclusion. There is hidden within the first books of the Old Testament an original core document upon which the subsequent revisions were cut and pasted. Named "Book of J" or "In the Day," the original work commences with 2:4 of Genesis, "In the day that the LORD God made the earth and the heavens, . . ." and ends with the death of King David. It is believed by some biblical scholars that the document was created by a single author—who may have been a woman.

During the 18th year of King Josiah's reign, the Bible reveals that a priest mysteriously found a scroll of the Torah in the Temple.

The book contained Moses's farewell speech in which he delivers a code of laws and appoints Joshua as his successor. Moses then climbs Mount Nebo, from which he can see into the promised land, and he dies.

There is a great deal of evidence showing that the Josiah period was a period of increased literacy in Jerusalem. Not only was the book of Deuteronomy produced then, but the next six books of the Bible were rewritten to include the reign of King Josiah. The books of Joshua, 1 and 2 Samuel, and 1 and 2 Kings are known as the Early Prophets. Deuteronomy and these books weave together a continuous story about the people of Israel from Moses to King Josiah. The collection draws upon literary forms of covenants in Iraqi literature, but it also reflects a familiarity with early Greek writings.

The laws of Deuteronomy were central to the history of Israel and Judah, and their kings were evaluated as being "good in the eyes of Yahweh" or "bad in the eyes of Yahweh" in fulfilling those laws. Ultimately, however, the nation's fate depended on whether the people kept the commandments of Deuteronomy. In all these matters, it was the priests who gained power and influence over the affairs of the kingdoms and their people.

Some believe the prophet Jeremiah may have personally produced the composition, or he may have simply served as its inspiration. The prophet began his ministry during Josiah's reign; he was a great admirer of the king, and he composed a lamentation for Josiah when he was killed. There is identical language in the book of Jeremiah and in Deuteronomy referring to Egypt as an "iron furnace," and there are similarities in the commentary regarding the justice of God's judgment.

Josiah held a mass ceremony in which the new book was read to the people, who then renewed their covenant with God. Josiah ordered a complete destruction of the high places and the altar at Beth-El, where one of the golden calves had once stood. Moreover, he destroyed all artifacts and locations of worship associated with Asherah, the ancient Mother Goddess of the Middle East including the people of Israel and Judah.

Throughout the eons, Asherah had been a source of comfort for woman troubled with menstruation, pregnancy, childbirth, and the nurturing of children. Archeological excavations in Jerusalem have uncovered hundreds of figurines of the Mother Goddess which were destroyed and buried at the time of Josiah. Deprived of the companionship and compassion of God's consort, the Yahweh cult became increasingly patriarchal, judgmental, and harsh.

The Deuteronomic Code was an attempt to transform the religious principles of the early prophets into daily practice. All pagan rites were forbidden, and actual sacrifice was reduced to a symbolic minimum. Functioning almost as a constitutional bill of rights, the Code defined the rights of the poor, orphans, widows, foreign visitors, and slaves. Debts had to be forgiven after seven years, and the people were admonished:

> If there is among you a poor man, one of your brethren, in any of your towns within your land which the LORD your God gives you, you shall not harden your heart or shut your hand against your poor brother, but you shall open your hand to him, and lend him sufficient for his need, whatever it may be. . . . therefore, I command you, You shall open wide your hand to your brother, to the needy and to the poor, in the land.

We will learn—as the story continues to unfold—it is this essence of *righteousness* in caring for one another that will be at the core of all subsequent developments in the Abrahamic religions.

Black clouds were gathering at this time in the East that would bring storms to Judah. Babylonia revolted against the Iraqi kingdom in 626 BCE and resumed its independence. The Medes of Iran were becoming increasingly powerful and stormed the ancient Iraqi capital of Ashur. The Persians formed an alliance with the Babylonians to attack the Iraqi capital at Nineveh. Egypt may have reached an agreement with Iraq giving it the right to occupy Syria west of the Euphrates in an alliance against the rising powers to the east.

Egypt dispatched an army through Palestine to aid the beleaguered Iraqis in 609 BCE. King Josiah, who had expanded the boundaries of Judah to include Samaria, moved to block the Egyptian army at Megiddo. He was defeated and killed; Judah lost its brief independence, and the Aramaic empire of Iraq was destroyed.

Josiah's early death curtailed his country's political independence and religious reform. Josiah's Davidic successors continued to rule Judah, but as Egyptian vassals. Given these geopolitical realities, it is easy to see why the Deuteronomistic History talked about a dominating and enslaving Egyptian pharaoh, which it placed earlier in time.

The Babylonians Destroy the Temple and Deport the People to Iraq

Nebuchadnezzar became the king of Babylon in 604 BCE and founded the Chaldean dynasty in Iraq. He built a great city in Babylon with streets paved with bricks and bitumen, and he constructed the Hanging Gardens, one of the Seven Wonders of the ancient world.[12]

Nebuchadnezzar quickly drove the occupying Egyptian forces out of Syria. In 597 BCE, he invaded Judah and carried the Davidic king off to Babylon along with "his mother, and his servants, and his princes, and his officers . . . and all the mighty men of valor, even ten thousand captives, and all the craftsmen and smiths."

Nebuchadnezzar placed a puppet on the throne of Judah, who was urged by nationalists to rebel against the Babylonians. At the same time, the Prophet Jeremiah warned that any resistance to the Babylonians was tantamount to rebellion against God's will. He said the Babylonian yoke had been placed on Judah by God as a punishment for its sin, and he walked around Jerusalem symbolically wearing a wooden yoke.

Despite the warnings, Judah rebelled, and Nebuchadnezzar struck back. His strategy was to blockade Jerusalem and destroy the surrounding cities and towns. Jerusalem held out for 18 months before falling in 587 or 586 BCE. The city was burned to the ground, its walls were torn down, and the Temple was looted and destroyed. The sacred Ark of the Covenant disappeared.

Nebuchadnezzar appointed a Jewish governor—who was not of the house of David and who was quickly assassinated. Terrified at Nebuchadnezzar's revenge, many of those remaining in Judah fled to Egypt.

---

[12] Babylon was located about 59 miles southwest of the modern city of Baghdad.

Jeremiah accompanied the refugees to Egypt, from which he maintained a correspondence with those who were exiled in Iraq. With Jeremiah came the idea of religion as the personal experience of communication with the Divine. He believed the discovery of God to be within the soul of every individual. Jeremiah died while a refugee in Egypt, but it is said that before he died, he wrote,

> Behold, the days are coming, says the Lord, when I will fulfill the promise I made to the house of Israel and the house of Judah. In those days and at that time I will cause a righteous Branch to spring forth for David; and he shall execute justice and righteousness in the land. In those days Judah will be saved, and Jerusalem will dwell securely. And this is the name by which it will be called: 'The Lord is our righteousness.

As with the prophecies of Isaiah, the words of Jeremiah would be relied upon in the future to create an expectation of a messiah who will save the people of Israel from their oppressors—including the birth and ministry of Jesus. Once again, the essential concept of *righteousness* was central to the prediction.

The Judahites had to face harsh realities during their exile in Babylon between 586 and 538 BCE. Did they continue to be a "chosen people" with a privileged relationship with God? A new philosophy and theology evolved, and the revision of the Bible continued.

Among the captives were the most literate of the Jews. They made a major contribution to the evolving Bible in explaining how the end of the Davidic Kingdom was not the end of the people of Judah. They organized religious Torah schools, formed synagogues in their homes, and formalized rituals such as circumcision, observance of the Sabbath, purity of foods, and commemorative feasts and holidays. It was during this time when the role of the teachers of the law, who studied and interpreted the Torah, was institutionalized. These rabbis (masters) would ultimately supplant the priesthood in the future of the Jewish people and their religion.

The synagogue evolved during the exile as a religious gathering place of the people and as an educational institution. The Aramaic language of Iraq became the vernacular, and the quadratic alphabet replaced the Phoenician alphabet.

In Exile, Ezekiel Created a Novel Theory of Sin and Redemption

The exiles studied the instructions of the prophet Ezekiel, who—building on an individual experience with God as taught by Jeremiah—introduced the concept of having a unique relationship with God and a personal responsibility for sin. People could change their behavior and atone for their sins, because the divine blessing could forgive guilt. Individuals are rewarded or punished for their own conduct, and, for the first time, the people learned that the faithful could survive death. The standard of behavior was evolving to one of simple righteousness.

Ezekiel was the only prophet who ever got a glimpse of God seated on his chariot-throne. The story goes that Ezekiel was transported by God to a valley full of bones, and God asked, "Son of Man, can these bones live? . . ." God said to the bones, "Behold, I will cause breath to enter you, and you shall live." Ezekiel prophesied, "and the breath came into them, and they lived, and stood upon their feet, . . ." God then told Ezekiel, "Behold, I will open your graves, and raise you from your graves, . . . and I will bring you home into the land of Israel. And you shall know that I am the Lord, when I open your graves, and raise you from your graves, . . . And I shall put my Spirit in you, and you shall live, . . ."

Thus, the doctrine of resurrection from death was created to encourage people to avoid sin and to live righteously. Once the doctrine was created, the question arose as to who defined and decided what behavior was sinful and what was righteous. The power of the priests and other religious leaders continued to grow.

Finally, during the exile, the Hebrew religion evolved to a belief that Yahweh was no longer just the God of Israel. He was to become the God of the whole world, *if* He was properly worshipped and witnessed by the Jews. An unknown author known as Deutero (or second) Isaiah wrote the final verses of the book of Isaiah, beginning at chapter 40. The prophecy commences with:

A voice cries: "In the wilderness prepare the way of the LORD, make straight in the desert a highway for our God. Every valley shall be lifted up, and every mountain and hill shall be made low; the uneven ground shall become level, and the rough places a plain. And the glory of the LORD shall be revealed, and all flesh shall see it together, for the mouth of the LORD has spoken."

As we will see in the next part, this prophecy played a part in the evolution of the Way of Righteousness.

Learning About the Good and Evil of Zoroastrianism From the Iranians

During their exile in Babylon, the Jews were exposed to the prevalent Iranian religion known as Zoroastrianism, which was to have a profound effect on their philosophy and religion. Zoroaster (Zaranthustra), the prophet by whose name the religion of Iran came principally to be known, is thought to have lived in western Iran somewhere in Azerbaijan or possibly north of present-day Iran. The time of his life is uncertain, but it could have been as late as 550-523 BCE.

Zoroaster's reform was a qualified monotheism that mandated perfectionist ideals of personal honesty and integrity—which may have influenced Ezekiel's theory of redemption. God provided man with the free will to resist evil and to conform his mind to the divine plan. Man's rewards will be the gifts of wholeness and immortality.

The culture and religion of Persia-Iran greatly influenced the future of the Hebrew religion. Previously, contact with heathen cultures had only awakened contempt and disgust by the Jews. The Iranian religion, however, was nobly ethical in character. It represented all existence as a struggle between two opposing principles or deities, one of light and goodness, the other of darkness and evil. Man's duty is to take part in the struggle, to conquer the evil nature within him, and to align himself on the side of light. The struggle will continue through many ages, but at last good will triumph. All those who have ever lived will be judged for their conduct—the wicked will be destroyed, and the immortal righteous will live in endless bliss. Combining the eastern personal duty of righteous living with Ezekiel's promise of resurrection for doing so, the stage was set for the arrival of a more enlightened religious philosophy in Jerusalem.

The release of the Jews from their exile came through the most unlikely messiah in the Bible—Cyrus the Persian, whom Deutero-Isaiah hailed as the LORD's anointed.[13] Cyrus quickly rose to power in Iran in the middle of the sixth century BCE. By 550 BCE, he was the ruler of the Iranian empire of the Medes, and then he conquered most of Asia Minor, leaving Babylon increasingly isolated and friendless.

Nebuchadnezzar died in 562 BCE, and the power of Babylon declined. The last ruler spent most of his time in the desert southeast of Edom, leaving his son Belshazzar as regent in Babylon. Although the Book of Daniel was composed at least four centuries after the Exile, it describes a feast where Belshazzar dared to use the gold and silver vessels of the Jerusalem Temple for a banquet. Symbolically, a man's hand appeared from thin air and wrote on the wall. When none could interpret it, the king summoned Daniel, who read *"Mene, mene, tekel, upharsin,"* translated "Numbered, numbered, weighed, divided."

The Babylonian empire become so enfeebled that Cyprus was able to walk into the city of Babylon unopposed. The city was spared, and Cyrus was welcomed as a liberator.

The Iranians Rescue the Jews and Fund the Rebuilding of Their Temple

Cyrus returned the Jewish exiles to their homelands and issued a decree in 538 BCE specifically ordering the restoration of the

---

[13] The Hebrew word *mashiach*, or Messiah, will be constantly used throughout this book. It means one who has been anointed, usually with oil. Prophets, kings, and high priests in Israel were anointed and were called messiahs. The anointed ones were selected and honored by God to achieve His purposes on Earth. "Christ" is the Greek translation (*christos*) of the Hebrew word, messiah. It is not a personal name—it is a title or honor.

Judah community and cult in Jerusalem, and the return of the sacred temple vessels.[14]

According to the Book of Ezra:

> In the first year of Cyrus the king the same Cyrus the king made a decree concerning the house of God at Jerusalem, Let the house be built, the place where they offered sacrifices, and let the foundations thereof be strongly laid . . . and let the expenses be given out of the king's house. (6:3-4)

Only a small party initially took advantage of the edict. They returned under the joint leadership of Zerubbabel, a prince of the house of David—who was appointed as the Persian governor—and Joshua bar Jozakak, a priest of the family of Zadok. A revolt soon occurred, and Zerubbabel was either executed or deported. Thereafter, Joshua became the priestly leader of the group. He was anointed as the first high priest of the restored temple, and his successors became known as the Sadducees.

It took more than 20 years to complete the Second Temple, which was much smaller than the original. It contained a seven-branched Menorah lamp stand in place of the lost Ark of the Covenant, and a High Priest—rather than a Davidic king—became Yahweh's on-site representative.

Although the Temple had been restored, Jerusalem remained a tiny province of the vast Persian empire. It was denoted with the Aramaic name of Yehud, and it was at this time that the people became known as *Yehudim*, or the Jews. Yehud was later changed to Judea by the Romans, but we will continue to refer to the local geographic area as Judah, to differentiate it from northern Israel.

---

[14] Reflecting upon what was earlier written about the DNA of the Jews including the settlers and conquerors from Syria, Iraq, and Egypt, it is unlikely that the DNA would include that of the Persians-Iranians—who never occupied the land of Israel. This is true even though at various times in history, great Persian empires extended throughout the Middle East.

Ezra, the Priest, Revises the Bible and Seizes Power Over the People

The walls were restored around the much-reduced city, and a new prophet appeared on the scene. Ezra was a priest and a scribe, who had access to all the existing documents of the law. The Bible says, "Ezra had his heart set on seeking out Yahweh's Torah . . . ," that "He was a ready scribe in the Torah of Moses," and that the Iranian emperor had authorized him to teach and enforce "the law of your God which is in your hand." As a priest of a Sadducee family and a "scribe of the law of the God of heaven," Ezra was a zealous reformer who greatly increased the power of the priests.

Ezra returned to Jerusalem some 50 to 75 years after the Second Temple had been rebuilt. According to the letter of authorization provided Ezra by the Iranian king, "The Law of your God . . . is in your care." "Ezra, (you are to) appoint magistrates and judges . . . who know the Law of your God . . . to judge and teach those who do not know. Let anyone who does not obey the Law of your God . . . be punished."

Ezra is most likely the writer-editor who finalized the work of Jeremiah in redacting the P, E, D, and J versions of the Law of Moses into the Torah as we generally know it today. With the Sadducees firmly in control, the role of their priesthood is emphasized. The first time the full Torah of Moses is heard in Judah, it is Ezra who is reading it at the water gate, and it was unlike anything the people had ever heard before.

The P source provides laws about holidays in Leviticus 23, where the main holidays are listed, including the feast of Passover, the feast of Weeks, and the feast of Booths, plus the New Year and Day of Atonement holidays. This holiday list begins and ends with the words "These are the appointed feasts of the LORD." Two verses below the list, a new law about the feast of Booths was added. Suddenly, the people were ordered to build actual booths and to live in them for seven days to remind them that they had to live in temporary huts when they were brought out of Egypt. Nehemiah says: "The children of Israel had not done so from the days of Joshua son of Nun until that day."

Irrespective of how the final composition came to be written, Ezra brought the Pentateuch and Early Prophets with him from Babylonia. He established the Pentateuch (the first five books of the Bible) as the central authority in Jerusalem, and his edition of the Torah (including the Prophets and Writings) became authoritative—as it was backed by the power of the Iranian government. It is significant that the Book of Ezra immediately follows Chronicles within the original foundational writings of Judaism—before the prophets who had yet to speak.

Just as the "Lost Tribes of Israel" never left the land when the leadership were taken away, and just as the Babylonian Exile only took away the learned religious few, the ordinary people of Israel, Samaria, and Judea never left the land. They continued their adherence to Abraham's covenant of righteousness, even without the exiled priests and rabbis.

Ezra began to break up the marriages of men who had married non-Jewish wives, including Samaritans. In doing so, he was following the harsh covenant of Phinehas, a grandson of Aaron, who killed a member of the Moses congregation and the Midianite woman he tried to marry. The covenant of Phinehas is very restrictive, holding that only Aaronites and Levites *who are righteous and zealous for the Law* can qualify for the high priesthood.

Ezra's action caused a permanent schism between the Jews and Samaritans, whose offer to help reconstruct the temple had been rebuffed. The Samaritans, the surviving members of the Kingdom of Israel in the north of Judah, built their own temple and adopted the Pentateuch—minus the Prophets and Writings—as their holy book. The Samaritans believed they practiced the true Judaic religion as maintained by those who remained in the land of Israel and were not exiled.[15]

The Samaritans claimed descent from the Hebrew tribes of Ephraim and Manasseh, the two sons of Joseph, and they occupied the area known today as the West Bank of the Jordan River. As we

---

[15] Genetic testing reveals that the modern Palestinians of this region are more closely related to the Jews than to their Arab neighbors. These Palestinians of both Samaritan and Israeli descent were forcibly converted to Christianity by the Byzantines and later to Islam by the Muslims. A small remnant in Israel cling to their ancient Samaritan religion. They are the last of the "Good Samaritans."

will see, their temple was later destroyed during the Hasmonean Revolution; however, they remained as a distinct group occupying the land that separated Judah in the south from the Galilee in the north. The Samaritans continue to exist to this day as a distinct group in the State of Israel, whose Jewish people primarily trace their descent from the Kingdom of Judah.

Although many of the patriarchs of the faith, including Abraham, Moses, David, and Solomon had descended from foreigners and had married foreign wives, the priestly leadership under Ezra now proclaimed that all such marriages were illegal and void.

Jewish political and religious power became combined in a tiny theocracy centered on the Second Temple in Jerusalem. It was exclusively controlled by the Aaronic priesthood, which, with time, became a hereditary theocratic monarchy. Taking their name from Zadoc, the priestly sect was known as the Sadducees.

Secular power would remain with the Iranians for another century. It would then pass to Alexander the Great and his Greek successors, and finally to the Romans.

THE BOOKS OF THE PEOPLE

In the year 332 BCE, a new conqueror arrived before the restored walls of Jerusalem. Educated by Aristotle, Alexander the Great had succeeded to the unified Greek kingdom established by his father, Philip II, and he mobilized its powerful military force. The tightly packed phalanx had proved itself unstoppable as Alexander had marched in lockstep through Asia Minor, the coastal cities of Phoenicia, Palestine, and Gaza. Jerusalem offered no resistance.

Over the next eight years, Alexander went on to conquer Egypt, Syria, Iraq, and Iran before arriving at the "ends of the earth" near the foot of the Himalayas in India. Before dying in Babylon in 323 BCE, Alexander introduced the Greek culture of Hellenism to Asia and the Middle East. Everywhere, the people began to speak an international dialect of Greek known as *Koine*, ultimately replacing Aramaic as the common language.[16]

Following his death, Alexander's empire was divided among his generals. Seleucus I established the Seleucid kingdom of Mesopotamia and Syria, and Ptolemy I Lagos established the 31st and last dynasty of Egyptian pharaohs. The tiny theocratic city-state of Judah was caught in the middle, as the two Greek kingdoms competed for power, and the people of Palestine-Israel suffered.

The Jews began to learn more than a new language. Their literature had been largely limited to religious matters, but they were now exposed to Greek philosophy, history, science, mathematics, poetry, and music. They learned about the concept of state citizenship—apart from religion—in which people had a democratic voice in their government, and the secular education of their children, including physical training in gymnasiums.

Confronted by the philosophical individualism and democracy of Hellenism, the Jewish theocratic leadership hunkered down behind fundamental legalisms. The books of Jonah and Job were written to illustrate how people could deal with foreign invaders and the suffering of life, while maintaining a faith in the justice of God's forgiveness. The Jews sought solutions to their secular problems by

---

[16] The Dead Sea Scrolls are written in both languages, as well as Hebrew.

obsessing on their sacred religious history in order to derive oral laws, or *halakha*, to serve as guidelines for daily living.

The Torah was finally compiled as late as the fourth century BCE, and the Prophets were formulated by the end of the third century. The Writings, including Chronicles, Proverbs, and Ecclesiastes, were created by priestly writers to expand upon and explain the Torah and Prophets, and to increase their own power. Altogether, the whole work came to be called the *Tanakh*, after the initial letter of its three parts, Torah, Neviim, and Khetuvim.

Greek cities were built in the Middle East and Egypt, including the Decapolis east of the Sea of Galilee in Jordan. Cities in Gaza and along the Palestinian coast were rebuilt with classical Greek architecture. It was in Alexandria, the city founded by Alexander at the mouth of the Nile on the Mediterranean coast, where Hellenization had its greatest influence on the Jewish people who came to live there.

Although the area of Palestine-Israel was relatively small compared to the great empires of Iran, Iraq, Greece, and Rome that would from time to time sweep through the region, its people maintained a literary tradition—primarily in regard to their religion—from an early period that prevailed throughout its history. A brief overview of that literature may assist an understanding of the events that are to come. The reader might want to consider this section a long footnote to be returned to when a discussion of these books is encountered.

The Masoretic Text of the Torah and the Septuagint Greek Translation

The first five books of the Torah (Old Testament)—Genesis, Exodus, Leviticus, Numbers, and Deuteronomy—are known as the Pentateuch (five books). Both Jewish and Christian dogma hold that they were personally written or dictated by Moses. The Sadducees and the Samaritans believed that only the Pentateuch was authoritative.

Over the centuries of strife, conquests, deportations, and revisions, the Torah, as finally edited by Ezra and added to by the later Prophets and Writings became known as the Masoretic, or Hebrew text of the Tanakh.

The Greek-Egyptian king, Ptolemy I Soter established the great royal library of Alexander and caused it to collect at least a half million books primarily written on papyrus scrolls. There is a story that his successor, Ptolemy II ordered that the Hebrew Torah be translated into Greek. Legend attributes the work known as the Septuagint (Greek-seventy) to the efforts of seventy translators. More likely, Greek-speaking Alexandrian Jews prepared Greek translations of the Torah for their own use during readings in the synagogues.

The Septuagint would become the Old Testament of The Holy Bible in the Christian religion. The Masoretic text would become the authoritative version used by Rabbinic Judaism. Together, along with the New Testament, they would influence the development of Islam.

The Historical Writings of Josephus Based on the Book of Maccabees

Until the middle of the twentieth century CE (Common Era), the Bible was the primary source of information about the origin, foundation, and evolution of the Jewish, Christian, and Islamic religions. The primary, alternative, secular source of knowledge was provided by the writings of Titus Flavius Josephus, who was born Joseph ben Matityahu into a priestly and aristocratic Jewish family in the Roman province of Judea. He served as a Jewish military commander in the First Jewish-Roman War in 66-73 CE, before surrendering to Vespasian's Roman forces.

A turncoat, Josephus quickly gained favor with the Romans by proclaiming that the Jewish messianic prophecies were about Vespasian becoming the Roman emperor. Josephus collaborated with Vespasian and served as his interpreter. He became friends with Vespasian's son, Titus, and personally participated in the destruction of Jerusalem and Herod's Temple.

When Vespasian became emperor, he granted Roman citizenship to Josephus, who adopted Vespasian's family name of Flavius. Thereafter, Josephus lived and wrote in Rome. In addition to his autobiography, Josephus' most significant books were the *Antiquities of the Jews* and the *Wars of the Jews*. Much of his work has survived intact and is readily available in most languages.

With his aristocratic upbringing, Josephus was literate in Greek and Latin and was knowledgeable about the Books of the Maccabees—which documented the Maccabean Revolution and the Hasmonean Dynasty. Writing in Rome for a critical and sophisticated audience, that included the Emperor, Josephus attempted to be an accurate historian, while defending the history and reputation of the Jewish people. His work is generally considered to be reliable. Josephus undoubtedly had access to many other books, which later came to be known as the Pseudepigrapha and Apocrypha, in writing his histories.

Specific references in Josephus' writings to Jesus as the messiah who was crucified by Pilate are not considered by biblical scholars to have been written by Josephus. However, his references to "the brother of Jesus, who was called Christ, whose name was James" have a greater recognition as being authentic. Equally validated is Josephus' reference to the imprisonment and decapitation of John the Baptist. He also introduced his readers to those who followed the Way of Righteousness, whom he referred to as the Essenes.

The Dead Sea Scrolls of The Way

The Dead Sea Scrolls are the remnant of a vast library of written materials accumulated over hundreds of years by the influential and widely practiced Way of Righteousness during the period that included the ministry of Jesus. Inasmuch as the Scrolls represent the doctrine of the Way that Jesus and his brothers taught, the Scrolls illuminate much of his ministry that was obscured by the later Pauline Christian authors who either rewrote the documents or used them out of context.

In November 1946, an Arab shepherd boy searching for a lost goat discovered a collection of ancient books in clay jars in a cave near Qumran by the Dead Sea within the West Bank of Jordan. These books and others later found in nearby caves became known as the *Dead Sea Scrolls*.

The Books of the People

Over the next year, the scrolls from the first, or Cave 1, made their way into Jerusalem, and four scrolls came into the hands of the Archbishop of the Syrian Orthodox Monastery of St. Mark. These consisted of a complete book of *Isaiah* (See Photo #6), a commentary on the book of *Habakkuk*, two parts of a single scroll later named the *Community Rule* or *Manual of Discipline*, and one badly decomposed Aramaic scroll.

The remaining scrolls, which included an ancient copy of *Deutero-Isaiah* and two previously unknown works later named *The War of the Sons of Light Against the Sons of Darkness* or *War Rule* and the *Thanksgiving Psalms* were directly purchased by Dr. E. L. Sukenik, Professor of Archeology at the Hebrew University, using funds contributed by the University.

Inasmuch as the Israeli war of independence had divided Jerusalem, Dr. Sukenik was unable to examine the scrolls at St. Marks. These were brought by the Syrian monks to the American School of Oriental Research where they were examined and photographed.

The St. Mark scrolls were later brought to the United States where they were advertised for sale. They were secretly purchased by the government of Israel through the efforts of Dr. Sukenik's son and were returned to Israel in 1953.

In the meantime, in October 1951, additional fragments of scrolls were found by Bedouin tribesmen about eleven miles south of Qumran near the Dead Sea. The next year a survey was made of all identifiable caves in the area and, in what became known as Cave 3, a team found two portions of the same scroll consisting of rolled copper, which was found to be an inventory of hidden Temple treasure.

Six months after the official survey, local Bedouins found the large Cave 4, the most spectacular find of all for it proved to have been an ancient library, or *geniza*, for the storage of documents. Cave 4 is not a natural cave, having been carved by hand from the soft marl stone and equipped with holes in the walls used to support shelves for the storage of documents. Careful shifting through the thick layer of dust on its floor produced fragments from more than 900 manuscripts. (See Photo #7)

The discovery of these additional scrolls aroused interest in the ruined structures located at Khirbet Qumran within easy walking distance of Caves 1 and 4. First believed to be the ruins of a Roman fort, excavations conducted there between 1951 and 1956 by Father Roland de Vaux of the École Biblique confirmed the likelihood that the structures and caves were connected with a community of Essenes[17] who lived there at the time of Jesus.

The Essenes were described by the Roman historian Pliny in the first century CE, and the *Community Rule* found in Cave 1 provides a comprehensive constitution and by-laws for the Qumran congregation who referred to themselves, not as Essenes, but as the Doers of the Law (Osim), the Sons of Zadok, the Sons of Light, the Saints, the Poor, or simply *the Way*. Among the fragments recovered from the dust of Cave 4 were those of a manuscript which was already known in history as the *Damascus Document* or *Damascus Rule*.

In 1896, Solomon Schecter, a lecturer at Cambridge University learned of old manuscripts stored in a loft above an ancient synagogue in Cairo. He obtained permission to explore the *"genizah,"* a place where old or worn out sacred manuscripts are stored, and he recovered 164 boxes containing 100,000 pieces of material. The most startling manuscript was the *Damascus Document* which revealed the existence of an Israelite community which entered a new covenant with God under a Righteous Teacher and who lived in the wilderness known as Damascus.

The scroll fragments found at Qumran also confirmed the antiquity of another document from the Pseudepigrapha known as the *Testament of the Twelve Patriarchs*. Long believed to have been the result of later Christian redaction due to its numerous predictions of a coming messiah, the scrolls proved that The Way had indeed possessed specific expectations of an immediate messianic rule by not one, but three messiahs: a suffering son of man messiah (son of the Most High); a Davidic messiah (a son of Judah); and a priestly messiah (a righteous son of Aaron).

The last major scroll discovery was made during the 1967 war when Bethlehem was captured by the Israelis. Suspecting that a

---

[17] For reasons discussed later, the Essenes will be called the Osim in this book.

dealer connected with the original scrolls might still possess some documents, the dealer was interrogated and led officers to his home where he produced a scroll which he had hidden for six years. This document became known as the *Temple Scroll* and was published in 1977.

The Dead Sea Scrolls were probably hidden in the caves during the period between the Roman destruction of Jerusalem and the Temple in 70 CE (following the deaths of Jesus and his brother, James) and 132-6 CE (when Judea was totally destroyed by the Romans after the Bar Kochba uprising was suppressed).

One of the earliest reports of the discovery of ancient books in the vicinity came in the third century CE, when Origen, a Christian leader, wrote about a manuscript "together with other Hebrew and Greek books [found] in a jar near Jericho." Writing in the ninth century, Timotheus, a Nestorian Christian Patriarch, reported that "some books were found some years ago in a rock dwelling near Jericho." Apparently, none of these documents survived.

Following their discovery in November 1946 in Cave 1, the seven major, largely intact, Dead Sea Scrolls were quickly published by the Israeli and American scholars who first obtained possession. As searches of other caves in the vicinity turned up additional fragments of ancient manuscripts, many of the fragments were purchased by a group of foreign archaeological and biblical research schools in east Jerusalem. Funds were contributed by various sources including the government of Jordan and the Vatican.

The pace of publication was very slow. As the years passed and very little original material was offered for publication by members of the International Team, increasing criticism was made by many scholars, including Géza Vermes of Oxford who wrote as early as 1977 that the situation was likely to become the academic scandal *par excellence* of the twentieth century.

By 1990, only about twenty percent of the scroll fragments had been published. There remained unavailable a large corpus of fragmentary manuscripts from the Dead Sea caves whose publication had been delayed over the years by the small group of scholars who had exclusive possession of them.

Although ownership of the scrolls was claimed by Israel's Department of Antiquities after the 1967 war (as a result of Israel's conquest of East Jerusalem and the Rockefeller Museum where the scrolls were housed) actual control continued to be maintained by the International Team controlled by the Dominican priests.

In 1991, The Biblical Archaeology Society in Washington, D.C. contracted to publish photographs of the remaining scrolls. The arrangement provided that Dr. Eisenman and Dr. James Robinson, Chair of the Religion Faculty, Claremont Graduate School—who had headed the Committee which prepared the English Edition of the Gnostic Gospels—would write an introduction and compile an index. Representing an "undisclosed client" and an "undisclosed donor" of publication funds, the author of this book signed the publication contract with the Biblical Archaeology Society.

A Facsimile Edition of the Dead Sea Scrolls in two volumes was published in November of 1991.

The Gnostic Gospels of Mary Magdalene

The Gnostic Gospels represent a small portion of the large library accumulated by the majority group of Jesus's followers following his execution. As we will learn later in the chapter about Mary Magdalene and her ministry, the Gnostics most closely represented the spiritual values taught by Jesus during his ministry. For the first several centuries following his death, the Gnostic version of Jesus's teaching was the prevalent view throughout the Eastern Mediterranean area, including Egypt and Syria.

The Gnostic Gospels were discovered in December 1945 (eleven months before the Dead Sea Scrolls) by two Arab farmers digging around the base of a large rock at the foot of a cliff along the banks of the Egyptian Nile. As they dug up the rich nitrates used to fertilize their fields, they uncovered a large sealed clay jar containing some fifty-two papyrus[18] books in twelve leather bindings. The language used in the books was Coptic, which is Egyptian written with Greek

---

[18] Papyrus is an early form of durable paper made from the pith of the papyrus plant.

letters. Some were originally composed as early as the first century, and they were probably buried for safekeeping around 360 CE.

Following the armed takeover of the Roman Empire by Emperor Constantine, Christianity became a recognized religion and official suppression ended. Orthodox Christian bishops gained the power to condemn heretical books, including those of the Gnostics, and to make their possession a criminal offense. Many such books were burned and destroyed, and it was at about this time that the great library at Alexandria was sacked and burned by an orthodox Christian mob.

Gnostics were particularly active in Egypt, both as a part of the Christian monastic movement and in opposition to, or as an alternative to, orthodoxy. Among the orthodox monasteries was St. Pachomius located near where the modern town of Nag Hammadi is found today and close to the cliff where the *Gnostic Gospels* were discovered.

In the face of the cliff, near the top, sixth dynasty tombs (which had been dug between 2350 and 2200 BCE) had been robbed in antiquity. These cool caves may have offered dissident monks—who separated from the nearby orthodox monastery—a place for spiritual retreat or living quarters for the solitary. The cave walls are covered with Christian crosses and the opening lines of biblical Psalms.

After being found in 1945, some of the Gnostic manuscripts from Nag Hammadi were burned by the widow of one of the discoverers who believed them worthless, or a source of bad luck. The remainder were sold through several sources, and Codex I was acquired in 1952 by the Jung Institute of Zurich. The "Jung Codex" was returned to Egypt between 1956 and 1975, as it was being published and joined the remaining manuscripts which had been brought together at the Coptic Museum of Old Cairo.

As these *Gnostic Gospels* came to be studied, it was learned that they too were like other finds of the past. The first known discovery was in 1769 when a Scottish tourist purchased a Coptic manuscript near Luxor in Upper Egypt. Later published in 1892, the document claims to record conversations of Jesus with his disciples, which included both men and women.

In 1773 a collector browsing through a London bookstore found a Coptic manuscript which also contained a discussion of mysteries between Jesus and his disciples. Finally, in 1896, a German Egyptologist purchased several Coptic manuscripts in Cairo which contained some of the books later found at Nag Hammadi, including the *Gospel of Mary* (Magdalene) and the *Apocryphon of John*.

Under an agreement originally reached during the early 1960s between UNESCO and the Minister of Culture and National Guidance of the United Arab Republic (Egypt), an International Committee for the Nag Hammadi Codices was finally appointed in 1970. The twelve-volume *Facsimile Edition of the Nag Hammadi Codices* began to appear in 1972 and was completed in 1978.

Based upon the availability of the facsimiles, complete editions in English, German, and French were prepared, including an eleven-volume English edition, entitled *The Coptic Gnostic Library*.

Finally, under the leadership of the late Dr. James M. Robinson, Chair, Religion Faculty, Claremont Graduate School, *The Nag Hammadi Library in English* was translated by the members of the Coptic Gnostic Library Project of the Institute for Antiquity and Christianity and published as a single volume in 1977.

The Authors and Editors of the New Testament

Following the crucifixion of Jesus, his followers may have conveyed the message of his ministry orally; however, when the Pauline Church came to be centered in Rome, the first three gospels were written to reflect an accommodation with the Roman government and to create a written dogma to unite the Pauline congregations. The Book of John was written later to help paper over differences between the original message of the Way of Righteousness at Qumran, the ministries of Paul, and the Gnostics led by Mary Magdalene.

The first four of these books written in the names of Matthew, Mark, Luke, and John are known as the Gospels, or good news. They are followed by the Acts of the Apostles, which is a continuation of Luke. There are thirteen letters either written by Paul, or in his name, and additional letters attributed to Peter, John, and James the Just and Judas (Jude), the brothers of Jesus. The Letter to the Hebrews may have been written in the Greek language by Joseph (Joses or Barnabas), another brother of Jesus, who may have also written the original Book of Matthew in the Hebrew language.

The authentic letters of Paul were among the earliest and were primarily addressed to the congregations he organized among the Gentiles of Asia Minor and Greece. These were not the only congregations of the teachings of Jesus, and there were other books written presenting alternative points of view and differing theologies. Among these were those written and circulated by the Gnostics (*those who know* from the Greek word, *Gnosis* or knowledge). They considered themselves to be followers but believed that they were in possession of secret knowledge and teachings of Jesus.

Perhaps in response to the Gnostic books, various orthodox church leaders began to circulate lists of books they held to be authoritative. There were disputes, including differences about the books of Hebrews and Revelations. It took several hundred years before a list prepared by the historian Eusebius of Caesarea received the widest acceptance. His list contained all the 27 books that ultimately form the canonical New Testament. This list was approved at the Third Council of Carthage in 397 CE and was confirmed by Pope Innocent I in 405 CE.

As we will come to see, *the deliberate omission of all the books* relied upon by the Gnostics deprived Christianity of the spiritual soul of the Way of Righteousness as taught by Jesus. The Christian community is only now becoming aware of this fact since the discovery of the Gnostic Gospels and the Dead Sea Scrolls. By minimizing the role of James, Judas, Simeon, and Joseph, the brothers of Jesus, in the Gospels and by relegating their writings to the end of the New Testament, Christianity failed to incorporate the balancing views offered by these works to the religion created by Paul.

The Books That Were Not Included in the Old or New Testament

The term *Pseudepigrapha* commonly refers to more than 60 religious texts written between 300 BCE and 300 CE, which were not included in the Old or New Testaments. Some are included in the Catholic Bible, but not the Protestant Bible, and others are included in the Septuagint, but not the Hebrew Bible. The name comes from the fact that many of the books were written using pseudonyms of various biblical authorities and personages.

Protestants refer to the books included between the Old and New Testaments of the Catholic and Eastern Orthodox Bibles as the Apocrypha.

Although fundamentalist Christians and Jews believe that the Bible is the inerrant word of God, there has to be some informed recognition that the dozens, if not hundreds, of other textual scriptures created at the same time as those ultimately included in the canons of these religions have value in understanding and interpreting the religions. Without consideration of this vast store of supplemental knowledge, the Bible can be viewed as only a summary of what was relied upon by those who practiced the religions at the time the documents were created.

Portions of Josephus' histories, the Pseudepigrapha, and the Old and New Testaments were validated and illuminated by the discovery of the Gnostic Gospels at Nag Hammadi in Egypt during December 1945 and the Dead Sea Scrolls at Qumran in the West Bank of Jordan the following year in November 1946.

Relying on these books and other related discoveries, it is now possible to more accurately define the origins of Judaism, Christianity, and Islam. To better understand the nature of the Way of Righteousness upon which Jesus based his ministry, and its effects, we will now skip forward to a period several hundred years before the life of the historical Jesus.

The Growth of the Way of Righteousness

Commencing about 200 years before the life of Jesus, the following is a brief history of the Hellenization of Israel by the Syrian Greeks, the resistance by the Hasideans and the Zaddik, the Maccabean Revolution and its establishment of the Hasmonean Kingdom, the Roman Conquest by Pompey, the Herodian Kingdom, and the growth of the Way of the Righteous.

THE HASIDEANS AND ZADDIKS

Shortly after the beginning of the second century BCE, Judah was a religious city-state, something like the Vatican of today. Consisting of little more than the immediate area around Jerusalem, it was an insignificant vassal of the Greek (Egyptian) Ptolemaic Kingdom.[19]

During the period of the Second Temple following the Babylon exile—after Ezra the priest seized power—the people of Judah had been ruled by a succession of high priests of the family lineage of Zadok, Solomon's priest. Known as the Sadducees, these families were the aristocrats of Jerusalem. They had become wealthy and powerful under Greek rule and generally supported the Hellenization of Israel.

Although the Sadducees were religiously orthodox—they recognized only the first five books of the written Torah as authority and rejected the later prophets—they bribed and connived for the financial benefits flowing from the high priesthood, including control of theatres, baths, and athletic gymnasiums in Jerusalem.

The Pious Hasideans Oppose the Corrupt High Priests

In opposition to the Sadducees was a group known as the Hasideans—from the Hebrew word *Hesed* meaning Piety—which was composed of both ordinary priests and laity. Because they lived under Greek pagan occupation and suffered from the corruption of their Sadducee religious leaders, the Hasideans believed the Last Times were imminent. They saw themselves as representatives of the Jewish people in practicing a love of God (Piety) and a love of their fellow man (Righteousness).

Under Persian influence during the Exile, the Hasideans had developed a belief in a succession of ages during which the forces of light and darkness would contend with each other—until a final

---

[19] This part is largely based on the historical writings of Titus Flavius Josephus (Yosef ben Matityahu) and the Books of the Maccabees, upon which he also relied.

age in which light would prevail. Those who lived a life of piety and righteousness would be rewarded by having their physical bodies raised up in the Last Times into the presence of God.

Drawing on the prophecy of Ezekiel, the Hasideans had come to believe in a bodily resurrection, a literal "standing up of the bones," which would occur at the end of the ages when the pious and righteous would be raised from Sheol, where they rested with the fallen of the Mighty Ones of Old, the *Nephilim* or the *Watchers*, who came to be known as the angels.

The Hasideans also developed an idea of a Hell as a place of torment for the wicked after death. The word they used meant "accursed valley," apparently a reference to the valley of Hinnon (Gehenna) southwest of Jerusalem where the trash of the city was burned. For the righteous, they predicted a paradise of delights.

A new literature of apocalyptic writings about the end time was born. The apocalypse would unveil the divine mysteries—and the future would be revealed. These apocalyptic writers followed in the footsteps of the biblical prophets with their warning and interpretations. Several of their books would be later redacted into the Book of Daniel, which personified the genre.

Appalled by the corruption of the high priesthood, the Hasideans believed the most important qualification for high priests was not that one should be a Sadducee—who inherited the name of Solomon's priest, Zadok. Rather, a high priest should actually be *Zaddik,* or righteous, toward the people and be *Hesed*, or pious, before God.

While most Hasideans emphasized a life of righteousness as expected by the Law, others directed their piety towards a worship of the Law of God itself. The most pious were those who were able to memorize and recite the oral Torah (*halakha*), which was conceived during the exile. They came to be known as teachers of the law, or rabbis (master). The rabbis administered a large body of oral Torah concerned with its practical daily applications, and a vast literature of apocalyptic and spiritual writings. From among these teachers, the first lawyers arose. They could recite both the restrictions *and,* for the benefit of their clients, the exceptions to the law. The rabbis organized synagogues in their homes for Sabbath services, and they became a sect known as the Pharisees (Aramaic *perishayya*, from the Hebrew *perushim*, those "set apart" or separated by their piety).

The Greek Syrians Conquer Judah-Israel and Force Hellenization on the People

The period of relative harmony in Judah-Israel under the benign rule of the Egyptian Greek Ptolemies—with its cultural and religious freedoms—was disrupted in 198 BCE. The Syrian Greek Seleucids challenged the Egyptian Ptolemies for control of the ancient land bridge of Palestine-Israel. After five "Syrian Wars," the Syrians seized control of the region.

The Syrians sought to forcibly impose Hellenization on the people, including the Greek language and secular practices. Could the Jewish religion adapt to these innovations? The Sadducees and some Doctors of the Law believed reform and accommodation was possible; however, the Hasideans and many ordinary Jewish people equated Hellenization with apostasy, and the Apocalypse they both feared and prayed for, descended upon them.

The Righteous Priests of the People Oppose the Corrupt Priesthood

At this time Simeon (Simon) son of Onias, who was known as the *Zaddik*, or Just, was appointed as high priest. Although a pureblood Sadducee, Simeon also conformed, spiritually, to the Hasidean requirements of piety to God and righteousness to the people. Simeon is described in *Ecclesiasticus (Wisdom of Sirach)*:

> He was like the morning star appearing through the clouds or the moon at the full; like the sun shining on the temple of the Most High or the light of the rainbow on the gleaming clouds; like a rose in spring or lilies by a fountain of water; like a green shoot upon Lebanon on a summer's day or burning incense in the censer; like a cup of beaten gold, decorated with every kind of precious stone; like an olive-tree laden with fruit or a cypress with its top in the clouds.

Simeon was succeeded by his son Onias III, who also served as a righteous high priest; however, when Antiochus IV Epiphanes took over the Syrian Seleucid kingdom in 187 BCE, the king was petitioned by Onias's brother Jeshua (or Joshua) to become the high priest instead of Onias. Joshua sweetened his petition with a bribe of 360 talents in silver coin and a promise of 80 talents from future revenue. In addition, Jeshua offered another 150 talents for the right to build a sports stadium in Jerusalem. Antiochus accepted the bribe and appointed Jeshua, who changed his name to the Greek Jason and began to impose the Greek way of life on the people.

The palace intrigue increased when Menelaus, Jason's traitorous ambassador to Antiochus, outbid Jason by 300 silver talents and was appointed high priest in his stead. Menelaus failed to produce the promised bribe and had to surrender some of the Temple gold plate, when held to an accounting by Antiochus. In the meantime, Onias III was murdered when he denounced Menelaus.

The people of Jerusalem rioted when they heard about the death of Onias and the diversion of the Temple treasure. A legal action was brought against Menelaus; however, after providing an additional bribe to Antiochus, he was acquitted, and his accusers were executed.

The Zaddik and Their Teacher of Righteousness Create the Way of His Heart

Onias IV, the son of Onias III, emigrated to Egypt with some dissident priests and founded a rival temple to Yahweh in Leontopolis along the Nile with the blessings of the Greek King Ptolemy Philometor.

At about this time, we can trace the beginning of a movement from within the Hasideans which even more closely identified with living a simple life of righteousness. The dissidents began to gather in Galilee and to withdraw from Temple worship in Jerusalem *and* the synagogues of the Pharisees. They established an alternative priesthood based on a succession of righteousness teachers, who were often confronted with "wicked priests" of the Sadducees and "scoffing liars" of the Pharisees.

The evolving group became known as the *Zaddik* or Zadokites, and from them a vast literature began to grow—some of which was undoubtedly shared with those of a similar mind in Egypt. The earliest of their documents may have been *Ecclesiasticus,* which traced all the heroes of Judah-Israel down through and including Simeon the Just. Fragments of *Ecclesiasticus* were found in the Cairo *genizah*, among the Dead Sea Scrolls, and during excavations at Masada. In addition to the Prophets and Writings, other books such as *Adam and Eve* and *Enoch* were probably in circulation and redaction by this time.

The Zaddik evolved over time into the Way of the Osim, as their literature increasingly reflected the influence of Eastern religions and Gnostic philosophies. The *Damascus Document*, one of the Dead Sea Scrolls, which was written later, may be referring to this period in its introduction. It makes the first mention of the Way, which came to denote the movement:

> Hear now, all you who know righteousness, and consider the works of God; for He has a dispute with all flesh and will condemn all who despise Him.
>
> For when they were unfaithful and forsook Him, He hid his face from Israel and His Sanctuary and delivered them up to the sword. But remembering the Covenant of the forefathers, He left a remnant to Israel and did not deliver it up to be destroyed. And in the age of wrath, three hundred and ninety years after he had given them into the hand of king Nebuchadnezzar of Babylon, He visited them, and He caused a plant root to spring from Israel and Aaron to inherit His land and to prosper on the good things of His earth. And they perceived their iniquity and recognized that they were guilty men, yet for twenty years they were like blind men grouping for the way.
>
> And God observed their deeds, that they sought Him with a whole heart, *and he raised for them a Teacher of Righteousness to guide them in the way of His heart.* And he made known to the latter generations that which God had done to the latter generation, the congregation of traitors, to those who departed from *the way.* (emphasis added)

In the next paragraph the Document describes the Righteous Teacher's adversary, "when the Scoffer arose who shed over Israel the waters of lies. He caused them to wander in a pathless wilderness . . . ."

The Epilogue of *Ecclesiasticus* gives thanks to God for "rescuing me from death, from the trap laid by a slanderous tongue and from lips that utter lies." It praises God for rescue "from the foul tongue and its lies—a wicked slander spoken in the king's presence." Both references may refer to Onias' denunciation by Jason or Menelaus. The Epilogue ends with an invitation to those who need instruction to lodge in a house of learning.

The Syrian Greeks and Egyptian Greeks continued to vie for power in the Middle East, and the Syrian king, Antiochus IV organized an invasion of Egypt in 169 BCE; however, there was a new player on the stage. Rome blocked the Syrian advance, and Antiochus turned his fury on Jerusalem.

There were two factions competing for power within the Sadducees. The Tobiads were the more worldly Hellenistic group which generally supported the Syrians, and the more righteous Oniads favored the Egyptians.

Responding to an appeal for assistance by the Tobiads, Antiochus IV killed thousands of people in Jerusalem, including many Oniads, and sold thousands more into slavery. Menelaus invited Antiochus into the Temple and handed over 1,900 talents of silver. A Greek was appointed commissioner of Jerusalem, and a mercenary army occupied the city.

In the "abomination of desolation" described in the Book of Daniel, the Second Temple was rededicated to the Greek sky god Zeus. The people were not allowed to observe the Sabbath or keep the religious festivals and holidays. It became a crime punishable by death to possess or adhere to the Law.

Daniel Imagined The Angels and Resurrected the Dead

For the Way, this had to be the end of times. It was in their Book of Daniel where—after several preliminary stages in prophetic literature—the apocalyptic proclamation came to be fully elaborated. Daniel was probably composed during the time of the Greek-Syrian invader, Antiochus IV, but, over time, the focus of evil shifted from the Greek oppressors to the Romans, who became the *Kittim* of the Fourth Kingdom.

Daniel contains the first mention of angels in the Hebrew Bible. In Daniel, the *Nephilim* or *Watchers*, who had heretofore all been killed, now came among the living and were given names, such as Gabriel and Michael.

Gabriel was the messenger angel who explains Daniel's visions to him. He would later appear to the Virgin Mary foretelling the birth of Jesus and to Muhammad telling him to recite the Quran.

Michael, one of the chief angels, was the Prince of Israel. There were other princes over Persia and Greece, who did battle with Michael and his allied princes. Daniel (12:1) predicts, "At that time shall arise Michael, the great prince who has charge of your people. And there shall be a time of trouble, such as never has been since there was a nation 'til that time; but at that time your people shall be delivered, everyone whose name shall be found written in the book."

The same chapter of Daniel also contains the earliest and undisputed reference in the Hebrew Bible to a resurrection of the dead:

> And many of those who sleep in the dust of the earth shall awake, some to everlasting life, and some to shame and everlasting contempt. And those who are wise shall shine like the brightness of the firmament; and those who turn many to righteousness, like the stars forever and ever. (12:2-3)

For the first time in Jewish history, belief in an individual resurrection from the dead came into being. Confronted with terrible persecution—with men, women, and children being cruelly tortured for holding to the Law—the old problem of retribution arose more sharply than ever. For the martyrs to the faith—those given the choice of apostasy or death—new questions are asked. How significant is a martyr's death, if the faithful receive nothing in the hereafter? Where is the just God with his righteousness—especially for those who are the most righteous of all?

Daniel's answer is that the epoch was a part of the end times. Israel will be saved, and the dead will rise again. Those who have slept in the "land of the dust" will awaken and return to a glorious life as whole human beings—not just as souls. This worldly existence will last eternally, without end—for the wise in the form of eternal light, for the sinners in the form of eternal shame.

THE MACCABEAN REVOLUTION FREES THE PEOPLE FROM THE SYRIANS

The forced imposition of the Greek culture expanded beyond Jerusalem and came to a head when a Syrian official ordered a priest named Mattathias in the northern village of Modi'in[20] to offer a sacrifice to the Greek gods. Mattathias displayed his zeal for the Law by refusing and by killing another Jew who offered to comply. Mattathias then killed the Syrian.

Mattathias had five sons: John, Simeon, Judas, Eleazar, and Jonathan. His grandfather was known as Asmoneus—which resulted in the family being known as the Hasmonaeans.

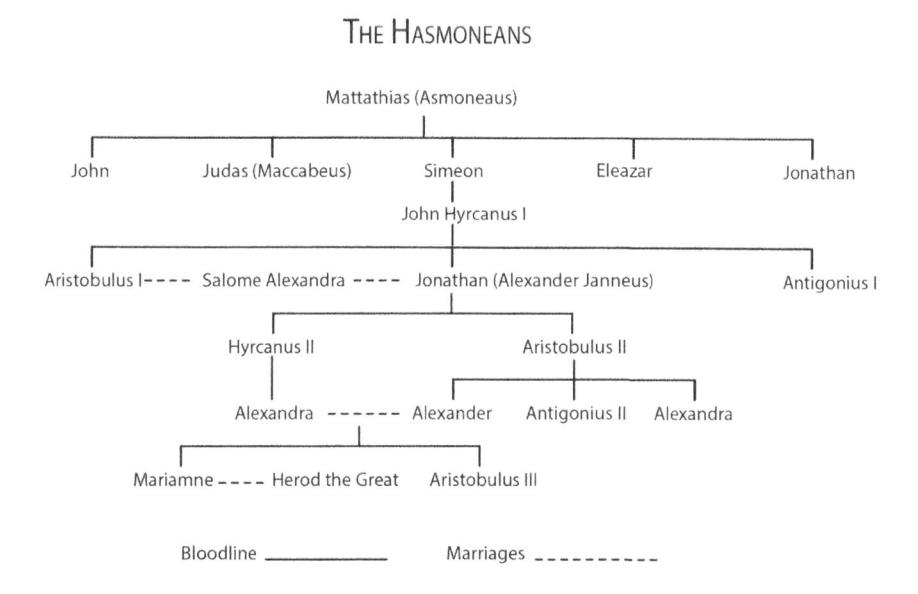

THE HASMONEANS

```
                        Mattathias (Asmoneaus)
                                |
   ┌──────────┬────────────────┬──────────┬──────────┐
  John    Judas (Maccabeus)  Simeon    Eleazar    Jonathan
                                |
                         John Hyrcanus I
                                |
   ┌──────────────────────────────────────────────────┐
Aristobulus I ---- Salome Alexandra ---- Jonathan (Alexander Janneus)        Antigonius I
                                |
           ┌────────────────────┴─────────────┐
       Hyrcanus II                       Aristobulus II
           |                                  |
       Alexandra  ------ Alexander    Antigonius II   Alexandra
           |                  |
   ┌───────┴──────────────────┴───┐
Mariamne ---- Herod the Great   Aristobulus III

       Bloodline _____        Marriages _ _ _ _ _
```

Mattathias and his sons took to the countryside with the cry, "Follow me every one of you who is zealous for the Law and strives

---

[20] The modern city of Modi'in-Maccabim-Re'ut is located 19 miles west of Jerusalem and 22 miles southeast of Tel Aviv on the main highway connecting the two cities.

to maintain the covenant." Judas, also called Maccabaeus (Aramaic *maggabay* the "hammer man"), escaped into the desert with nine *Zaddikim*, where they lived in the wild. They were joined by many others of the Way who wanted to maintain their religion and law.

Many of the Zaddiks and those of the Way took their families and livestock and gathered in caves in the vicinity of Qumran (where the scrolls were discovered) to keep the Sabbath in secret. They were denounced to the Syrian governor, who sent soldiers to attack them. When the Zaddik refused to come out of the caves, or to defend themselves on the Sabbath, hundreds were killed and burned.

When Mattathias and his group heard about the slaughter at Qumran, they resolved to fight on the Sabbath if attacked. The Hasmonaeans were joined by the Hasideans, who accepted Mattathias and his son Judas as "guides of righteousness." The combined force swept through the country, destroying pagan altars and forcibly circumcising all the uncircumcised boys they encountered.

Restoration of the Temple by Judas Maccabaeus

Mattathias became ill in 166 BCE, and on his deathbed, he called his sons together and said, "my sons, draw your courage and strength from the law, for by it you will win great glory. Now here is Simeon, your brother; I know him to be wise in counsel; always listen to him, for he shall be a father to you. Judas Maccabaeus has been strong and brave from boyhood; he shall be your commander in the field and fight his people's battles." (1 *Maccabees* 2:65-68)

Judas assembled an army of religious partisans, which fought and won a series of battles, throughout Judah and neighboring areas, including Hebron and Idumaea. He and his brothers confronted and defeated a much larger Syrian army with the battle cry "God is our help." The rebels seized money and weapons allowing them to later defeat an even larger Syrian army.

In 164 BCE, Judas Maccabaeus recovered control of Jerusalem and the Second Temple. The sanctuary of the Temple was cleansed; a new altar was constructed, and sacrifices were offered for the first time in three-and-one-half years.

According to tradition, when Judas first entered the Temple, he found only one small lamp there, containing enough oil to burn for only one day. When the lamp was lighted and placed in the sanctuary, God caused it to burn for eight days. Jews celebrate the purification of the Temple by the feast of Hanukkah, known as the "Feast of Lights," which features an eight-branched candelabra.

The Hasideans Split Into the Pharisee Party and the Essene (Osim) Congregation

During this time, the Hasideans divided when the smaller Pharisaic sect withdrew from the group, as the Pharisees were content with spiritual and religious autonomy under the Syrian Seleucids. The focus of the Pharisees was on education and teaching, believing that those who were ignorant of the Torah lacked culture. They considered themselves to be "set aside" as religious reformers—who were able to interpret the Mosaic Law to identify ways to get around its more severe applications, considering contemporary conditions. Through their memorized interpretations and commentary on the Law, the Pharisees developed an extensive oral Torah, which they believed was as divinely inspired as the written Torah. By "building a wall" of ordinances and interpretations around the Torah concerning every imaginable situation or possibility, the Pharisees sought to avoid violating the Law itself.

The remainder of the Hasideans and Zaddiks became known in history as the Essenes, or the Way. The members of the Way rejected the oral Torah and despised Pharisaic practices, "But all these things those who built the wall and daubed it with whitewash did not understand, for a raiser of wind and preacher of lies preached to them . . . . In God's love for the forefathers, who stirred up after him, he loved those who came after them, for theirs is the covenant of the fathers. But in his hatred of the builders of the wall his anger was kindled." (*Damascus Document*, IX)

There have been numerous suggestions as to the origin of the name Essenes, some believing it means pious or righteous, while others think it means healer. Dr. Robert Eisenman proposes that members of the Congregation would refer to themselves as the

Osim, pronounced Oseem, which was a contraction or acronym of the Hebrew words, *Osei ha-torah* which means, *"Doers of the Law."* They were less worried about what the Law said or did not say but were dedicated to living the spirit of Abraham's ancient covenant of righteousness, as it was intended. Their name has been historically written as Essenes—which is generally accepted; however, because it best represents their most deeply held conviction, these "Doers of the Law" will be referred to hereafter as the Osim, or the Way.

The Way spread to all places in the Diaspora where Jews lived, including Egypt where they were called *Therapeutae*. There may have been direct connections with the breakaway group in Egypt, as they seem to have shared the same literature. Although members referred to themselves in a variety of ways in their extensive literature, righteousness was the way they chose to live their lives, and its attainment was the essence of their message.[21]

Those who were referred to as Essene by others called themselves the Saints, the Poor (*Ebionim*), the Meek, the Congregation, or the Way. They believed the great suffering of the Jews was brought on by heathen pressure to forsake their ancient faith, resulted from the last gasp of evil exerting itself to gain victory. For those of the Way, the drama was approaching its climax and the faithful had to intensify their resistance by a total devotion to God and His Law. They accepted persecution and isolation as the price to be paid for winning through to a share in the bliss of the age to come—which could not be long delayed.

Development of a Jewish Missionary Movement Beyond the Land

The astounding victory of tiny Israel over the great Syrian

---

[21] *The Way of Righteousness* is not only the title of this book, it is a golden literary thread that binds the silver cloth of all monotheistic religions into a spiritual covering intended to comfort all those, of every faith, who wear it. From this point forward, the Way will be referring to this evolving group of faithful, as they came to represent the hopes and aspirations of most Jewish people at the time of Jesus, and it provided the foundation of his spiritual mission to the world.

Seleucid empire filled the Jewish people with pride and enthusiasm. One of the most remarkable results was the development of a Jewish missionary movement. After the Maccabean successes the Jews became filled with the sense of a great destiny, and their missionary efforts became more aggressive and systematic. Both in Israel and in the Diaspora among other nations, great numbers were converted to the Jewish faith and its Way of Righteousness.

The world was ready for the message of the Way. The old pagan cults were stagnant, and intelligent people questioned them and looked for deeper meaning. Greek philosophy was too cold and abstract to fill the hearts of most people, and a real hunger for a moral religion was keenly felt.

People were experimenting with all sorts of oriental cults, and various mystery religions had become fashionable. The Jewish religion was a simple, rational belief; its ethical standards were high and inspiring, and its message was comforting. Moreover, it was based on an extensive library of writings that helped to explain its meaning and mission.

In addition to those who formally converted to Judaism, many Gentiles attached themselves unofficially and were known as "the God-fearing" or "strangers within the gate." These Gentiles were not required to undergo circumcision or abide by the food laws of the Jews; however, they had to vow to obey the basic laws that Noah established for all humans, which prohibited cursing God, idolatry, illicit sexuality, bloodshed, robbery, and eating flesh from a living animal. Essentially, the Noahic covenant with God required a respect for all living things.

Outside evidence of this evangelical activity can be found as early as 139 BCE, when there was an expulsion of Jews from Rome by the praetor Hispalus because of their attempts "to contaminate Roman beliefs by foisting upon them the worship of Jupiter Sabazios," their name for Yahweh Sabaoth, the Lord of Hosts.

THE PRIEST KINGS OF THE HASMONEAN DYNASTY

While the Greek Syrians continued to control the territory including and between the modern nations of Syria and Iran, its attempt to extend its empire westward into Greece was met with defeat by the Romans in 190 BCE. A peace treaty in 188 BCE required the payment of a significant indemnity to the Romans. During the ensuing decades, the Syrian kingdom was racked by continual palace intrigues, as a succession of kings attempted to maintain control and to meet the demands of the Romans. In addition, there was the ongoing conflict with Egypt. The power of the Syrian kingdom was also challenged by the Maccabees, who had occupied Jerusalem, the Temple, and surrounding areas. The Syrian army, however, continued to hold the Akra citadel in Jerusalem, which overlooked the Temple, and the Syrian king retained the power to appoint the high priest and governor of the district around Jerusalem.

Roman power continued to expand into the Middle East, and Demetrius I Soter, son of Seleucus IV, had been living and studying in Rome. Sailing under Roman protection, he landed on the coast of Asia Minor and declared himself king of Syria. The Syrian army revolted against Antiochus V and murdered him, and Demetrius I ascended the Syrian throne.

The Hasmonean brothers continued to be intent on political autonomy for Judah-Israel. Recognizing the growing power of Rome, Judas Maccabaeus sent envoys to the Roman Senate and negotiated a mutual defense agreement in 161 BCE. The agreement warned the new Syrian king Demetrius to stop his efforts to defeat the Maccabean rebellion.

Judas Maccabeus was killed in 160 BCE while defending against a Syrian invasion, and he was buried in the family tomb at Modi'in.

Jonathan Establishes the Congregation of Israel

Following the death of Judas Maccabeus, his brother, Jonathan was chosen to lead the Maccabean rebellion.[22] Shortly thereafter, another brother, John was kidnapped and murdered, and Jonathan led an attack to avenge his death.

The Maccabees were not of the genealogical lineage of Zadok; however, they were members of another large priestly family. At least initially, the Maccabees were Zaddiks in the spiritual lineage of Simeon the Just. Coins minted during this period bore the title, "Congregation of Israel." Jonathan's designation of "Israel" was likely intended to combine the territories of Judah and Northern Israel, ideologically, if not yet as a political and military reality.

Jonathan was able to take advantage of the internal Syrian civil war—and the Syrian conflicts with Rome and Egypt—by adroitly aligning himself with one side, and then another. In return, Jonathan was appointed by the Syrians to the high priesthood in Jerusalem and given the title of "King's Friend." Jonathan received a purple robe and gold crown, and he assumed the vestments of high priest at the Feast of Tabernacles.

Aligning himself with the Syrian king Balas Alexander—who had made an alliance with Egypt in 150 BCE and married Cleopatra, daughter of King Ptolemy of Egypt—Jonathan attended the wedding and was appointed by Alexander to command the Jewish forces. After Jonathan defeated another pretender to the Syrian throne in 147 BCE at Joppa, he was rewarded by Alexander with additional territory.

War broke out between the Syrians and the Egyptians, and Balas Alexander was defeated in 145 BCE; however, Ptolemy died soon thereafter, and Demetrius II seized the Syrian throne. Jonathan made

---

[22] Among the children of Jonathan was a daughter who married Matthias Ephlias, the great, great grandfather of Joseph ben Matthias, known to history as Flavius Josephus. Josephus was an observer of the fall of Jerusalem in 68 CE, and later wrote several books including an autobiography, the *Antiquities of the Jews* and the *Wars of the Jews,* all of which form the primary basis of all histories of the period, including this effort.

The Priest Kings of the Hasmonean Dynasty

peace with Demetrius, who confirmed him in the high priesthood. Demetrius agreed to exempt Judah and three Samaritan districts from taxation in exchange for 300 talents of silver.

Later, when Jonathan requested the Syrian troops to be withdrawn from the Akra citadel in Jerusalem, Demetrius promised to do so, but he requested the assistance of Jewish troops to help him overcome a revolt of his own troops in Antioch. Jonathan sent 3,000 fighting men and helped save the life of Demetrius; however, before he could keep his promise, Demetrius was defeated by the Greek general, Diodotus, who controlled yet another Greek pretender to the Syrian throne. The young Antiochus VI was crowned, and he continued Jonathan's confirmation as high priest with authority over the Samaritan districts.

Jonathan's brother, Simeon was appointed as the commanding officer of the coastline area from Tyre to the Egyptian border. Jonathan and Simeon captured Gaza, and they routed the remainder of Demetrius' Syrian army in a battle by the Sea of Galilee. Jonathan built fortresses in Judah, heightened the walls of Jerusalem, and built a high barrier to isolate the Akra citadel, which remained under Syrian control.

After Jonathan concluded a treaty of friendship with Rome, the Syrian General Diodotus invaded Israel and confronted Jonathan. Seeing the size of the Maccabean force, the general pretended to come in peace and offered to turn over the city of Ptolemais to Jonathan—but it was a trap. When Jonathan, accompanied by a reduced force of 1,000 men, moved to occupy the city, his men were slaughtered, and he was taken captive.

General Diodotus sent envoys to Simeon with a ransom demand of 100 talents of silver and two of Jonathan's sons. Simeon met the demand, but Jonathan was not released. There followed a running series of battles which culminated in Diodotus withdrawing into Gilead (east of the Jordan River), where he had Jonathan put to death. Diodotus then murdered his ward, the young Antiochus VI, and assumed the crown of Asia under the name of Typhon.

Simeon's Covenant With the People

Following the death of Jonathan in 142 BCE, the Jewish people acknowledged his older brother Simeon as "our leader in place of Judas and your brother Jonathan. Fight our battles, and we will do whatever you tell us." Simeon became the high priest and the first prince of the Hasmonean Dynasty.

Judah retained all its fortifications, and the Akra citadel was finally surrendered by the Syrians in 141 BCE. Simeon fortified the temple hill opposite the citadel, and he took up residence there. Simeon appointed his son, John as commander of the armed forces with his headquarters at Gaza, as Egypt appeared to be a greater threat than the Syrians.

To the now Romanized outside world, Judah was becoming known as Judea, and its people called themselves Jews. The coins issued by Simeon for the first time identified the people as the "Congregation of the Jews," and each local unit was known as the "Congregation of the City."

Under Simeon, Israel was at peace. He sent envoys to Rome with a large gold shield worth a thousand minas, to confirm his alliance with the Roman empire. The Roman Senate officially recognized the Hasmonean dynasty in 139 BCE.

The people showed their gratitude to Simeon and his sons by a covenant in which Simeon was confirmed as their leader and high priest in perpetuity "until a true prophet should appear." This covenant confirmed the Hasmonean dynasty, but it would last only until the appearance of a prophet of Israel, who would bring the dynasty to an end and who would anoint a new Messiah over Israel.

The ongoing Syrian civil war took another turn in 138 BCE, when Antiochus VII Sidetes, brother of Demetrius II, seized power over a much-reduced Syrian kingdom. When Simeon offered to send 2,000 picked men to assist Antiochus, he refused the offer and repudiated all previous agreements. Antiochus demanded the return of Joppa, Gaza, and the Akra citadel—or the payment of 1,000 talents of silver. Simeon counteroffered 100 talents, which was refused.

Antiochus invaded, and Simeon sent his sons John and Judas to meet him. The Syrian army was routed during a battle near Modi'in.

Simeon's son-in-law, Ptolemy, had been appointed governor of the Jericho region by the Syrians and was reconfirmed by Simeon. Ptolemy, also known as Ptolemaeus, however, harbored ambitions to seize control of Israel.

When Simeon and his sons, Mattathias and Judas arrived at Jericho in 135 BCE to inspect its fortifications, Ptolemaeus entertained them lavishly. After Simeon and his sons became drunk, they were attacked and killed.[23] Ptolemy dispatched a force to Gaza to kill John, the remaining son. Having received a warning, however, John killed the assassins when they arrived.

These events may be referred to in a *List of Testimonia* found in Cave 4 at Qumran. One of the *Testimonia* (the fourth) discusses a "cursed one," predicted in Joshua 6:26. The passage of Joshua follows the account of the ancient destruction of Jericho and reads:

> May the LORD's curse light on the man who comes forward to rebuild this city of Jericho: The laying of its foundations shall cost him his eldest son, the setting up of its gates shall cost him his youngest.

The Regrettable Conquest and Forced Conversion of Idumea to Judaism

John, the only remaining son of Simeon, became the first combined king and high priest of the Hasmonean dynasty. Known as Hyrcanus I, John reigned for more than 30 years (from 135 to 104 BCE), as Israel increasingly became politically independent.

Hyrcanus I aggressively sought to expand the boundaries of his kingdom by conquering Idumea, an area to the south of Judah. Ancient enemies, the Idumeans were descended from the Nabataeans who ruled from Petra located in a desert canyon about

---

[23] Dante Alighieri in his *Inferno*, designated Ptolemaea as a place in hell for traitors who harm guests in their home.

halfway between the Dead Sea and the Gulf of Aqaba. The "King's Highway," a caravan route, passed through the canyon allowing for the lucrative collection of tolls from merchants. From about 200 BCE, the Nabataeans became very wealthy and carved a magnificent city in the canyon out of the surrounding rock. The Idumeans expanded to control the area of Judah surrounding the cities of Hebron and Beersheba.

Although the evolving religion of the Jewish people was attracting converts from among other nations, the conquest and conversion of the Idumeans was more likely associated with military necessity than religious proselytization. With Ptolemaic Egypt remaining a threat, John was able to secure the southwest flank of Judah by incorporating Idumea into the Hasmonean kingdom, and its religion. As we will see, several generations later the conversion and forced circumcision of the Idumeans would have unforeseen consequences for the Jewish people.

The Growing Political Power of the Pharisee Party as Roman Collaborators

Having become a unified theocracy under the Hasmoneans, and with Hyrcanus I now installed as priest-king, the nation and religion of the Jews was not, however, free from internal strife. Opposition to the dynasty was primarily led by the Pharisees. They believed in observing the Law—as interpreted by their oral tradition—according to rules that governed daily life, and which sought to explain and understand all possibilities. The Pharisees believed that God revealed both the written and oral Torah, and it was the role of the Pharisees to contemplate and explain the demands and expectations of God to the people.

The Pharisees considered their doctrine to be superior to the Hasmonean theocracy, and while they generally accepted John Hyrcanus, the Pharisees thought the new priest-kingship had become too secular. They believed the king should focus on governing and should not serve as the high priest.

Opposition by the Pharisees caused Hyrcanus I to ally with the Hellenistic party of the Sadducees. The orthodox Sadducees believed that only the Pentateuch was binding, and they discounted the writings of the prophets and the Pharisee's oral Torah.

Following the death of Hyrcanus I in 104 BCE, the household battle over his succession was worthy of a television soap opera. His son, Aristobulus I, took the throne and imprisoned all his brothers, except Antigonus—who was killed by Hyrcanus' guards with the connivance of his wife, Salome Alexandra. Although his reign only lasted one year, Aristobulus I was the first Hasmonean to openly call himself king of Israel, and he undertook a campaign to extend his kingdom. Acting to secure his northern flank, Aristobulus forcibly converted the population of Galileans and Itureans into the Judaic religion.

When Aristobulus I died by unknown causes, Salome freed his brothers from prison. The eldest, Jonathan—known as Alexander Janneus—married the widowed Salome and was anointed king and high priest. He was only 24 years old, but his reign would endure for 27 years. Having formally assumed the title of king—which traditionally was reserved for a son of David—Janneus maintained his rule by military force. Janneus attempted to extend the boundaries of Israel and successfully defended against an Egyptian invasion; however, an internal rebellion arose against him. Relying on foreign mercenaries, Janneus killed 6,000 of his own subjects.

Following a defeat by the Nabataeans in which Janneus lost his entire army, he escaped to Jerusalem. A six-year civil war followed in which 50,000 Jews died. When Janneus asked the people what he could do to make peace, they told him that he should kill himself.

In opposition to Janneus, the Pharisees invited Demetrius III Eucerus, another Greek pretender to the Syrian throne, into Israel and Judah. Six thousand Jews joined Janneus' force of 10,000 partisans and 8,000 mercenaries to defeat the Syrians and the Pharisees.

Janneus crucified 800 of traitorous Pharisee leaders, after executing their wives and children in front of them. Found among the Dead Sea Scrolls, the Temple Scroll expanded the crimes for which *talah 'al-ha'es* (executed by hanging the body on a pole) to include any Jew who "passes on information about my people and betrays my people to a foreign people." This passage is believed to refer to Janneus' crucifixion of the Pharisaic collaborators.

Janneus went on to conquer Pella, Golan, and Gamala before dying in 76 BCE. Under Hasmonean rule, Judah incorporated the coastal cities, the Galilee, and a large portion of Transjordan into its theocracy. But, the eight decades of Jewish independence could last only so long as external forces were weakened or preoccupied. The expansionist Roman empire in the West now included Greece, and Caesar's general, Pompey the Great, was making plans for the conquest of Asia Minor and Egypt.

Following the death of Alexander Janneus, the Hasmonean dynasty again disintegrated into a fantastic drama. He was succeeded by his widow, Salome Alexandra—one of only two queens to ever rule in Judea-Israel. She reigned from 76 to 67 BCE; however, the Pharisees, led by her brother, Simon ben Shetach, became the real administrators of public affairs. Her two sons were Aristobulus II and Hyrcanus II, whom she appointed as high priest.

Under normal succession, Hyrcanus II should have become king following Salome's death; however, Aristobulus II, backed by mercenaries and a group of supporters, confronted him in a battle near Jericho. When many of his troops defected to Aristobulus, Hyrcanus fled to the Akra citadel at the Temple, where Aristobulus's family was being held as hostages. The two brothers arranged a compromise in which Hyrcanus retained royal dignities; however, Aristobulus II became both king and high priest. He reigned for four years, between 67 and 63 BCE.

The Romans Conquer Judah and Install Antipater the Idumean Over the People

The earlier forceful conversion of the Idumeans and their incorporation into Judea-Israel now had unforeseen consequences for the Hasmoneans. Among those forced to undergo circumcision and conversion to Judaism by John Hyrcanus was a leading Idumean family headed by a man named Antipater. His son, also named Antipater, was married to a Nabataean princess and enjoyed a close relationship with King Aretas, who was called "Aretas the Arabian" by Josephus. Antipater II was ambitious and had been appointed by King Alexander Janneus and Queen Salome Alexandra as their governor of Idumea.

Aristobulus II, the new Hasmonean king, hated Antipater; however, and more importantly, the ambitious Antipater had formed a protective friendship with Mark Antony, the Roman general.

Antipater began to actively meddle in Jerusalem politics by helping Hyrcanus II escape to Petra and to obtain military assistance from the Nabataeans. The Nabataeans, who had no love for the Jews (since their own attempted forcible conversion by Alexander Janneus) and who were promised the return of certain towns, raised a force of 50,000 and attacked Judah. Aristobulus II and his supporters, including members of the Way, were driven back into Jerusalem, and the city was placed under siege.

By 64 BCE, Pompey had broken the resistance of the last Greek pretenders to the Syrian throne, and he annexed Syria into the Roman Empire. Both the Idumean Antipater and the Roman Pompey were quick to take advantage of the battle over the Hasmonean dynastic succession in Judea. In 65 BCE, Pompey's legate intervened on behalf of Aristobulus II, and the siege of Jerusalem was raised.

In 63 BCE, Pompey received appeals from the two contending brothers. Complaints were also received from the people and the Pharisees, who were tired of Hasmonean royal rule and who once again called for a separation of religious and political rule. The Pharisees wanted a restoration of priestly rule—limited to the religious and cultic sphere. They were also prepared to cede secular rule to Rome, the new world power.

Finding the brother they had first supported, Aristobulus II, to be insufficiently pliable, the Romans arrested him. At Jerusalem, the Romans were allowed by the Pharisaic party of Hyrcanus II to enter the city, but the ordinary priests of the Way who supported Aristobulus took refuge in the Temple.

Only after a siege of three months was Pompey able to capture the Temple stronghold. The Pharisees allied themselves with Pompey and Antipater and aided the Roman troops in overwhelming Aristobulus' supporters in the Temple. During the attack within the Temple, the righteous priests of the Way continued their priestly duties at the altar, even as they were being slaughtered. Most were killed by the Pharisaic collaborators of the Romans and Herodians.

The high priesthood was restored to Hyrcanus II, who held it until 40 BCE as a vassal of Rome. Aristobulus II and his children, except Alexander, were led in chains in Pompey's triumphal procession at Rome celebrating the capture of Jerusalem.

The territory was renamed Judea and became a vassal state of Rome. It was very much reduced, without the coastal cities and without access to the Mediterranean. Hyrcanus II remained as the high priest, but he was stripped of his powers and denied the title of king with the right to levy and collect taxes. He ruled only over the faithful religious community in Jerusalem, and he was ethnarch only by courtesy of the Romans.

Alexander, the only child of Aristobulus II to escape capture by the Romans in 57 BCE, raised a rebellion, which was quickly defeated by Mark Anthony. Aristobulus II was able to escape from Rome and upon his return, he attracted a partisan army, which included members of the Way. Allied with his son Antigonus, Aristobulus fought several battles with the Romans, before being defeated and captured. In 55 BCE, Aristobulus' surviving son, Alexander, organized another army of the people and fought a series of losing battles with the Romans and their ally, Antipater. Following the defeat of Alexander, the Romans relied upon Antipater the Idumean to pacify the country.

Because of the civil war going on within the Roman empire between Julius Caesar and Pompey, Caesar released Aristobulus II and gave him command of two legions of troops to occupy and conquer Syria. However, Aristobulus was poisoned by followers of Pompey in 49 BCE. Alexander was beheaded on the orders of Pompey, who died shortly thereafter in Egypt.

In the Book of Daniel (9:24), the angel Gabriel set the period of seventy weeks of years from the time of the return from Babylonian exile to, "finish the transgression, to put an end to sin, and to atone for iniquity, to bring in everlasting righteousness, to seal both vision and prophet, and to anoint a most holy place." Seventy weeks of years equals 490 years from the year 538 BCE, ending in 48 BCE, the year of Pompey's death in Egypt.

The *Psalms of Solomon*, which was written at about this time by the Way lament the invasion of the Temple by Pompey. The *Psalms* ask for mercy on the righteous and pious of God and offers prayer as a substitute for sacrifice, "A new psalm with song in gladness of heart, the fruit of the lips with the well-tuned instrument of the tongue, the first fruits of the lips from a pious and righteous heart." (*Psalms of Solomon*, XV)

Regarding the same events, a revised Book of Daniel raises the hopes and dreams of the people for salvation:

> I saw in the night visions, and behold, with the clouds of heaven there came one like a son of man, and he came to the Ancient of Days and was presented before him. And to him was given dominion and glory and kingdom, that all peoples, nations, and languages should serve him; his dominion is an everlasting dominion, which shall not pass away, and his kingdom one that shall not be destroyed. (7:13-14)

THE OSIM: FOLLOWERS OF THE WAY OF RIGHTEOUSNESS

Primarily, there were three political-religious groups existing in Israel at the time Antipater and his son, Herod, came to power. The Sadducees consisted of the wealthy and aristocratic families who traditionally produced the high priests and who had supported and profited from the Greek Hellenization of Israel. They only recognized the first five books of the Torah as authoritative and rejected the oral tradition, resurrection, and angels of the Pharisees. The Pharisees, who had become powerful from their collaboration with the Romans and Herod, used their oral traditions to "build a fence," or hedge, around the law to encourage, or to excuse compliance. Regarding these two groups, the Book of Matthew (3:7-10) has John the Baptist calling them a "brood of vipers" and Jesus saying:

> "Beware of the leaven of the Pharisees and Sadducees." Then they understood that he did not tell them to beware of the leaven of bread, but of the teaching of the Pharisees and Sadducees. (16:11-12)

The Sadducees and the Pharisees were powerful minority sects because of their alliance with the Romans and Herodians, but they represented only a small portion of the people of Judea and Israel. Most of the people had abandoned their faith in these corrupt parties and were increasingly attracted to the simple life of the Way of Righteousness.

The Way—the successors to the Hasideans and Zaddiks—continued to provide an alternative priesthood to the Sadducees based on righteousness and piety, and to increasingly challenge the secular authorities through their spiritual leadership of the rebellious Zealots. The Way did, however, share the view with the Pharisees that the Prophets and Writings of the Bible were authoritative, including a belief in angels and the resurrection.

The followers of the Way saw themselves as "doers of the law" who lived among the people and demonstrated a life of righteousness (instead of being teachers and interpreters of the law who held themselves above and apart from the people). The Way rejected the oral Torah of the Pharisees as being too permissive and not the word of God. The followers of the Way were guided by their consciences in living lives of righteousness and poverty, rather than by what the Law permitted or prohibited. They were strongly influenced by the Eastern religions in developing an intellectual life of spiritual freedom, rather than being bound by the Law.[24]

Members of the Way were present in every village of Israel and Judah and were particularly concentrated in the Galilee. It was not that they obeyed every letter of the Mosaic Law, but as doers of the law, they lived the spirit of the Law in lives of simplicity, poverty, and righteousness. They cared for others and forgave their debts—they loved one another. The Way did not need the Law to tell them what to do; they found the correct answer in their hearts and consciences. They were a community of righteousness, and their popularity spread among the people until they became the face of Judaism in the land.

Although the Osim are not mentioned by name in the New Testament, the Way is, repeatedly, as Jesus's Congregation of the Poor in Jerusalem were followers of the Way. The related beliefs of the Way were recorded by historians at the time and has been confirmed by the discoveries of the Gnostic Gospels and the Dead Sea Scrolls.

Philo of Alexandria (20 BCE - 50 CE) was a Hellenistic Jewish philosopher from Egypt who attempted to reconcile the Torah and other Jewish scriptures with Greek philosophy. He was a member of the Therapeutae, who associated with the Way. Among his writing are the following observations about the congregation:

> They have an internal rule which all learn, together with rules on piety, holiness, justice and the knowledge of good

---

[24] The basis of the word Sadducee is from the Hebrew foundational word for righteousness and is derived from the priestly sect being in the lineage of Zadok, who was Solomon's high priest. The same foundation applies, however, to the Maccabees, who were zealous for the law, and to the Osim because of their dedication to righteousness to their fellow man and piety to their God. Later, we will see that the same foundation also applies to James the Just (a *Zaddik*) and his Congregation of the Poor in Jerusalem.

and bad. These they make use of in the form of triple definitions, rules regarding the love of GOD, the love of virtue, and the love of men. They believe GOD causes all good but cannot be the cause of any evil. They honor virtue by foregoing all riches, glory and pleasure. Further, they are convinced they must be modest, quiet, obedient to the rule, simple, frugal and without mirth. Their lifestyle is communal. They have a common purse. Their salaries they deposit before them all, in the midst of them, to be put to the common employment of those who wish to make use of it. They do not neglect the sick on the pretext that they can produce nothing. With the common purse there is plenty from which to treat all illnesses. They lavish great respect on the elderly. With them they are very generous and surround them with a thousand attentions. They practice virtue like a gymnastic exercise, seeing the accomplishment of praiseworthy deeds as the means by which a man ensures absolute freedom for himself.

The Essenes live in a number of towns in Judea, and also in many villages and in large groups. They do not enlist by race, but by volunteers who have a zeal for righteousness and an ardent love of men. . . . They are farmers and shepherds and beekeepers and craftsmen in diverse trades. They share the same way of life, the same table, even the same tastes; all of them loving frugality and hating luxury as a plague for both body and soul. Not only do they share a common table, but common clothes as well. What belongs to one belongs to all.

Pliny the Elder (23 - 79 CE) was a Roman author and natural philosopher who lived at the time of Jesus. In his encyclopedic book, *Naturalis Historia (Natural History)*, he recorded a quasi-factual fantasy about the Way:

To the west [of the Dead Sea] the Essenes have put the necessary distance between themselves and the insalubrious shore. They are a people unique of its kind and admirable beyond all others in the whole world; without women and renouncing love entirely, without money and having for company only palm trees. Owing to the throng of newcomers, this people is daily reborn in equal number; indeed, those whom, wearied by the fluctuations of fortune, life leads to adopt their customs, stream in in great numbers. Thus, unbelievable though this may seem, for thousands of centuries a people has existed which is eternal yet into which no one is born: so fruitful for them is the repentance which others feel for their past lives!

Titus Flavius Josephus, born Joseph ben Matiyahu (37 - 100 CE), was a Jewish turncoat who allied himself with the Romans in the First Jewish-Roman War and was accepted into the household of the Roman Emperor Vespasian. Writing in *The Jewish War*, Josephus had this to say about the Way:

> The sect of the Essenes . . . despise riches. When they enter the sect, they must surrender all of their money and possessions into the common fund, to be put at the disposal of everyone; one single property for the whole group. Therefore neither the humiliation of poverty nor the pride of possession is to be seen anywhere among them. . . . They are not just in one town only, but in every town several of them form a colony. They welcome members from out of town as coequal brothers, and even though perfect strangers, as though they were intimate friends. For this reason, they carry nothing with them as they travel: they are, however, armed against brigands. They do not change their garments or shoes until they have completely worn out. They neither buy nor sell anything among themselves. They give to each other freely and feel no need to repay anything in exchange. . . . They are very careful not to exhibit their anger, carefully controlling such outbursts. They are very loyal and are peacemakers. They refuse to swear oaths, believing every word they speak to be stronger than an oath. They are scrupulous students of the ancient literature. They are ardent students in the

healing of diseases, of the roots offering protection, and of the properties of stones. . . . They despise danger: they triumph over pain by the heroism of their convictions, and consider death, if it comes with glory, to be better than the preservation of life. They died in great glory amidst terrible torture in the war against the Romans. They believe that their souls are immortal, but that their bodies are corruptible. They believe the soul is trapped in the body and is freed with death.

The wilderness area on the west shore of the Dead Sea described by these writers was listed in the Book of Joshua (15:61) as granted to the tribe of Judah and included the village known as Seca'ah. Now known by its Arabic name as Khirbet Qumran, the ruins of a Maccabean fort were also called the *Metzad Hasidim*, or Fortress of the Pious Ones. Here—not the manger in Bethlehem—is the true cradle of Christianity. (See Photo #8)

Building probably began at Qumran around 150 BCE. The original foundations of an abandoned Maccabean fort were completely built over, and a heavy non-fortified structure was erected. With later additions, the main building was about 118 feet long and 94 feet wide and was roofed with palm timbers covered with plastered reeds. Dams were built in the cliffs at the head of the Wadi Qumran and water was directed through a tunnel into an aqueduct which fed two large cisterns. The cisterns were well-plastered and had steps leading down into them to allow for the drawing of water as the level dropped in the dry season. The water was channeled through the settlement into smaller cisterns of a size and shape consistent with their use as ritual baths, or baptisteries of the Way.

As reported by Philo and Josephus, the Way was headquartered at Qumran, but lived throughout Judea, the Galilee, and the Diaspora. Beyond these early brief accounts, little was known about the Way until the discovery of the Dead Sea Scrolls. It is from these Scrolls and the earlier discovery of the *Damascus Document* in Cairo, that a more complete understanding of the doctrine of the Way of Righteousness and its influence on the ministry by Jesus could be determined.

The Osim: Followers of the Way of Righteousness

It was this new knowledge that allowed us to adjust our thinking about the Way from being a small isolated congregation to become a vibrant community throughout Judah-Israel and the Diaspora that was the predominate practice of Judaism at the time. They adopted their piousness from the Hasideans and the Way of the Heart from the Zaddik. They were highly literate, and the extensive literature they developed to describe and define their life of righteousness was the foundation of the mission of Jesus.

The Way was led by the Sons of Zadok, priests of the New Covenant predicted by Jeremiah and established by the Zaddik at the time of the Maccabean Revolution. It may be that the priests of the Way were restricted to being of the lineage of Zadok (like the Sadducees), or even of the family of Aaron; however, it is much more likely the new alternative priesthood included priests from all of the priestly lineages as long as they were of the Levite family of Moses.

Emphasizing piety and righteousness, the priests of the Way considered themselves to be a purer alternative to the Sadducees. In the righteous lineage of Onias, the high priest and his son, Simon, the first Righteous Teacher, their leaders were chosen by lot, rather than by family lineage.

All those who renewed their covenant each year did so as the Sons of Dawn and the Sons of Light, and altogether, they saw themselves as the *Ebionim,* or the Poor, who cared for others and shared what they had.

Members of the Way were known as physical healers, and they shared the study and use of herbs in their practice of common medicine. But in addition, the Osim were known as healers of the mind because of their empathy and righteous powers. Because they were in fact doers of the law and lived lives of both piety and righteousness in their daily practice of the true meaning of the Law, it was believed that they could lay hands on people and drive away the evil thoughts and spirits that inhabited their minds. It was also said they were truth seers, in that liars could not stand before them.

As the Way continued to attract new converts it became necessary to document the practices and beliefs of the community. One of the books found among the Dead Sea Scrolls at Qumran was the *Community Rule*, or *Manual of Discipline*.[25] The *Rule* begins with the goals established for members of the Community:

> Seek God with a whole heart and soul, and do what is good and right before Him as He commanded by the hand of Moses and all His servants the Prophets; that they may love all that He has chosen and hate all that he has rejected; that they may abstain from all evil and hold fast to all good; that they may practice truth, righteousness, and justice upon earth and no longer stubbornly follow a sinful heart and lustful eyes committing all manner of evil. He shall admit into the Covenant of Grace all those who have freely devoted themselves to the observance of God's precepts, that they may be joined to the counsel of God and may live perfectly before Him in accordance with all that has been revealed concerning their appointed times, and that they may love all the sons of light, each according to his lot in God's design, and hate all the sons of darkness, each according to his guilt in God's vengeance. (*Community Rule*, I)

Once members were accepted into the community—which they repeatedly refer to as the Way in their writings—initiates agreed that they would abide by the rules and that:

> They shall separate from the habitation of ungodly men and shall go into the wilderness to prepare the way of Him; as it is written, Prepare in the wilderness the way of . . . , make straight in the desert a path for our God. This [path] is the study of the Law which He commanded by the hand of Moses, that they may do according to all that has been revealed from age to age, and as the Prophets have revealed by his Holy Spirit. (*Community Rule*, VIII)

Those seeking to come into "the Council of the Community" were required to "enter into the Covenant of God in the presence

---

[25] These quotations from the Dead Sea Scrolls and, except as otherwise noted, all of the following quotations are from *The Complete Dead Sea Scrolls in English*, (Penquin, 1977), as translated and interpreted by Géza Vermes (1924-2013), who is generally considered to be one of the greatest Jesus scholars of all times.

of all who have freely pledged themselves." Initiates were required to "undertake by a binding oath to return with all his heart and soul to every commandment of the Law of Moses in accordance with all that has been revealed of it to the sons of Zadok, the Keepers of the Covenant and Seekers of His will, and to the multitude of the men of the Covenant who together have freely pledged themselves to His truth and to walking in the way of His delight." (*Community Rule*, V)

Following a year of probation during which members were evaluated regarding their "understanding and observance of the Law," they were judged by the "Priests and the multitude of the men of their Covenant." If allowed "to enter the company of the Community," the initiates could eat with the others during a second year of probation. If he passed another examination, the initiate would be allowed "to enter the Community, then he shall be inscribed among the brethren in the order of his rank for the Law, and for justice, and for the pure Meal; his property shall be merged and he shall offer his counsel and judgment to the Community." (*Community Rule*, V)

The *Rule* includes many passages that reflects the influence of Zoroastrianism—acquired by the Jews from the Iranians during their Exile—which presents the continual, but unseen, battle between the darkness and the light. Since the choice between the two always lies within human ability, the battle necessarily involves the moral duty of every individual. The Way combined Eastern and Gnostic thinking in raising the imagery of dualism to new heights.

> The God of Knowledge created man to govern the world and has appointed for him two spirits in which to walk until the time of His visitation: the spirits of truth and falsehood. Those born of truth spring from a fountain of light, but those born of falsehood spring from a source of darkness. All the children of righteousness are ruled by the Prince of Light and walk in the ways of light, but all the children of falsehood are ruled by the Angel of Darkness and walk in the ways of darkness. (*Community Rule*, III)

Repeatedly throughout the Dead Sea Scrolls, there is also language that reflects Gnostic thinking, including this imagined future for those who walked in righteousness:

> And as for the visitation of all who walk in this spirit, it shall be healing, great peace in a long life, and fruitfulness, together with every everlasting blessing and eternal joy in life without end, a crown of glory and a garment of majesty in unending light. (*Community Rule*, IV)

Overseeing all aspects of the community was a "Master," who "shall instruct all the sons of light and shall teach them the nature of all the children of men according to the kind of spirit which they possess, the signs identifying their works during their lifetime, ..."

There was also a Council of the Community consisting of twelve men and three Priests to manage the affairs of the community. They were required to be "perfectly versed in all that is revealed of the Law, whose works shall be truth, righteousness, justice, loving kindness and humility." (*Community Rule*, VIII)

The community prepared itself for the day:

> When these are in Israel, the Council of the Community shall be established in truth. It shall be an Everlasting Plantation, a House of Holiness for Israel, an Assembly of Supreme Holiness for Aaron. They shall be witness to the truth at the Judgment and shall be the elect of Goodwill who shall atone for the Land and pay to the wicked their reward. It shall be that tried wall, that precious cornerstone, whose foundations shall neither rock nor sway in their place. (Isaiah 28:16, *Community Rule*, VIII)

The Way was expecting a prophet in the manner of Elijah, who would announce the appearance of a savior messiah—in addition to an expected priestly messiah *and* a kingly messiah of the manner of David. The book of *Jubilees*, fragments of which were found in Cave I at Qumran, was probably written at this time by the Way. *Jubilees* reveals that the community had evolved a specific expectation of a suffering and redeeming messiah.

The Osim: Followers of the Way of Righteousness

Another fragment from Cave 4, titled "On Resurrection," or "Messianic Apocalypse," reveals the Way's hoped for messiah:

> ... The heavens and the earth will obey His Messiah, The sea and all that is in them. He will not turn aside from the commandment of the Holy Ones. Take strength in His mighty work, all ye who seek the Lord. Will you not find the Lord in this, all ye who wait for Him with hope in your hearts? Surely the Lord will seek out the pious and will call the righteous by name. His spirit will hover over the poor; by his might he will restore the faithful. He will glorify the pious on the throne of the eternal kingdom. He will release the captives, make the blind see, raise up the downtrodden.[26]

The Osim not only possessed a wealth of literature at their refuge at Qumran, including a library containing a thousand books, the essence of their philosophy embraced the most enlightened thinking of the Eastern and Greek philosophies they were exposed to in the real world in which they lived.

With the followers of the Way of Righteousness headquartered at Qumran and residing throughout Israel-Judea and the diaspora, let's take a closer look at the Herodians who came to rule the nation. We will thereafter return for another visit with the Way, before considering the mission of Jesus.

---

[26] Eisenman, Robert & Wise, Michael, *The Dead Sea Scrolls Uncovered*, (Element, 1992), p. 23.

HEROD BECOMES KING AND MARRIES INTO THE HASMONEAN DYNASTY

Antipater the Idumean, who had been supporting Pompey, now switched his allegiance to Julius Caesar and, in several battles, he provided armies in support of Caesar's efforts to pacify the Middle East. Antipater was rewarded with Roman citizenship and made procurator of Judea-Israel. Antipater appointed his son, Phasael (Phasaelus) prefect of Judea, and his twenty-five-year-old son, Herod was made prefect of Galilee.

Hyrcanus II, the Hasmonean king and high priest, became concerned that Antipater and his family were challenging his rights to the monarchy. When Herod caused the deaths of many in Galilee, Hyrcanus brought charges against Herod before the Sanhedrin in Jerusalem. Influenced by Antipater, the Sanhedrin acquitted Herod (perhaps because Herod's army had accompanied him to the trial).

Herod contributed his military support to Octavian Caesar (Augustus) and Mark Antony in their efforts to conquer Syria. For his efforts, Herod was made procurator of Syria, as well as Galilee and Samaria. When Antipater was poisoned by an opponent, Herod took revenge for his father's death and succeeded to the powers Antipater had accumulated under the Romans.

Antigonus, the Hasmonean contender for the throne, continued his rebellion aided by the people and followers of the Way. Herod defeated Antigonus in several battles, forcing Antigonus to seek the assistance of the Parthians from Iran—who had conquered Iraq and Syria. The Parthians gained entrance to Jerusalem and put Hyrcanus II and Phasael, Herod's brother, into prison, and plundered the city.

The Parthians installed Antigonus, the surviving son of Aristobulus II, as high priest and king. Antigonus then bit or cut off Hyrcanus' ears, which disfigurement rendered him unfit for the high priesthood. Antigonus became king and high priest for the next three years (40-37 BCE)—the last of the Hasmoneans to sit on the throne.

Herod retreated with his family and Idumean supporters to the fortress at Masada near the south end of the Dead Sea and sought the assistance of the Nabataeans at Petra. When Arabian assistance was refused, Herod made his way to Rome where he obtained the patronage of his father's allies, Caesar Augustus and Mark Antony, in being declared king of Judea by the Roman Senate.

Herod returned to Judea, where Antigonus continued to besiege Masada. With the support of mercenaries and Roman troops, Herod began a march through Galilee, south through Judea, toward Masada. After taking Joppa, Herod relieved the siege of Masada and surrounded Jerusalem where Antigonus had taken refuge.

Leaving his brother, Joseph, in charge of the siege, Herod occupied Jericho with ten cohorts of Roman troops and sacked the city; then turned north and took Sepphoris, the capital of his former governorship of Galilee. Herod burned out and slaughtered the followers of the Way and other rebels who had fled with their families into caves, many of whom committed suicide rather than suffer capture. Herod chased the survivors to the east bank of the Jordan River.

When Herod's brother, Joseph, led newly arrived and untrained Roman troops toward Jericho to seize the annual grain harvest, they were attacked by Zealots. Joseph was slain along with most of the inexperienced troops. Herod received word of his brother's death and marched with a large contingent of Roman troops toward Jerusalem, going by way of Jericho and defeating a large group of the people in the mountain villages.

Certainly, during one of these campaigns near Jericho, Herod's army destroyed defenseless Qumran. Modern excavations reveal large cracks resulting from a great earthquake which history records as having struck six years later in 31 BCE, followed by a later rebuilding. Some scholars continue to follow the initial impressions of the original excavators of Qumran that the community was still in existence when the structure was destroyed by the earthquake. The hatred, however, expressed by the community for all things Herodian and the fact that Herod later constructed a great pleasure palace at nearby Jericho, argues for its destruction during Herod's assault on Jerusalem. Moreover, if the structures were only destroyed during the earthquake, there is no reason why they could not have been rebuilt at the time, rather than a generation later in 4 BCE after the death of Herod.

While continuing the siege of Jerusalem, Herod (who was to ultimately have nine or ten wives) went to Samaria and married Mariamne, the daughter of Alexander (son of Aristobulus II) and Alexandra (daughter of Hyrcanus II). She was also the niece of Antigonus, who remained under siege in Jerusalem. Herod thus sought to legitimize his regime by marrying into the Hasmonean dynasty.

In 37 BCE, after a five-month siege—which involved bloody and savage fighting—Herod's Roman troops were able to penetrate the walls of Jerusalem and slaughter all the Zealot fighters and followers of the Way who had rebelled. Antigonus was captured and later beheaded.

Herod was able to gain control of the city and avoid its complete destruction by paying off the Roman troops. While the Sadducees were opposed to Herod, two prominent Pharisees advised the people to welcome him into the city.

Herod ransomed his wife, Mariamne's grandfather, who had been detained by the Parthians with the Jewish Diaspora in Babylon. Hyrcanus II was returned to Jerusalem, where he was treated with dignity by Herod—at least initially.

The Pharisees Extend Their Collaboration With the Romans to Herod

In 31 BCE, Herod came to the assistance of Mark Antony, who was still fighting a war against the Arabians of Petra at the urging of his Egyptian lover, Cleopatra. The war did not go well for Herod and—following the great earthquake which killed more than 30,000 people—the Arabians were encouraged by the disaster and invaded Judea. They were finally defeated by Herod in a great battle at Philadelphia (modern Amman, Jordan).

Herod established a state which—while dependent on Rome—was relatively independent and was approximately the same size as the Hasmonean kingdom. His reign lasted 33 years, and a bloody and murderous reign it was. He chiseled his mark into history, but he cut it even more deeply into the people he ruled.

Herod Becomes King and Marries Into the Hasmonean Dynasty

In Jerusalem, Herod ostentatiously acted as a Jew; he did not directly attack the Yahweh cult, and he generally supported the rights of Jews in the Diaspora. He developed Jerusalem and the Temple to give them great splendor and secured peace and prosperity for the city and the whole country through the *Pax Romana*. He was deeply hated by the people, however, particularly by the Way, because of his slaughter of its members and their exile into Jordan.

The central organ of government, administration, and justice, responsible for all religious matters and matters of civil law, was the Supreme Council of Jerusalem—in Greek *synkedrion* (assembly, Aramaic *sanhedrin*)—formerly headed by the high priest. The ruling classes of the country were represented in it; in addition to the Sadducean priests and aristocrats, there were the Sadducean scribes and Pharisaic doctors of the law.

The Sanhedrin, consisting of seventy men, came under the presidency of Hillel, the leading Pharisee, whose descendants would thereafter hold the title of *Nasi*. Although totally dependent on Herod and the Roman occupying forces, the Sanhedrin was still regarded as the supreme representative of the Jewish people.

Herod ostensibly recognized the separation of state and religion, but he appointed and discharged high priests at will. While still under the protection of Mark Anthony, Herod had appointed an obscure priest from Babylon as high priest, but following the objection of Alexandra, his Hasmonean mother-in-law, he appointed his wife's sixteen-year-old brother, Aristobulus III, as the high priest. Although Aristobulus was well received by the people in memory of his grandfather by the same name, he and his mother, Alexandra, made secret plans to escape to Cleopatra in Egypt. Learning of this betrayal, Herod contrived to have Aristobulus drowned while swimming in the fishpond at the Jericho palace.

Herod, who had fallen in love with a beautiful Jewish woman named Mariamne (II), appointed her father, Simon ben Boethus, as high priest in order to elevate the status of the family enough for Herod to marry the daughter, which he did.

Responding to a complaint by Cleopatra to Mark Anthony, Herod was summoned to Laodicea to justify Aristobulus's murder. He left his wife Mariamne I in the care of his brother Joseph, who was also married to Herod's daughter, Salome. Upon Herod's return, Salome told him that Joseph had been having a sexual affair with Mariamne. Herod executed his brother, but he allowed Mariamne to live.

Herod then travelled to Rhodes and a meeting with Caesar Augustus, during which he switched his allegiance directly to Caesar. Herod then turned against his old friend, Mark Antony, and assisted Caesar in his military campaign in Egypt against Antony. Following the suicide of Antony and Cleopatra, Herod was rewarded with a much larger kingdom that included Samaria, Galilee, the coastal cities, and Judea.

From the time of the Hasmoneans, the internal political struggle in Israel was mainly dominated by a battle between the rich Hellenized upper class of the Sadducees and the Pharisees—who now joined in a wholehearted alliance with the Romans and Herodians. By their unflinching support of Herod, the Pharisees prevailed and achieved dominance over the Sanhedrin and other organs of political power, and they were able to inveigle the women of the Herodian court to do their bidding.

Hillel the Elder was the outstanding Pharisee in the days of King Herod. A native of Babylonia, he arrived in Jerusalem at about the same time as the destruction of the Sadducean Sanhedrin, which had opposed Herod. Hillel stepped into the power vacuum and was soon recognized as a great legalist and leader of the Sanhedrin.

One of Hillel's innovations led to a reversal of a law of the Torah, which provides for a general cancellation of debts every seven years during the sabbatical of the land. This law originated in the agricultural civilization of earlier Israel, where a loan was usually a favor extended to someone who had a crop failure. But as commerce became based on a money economy, the law worked hardships on both creditors and debtors. In the last year or so of each cycle, credit became unavailable as lenders refused to lend money which might not be repaid. Hillel therefore introduced a legal fiction called the *prosbol* or *prozbul*, which allowed the creditor to file a document at the Temple at the time of a loan, which allowed collection even in the sabbatical year. To all intents and purposes, Hillel repealed a biblical law to favor the rich and upper-middle class, as against the poor and downtrodden the law was intended to protect.

Another matter in which Hillel accommodated Herod was when the king wanted to build Tiberias on the site of an Israelite cemetery. Hillel concluded that the grounds were not forever unclean, only for so long as it took to undergo a ritual cleansing, and he advised Jews that they should settle in the city.

His most significant accommodation to Herod was Hillel's ruling regarding divorce in which he said that a man may divorce his wife for any reason, even if she burns his soup.

The Pharisee establishment position was not popular with the ordinary people, who continued to view, as outsiders, all those who held positions of power. Whether expressed openly or in secret, the expectations widespread among the people were quite different from those of the establishment.

According to Josephus, Herod maintained his rule through the imposition of a police state and violence:

> The people were uneasy about Herod because of the innovations he had introduced in their practices to the dissolution of their religion, and the disuse of their own customs and the people everywhere talked against him, like those that were still more provoked and disturbed at this procedure. Against which discontents he greatly guarded himself, and took away the opportunities they might have to disturb him, and enjoining them to be always at work; nor did he permit the citizens either to meet together, or to walk, or eat together, but watched everything they did, and when they were caught they were severely punished; . . . And there were spies set everywhere, both in the city and on the roads, who watched those that met together.

Herod Builds Magnificent Palaces and Remodels the Temple

As a builder-king, Herod was virtually unequaled in the world at the time. An Arab of mixed birth with Roman citizenship, he built or enlarged Hellenistic and Romanized palaces, temples, and cities everywhere in Israel. Herod encouraged emperor worship by renaming Samaria as Sebaste (Greek - Augusta) and establishing the magnificent port city of Caesarea on the Mediterranean coast, both in honor of his patron, Caesar Augustus.

Herod rebuilt the winter palace of the Maccabees at Jericho and built a new palace-fortress at Herodium at the edge of the Judean desert within a hollowed-out-cone at the top of a natural hill. He also built or rebuilt numerous fortresses including Macherus east of the Jordan River, and Masada on the southwest shore of the Dead Sea (where he had been besieged by Antigonus). Masada, which was to become famous in later history, was constructed on a series of engineered terraces on the northern cliff of an ancient mountain fortress, which provided swimming pools and a view of the Dead Sea and the Judean desert. It was Herod's retreat of last resort.

At the northwest corner of Jerusalem, he built a new administrative and defensive center as a grandiose royal palace. The palace was enclosed by a wall thirty cubits high with three massive towers, or citadels. Josephus described it as containing:

> immense banqueting halls and bedchambers for a hundred guests . . . the host of apartments with their infinite varieties of design, all amply furnished, while most of the objects in each of them were of silver or gold. All around were many circular cloisters, leading one into another, the columns in each being different, and their open courts all verdant; there were groves of various trees intersected by long walks, which were bordered by deep canals, and ponds everywhere studded with bronze figures, through which the water was discharged, . . ."

Herod also tore down the old Temple and rebuilt a massive masonry foundation or mount upon which he constructed the Antonia Fortress on the northwest corner which commanded the Temple site and the old City of David on Mount Zion. Once he completed the Temple Mount, it was (at almost 500 meters square) the largest structure in antiquity. Upon this foundation, he built one of the most magnificent temples in the world, which eclipsed in size both Solomon's original Temple and the Second Temple built following the return from the Babylonian exile. For his personal access to the Antonia Fortress and the Temple, Herod built a causeway from his palace to the Temple Mount, which spanned the Valley of the Cheese makers where the poor lived.

Although there were massive bronze doors located on the east side of the Temple facing the Mount of Olives and the rising sun, the Temple was primarily approached by the people from the southwest in the area of King David's original city site on the Ophel Hill, or Mount Zion. To approach this entrance, Herod constructed a grand sweep of stairs about 65 meters wide running down toward the Mount Zion corner. The steps alternated between wide and narrow, requiring two paces forward and one up. The effect was to slow the ascent and arrival at the threshold of the Temple in a proper frame of mind to enter the House of the LORD.

A wide, stone-paved road, the major north-south thoroughfare of the expanded Jerusalem, ran alongside the west side of the Temple Mount by where the Wailing Wall is today. It continued under the arched stairways, and past the cornerstone at the southwest, or Mount Zion, corner of the Temple Mount. Modern excavations at this location have uncovered the original massive cornerstones. (See Photo #9)

On nearby Mount Zion, or Ophel Hill, lived many of the ordinary Levite priests who attended the Temple—the survivors of those slaughtered by the Roman troops and Pharisees. Many of these priests were probably Sons of Zadok, the priests of the Way, who supported the nationalistic and theocratic aims of the Zealot rebellion and provided resistance to the hedonistic Herodians.

THE WAY FLEES INTO JORDAN AND MAKES A NEW COVENANT WITH GOD

During the military campaign of Herod the Great in 37 BCE against the Jewish partisans, Qumran was destroyed and members of the Way were forced to flee to an area east of the Jordan River known to the Zadokites as the land of Damascus and the "wilderness of the peoples." It was in this same area that the Hasideans had sought refuge from Antiochus IV around 159 BCE following the death of Judas Maccabaeus.

The Way retreated to this region when they were persecuted by Herod, and it was during this period the *Damascus Rule* was likely written. The *Rule* discusses a "Unique Teacher" who lived in the past and a "Righteous Teacher" who was either living at the time, or whose imminent appearance was expected.

The *Rule* discusses a new covenant which has been made in the land of Damascus and from which we can begin to foresee the mission of Jesus: "They shall love each man his brother as himself; they shall succor the poor, the needy, and the stranger. (*Damascus Rule*, VI)

The Way continued to be "doers of the Law," but for them, the law they piously worshipped was that defined by their own scriptural interpretations and the new covenant they made in the wilderness of Damascus. They sought the spiritual meaning of the Law and translated it into the simple life of righteousness they lived on a daily basis.

> All those who hold fast to these precepts, going and coming in accordance with the Law, who heed the voice of the Teacher and . . . who have listened to the voice of the Teacher of Righteousness and have not despised the precepts of righteousness when they heard them; they shall rejoice and their hearts shall be strong, and they shall prevail over all the sons of the earth. God will forgive them, and they shall see His salvation because they took refuge in His holy Name. (*Damascus Rule*, XIV)

How Did the Way Organize its Community?

All members of the Way were under the general direction of a *Mebakker,* Master, or Overseer, who taught, evaluated, and ranked all members:

> He shall instruct the Congregation in the works of God. . . . He shall love them as a father loves his children and shall carry them in all their distress like a shepherd his sheep. He shall loosen all the fetters which bind them that in his Congregation there may be none that are oppressed or broken. He shall examine every man entering his Congregation with regard to his deeds, understanding, strength, ability and possessions, and shall inscribe him in his place according to his rank in the lot of Light. (*Damascus Rule*, XIII)

Members of the congregation who lived in cities were known as the "seed of Israel." They were bound by ordinance to separate the clean from the unclean, and to make known the difference between the holy and the common. Rather than surrendering all their possessions, those who lived and worked among the people were required to tithe, "They shall place into the hands of the Guardian and the Judges, and from it they shall give to the fatherless, and from it they shall succor the poor and the needy, the aged sick and the homeless, the captive taken by a foreign people, the virgin with no near kin, and the ma[id for] whom no man cares." (*Damascus Rule*, XIV)

Contrary to the fantasy related by Pliny the Elder, it appears that even those who lived at Qumran were able to marry and have children. "And if they live in camps according to the rule of the Land and begetting children, they shall walk according to the Law and according to the statute concerning binding vows, according to the rule of Law which says, 'Between a man and his wife and between a father and his son.'" (Numbers 30:17, *Damascus Rule*, VII)

It is easy enough to imagine the followers of the Way living throughout the land, primarily in the towns and villages, rather than the city. They shared what they had and cared for one another.

Although they were poor, their faith in the Way of Righteousness brought them joy and they were able to marry, sing and dance, and to raise children amid the violent occupation of their land.

What Did the Covenant Believe?

Reflecting Eastern and Gnostic principles, the *Rule* establishes the two ways of right and wrong, and emphasizes the value of knowledge and wisdom:

> God loves knowledge. Wisdom and understanding He has set before Him, and prudence and knowledge serve Him. Patience and much forgiveness are with Him towards those who turn from transgression; but power, might, and great flaming wrath by the hand of all the Angels of Destruction towards those who depart from the way and abhor the Precept. (*Damascus Rule*, II)

The righteous members of the Covenant who have not gone astray are promised hidden Gnostic knowledge and everlasting life. For the Way, the resurrection became spiritual, rather than physical:

> But with the remnant which held fast to the commandments of God He made His Covenant with Israel forever, revealing to them the hidden things in which all Israel had gone astray. He unfolded before them His holy Sabbaths and his glorious feasts, the testimonies of His righteousness and the ways of His truth, and the desires of His will which a man must do in order to live. (*Damascus Rule*, III)

Who Were the Opponents of the Congregation?

The opponents of the Way are identified as the Herodian Monarchy and the Pharisees whom they derisively called, "The 'builders of the wall." One has only to consult the tangled family tree of the Herod family to see that not only did Herod have many wives, but his family made it a practice to divorce and to intermarry with nieces, nephews, and cousins. Several Pharisaic rulings are alluded to and condemned in the *Damascus Rule*, including pro-Herodian rulings allowing remarriage after divorce and marriage with one's niece.

The designation "builders of the wall" is apparently an adaptation of the concept, known from the Mishnah which teaches, "build a fence around the Torah." According to the rabbinic tradition, laws not found in the Bible may be created to make certain that those laws which it does contain are not transgressed. These additional laws are the "fence around the Torah" known as the *halakha*. The Way opposed this approach, not only because they may not have agreed with the non-biblical laws, but also because they rejected the idea of expanding the biblical commandments in this way. For them, these oral laws were without biblical basis and were unnecessary for those who actually lived the spirit of the Law, without seeking excuses for noncompliance.

Perhaps in a reference to Hillel's innovation reversing the law requiring the cancellation of debts at the end of each Sabbatical Jubilee, the *Damascus Rule* says, "But all these things the *builders of the wall and those who daub it with plaster* have not understood because a follower of the wind, one who raised storms and rained down lies, had preached to them, against all of whose assembly the anger of God was kindled." (emphasis added, Damascus Rule, VIII)

The *Damascus Rule* is referring to the Pharisees when it talks about those who "interpreted false laws" and choose falsehoods, sought out opportunities to violate the Law, choose luxury, and declared the guilty to be innocent and the innocent to be guilty. The Pharisees violated the covenant, annulled the Law, and bound together to do away with the righteous.

How Many Messiahs *Did* the Way Expect?

With the ascension of Herod the Great, the Community became increasingly Messianic in reliance upon the "Star" prophecy of Numbers 24:17, among other predictions.

> The Star is the Interpreter of the Law who shall come to Damascus; as it is written, A star shall come forth out of

Jacob and a scepter shall rise out of Israel. The scepter is the Prince of the whole congregation, and when he comes, he shall smite all the children *of Seth*.[27] (emphasis added, *Damascus Rule*, VII)

What the movement now anticipates is the coming of the Messianic Kingdom, the kingdom of the Messiah of Israel, the "Star." The *Community Rule* and *Damascus Rule* talk about at least two messiahs. One is a kingly messiah of Israel, not necessarily from the family of David, and a priestly messiah of the family of Levi, who possesses the twin attributes of piety and righteousness, both of whom are to be selected by lot by the people.

With the destruction of their national independence, the Way awaited the arrival of a prophet in the manner of Elijah (who had been expected since the time of Simeon Maccabee's ascension to the high priesthood), followed by a priestly messiah, a kingly messiah, *and a suffering spiritual messiah representing not only all of the children of Israel, but all of the children of Adam*. The Saints of the Way saw themselves as Daniel's collective Son of Man who—by their faithfulness to the Law and their suffering at the hands of the Romans and their collaborators—were performing an atoning work for the sins of everyone, including the Gentiles.

The *Testament of the Twelve Patriarchs* was likely written by members of the new covenant during the reign of the Maccabees. Complete copies have been preserved through history; however, they were long thought to have been edited later by Christians to include the numerous references to messiahs. The *Testament* was validated, as written, when fragments containing the identical text were identified among the Dead Sea Scrolls. Beginning with the oldest, Reuben, all the sons of Jacob recite their life stories and provide directions and blessings from their deathbeds. Emphasis has been added to the following quotes.

The *Testament of Simeon* says, "And now, my children, obey Levi and Judah, and be not lifted up against these two tribes, for from them shall arise unto you the salvation of G od. For the Lord shall

---

[27] Seth was the replacement son born to Adam and Eve following the murder of Abel by Cain, and whose descendants include Noah and all humanity.

raise up from Levi as it were a High Priest, and from Judah as it were a King, God and man, He shall save all the Gentiles and the race of Israel." (3:10-11)

The *Testament of Levi* speaks of the priestly messiah of the lineage of Levi, who, as a prophet, will establish a new priesthood, which will include the Gentiles. In chapter five, *Levi* discusses seven jubilees during each of which there will be a priesthood. Beginning with the first who shall be "perfect with the LORD, and in the day of his gladness shall he arise for the salvation of the world;" finally, in the seventh jubilee, following the exile, there is a failure of the priesthood (the Sadducees), whose priests had become "idolaters, adulterers, lovers of money, proud, lawless, lascivious, abusers of children and beasts." (5:2-12)

> Then shall the Lord raise up a new priest. And to him all the words of the Lord shall be revealed; and he shall execute a righteous judgment upon the earth for a multitude of days. And his star shall arise in heaven as of a king. Lighting up the light of knowledge as the sun the day, and he shall be magnified in the world. He shall shine forth as the sun on the earth, and shall remove all darkness from under heaven, and there shall be peace in all the earth . . . . And there shall none succeed him for all generations forever. And in his priesthood the Gentiles shall be multiplied in knowledge upon the earth and enlightened through the grace of the Lord. In his priesthood shall sin come to an end, and the lawless shall cease to do evil. And he shall open the gates of paradise, and shall remove the threatening sword against Adam, and he shall give to the saints to eat from the tree of life, and the spirit of holiness shall be on them. And Beliar shall be bound by him, and he shall give power to His children to tread upon the evil spirits. And the Lord shall rejoice in His children, and be well pleased in His beloved ones forever . . . . And now, my children, ye have heard all; choose, therefore, for yourselves either the light or the darkness, either the law of the Lord or the works of Beliar. (5:13-30)

The *Testament of Judah* speaks of Israel following the return from the exile and goes on to describe the attributes of the expected kingly messiah:

> And after these things shall a star arise to you from Jacob in peace. And a man shall arise from my seed, like the sun of righteousness. Walking with the sons of men in meekness and righteousness; And no sin shall be found in him. And the heavens shall be opened unto him, to pour out the spirit, even the blessing of the Holy Father; and He shall pour out the spirit of grace upon you; And ye shall be unto Him sons in truth, and ye shall walk in His commandments first and last. Then shall the scepter of my kingdom shine forth; and from your root shall arise a stem; and from it shall grow a rod of righteousness to the Gentiles, to judge and to save all that call upon the Lord . . . . And ye shall be the people of the Lord and have one tongue; and there shall be there no spirit of deceit of Beliar, for he shall be cast into the fire forever. (4:20-30)

From the *Testament of Benjamin*, the last of the sons of Jacob there comes a description of the third combined messiah, who by his work and word will enlighten the Gentiles:

> And there shall arise in the latter days one beloved of the Lord, of the tribe of Judah and Levi, a doer of His good pleasure in his mouth, with new knowledge enlightening the Gentiles . . . . And he shall be inscribed in the holy books, both his work and his word, and he shall be a chosen one of God for ever. (2:26-28)

A primary difference between the Pharisees and the Way was the manner in which the Pharisees acted almost as lawyers in creating a bewildering set of oral laws that, on one hand established precise ways to obey the basic injunctions of the Law, and on the other, sought interpretations to excuse compliance with the original Law. The Way rejected all these legalisms; however, they did engage in extensive analysis of the scriptures to provide inspiration and guidance during the violently insane times in which they lived.

The Way Flees Into Jordan and Makes a New Covenant With God

The messianic dreams of the Way were based on their changing attitude towards the scriptures. As their biblical canon came to include the Prophets and Writings, these books were viewed as the Oracles of God. They were interpreted to identify hidden meanings and to project these findings onto the horrific events taking place around them.

They expected their kingly messiah to act as prophesized by Isaiah: ". . . but with righteousness he shall judge the poor, and decide with equity for the meek of the earth; and he shall smite the earth with the rod of his mouth, and with the breath of his lips he shall slay the wicked." (11:4) For the Way, the sharp two-edged sword of the Messiah would be no physical weapon, but justice and righteousness.

The *Psalms of Solomon* were written by the Way to predict that the rule of the Messiah would not result from force, but from righteous example:

> And a righteous king and taught of God is he that reigneth over them; and there shall be no iniquity in his days in their midst, for all shall be holy and their king is the Lord Messiah. For he shall not put his trust in horse and rider and bow, nor shall he multiply unto himself gold and silver for war, nor by ships shall he gather confidence for the day of battle . . . For he shall smite the earth with the word of his mouth even for evermore . . . He himself also is pure from sin, so that he may rule a mighty people, and rebuke princes and overthrow sinners by the might of his word. And he shall not faint all his days, because he leaneth upon his God; for God shall cause him to be mighty through the spirit of holiness, and wise through the counsel of understanding, with might and righteousness.

Increasingly, however, the Way expected that a Messiah would arise out of Israel—not necessarily Judah or David—and that the Messiah would be a son of God. The scroll fragment found in Cave 4, entitled *Son of God* indicates that while the Messiah would be an earthly leader, his power would be that of a son of God.

Founded by a suffering Teacher of Righteousness, the Way expected that another Teacher of Righteousness would arise in the Last Times. This suffering Just One would "instruct the upright in the knowledge of the Most High." As stated in the Way's *Testaments of the Twelve Patriarchs*, Jacob blessed Joseph, the purest of his twelve sons, saying, "In thee shall be fulfilled the prophecy of heaven, which says the blameless one shall be defiled for lawless men, and the sinless one shall die for godless men."

For the Way, it was time for the Son of Man prophesized by Daniel to appear and save humanity:

> I saw in the night visions, and behold, with the clouds of heaven there came one like a son of man, and he came to the Ancient of Days and was presented before him. And to him was given dominion and glory and a kingdom, that all peoples, nations, and languages should serve him; his dominion is an everlasting dominion, which shall not pass away, and his kingdom one that shall not be destroyed. (7:13-14)

Among all there was a growing conviction that the Last Days had begun, and the stage was set for the entry of a messianic figure who would refer to himself as the Son of Man. His mission would be to offer himself as a sacrifice against the might of the Roman Empire.

GNOSIS AND SOPHIA (WISDOM)

Most readers understand the meaning of the word agnostic, which is commonly used to describe someone who does not know if God exists, or if Jesus is His son. A Gnostic, on the other hand, is one who knows, and the word gnosis describes an ancient philosophy often associated with religious worship. There were pagan Gnostics, Eastern Gnostics, Jewish Gnostics, and elements of Gnosticism were involved in the belief system of the Way and their related group, the Therapeutae in Egypt.

The most ancient religious figure was the Earth Mother, or Mother Goddess. When she later became paired with male pagan gods, such as Aphrodite and Adonis, they each took on differing, but supporting roles. As we saw earlier, Asherah—the comforter of women—was the consort of YAHWEH until the religious reformations of King Josiah. Even thereafter, the Jews adopted and continued to write about the Goddess Sophia in Proverbs (8) and other texts. In these texts, "wisdom" is Sophia; she was the first of the Lord's "works" and "was constantly at His side." The Greek word "philosopher" comes from "lover of Sophia."

Philo, the Jewish philosopher, who wrote about the Way, described Sophia as the "mother of the Logos," which is the guide to Gnosis.

The essence of Gnosticism is knowledge, of one's own self—and of the Divine. As used by Plato, it is intellectual, rather than practical; it is inward looking and creates insights that provide a deeper understanding of the role of consciousness in life, and in religion. Gnosticism is not for everyone; the outward forms of religion, with its ethical lessons and injunctions, are for those who do not possess the often secret, or difficult to obtain and comprehend, knowledge.

For Gnostics, God equates with the universal consciousness, and the task for initiates is to become aware of one's own self in order to unite with an Abiding Mind extant throughout the universe and eternity. The Abiding Mind includes everything that has ever been imagined or created within a universe without boundaries during an eternity with neither a beginning, nor end.

Often, baptism with water is the first step as a recognition of shared divinity and a commitment to continually search for enlightenment. This was the nature of baptism among members of the Way, who built extensive baptism facilities at Qumran.

The Gnostics believed that at our core we all share in the Abiding Mind and that our soul connects this universally connected core with the outer person or body seen by others. We (or I, as we call our individual self) are the totality of our experiences, creations, and learned knowledge—our consciousness, which is joined with the combined consciousness as a shared identity. Much like an aspen tree, we may look different on the surface, but we are all part of a larger, single connecting organism.

Learning from the more ancient Vedic and Buddhist religions of India, the Gnostics believed in reincarnation. Those who achieve self-knowledge or salvation in this life are permanently rejoined with the Abiding Mind at death, but those who fail to achieve repentance, or change of heart, are destined to be reborn. Those who engaged in harmful behavior in this life, will experience it at the hands of others in the next, and those who cared for others will be equally nurtured in the next.

The Gnostics equated the "Mystery of God" as the "Good." It is not that we *become* good by seeking self-awareness, but that in becoming conscious, we come to understand that our essential nature is good. God is not judgmental and punishing but represents unconditional love and forgiveness. When we become "One" with God—with the Abiding Mind—we become aware that we are selfless and good amid pure love.

While our true nature is good, we sometimes fail to act as we could and should. The Gnostics view this as "missing the mark," which the Greeks called *hamartia,* or "sin."

Plato believed that we are already dead and that the body is the tomb of the soul. For the Gnostics, those who are spiritually dead exist in this underworld we call life; however, through the process of becoming self-aware, we can learn to elevate ourselves. For those who achieve gnosis, death allows them to escape this Hell on earth and to unite with the Abiding Mind in the hereafter.

Philo of Alexandria, a fellow traveler of the Way, believed the entire Old Testament contained fables that had to be read and understood as allegories instead of literal truths. He wrote books on how to determine what the scriptures meant. For Philo, the statement in Genesis that "giants" walked the earth really means that they were men possessed of great wisdom.

When combined with the ancient Iranian Zoroastrian belief in a deity of wisdom, members of the Way were able to live the ethical laws of the Torah by choice in dedicating their lives to righteousness. They were waiting to receive the promised teaching of the suffering Son of Man who would instruct them in the "knowledge of the Most High." (Numbers 24:16)

THE BLOODY LEGACY OF HEROD, WHO MURDERED HIS WIVES AND CHILDREN

Following the battle of Actium in 31 BCE, in which Caesar Augustus (Octavian) decisively defeated Marc Antony, Herod—who had adroitly switched his support from Antony to Augustus—significantly improved his position with his Roman benefactors. Among other favors, Augustus ruled that Herod had the right to name his own successor. That decision would have deadly consequences for his descendants.

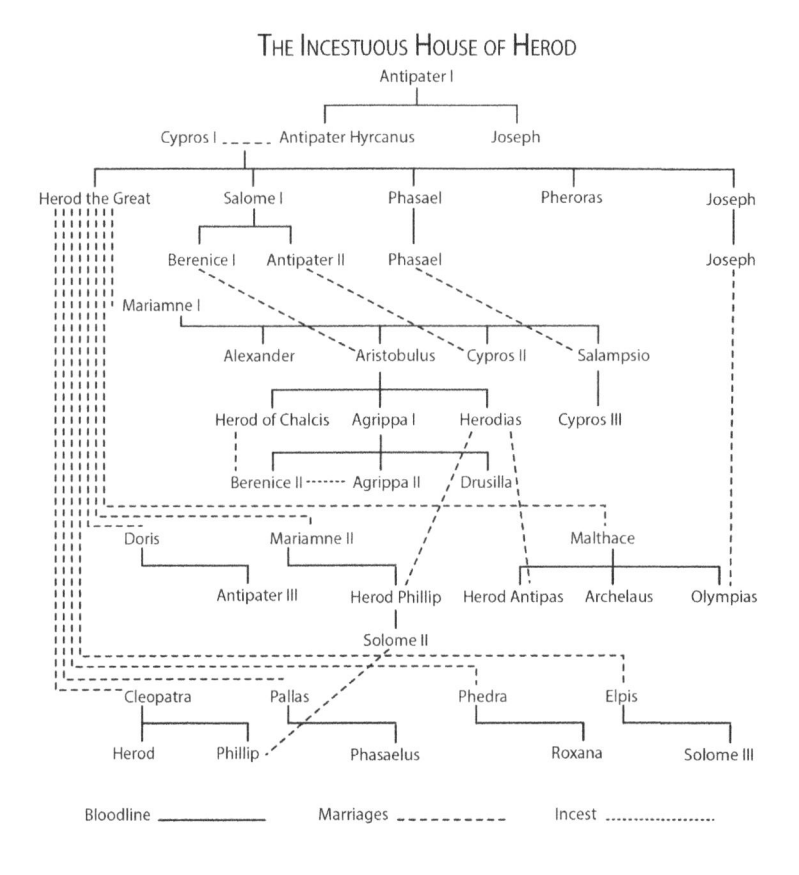

THE INCESTUOUS HOUSE OF HEROD

Antipater I
├── Cyros I — Antipater Hyrcanus — Joseph

Herod the Great — Salome I — Phasael — Pheroras — Joseph
                  Berenice I   Antipater II   Phasael   Joseph
Mariamne I
         Alexander   Aristobulus   Cyros II   Salampsio
              Herod of Chalcis   Agrippa I   Herodias   Cyros III
                   Berenice II ---- Agrippa II / Drusilla
         Doris   Mariamne II   Malthace
                  Antipater III   Herod Phillip   Herod Antipas   Archelaus   Olympias
                                  Solome II
     Cleopatra   Pallas   Phedra   Elpis
         Herod   Phillip   Phasaelus   Roxana   Solome III

Bloodline ———   Marriages ---------   Incest ....

129

Hyrcanus II, whom Herod had ransomed from the Parthians, was the senior member of the Maccabean dynasty who was still alive. Herod, however, intercepted a letter sent by Alexandra, Hyrcanus's daughter, to the governor of Arabia proposing a meeting with Hyrcanus. Herod brought the matter before the Herodian- and Pharisaic-dominated Sanhedrin and executed Hyrcanus II.

Herod again left his wife Mariamne, the Maccabean princess, and her mother, Alexandra under close supervision at Alexandrium, outside of Jerusalem, while he traveled to meet Caesar. He left instructions that—if he for any reason was unable to return—his wife and her family were to be put to death. During his absence, Mariamne learned of these instructions, and upon his return, she wanted little to do with Herod. When she refused to come to his bed, his sister, Salome and his mother Cypros, who hated the Maccabean women, caused Herod to be informed that Mariamne had arranged for him to receive a love-potion to excite him, before denying him conjugal privileges. Herod accused Mariamne and brought her to trial where she was condemned to death and executed.

When Mariamne's mother, Alexandra conspired to organize a resistance to Herod and to seize fortifications at Jerusalem, Herod gave orders for her to be put to death as well. Two remaining Maccabean descendants were also slain shortly thereafter.

Herod sent his two sons by Mariamne, Alexander and Aristobulus, to Rome to study and to "enjoy the company of Caesar." Herod then set about securing his kingdom by serving Caesar Augustus in every way possible, and by rooting out all opposition through the deployment of spies and mercenaries. He imposed an oath of fidelity on all citizens, except the Pharisees and followers of the Way—who refused to take the oath.

When Herod's two sons by Mariamne returned from Rome, Herod arranged marriages for them. Alexander was married to Glaphyra, daughter of Archelaus, king of Cappadocia (Central Anatolia in Turkey). Aristobulus married Herod's niece Berenice I, daughter of Herod's sister, Salome—who immediately began to intrigue against the two brothers.

Herod began to groom another heir, his son Antipater III—who was born to his first wife, Doris. Antipater was sent to Rome to study, while Mariamne's sons remained in Jerusalem. Alexander and Aristobulus spoke badly to others in private about their father, who had, after all, murdered their mother and grandmother. When gossip of this came to Herod, he brought them before Caesar for trial in Rome. They were acquitted by Caesar and reconciled with Herod and their brother, Antipater III.

Herod named Antipater in his will to be his successor, and the accusations by Salome and Antipater against his other two sons continued. Following the torture of their intimates and testimony that the two had wished for the death of Herod, Alexander and Aristobulus were again brought to trial by Herod. This time, the two were condemned to be strangled to death.[28]

At this point, Herod had at least nine wives: In addition to Mariamne I, there was Doris, who was Antipater's mother, and Mariamne II the daughter of the high priest, Simon ben Boethus, by whom he had a son named Herod Philip. Herod also married two nieces, a daughter of his sister and a brother's daughter, neither of whom had children. His wife, Malthace was a Samaritan who had two sons, Herod Antipas and Archelaus, who had been raised in Rome, and two daughters who married two of Herod's nephews. Another wife was Cleopatra of Jerusalem with whom he had two sons, one also named Herod and the other Philip. His wife, Pallas, bore him a son named Phasaelus, and his wives Phedra and Elpis provided him daughters, Roxana and Salome. There may have been others, but these were the primary actors in the Herodian tragedy.

Herod's brother, Pheroras was influenced by his wife, his mother, and his aunt, over whom the Pharisees had gained control. When Herod fined the Pharisees for failing to take the loyalty oath to him, the women paid their fines. The Pharisees began to prophesize that Herod's rule was coming to an end and that Pheroras and his wife would take over the kingdom. When Herod learned of this from his sister, Salome, he had the Pharisee ringleaders put to death,

---

[28] These serial murders of children, including his own, by Herod may be the historical basis for the "Massacre of the Innocents" recounted in the Book of Matthew (2:16-18), as there are no other references to the alleged biblical massacre in the historical record, including the writings of Josephus.

along with those members of his own family who had encouraged the prediction.

Antipater III became concerned for his own safety and arranged for friends in Rome to request his presence there. Herod sent Antipater to Rome along with his last will and testament, in which he appointed Antipater as his heir and successor; however, if Antipater did not survive Herod, his son Herod Philip by Mariamne II would become king.

Shortly thereafter, Pheroras died, and his Pharisaic wife was accused of having poisoned him. When the woman was questioned under torture, she revealed knowledge of information Herod had entrusted in secret to his son, Antipater. In addition, Antipater's procurator admitted under torture that Antipater had prepared a poison for Herod, which he had given to Pheroras to administer in his absence. Moreover, it was learned that Mariamne II had knowledge of these events and had concealed it.

Herod divorced Mariamne II, removed her son, Herod Philip from his testament, and dismissed her father Simeon from the high priesthood, appointing another in his stead.

In the history of despot monarchs, Herod is unsurpassed in having murdered so many members of his own family. Writing about Herod's reign of terror, Josephus wrote:

> There were none left of the kindred of Hyrcanus and no one left with sufficient dignity to put a stop to what he did against the Jewish Laws. Herod rebelled against the Laws . . . polluting the ancient constitution by introducing foreign practices . . . by which means we became guilty of great Wickedness thereafter, while those religious observances that used to lead the multitude to Piety were now neglected.

Herod summoned Antipater to return from Rome and put him on trial. After an impassioned defense, Antipater was imprisoned. In a new will, Herod left his kingdom to his youngest son, Herod Antipas, of Malthace, his Samaritan wife.

All these arrangements were pertinent, as Herod had become disabled in his old age, suffering from ulcerated intestines and putrefacation of his genitals. As he lay dying, he heard that Antipater was trying to get out of prison and ordered that his son be immediately killed.

Whereupon, Herod changed his will for the last time. He appointed Herod Antipas—to whom he had previously left the entire kingdom—to the small tetrarchy of Galilee, and he gave the kingdom of Judea to Archelaus. He also gave Gaulonitis and Trachonitis to Philip, his son by Cleopatra. Writhing in great (and well deserved) pain, Herod was prevented from stabbing himself to death, but died five days later. He was buried in the mausoleum he had constructed at Herodium 7.5 miles south of Jerusalem.

Following the death of Herod, there was a riot at the Temple in support of the appointment of a new high priest. Archelaus violently suppressed the disturbance, killing 3,000 demonstrators, but many escaped into the surrounding hills.

Archelaus, Herod Antipas, and Philip all sailed for Rome in a competition for the blessing of Caesar Augustus. Following their departure, there was another uprising at the Temple which resulted in its being partially burned, and the retreat of the Roman and Herodian forces into the citadels of Herod's palace. There were also riots throughout the country and many of Herod's palaces and buildings were destroyed. During this time, there were several popular pretenders to the throne who gained followers, but all were ultimately killed or imprisoned.

Augustus finally ruled on Herod's succession by appointing Archelaus as ethnarch of one-half of Herod's former kingdom, including Judea, Samaria, and Idumea and promised him the kingship if he governed well. Augustus divided the other half, giving Batanea, Auranitis, and Trachonitis to Philip, with Herod Antipas receiving Galilee and Perea.[29] The Grecian cities of Gaza, Gadara, and Hippos were severed from the kingdom and placed under the Roman procurator of Syria.

---

[29] In 39 CE, Herod Antipas was accused by his nephew, Agrippa I of conspiring against the new emperor, Caligula. Accompanied by Herodias, Antipas was exiled to Gaul, where he died.

Upon his return to Judea, Archelaus was confronted with a continuing rebellion against his rule and appointments. He accused the current high priest, Joazar son of Boethus of sedition and replaced him with his brother Eleazar, who was shortly replaced by Jesus son of Sie. Archelaus did other things to enrage the Jews. Charges were brought against Archelaus, and Caesar banished him to Gaul. Augustus then appointed the Roman procurator of Syria to govern the former Herodian dominions of Judea, Samaria, and Idumea.

THE WAY WAS THE
SPIRITUAL LEADER OF THE ZEALOTS

It is likely that the Way continued to occupy caves in the vicinity of Qumran during the reign of Herod the Great; however, the structures they had built during the Hasmonean reign and destroyed by Herod in 31 BCE, were not rebuilt until after Herod's death in 4 BCE. As predicted by the *Damascus Document*, the Way returned to the "Desert of Jerusalem" and reestablished Qumran as the headquarters of their congregation.

Among the Galileans, there arose a violent reaction to the events which followed the death of Herod. When Caesar sent a procurator to assess the estate of Herod, the high priest Joazar, son of Boethus, encouraged the Jews to fully disclose their wealth to the census takers. There was, however, a resident of Gamala named Judas the Galilean who refused to cooperate—believing the taxation to be no better than slavery. He united with others and organized a revolt against the Romans. Following the cry, "No Lord but God," the "Zealots," as they became known, gathered supporters in violent resistance. Josephus reports that those who had a "zeal for the law" did not value dying any kinds of death, nor heed the deaths of their friends and relations, nor could fear cause them to call any man Lord.

Under the leadership of Judas, the Zealots seized the armory at Sepphoris, armed themselves, and began to overrun the countryside. At the same time other would-be messiahs gathered supporters and assaulted the Roman and Herodian troops throughout Israel.

The Romans responded with a large army allied with Arabian forces under King Aretas and violently put down the rebellion. Sepphoris was again destroyed, and Judas the Galilean was killed. Other cities and towns were plundered in the allied drive towards Jerusalem, where the Roman army was welcomed by the establishment Sadducees and Pharisees. The Roman forces chased the Zealots into the surrounding countryside and crucified more than 2,000. The countryside was pacified, but the Zealots continued to pursue an underground guerilla war as a militant wing of the Way, whose philosophy and theology they shared.

The Way Was the Spiritual Leader of the Zealots

A violent element of the movement came to be called the *Sicarii*, or "dagger men." A *sica* was a curved dagger which these rebels carried concealed in their belts under their robes. Josephus reports that these dagger men managed to penetrate the innermost precincts of the Temple on several occasions, and even to assassinate a High Priest in 27 CE (Current Era) and a procurator in 46 CE. The Sicarii were the extremists among the Zealots, who were inclined to immediate and violent response to crises. They engaged in constant subversion, and their specialty was assassinating establishment Jews who collaborated with the Romans.

As these events unfolded between Herod's death in 4 BCE and the Roman destruction of Jerusalem and Qumran in 70 CE, the Way, as descendants of the Zadokites and in association with the Zealots, remained convinced that the last days were upon them. They grew in strength and awaited the appearance of the multiple messiahs predicted in their books.[30]

---

[30] This was approximately the time of the birth of Jesus and Judas and the rebuilding of Qumran by the Osim.

Perfecting the Way of Righteousness

On any given Sunday—within Christian churches around the world—there are thousands and thousands of ministers and priests interpreting and preaching the message of Jesus to their congregations. Each of them differs from all others in his or her own sermon—which each proclaims to be the true message and that others are in error.

If we are to discern the truth about Jesus and his mission for the Way of Righteousness, we must first understand the circumstances surrounding his life and teachings; we must cut through the distortions which have accumulated since his death; and we must study to grasp the deeper and more accurate meaning of that which remains.

SETTING THE STAGE FOR JESUS

Accustomed as we are to Christmas nativity scenes of the birth of Jesus in a manger or cave, attended by shepherds and wise men, most people tend to imagine the land of Palestine-Israel at the time as being a rather crude and backward place. To the contrary, located at the crossroad between the ancient advanced civilizations of Egypt, Syria, Iraq, and Iran, and having been exposed to hundreds of years of Greek influence, Judea had a thriving, literate, and commercially productive society that competed with that of Alexandria, Athens, Baghdad, or Rome.[31]

Technologically speaking, there was little difference between Herod's Jerusalem and London or Paris before the introduction of steam power in the eighteenth century. All transportation—personal and commercial—was by animal power, and lighting was by oil lamps. Literacy was perhaps even more widespread, with many people speaking not only the common language of Aramaic, but also Greek and Latin. Just to the west in Egypt, the great Library of Alexandria held hundreds of thousands of books in multiple languages, including geographies, histories, and encyclopedias.

Over the centuries of their religious development, the Jewish people had written, revised, copied, and treasured many books presenting a wide variety of views. Papyrus paper had been in widespread use for hundreds of years and the literary works of writers, artists, philosophers, and scientists had filled libraries and the homes of the wealthy.

Most Jewish men could speak and understand the ancient Hebrew language sufficiently to participate in and to understand worship activities. For almost a thousand years, however, the common language of the Middle East had been Aramaic—which was still spoken by most people. Since the conquest of Alexander more than 300 years earlier, the Greek language had become the common international language and had to be spoken by those engaged in trade, travel, or higher education. Finally, with the rise of the Roman

---

[31] A True Story in the Summations provides a dramatic expression of the historically accurate essence of the life of Jesus.

Empire, those who would benefit from rights of citizenship or those who sought the protection of the Emperor or to trade with Rome, had to be fluent in Latin. Thus, any or all these languages might have been used in families and different parts of the Jewish society, dependent upon the needs of translation and understanding.

As we have learned, Herod had constructed some of the most impressive structures in the world, including Rome. We have only to walk the streets of ancient Pompeii—which was sealed in time by volcanic ash in 79 CE—to appreciate the level of commercial and personal development at the time of Jesus. Take-out food was available from street corner cafes, streets were paved and drained, people bathed at public baths with hot and cold water, their homes were nicely furnished and decorated, and they were entertained in large outdoor auditoriums.

Now, with the discoveries of the Gnostic Gospels and the Dead Sea Scrolls—and with new archeological discoveries documenting the thousands of years of human development which produced Jesus and the religion he worshipped—we can more clearly see that the world in which Jesus lived and functioned was an intelligent and cultured society. While literacy may not have been widespread in the countryside, the Congregation of the Way, at Qumran and throughout the towns and villages of Israel, were a book-oriented society that encouraged a high level of literacy.

Although it is unlikely that Jesus was born at Bethlehem in the south, or that he resided in Egypt for a time with his parents, it is more certain that he was born in the northern area of Galilee. His hometown is given as Nazareth in the Bible; however, a town by that name was not in existence during his lifetime and was probably established or renamed later. He became known as Jesus, the Nazarene, not because he was from Nazareth, but because he was a Nazarite—one who had taken a vow of consecration to the service of God. This would also be indicated by his name, Joshua or Yeshua, which meant "Yahweh is Salvation." It is probable that his brothers James and Simeon were also under Nazarite vows.

Geographically separated from southern Judea by the land of Samaria, northern Galileans violently resisted Hellenization, Herodian practices, Pharisaic accommodation, and Roman occupation. Practicing the ancient Judaic religion, as refined by the Way of Righteousness, the Galileans were at the vanguard of the Zealot rebellion. Most members of the Way did not participate in the monastic life at Qumran but lived and worked in the towns and villages of the Galilee. While they were dedicated to living lives of poverty and righteousness, they were not pacifists, and they were prepared to take up arms in defense of their beliefs and families.

Living as they had under the occupation and domination of the Greeks and Romans for centuries, the physical burden of taxes and forced labor was difficult, but bearable; however, other events were becoming intolerable. In 27 BCE, the Roman emperor, Caesar Augustus declared himself to be the son of god and the savior of humanity, and Herod began to build elaborate temples in which to worship Caesar. Moreover, following the death of Herod and the removal of his sons from the kingship, most of Judea and Galilee came under the direct administration of Rome. Its legions marched throughout the land displaying the abominable wild boar on their standards and worshipping their weapons of death and destruction. It was then that the final blow was delivered, the people were commanded to take an oath of allegiance to the divine emperor, and daily sacrifices had to be offered on his behalf by the priests in the Holy Temple in Jerusalem.

The outrage of the people knew no bounds—even their sacred religion, which had comforted them through exile, defeat, torture, and occupation, was now to be forfeited. They began to arm themselves in revolt and to cry out to God for relief. The prophesized End of Time was drawing near! No other conclusion was possible.

Galilee would have been a horrible and frightening place for Jesus to come of age. Heavily taxed to pay for Herod's building program and living in the police state he created, the Galileans also suffered under the oppressive Roman military occupation. Responding to the Zealot uprising by Judas the Galilean, the Romans brutally and violently put down the rebellion. Thousands were killed, hundreds of rotting corpses could be seen hanging on crosses along the roads in Galilee feeding the birds of prey, and the towns and villages were destroyed and laid to waste. The suffering of the people would have made a deep impression upon any child growing up in this area at this time. The images would have remained with Jesus, even as he and his parents decided he should study at Qumran—which became the *de facto* spiritual and intellectual headquarters of the Zealot resistance to Roman rule. Jesus almost certainly went there to prepare himself for the Way upon which he was destined to journey. He was most likely followed by his brothers James and Simeon.

JESUS AND HIS NAZARITE FAMILY

"Jesus" was one of the most common names in Israel at the time of his life. It is the Greek translation of the Hebrew name Joshua, or Yeshua, which is written in the Hebrew language using the same consonant letters (YHWH) as the unspoken name of Yahweh, God, or Lord. The name implies "salvation," and it was Joshua who traditionally saved the Israelites and led them in their occupation of Canaan. "Christ" is not a name—it is an honorary title. It is the Greek translation (*christos*) of the Hebrew word, messiah, which means an "Anointed One."

Today, there are serious scholars who doubt the existence of an historical Jesus. In making their case, they point to the absence of any mention of Jesus in the extensive contemporary histories of the period, the common nature of his name and titles, and the correlation of his life, experiences, ministry, and death as reported in the New Testament, with other well-documented teachers and philosophers who lived at the time.[32]

The extant histories of the time fail to report the "multitudes" that accompanied Jesus in the closing days of his ministry, the three-hour darkness that enveloped the earth upon his death, the multiple earthquakes that shook the land and split rocks open, or the mass resurrection of Jewish saints who appeared to many in Jerusalem (all of which is vividly described as fact in the New Testament). Philo of Alexandria, who lived and wrote a book at the same time about the horrific persecution of the Jews by the Roman procurator Pilate and who was sympathetic to the Way, did not mention Pilate's execution of Jesus.

---

[32] A contemporary of Jesus, Apollonius of Tyana (15-100 CE) was a Greek Pythagorean philosopher from the Cappadocia province of Anatolia. His written works were available to his biographer, who recorded that Apollonius was one of the greatest men of his era. He was recognized throughout the Roman Empire as a philosopher, social leader, moral teacher, religious reformer, and healer. Among his surviving work is a fragment which holds that God does not wish to be worshipped and cannot be reached by prayers or sacrifices. Instead, God is only accessible through the *nous,* or intellect—inasmuch as God is pure intellect. Apollonius died at the age of 85, and more than 17 temples were erected in his honor in the Empire.

The Gospels that document the life and ministry of Jesus did not come into existence for at least a half century after his death, and when they did, they primarily relied on a single source—the author of the Gospel of Mark. Early Christian writers mention Paul's epistles, but do not make any reference to the Gospels. Paul's letters predated the Gospels by several decades, but they fail to relate any of the historical events later attributed to the life of Jesus in the Gospels. Matthew, Mark, Luke, and John were not written by the named disciples, but by anonymous authors and editors using their names. The actual disciples did not write anything, or at least nothing that has survived.[33]

It is possible that the ministry of Jesus was a myth created later to compete with other mystery religions, or that it was too insignificant to warrant notice by contemporary historians. There is, however, historical evidence that Jesus was survived by family members who carried on his mission—which is solid evidence of his historical existence.

Writing in the *Antiquities of the Jews,* Josephus mentions the murder of Jesus's brother, James the Just at the hands of the high priest Ananus. James is the Greek translation of the Hebrew name of Ya'akov (Israel), or Jacob. Although Catholic dogma holds that James was not the actual physical brother of Jesus (because of Mary's perpetual virginity), Josephus writes:

> But the younger Ananus who, as we said, received the high priesthood, was of a bold disposition and exceptionally daring; he followed the party of the Sadducees, who are severe in judgment above all the Jews, as we have already shown. As therefore Ananus was of such a disposition, he thought he had now a good opportunity, as [Roman procurator] Festus was now dead, and [his replacement, Roman procurator] Albinus was still on the road; so he assembled a council of judges, and brought before it the brother of Jesus the so-called Christ, whose name was

---

[33] Mark itself may have been based, in part, on an early version of the Book of Matthew, which may have been written in Hebrew by Jesus's brother Joseph, who was known as Joses or Barnabas.

James, together with some others, and having accused them as lawbreakers, he delivered them over to be stoned.

There is another glowing reference in Josephus to "Jesus, a wise man," which is generally considered to be a later forgery; however, most scholars accept the reference to James as genuine.

In Galatians (1:18-2:10), Paul refers to "James the Lord's brother" and called him one of the "pillars" of the Church. The last mention of James was in Acts (21:17-18) just prior to Paul's arrest, "And when we were come to Jerusalem, the brethren received us gladly. And the day following Paul went in with us unto James; and all the elders were present."

Early Christian writers also considered James to be the brother of Jesus. Clement of Rome said that James was the "bishop of bishops, who rules Jerusalem, the Holy Church of the Hebrews, and all the Churches everywhere." Hegesippus reported that, "After the apostles, James the brother of the Lord surnamed the Just was made head of the Church at Jerusalem." Clement of Alexandria wrote, "The Lord after his resurrection imparted knowledge (Gnosis) to James the Just and to John and Peter . . .."

The Gospel of Matthew (13:55) asks, "Is not this the carpenter's son? Is not his mother called Mary? and his brethren, James, and Joses, and Simeon, and Judas?" Judas is also known as Thomas, which means "twin" in Aramaic. Discovered among the Gnostic Gospels is the *Gospel of Thomas*, which is ascribed to Didymos Judas Thomas. Since Didymos also means "twin" in Greek, it appears the author not only believed Jesus had a brother, but that the brother may have been an actual twin. In the Gnostic tradition, Jesus instructs Thomas:

> Brother Thomas, while you are in the world for a time, listen to me, and I will reveal to you the things you have been thinking about. Since it has been said that you are my twin and true companion, examine yourself and learn who you are, in what way you exist, and how you will come to be. Since you will be called my brother, it is not fitting that you be ignorant of yourself.

In First Corinthians, Paul complains about the lack of support by the congregation saying, "Do we not have the right to our food and drink? Do we not have the right to be accompanied by a wife, as the other apostles and the brothers of the Lord and Ce'phas [Peter]?" (9: 4) This passage would indicate that Jesus's brothers Judas Thomas and perhaps Joseph (Barnabas or Joses) may have been married. James and another brother, Simeon (Symenon-Simon) had probably taken lifetime Nazirite vows—as had Jesus. As such, they would not have married.

The entire family may have been of the Rechabite Clan, many of whom were members of the Way. The Rechabites took lifetime vows to never drink alcohol or to live in cites. They tended to pursue trades that allowed for a nomadic life, such as house building. Jesus's father may really have been a carpenter. The father's name was Cleopas (not Joseph) and Mary was the mother. They had at least one daughter named Salome, and there were five sons, Jesus, Judas Thomas, James, Simeon, and Joseph. As far as we know, only Judas gave them grandchildren. They all followed the Way of Righteousness.

The Jesuit historian Malachi Martin reports that Pope Sylvester met personally in 318 CE with eight descendants of Jesus's brother, Judas Thomas, who were known as the Desposyni (The Master's People).

The only reliable information we have about lineal kin of Jesus is through his brother Judas. Thus, somewhere in the world today, there are likely those who are related by blood to Jesus. As the narrative continues, we will learn that almost all members of Jesus's immediate family were engaged in the ministry of the Way following his crucifixion and were also executed by the authorities.

It is not possible, at this late date, to ascertain or know as a scientific certainty that Jesus existed as an historical person. What we can do, if we accept the reliable circumstantial evidence of his existence, is to determine, as best we can, his education and the lessons he taught.

THE EDUCATION AND MATURITY OF JESUS

Whether Jesus did in fact travel to and study in Britain, Egypt, Syria, or India—as some believe—is speculative; however, from the message content of his ministry we can be more certain that he was a member of the Way of Righteousness. He may have been accepted as early as age ten for instruction and gained full membership or enrollment upon maturity at age 30.

We have earlier seen how the congregation of the Way lived in the towns and villages throughout Israel and how a core group came to live a monastic life at Qumran. While most Jewish men had a duty to marry and to multiply, most of those who resided at the camp chose to devote their lives to preparing the Way for the arrival of the Savior. It is more likely that Jesus spent his youth and early manhood studying at Qumran, than working as a woodworker with his father in Galilee. It is also probable that Jesus's parents were followers of the Way of Righteousness.

Among the Dead Sea Scrolls is the *Messianic Rule*, which contains the statutes regarding age and responsibility of those who dedicated their lives to God for the benefit of humanity. The rules, which are briefly quoted below, allow for the reception of young boys—who are raised by the Community—and follows their development until they obtain maturity at age 30.

> This is the Rule for all the congregation of Israel in the last days, when they shall join the Community to walk according to the law of the sons of Zadok the Priests and of the men of their Covenant who have turned aside from the way of the people, the men of His Council who keep his Covenant in the midst of iniquity, offering expiation for the Land.
>
> From his youth they shall instruct him in the *Book of Meditation* and shall teach him, according to his age, the precepts of the Covenant. He shall be educated in their statutes for ten years . . ..

The Education and Maturity of Jesus

At the age of twenty years he shall be enrolled, that he may enter upon his allotted duties in the midst of his family and be joined to the holy congregation. He shall not approach a woman to know her by lying with her before he is fully twenty years old, when he shall know good and evil. And thereafter, he shall be accepted when he calls to witness the judgments of the Law and shall be allowed to assist at the hearing of judgments.

At the age of twenty-five years he may take his place among the foundations [the officials] of the holy congregation to work in the service of the congregation.

At the age of thirty years he may approach to participate in lawsuits and judgments, and may take his place among the chiefs of the Thousands of Israel, the chiefs of the Hundreds, Fifties, and Ten, the Judges and the officers of their tribes, in all their families, under the authority of the sons of Aaron the Priests. And every head of family in the congregation who is chosen to hold office, to go and come before the congregation, shall strengthen his loins that he may perform his tasks among his brethren in accordance with his understanding and the perfection of his way. According to whether this is great or little, so shall one man be honored more than another.

From this document, we can see how Jesus would have advanced through the various stages in the Covenant, until finally undertaking his mission after gaining full spiritual maturity at age thirty. It is not difficult to imagine Jesus at various times during his initiation and training to be reading the hundreds of books collected by the Congregation, as he envisioned his destiny. Thus, of all the artifacts available in the world today which may have been personally handled by Jesus, the fragments of parchment and papyrus found in the dust of the Qumran caves may be most likely to carry his fingerprints.

JUST WHO ON EARTH DID JESUS THINK HE WAS?

If we are to accept the proposition that there was an historical Jesus, we must at least allow him the knowledge and experiences of other young men of his station and at his time. All young Jewish boys were required to understand Hebrew to commence their participation in worship; Aramaic, the vernacular, was a related language using the same letters; Greek had been commonly spoken in the land for hundreds of years; and Jesus was probably literate in all of these languages. He would also have had access to a vast library of books written in these languages, and he would have been aware of the messianic expectations expressed in many of them. When we combine these reasonable assumptions with the fact that the religions that flowed from his ministry of the Way are presently practiced by billions of people around the world, Jesus must have had a remarkable intelligence and a valid message. Thus, we should ask ourselves the question, who and what did Jesus believe about himself and his mission?

Jesus was surely a member of the Way of Righteousness. He would not have been a Pharisaic rabbi, as some have claimed. That group was detested not only by the Way, but by Jesus himself. With the Way seeing themselves as suffering for all of humanity, an empathetic and intellectually gifted young man in these circumstances may have come to see himself on a mission to establish a congregation of the Way in Jerusalem to help alleviate the suffering of his people. He was prepared to acknowledge he was one of the messiahs predicted by the scriptures and expected by the Way.

As the messianic fervor boiled to the point of explosion, many people relying on the prophetic writings came to believe that the End of Time was upon them. Just as things appeared to be unbearable—they got worse. We earlier saw how the Book of Daniel was revised by the Zadokites to predict that a "prince" would defile the Temple, bringing about the end times during which Israel would be restored and its Temple cleansed. With the land under the heel of the Herodians and Romans, and the Temple controlled by a corrupt priesthood, the people longed for the saviors promised by the scriptures to defeat and destroy their oppressors.

> Throughout the Gospels, Jesus repeatedly referred to himself as the "Son of Man." The apocalyptic vision in Daniel is one of the few places in the Old Testament that contains that phrase:

> ... and behold, with the clouds of heaven there came one like a son of man, and he came to the Ancient of Days and was presented before him. And to him was given dominion and glory and kingdom, that all peoples, nations, and languages should serve him; his dominion is an everlasting dominion, which shall not pass away, and his kingdom one that shall not be destroyed.

Along with Daniel, the prophet Isaiah was a major inspiration of the Way:

> There shall come forth a shoot from the stump of Jesse, and a branch shall grow out of his roots. And the Spirit of the LORD shall rest upon him, the spirit of wisdom and understanding, the spirit of counsel and might, the spirit of knowledge and the fear of the LORD. (11:1-2)

> By his knowledge shall the righteous one, my servant, make many to be accounted righteous; and he shall bear their iniquities. (53:11)

> Go through, go through the gates, *prepare the way* for the people; build up, build up the highway, clear it of stones, lift up an ensign over the peoples. Behold the LORD has proclaimed to the end of the earth: Say to the daughter of Zion, "Behold, your salvation [Yeshua] comes; behold, his reward is with him, and his recompense before him." And they shall be called The holy people, The redeemed of the LORD; and you shall be called Sought out, a city not forsaken. (emphasis added) (62:10-12)

Located among the Dead Sea Scrolls is prophetic language about Isaiah's suffering servant who is anointed by God, pierced through for human transgressions, and who dies for the forgiveness of everyone's sins. (11Q13 and 1Q1sa)

Also, among the writings treasured by the Way is their *Book of Enoch*, which introduces:

> This is the Son of Man, to whom righteousness belongs; with whom righteousness has dwelt; and who will reveal all of the treasures of that which is concealed: for the Lord of spirits has chosen him; and his portion has surpassed all before the Lord of spirits in everlasting uprightness. This Son of Man, whom you behold, shall raise up kings and the mighty from their dwelling places, and the powerful from their thrones; shall loosen the bridles of the powerful from their thrones; and break in pieces the teeth of sinners.

The final words written in the Old Testament provide the prophecy of Malachi:

> Behold, I will send you Elijah the prophet before the great and terrible day of the Lord comes. And he will turn the hearts of fathers to their children and the hearts of children to their fathers, lest I come and smite the land with a curse.

Although the Way had a firm belief in the spirit of Law, and as "doers of the law," they chose to live a life of righteousness; they also were liberally influenced by Eastern religions (such as the dualism of Zoroastrianism) in believing they were the Sons of Light. Like the Greek Cynics, they believed in living a life of virtue and rejecting wealth and power, and much like the Stoics, they sought to treat others in a fair and just manner.

Finally, through their understanding of the Wisdom of Sophia and other Gnostic thinking, they were the leaders of a spiritual renaissance. We must remember that Philo of Alexandria, a close associate of the Way, was writing prolifically about philosophical matters in Egypt at the same time Jesus was preaching in Israel, and that a copy of Plato's *Republic* was found among the Gnostic Gospels at Nag Hammadi.

With a sense of destiny, an empathetic and caring Jesus stood at the confluence of powerful social and political currents, uniquely equipped with the prophecies of his ancient religion, refined by Gnostic and Eastern religions, influenced by the Hellenistic philosophies, educated and encouraged by his teachers, politically and militarily supported by a zealous rebellion against the established powers, and sincerely seeking to provide a helpful and hopeful spiritual message for the comfort and future of his oppressed people. Along with his fellow congregants, he must have longed for the freedom of his people, and he must have decided to do what he could to achieve it.

If we are to accept that the living Jesus taught the message of righteousness to his Congregation of the Poor in Jerusalem, and that he was able to express it in a way that has survived for 2,000 years—and that billions of people continue to worship in several religions that were influenced by his mission—he has to have been a wonderfully gifted person of vast intelligence with a broad grasp of human knowledge. He may have been charismatic, but it was more likely his great wisdom and deeply felt empathy for the poor and downtrodden that helped and enlightened those who listened to him.

Following in the tradition of the Hasidean missionary movement that evolved 200 years earlier, and as a follower of the Way, Jesus came to believe he had words of comfort and encouragement to offer his fellow Jewish people, who were suffering unendurable agony under the Herodians and Romans. Achieving intellectual maturity and spiritual self-awareness, he must have recognized that the expansion in his vision—beyond even that seen by his fellow congregants—mapped a Way to salvation for all of humanity. As he combined and refined all he had learned and experienced, he must have concluded he had a gospel to share—good news for humanity. As a thoughtful and spiritual person, he would have recognized the need for his mission and, undoubtedly, was aware of the personal consequences, if he pursued it.

Did Jesus perceive himself to be God, or equal to God? Certainly not—for him that would have been a blasphemy. Did he believe the End of Days was near? Apparently. Did he think that—if he were able to convey a religious philosophy that saved humanity—he might be favored by God? Probably. Did he believe a terrible and painful death as a martyr awaited him at the end of his Way? Likely. Did he share the outrage of his Congregation about the occupation of their land by a brutal and heartless enemy—did he hate evil? Surely. Did he see himself as a teacher? Undoubtedly. Did he act with his eyes wide open? Yes.

The Way longed for the appearance of several messiahs, including a kingly messiah, a priestly messiah, and a suffering servant messiah. Which of these burdens, if any, might Jesus have believed that God had laid upon him, or called him to bear? There is no claim that Jesus was among the priests of the Sons of Zadok, like his brothers James and Simeon, nor is there any indication in the Gospels—or any of the recovered documents—that he may have seen himself as leading an armed revolution against the Herodians and Romans.

Aware of the personal dangers involved in teaching a message that would undercut and dilute the power and control of the Herodians and Romans, Jesus apparently choose to accept his destiny as the suffering Son of Man. In doing so, he necessarily had to offer his life as a sacrifice for the redemption and salvation of his fellow Jews—and for all of humankind. All that was required was for him to be baptized in the spirit and power of Elijah in order to commence his public journey along the Way.

JOHN BAPTIZED FOR THE WAY

As Jesus approached his maturity and mission, the Roman emperor Caesar Augustus died and was succeeded by his adopted stepson Tiberius. Herod's extensive kingdom had been divided among his sons, with Philip in the far north and Antipas in Galilee. Archelaus, however, was removed from Samaria, Judea, and Idumea by Caesar and banished to Gaul because of his extreme cruelty. The regions surrounding Jerusalem were placed under a Roman governor.

In 26 CE, Tiberias dispatched a new procurator named Pontius Pilate to govern Judea. Based in Caesarea (between modern Tel Aviv and Haifa) by the Mediterranean Sea, Pilate deployed Roman soldiers to occupy Jerusalem and the Antonia Fortress overlooking the temple. Insurrections arose in the city over the open display of the detested Roman standards and Pilate's appropriation of temple funds to construct an aqueduct for the city. A large crowd of protesters was infiltrated by Roman soldiers who, upon a signal from Pilate, began to beat and kill the demonstrators.

Philo of Alexandria described Pilate's "corruption, and his acts of insolence, and his rapine, and his habit of insulting people, and his cruelty, and his continual murders of people untried and uncondemned, and his never ending, and gratuitous, and most grievous inhumanity." Pilate was ultimately removed from office by Tiberius after he killed a large group of Samaritan protesters[34] and executed many prisoners without trial. It was Pilate who governed Judea during the mission of Jesus.

Having suffered for decades under the brutality of Herod and his progeny, and now under Roman domination, the Jews in the north and Judea were desperate for the appearance of a Messiah to free them from oppression and to lead them to victory. First, however, they believed that a prophet in the manner of Elijah must appear to anoint the new Messiah.

---

[34] Even though the Samaritans had been suppressed during the Hasmonean Dynasty, they remained as a distinct group occupying the area of the "West Bank" between Galilee in the north and Judea in the south. It was when they attempted to gather at their sacred Mount Gerizim that they were attacked by Roman soldiers.

Luke recites a fable about the birth of a son to Jesus's elderly great-aunt who was proclaimed to act with "the spirit and power of Elijah, to turn the hearts of the fathers to the children, and the disobedient to the wisdom of the just, to make ready for the Lord a people prepared." The child, John, was six months older than his cousin, Jesus.

Becoming known as the Baptist, John came to preach in the area around the Jordan River just east of Jerusalem in the vicinity of Qumran and the Dead Sea. (See Photo #10) His ministry was prophesized by Isaiah, Malachi and *Enoch*, "The voice of one crying in the wilderness; prepare the way of the Lord, make his paths straight." The *Community Rule* of the Way quoted the same scriptures as the basis for their going into the wilderness to prepare the Way of the Lord by studying and living the Law of Moses. Most scholars accept the likelihood that John the Baptist was a follower of the Way of Righteousness at Qumran.

Mark commences his gospel with the Isaiah prophecy and the baptism of Jesus:

> John the baptizer appeared in the wilderness, preaching a baptism of repentance for the forgiveness of sins. And there went out to him all the country of Judea, and all the people of Jerusalem; and they were baptized by him in the river Jordan, confessing their sins. Now John was clothed with camel's hair, and had a leather girdle around his waist, and ate locusts and wild honey. And he preached, saying, "After me comes he who is mightier than I, the thong of whose sandals I am not worthy to stoop down and untie. I have baptized you with water; but he will baptize you with the Holy Spirit." (1: 4-8)

Baptism in water was a central precept of the Way of Righteousness. In the *Community Rule* (II-III), those who refuse to enter the "Community of his truth" and who walk "in the stubbornness of his heart" shall "not be reckoned among the perfect; he shall neither be purified by atonement, nor cleansed by purifying waters, nor sanctified by seas and rivers, nor washed clean with any ablution."

For those who accepted the spirit of true counsel, "He shall be cleansed from all his sins by the spirit of holiness uniting him to His truth, and his iniquity shall be expiated by the spirit of uprightness and humility. And when his flesh is sprinkled with purifying water and sanctified by cleansing water, it shall be made clean by the humble submission of his soul to all the precepts of God."

The Way believed that at the "time of the visitation, . . . God will then purify every deed of man with his truth; He will refine for Himself the human frame by rooting out all spirit of falsehood from the bounds of his flesh. He will cleanse him of all wicked deeds with the spirit of holiness; like purifying waters He will shed upon him the spirit of truth (to cleanse him) of all abomination and falsehood. And he shall be plunged into the spirit of purification that he may instruct the upright in the knowledge of the Most High and teach the wisdom of the sons of heaven to the perfect of way." (*Community Rule* IV)

Most likely, when Jesus became 30 years old and achieved the most mature and enlightened status within the Way, he was ritually baptized by John, with full knowledge of the significance of its being in the spirit and power of Elijah.

According to the Book of Mark, when Jesus was baptized by John, he heard a Voice from heaven, and the Spirit of God descended upon him like a dove and entered him, signifying that he was the Messiah. After spending a period in the wilderness, perhaps in a cave near Qumran, Jesus emerged to commence his mission. Such a baptism, followed by a period of reflection, would follow the precepts of the Way *and* the Gnostics.

Shortly thereafter, John the Baptist was arrested by order of Herod Antipas and incarcerated. Herod was threatened with war by the Nabataean king of Arabia, whose daughter had been Antipas's wife and whom Antipas had discarded for Herodias, former wife of his brother Philip. John the Baptist had condemned the marriage as illegal, and many people were ready to revolt against Herod.

At a party held to celebrate Herod Antipas's birthday, Herodias' daughter by Herod Philip, Salome II danced for Herod and the guests. Enchanted, Herod offered her a gift, to which she replied, "I want you to give me at once the head of John the Baptist on a platter." Herod ordered John's execution and presented his head to Salome.

Josephus provides an historic basis for John the Baptist in Book XVIII, Chapter V of the *Antiquities of the Jews*:

> Now, some of the Jews thought that the destruction of Herod's army came from God, and that very justly, as a punishment of what he did against John, that was called the *baptist*; for Herod slew him, who was a good man, and commanded the Jews to exercise virtue, both as to righteousness towards one another, and piety towards God, and so to come to baptism; for that the washing (with water) would be acceptable to him, if they made use of it, not in order to the putting away, (or the remission) of some sins (only,) but for the purification of the body: supposing still that the soul was thoroughly purified beforehand by righteousness. Now when (many) others came to crowd about him, for they were greatly moved (or pleased) by hearing his words, Herod, who feared lest the great influence John had over the people might put it into his power and inclination to raise a rebellion, (for they seemed ready to do anything he should advise,) thought it best, by putting him to death, to prevent any mischief he might cause, and not bring himself into difficulties, by sparing a man who might make him repent of it when it should be too late. Accordingly, he was sent a prisoner, out of Herod's suspicious temper, to Macherus, the castle I before mentioned, and was there put to death. Now the Jews had an opinion that the destruction of this army was sent as a punishment upon Herod, and a mark of God's displeasure against him.

Note that Josephus explicitly describes John's baptism as an initiation purification of the body in preparation for one to engage in a life of righteousness—as practiced by the Way—instead of being for the remission of sins as related by Mark. Such an innovation would only arise later in the religion created by Paul.

Herod Antipas's military campaign to confront the southern Arabian threat was defeated by the Nabataeans in 36 CE. This defeat was seen by the people as a divine punishment for Antipas's execution of John the Baptist and as another portend of the End Times.

Having reached his full maturity as a teacher of the Way of Righteousness, and baptized and purified by the Spirit of Wisdom, Jesus departed along the Way on a mission to his own Congregation of the Poor in Jerusalem. What he had to say, and what he did, would change the world—forever.

SEARCHING FOR THE TRUTH IN THE NEW TESTAMENT

Throughout the Old Testament, the word "gospel" is used to mean the "good news" of God's salvation, which is widely proclaimed and joyfully received. For modern Christians, the Gospels are the New Testament books of Matthew, Mark, Luke, and John which present the "glad tidings" of Jesus, the Son of God, who died for the sins of humanity and who arose from the dead and was reunited with his Father God in Heaven. For many Christians, the Gospels also teach a unity of Jesus and his Father God with the Holy Spirit in an indivisible Divine Trinity.

If we are to ascertain an accurate picture of the personality of Jesus and his mission, we must look backward in time and peel away the layers of distortion added over the last 2,000 years—much like archeologists carefully and slowly scraping dirt and debris away from ancient buried treasures. Initially, we must understand that Christianity, as currently practiced by most Catholics and Protestants, began as a mystical revelation by Paul intended as an interpretation of the original message of Jesus. Paul, a Pharisee, crafted a lawyerly alternative to the mission of Jesus and the Way, which was easier to practice and more acceptable to his Gentile converts.

Following his own conversion from being a murderous persecutor of the followers of Jesus, Paul apparently spent three years in the wilderness studying with the Way. Later, the *mysteries* he writes about in his early epistles (the ones he wrote) generally followed the Gnostic theology of Jesus and the Way. Although Paul mentions Jesus or Christ more than 300 times, he does not include any stories about an historical Jesus, nor does he quote the words of an historical Jesus—only what he claims to have received by revelations. The crucifixion and resurrection of Jesus are mentioned in a spiritual sense; however, no historical details are provided.

For the Way and the original followers of Jesus, Gnosis *was* the only gospel required. A glimpse of this can be observed in Mark where Jesus is reported to have said, "To you has been given the secret [mysteries] of the kingdom of God, but for those outside everything is in parables; so that they may indeed see but not perceive, and may indeed hear but not understand; . . ." (4: 11-12)

For the original followers of Jesus (and apparently for Paul) there was no need for a biography of Jesus. His birth, life, and death—except for the lessons he taught and the insights that could be drawn from them—were irrelevant to the message. This is not surprising because there are no biographical or historical details in the Dead Sea Scrolls or the Gnostic Gospels—which were primarily written and intended for allegorical purposes.

The biographical Gospels of the New Testament were not written because these stories were initially passed along orally, but because there was no need, initially, for a virgin birth, miracles, and a supernatural resurrection to derive spiritual inspiration from Jesus's ministry of the Way of Righteousness. It was only later in order to compete with other major religions of the Roman Empire (such as Mithraism and Sol Invictus), to react to the Roman destruction of Jerusalem and the Temple, and to prove that Jesus was the expected messiah, that the Gospels were created.

Even after the written gospels diluted and obscured the true message of Jesus, the Gnostic Christian search for spiritual knowledge, universal consciousness, and self-awareness by the followers of Jesus was widespread throughout the Mediterranean world and flourished in all its major cities. Gnosticism *was* the most prevalent form of Christianity throughout the first centuries. Christian Gnosticism was a rich spiritual culture that relied on many books which were later destroyed during the Orthodox takeover and the creation of Roman Christianity in the fourth century. Some of these Gnostic teachings were revised and included in the Orthodox Gospels, others survived as the Apocrypha, and a few were recovered at Nag Hammadi in Egypt and at Qumran by the Dead Sea in Israel.

For understanding, we must look back beyond the fourth century, when Constantine the Great recognized the minority, Rome-centered, Pauline Christian sect as a state religion alongside Sol Invictus, and when—using that imperial authority—the Romans decided in 393 CE which books to keep and which to destroy as being heretical.

In a reversal of the manner in which the original mission of Jesus was to transform the Jewish religion from a fear-based worship into an individual search for enlightenment and spiritual awareness, the Paulines destroyed that which was good, wholesome, and independent in the mission of Jesus and replaced it with a priest and bishop-dominated religion that emphasized guilt, fear, suffering, and obedience. The Roman Christians rejected the Gnostic's belief in the inherent goodness of people and replaced it with the psychologically harmful doctrine of original sin. That which was recognized by the Gnostics as allegorical in the lessons taught by Jesus was converted into convoluted literalisms. The encouragement of an individual's search for truth was replaced by a demand for blind faith. Salvation through self-awareness was replaced by salvation through a belief in Jesus as a God who walked the earth, died and was resurrected, and who ascended to Heaven. Centuries of progress in the evolution of human consciousness and psychological healing was reversed in a return to the pagan worship of an all-powerful, judgmental God.

Paul said, ". . . for the written code kills, but the Spirit gives life." In lieu of searching the scriptures allegorically for spiritual guidance, his Roman followers insisted that the New Testament they created was the unquestionable, absolute word about Christianity. While the original ministry of Jesus offered freedom from the rigors of the Old Testament, the Paulines reimposed it on all Christians as the inerrant word and acts of God—barbarities and all.

To the extent that Paul's original epistles included a few of the Gnostic principles he learned during his initiation at Qumran, forgeries allegedly written by him were added to spout principles inimical to his more inspired lessons. Women—who had been leaders among the original followers of Jesus—were relegated to second-class status in what was ultimately transformed into the Roman Christianity practiced today.

With the suppression of science and spiritual inquisitiveness, the Roman Catholic Church created by Paul plunged most of the world and its people into a Dark Age that would last for centuries, and, in some respects, even until this day.

We must, however, look even further back in time to identify the depth of harm that Paul caused to the original mission of Jesus by his legalistic manipulations. While he may have learned and later repeated some of the Gnostic doctrine from the Way during the three years of his indoctrination, Paul did not abandon his lawyerly Pharisaic training in his attempts to "smooth" the basic principles believed in by the Way and taught by Jesus. This can best be demonstrated by a careful perusal of the 30 pages of Paul's Letter to the Romans. In his masterful legalistic brief, Paul begins with an acceptance of one the basic principles of the Way, the "doers of the law":

> For he will render to every man according to his works: to those who by patience in well-doing seek for glory and honor and immortality, he will give eternal live. (2:6-7)

> All who have sinned without the law will also perish without the law, and all who have sinned under the law will be judged by the law. For it is not the hearers of the law who are righteous before God, but the doers of the law who will be justified. (2:1-13)

Paul then commences his legalistic analysis with his own alternative proposition:

> Then what becomes of our boasting? It is excluded. On what principle? On the principle of works? No, but on the principle of faith. For we [Paul] hold that a man is justified by faith apart from works of law. (3:27-28)

Turning against James the Just and the other Poor of the Way in Jerusalem, Paul attacks,

> What shall we say, then? That Gentiles who did not pursue righteousness have attained it, that is righteousness through faith; but that Israel who pursued the righteousness which is based on law, did not succeed in fulfilling that law. Why? Because they did not pursue it through faith, but as if it were based on works. (9:30-32)

> For, being ignorant of the righteousness that comes from God, and seeking to establish their own, they did not

submit to God's righteousness. For Christ is the end of the law, that everyone who has faith may be justified. (10:3-4)

Paul directly contradicts Jesus when he says in Romans (10:13), "For, everyone who calls upon the name of the Lord will be saved." To the contrary, Matthew quotes Jesus as saying, "Not everyone who says to me, 'Lord, Lord,' shall enter the kingdom of heaven, but he who does the will of my Father who is in heaven." (7:21)

Paul concludes Romans with his intention to return to Judea carrying aid to make some "contribution for the poor among the saints at Jerusalem." (15:25-26) He goes on to ask for prayers on his behalf "that I may be delivered from the unbelievers in Judea, that my service for Jerusalem may be acceptable to the saints." (15:31)

Several books relegated to the back of the New Testament conform most closely with the original ministry of Jesus. The first of these, The Letter of James, resonates with the Dead Sea Scrolls and may be an authentic writing by James the Just. He says, "Blessed is the man who endures trial, for when he has stood the test, he will receive the crown of life which God has promised to those who love him." (1:12)

Contrary to Paul's arguments in Romans, James says:

> But be doers of the word, and not hearers only, deceiving yourselves. For if anyone is a hearer of the word and not a doer, he is like a man who observes his natural face in a mirror; for he observes himself and goes away and at once forgets what he was like. But he who looks into the perfect law, the law of liberty, and perseveres, being no hearer that forgets but a doer that acts, he shall be blessed in his doing. (1:22-25)

Rebuking Paul, James explains that "if you judge the law, you are not a doer of the law, but a judge," (4:11), and asks:

> What does it profit, my brethren, if a man says he has faith but has not works? Can his faith save him? If a brother or sister is ill-clad and in lack of daily food, and one of you says to them, "Go in peace, be warmed and filled," without

giving them the things needed for the body, what does it profit? So, faith by itself, if it has no works, is dead. But someone will say, "You have faith and I have works." Show me your faith apart from your works, and I by my works will show you my faith." (2:14-18)

Paul was also chastised in The First Letter of John which holds that, "He who says, 'I know him" but disobeys his commandments is a liar, and the truth is not in him; but whoever keeps his word, in him truly love for God is perfected. By this we may be sure that we are in him: he who says he abides in him ought to walk in the same way in which he walked." (2:4-5)

Thus, we arrive back at a point in time at which we can make a better determination of what Jesus said. In doing so, in addition to removing that which was later added, we must consider what he was likely reading—for we know he had access to many books that were lost or were later suppressed and destroyed by the Roman Christians. These include the *Book of Enoch*, that is quoted in The Letter of Jude (14)—which was written by the "brother of James" (and Jesus). Other books include *The Wisdom of Solomon, Maccabees, Psalms of Solomon,* and *Sirach*.

Written at, or near, the time of Jesus, *The Wisdom of Solomon* is included in the Septuagint, along with *Sirach*. In describing Sophia, or Wisdom, it is written that she existed from Creation with God as her source and guide. She is to be loved and desired and will come to the aid of the righteous. Surely, Jesus's acceptance of women as leaders among his followers—including his designation of Mary Magdalene as his most honored disciple—was based on his belief in the wisdom of Sophia and the Spirit of Wisdom.

Believed to have been written in the centuries preceding Jesus, *Sirach*, which is also known as the *Book of Ecclesiasticus*, is a collection of ethical teachings which recognizes "Simeon, the high priest, son of Onias" as one of the "men of renown." Simeon was probably the first Righteous Teacher of the Zaddik and Osim. Some of the words of *Sirach* are put in the mouth of Jesus in the New Testament, including his warning of false prophets in Matthew, "You will know them by their fruits. Are grapes gathered from thorns, or figs from thistles? So, every sound tree bears good fruit, but the bad tree bears evil fruit. . . . Thus, you will know them by their fruits." (7:16-20) James, quotes *Sirach* when he says, "Know this, my beloved brethren. Let every man be quick to hear, slow to speak, slow to anger, for the anger of man does not work the righteousness of God." (1:19-20)

As a doer of the law, Jesus probably did not see the need to document his mission. He was living the lessons of righteousness he taught and personally instructing the most enlightened of his followers about the Mysteries of Existence and the Spirit of Wisdom.

What if—drawing upon his education, experiences, and the books he had read—Jesus had chosen to personally write out his beliefs and expectations? What, exactly, was his message? If his Gospel were found sealed with tar in a clay jar today, what words would we read? Would any existing Christian minister or priest accept and preach that message, or would it be declared by most to be a heresy? Would the Gospel of Yeshua be burned, or would it be deemed by professional counselors to be a psychologically healthy religious philosophy for modern people to follow?

THE GOSPEL OF YESHUA

I Judas, known as Thomas, the brother of Jacob the Just, have carefully preserved these writings entrusted to me by our brother, Yeshua. These are the words he spoke and wrote during the time he walked the Way with us before his crucifixion by the Romans.[35]

1Think not that I have come to abolish the law and the prophets; I have come not to abolish them but to fulfill them. For truly, I say to you, till heaven and earth pass away, not an iota, not a dot, will pass from the law until all is accomplished.

2You are the light of the world. A city set on a hill cannot be hid. Nor do men light a lamp and put it under a bushel, but on a stand, and it gives light to all in the house. Let your light so shine before men, that they may see your good works and give glory to your Father who is in heaven.

3You shall love the Lord your God with all your heart, and with all your soul, and with all your mind. This is the great and first commandment. And a second is like it, You shall love your neighbor as yourself. So, whatever you wish that men would do to you, do so to them; for this is the law and the prophets.[36]

4A new commandment I give to you, that you love one another; even as I have loved you, that you also love one another. By this all men will know that you are my disciples, if you have love for one another.

---

[35] The careful reader could profit from a brief review of the earlier chapter, *Gnosis and Sophia (Wisdom)*, to better grasp the meaning of Jesus's words.

[36] When Jesus was asked in Matthew (22:36-40) about the greatest commandment in the Law, his answer is similar to words in the *Testament of the Twelve Patriarchs*, fragments of which were found among the Dead Sea Scrolls: The *Testament of Dan* (5:3) says, "Love the Lord through all your life, and one another with a true heart," and the *Testament of Joseph* (18:2) says, "And if anyone seeketh to do evil unto you, do well unto him, and ye shall be redeemed of the Lord from all evil."

Perfecting the Way of Righteousness

2Blessed are the poor in spirit, for theirs is the kingdom of heaven. Blessed are those who mourn, for they shall be comforted. Blessed are the meek, for they shall inherit the earth. Blessed are those who hunger and thirst for righteousness, for they shall be satisfied. Blessed are the merciful, for they shall obtain mercy. Blessed are the pure in heart, for they shall see God. Blessed are the peacemakers, for they shall be called sons of God. Blessed are those who are persecuted for righteousness' sake, for theirs is the kingdom of heaven. Blessed are you when men revile you and persecute you and utter all kinds of evil against you falsely on my account.[37]

3To you it has been given to know the secrets of the kingdom of God; but for others they are in parables, so that seeing they may not see, and in hearing they may not understand.

4I tell my mysteries to those who are worthy of my mysteries.

2I am not your teacher. For you have drunk, you have become intoxicated at the bubbling spring that I have measured out.

3I will give you what no eye has seen, and what no ear has heard, and what no hand has touched, and what has not occurred to the human mind.

4Whoever has ears should hear! Light exists inside a person of light, and he shines on the whole world. If he does not shine, there is darkness.

5If someone becomes like God; he will become full of light. But if he becomes one, separated from God, he will become full of darkness.

---

[37] The blessings of the Beatitudes are also like many of the testimonies in the *Testament of the Twelve Patriarchs*.

6If they say to you: "Where do you come from?" then say to them: "We have come from the light, the place where the light has come into being by itself, has established itself and has appeared in their image.

7Come to know what is in front of you, and that which is hidden from you will become clear to you. For there is nothing hidden that will not become manifest.

8The one who seeks should not cease seeking until he finds. And when he finds, he will be dismayed. And when he is dismayed, he will be astonished. And he will be king over the All.

9When you come to know yourselves, then you will be known, and you will realize that you are the children of the living Father. But if you do not come to know yourselves, then you exist in poverty, and you are poverty.

10If you bring it into being within you, then that which you have will save you. If you do not have it within you, then that which you do not have within you will kill you.

11Whoever will drink from my mouth will become like me. I myself will become he, and what is hidden will be revealed to him.

12Have you already discovered the beginning that you are now asking about the end? For where the beginning is, there the end will be too. Blessed is he who will stand at the beginning. And he will know the end, and he will not taste death. Blessed is he who was, before he came into being.

13Many times have you desired to hear these words, these that I am speaking to you, and you have no one else from whom to hear them. There will be days when you will seek me, and you will not find me.

14When you make the two into one, and when you make the inside like the outside and the outside like the inside and the above like the below—that is, to make the male and the female into a single one, so that the male will not be male and the female will not be female—and when you make eyes instead of an eye and a hand instead of a hand and a foot instead of a foot, an image instead of an image, then you will enter the kingdom.

15Love your brother like your life! Protect him like the apple of your eye!

16Judge not, that you be not judged. You see the splinter that is in your brother's eye, but you do not see the beam that is in your own eye. When you remove the beam from your own eye, then you will see clearly enough to remove the splinter from your brother's eye.

17If the flesh came into being because of the spirit, it is a wonder. But if the spirit came into being because of the body, it is a wonder of wonders. Yet I marvel at how this great wealth has taken up residence in this poverty.

18Blessed are the solitary ones, the elect. For you will find the kingdom. For you come from it and will return to it.

19If you would be perfect, go, sell what you possess and give it to the poor, and you will have treasure in heaven; and come follow me. Truly I say to you, it is easier for a camel to go through the eye of a needle than for a rich man to enter the kingdom of God.

20You shall not swear falsely but shall perform to the Lord what you have sworn. But I say to you, do not swear at all, either by heaven, for it is the throne of God, or by the earth, for it is his footstool, or by Jerusalem, for it is the city of the great King. And do not swear by your head, for you cannot make one hair white or black. Let what you say

The Gospel of Yeshua

be simply "Yes" or "No"; anything more than this comes from evil.[38]

21Do not tell lies and do not do what you hate.

22If those who lead you say to you: "Look, the kingdom is in the sky!" then the birds of the sky will precede you. If they say to you: "It is in the sea," then the fishes will precede you. Rather, the kingdom is inside of you and outside of you.

23No matter where you came from, you should go to James the Just, for whose sake heaven and earth came into being.

5If the things that are visible to you are obscure to you, how can you hear about the things that are not visible? If the deeds of the truth that are visible in the world are difficult for you to perform, how indeed, then, shall you perform those that pertain to the exalted height and to the Pleroma which are not visible? And how shall you be called "Laborers?" In this respect you are apprentices and have not yet received the height of perfection.

2Blessed is the wise man who sought after the truth, and when he found it, he rested upon it forever and was unafraid of those who wanted to disturb him.

3Watch and pray that you not come to be in the flesh, but rather that you come forth from the bondage of the bitterness of this life. And as you pray, you will find rest, for you have left behind the suffering and the disgrace. For when you come forth from the suffering and passion of

---

[38] Jesus shared with the Way a hatred of oaths. According to Josephus, the members of the Way "are eminent for fidelity, and are the ministers of peace; whatsoever they say also is firmer than an oath; but swearing is avoided by them, and they esteem it worse than perjury; for they say, that he who cannot be believed without (swearing by) God, is already condemned." (*War* II:VIII:6) Paul, however, contrary to the lessons he received at Qumran, frequently swears to God in his epistles that he is telling the truth.

the body, you will receive rest from the Good One, and you will reign with the King, you joined with him and he with you, from now on, forever and ever.

6When you pray, you must not be like the hypocrites; for they love to stand and pray in the synagogues and at the street corners, that they may be seen by men. But when you pray go into your room and pray in secret. Pray like this:

2Our Mother who art in heaven, hallowed be thy name. Thy kingdom come, Thy will be done, on earth as it is in heaven. Give us this day our daily bread; and forgive us our debts, as we also have forgiven our debtors; and lead us not into temptation but deliver us from evil.

7Do homage to those who give you Glory, and praise His name continually, because out of poverty has He lifted your head, seating you among the nobles. He has given you authority over an inheritance of Glory, so seek His favor continuously. Though you are Poor, do not say "I am penniless, so I cannot seek out Knowledge." Rather, bend your back to all discipline, and through all Wisdom, purify your heart, and in the abundance of your intellectual potential, investigate the Mystery of Existence. And ponder all the Ways of Truth and consider all the roots of Evil. Then you will know what is bitter for a man, and what is sweet for a person.

2Honor your father in your poverty and your mother by your behavior. For a man's father is like his arms, and his mother is like his legs. Surely, they have guided you like a hand, and just as He has given them authority over you and appointed them over your Spirit, so should you serve them. And just as He has opened your ears to the Mystery of Existence, thus should you honor them, for the sake of your own honor.

The Gospel of Yeshua

3If you take a wife in your poverty, take her from among the daughters of the Mystery of Existence. In your companionship, go forward together, with the helpmate of your flesh.[39]

8My companion, Mary Magdalene is the woman who knows the All. She is the most honored and loved of all those who follow me. Why do I not love you as I love her?

2I will pray to our Mother, and she will give you the Spirit of Truth to be with you forever, for she dwells with you, and will be in you. Yet a little while, and the world will see me no more, but the Holy Spirit of Wisdom, whom the Mother will send in my name, she will teach you all things and bring to your remembrance all that I have said to you.

3The light is with you for a little longer. Walk while you have the light, lest the darkness overtake you; those who walk in the darkness do not know where they go. While you have the light, believe in the light, that you may become sons of light.

9The covenant of Abraham, made at Jerusalem with Melchizedek, is to peacefully live the Way of Righteousness.

10This is my testament: Mary will be the messenger of the Way to the West, Judas to the East, Joseph to the Gentiles, Jacob and Simeon to tend to the flock and to see to our father Cleopas, and Salome to care for our mother, Mary.

I, Judas Thomas, add these final words to those written here by the hand of Yeshua. Following his cleansing of the Temple and his crucifixion by the Romans, a spear was thrust into our brother's side by a centurion to prove he was dead. We removed Yeshua from the cross and carried him to our refuge by the Dead Sea. Here we

---

[39] Chapter 7 contains the only words from the Dead Sea Scrolls that are included in the Gospel of Yeshua. They very concisely state the essence of the Way of Righteousness.

dug his grave and buried him among the Saints of the Way. We placed his Gospel and these words in a clay jar, sealed it with tar, and laid it on his chest in the grave. We covered his body with clay, and placed rocks upon the remains of his body. Among those who placed rocks upon his grave was our father, Cleopas, our mother, Mary, our brothers Jacob, Simeon, and Joseph, our sister Salome, and me, Judas. Many of the Way and Yeshua's Congregation of the Poor walked the distance with us and are gathered here as witnesses to the release of the Spirit of Yeshua from his body. They were led by Mary Magdalene, our companion and our brother's most honored messenger, who anointed him as our Savior, and who is now going forth to share the Spirit of Wisdom.[40]

---

[40] If it is truly possible that Jesus and his brothers are buried at Qumran, then might it also be true that it is also the final resting place of his mother, father, and sister, who also followed the Way of Righteousness?

Chapter Sources

1:1 Matthew 5:17
1:2 Matthew 5:14
1:3 Matthew 22:36-40
1:4 John 13:34
2 Matthew 5:3
3 Luke 8:10
4 *Gospel of Thomas* from the *Nag Hammadi Library* as translated by Stephen J. Patterson and James M. Robinson.
5 *The Book of Thomas the Contender* from the *Nag Hammadi Library* as translated by John D. Turner.
6 Matthew 6:5
7 *Your Holy Spirit,* Fragment 9, *The Dead Sea Scrolls Uncovered* as translated by Robert Eisenman & Michael Wise.
8:1 *The Gospel of Philip* from the *Nag Hammadi Library* as translated by Wesley W. Isenberg.
8:2 John 14:26
8:3 John 12:35

THE CRUCIFIXION AND RESURRECTION OF JESUS

Although the cross has become the ubiquitous symbol of Roman Christianity representing the sin atonement of Jesus's crucifixion, it is probable that little of the story told in the New Testament Gospels about his death and resurrection has an historical basis. That he survived his crucifixion, as believed by some, is as unlikely as his bodily resurrection.

The fact that decades passed between the time of Jesus's death and the fabrication of the Gospels, combined with the authors' motivation to weave a narrative that could compete with the similar stories of deaths and resurrections offered by other more prevalent religions in the Roman Empire at the time, and the need to comport the narrative with the scriptures predicting Israel's messianic savior, there is little in the Gospels to recommend as an historical fact, notwithstanding the faithful and wholehearted belief of billions of devoted Christians who worship Jesus as their personal Savior and God.

How then can we arrive at a reasonable understanding of the events surrounding the death of one of greatest individuals in human history, particularly as it affects the religions and beliefs of billions of people based on that fact? What motivated the Romans to execute Jesus in the way they did? What became of his body?

We have already examined the question about who Jesus thought himself to be and why the role he played necessarily resulted in his violent death. We have reviewed the history of the period, considered how that history would have impinged on Jesus's mission, and we have sought an understanding of the spiritual expectations of the Jewish people at the time. We now consider the threat of his mission to the Herodian and Roman authorities—and their Pharisaic and Sadducean collaborators—and examine the consequences.

The mission of Jesus was very short—at most a couple of years, and as short as a few weeks—and it is highly improbable that he attracted the "multitudes" described in the Gospels. He may have called himself the "Son of Man," but there is no evidence he believed himself to be the hoped for kingly Davidic Messiah who would lead the Jewish people to militarily defeat the oppressive Herodians and Romans. Most likely Jesus became an esteemed Righteous Teacher of the Way and upon his full spiritual maturity at age 30, he left Qumran and established a Congregation of the Poor in Jerusalem to reveal the gospel of the Way of Righteousness to a larger following, that included women, the poor and disadvantaged, and Gentiles.

It may also be true that Jesus reached out to a larger audience in the last weeks before his death, and he may have debated the Pharisees—whose oral Torah was opposed by the Way. Reports of his preaching would have aroused the powerful, but there is one event—the cleansing of the Temple—ascribed to Jesus in the New Testament that resonates with the history of the Way and which Jesus might have actually done to defy the established authorities and to bring about his passion.

After recapturing Jerusalem from the hated Greek Syrians in 164 BCE, Judas Maccabee cleansed the Temple, rebuilt the altar, and began to offer sacrifices for the first time in years. Attending the Temple at that time, and subsequently, were members of the alternative Zaddik priesthood, who were chosen for their piety and righteousness, instead of their membership in the family clan of Sadducees. These were the lower Levite priests who continued their priestly duties at the Temple altar during Pompey's conquest of Jerusalem in 63 BCE, and who were slaughtered by the Roman's Pharisaic collaborators. At the time of Jesus, the Way considered the Sadducean high priesthood to be entirely corrupt, and the Congregation maintained its own alternative priesthood and a separate, more accurate calendar for Temple attendance.

In the Gospels, Jesus arrives in Jerusalem riding a colt along a path of palm fronds to the cries of "Hosanna in the highest." It is more likely he would have quietly arrived with his small band of spiritual priests and warriors of the Way of Righteousness, including members of his family, determined to symbolically cleanse the Temple. The Way established a congregation in the Wilderness to rally the Sons of Light against the forces of darkness, and it was one of their greatest Teachers who set forth along the 29 miles of the Way from Qumran to Jerusalem. He did not believe he was a God, but reluctantly accepted a mission to become the messianic Suffering One, prepared to accept his fate and to suffer a violent death on behalf of his people and all humanity.

The road from Qumran would have taken him through Bethany, located a short distance east of the Mount of Olives and the Temple. There is one story found in the Gospels that—if not based on fact—is nonetheless poignant. If Jesus was to be the Messiah, he had to be anointed. In Matthew and Mark, the one who anoints him is identified only as a "woman." In Luke, the anointing unbelievably occurs in the home of a Pharisee and is performed by a prostitute, but in John, the woman is identified as Mary, the sister of Martha and Lazarus. Keeping in mind that the resurrection of Lazarus was most likely a Gnostic initiation and that the woman could have been Mary Magdalene, the companion of Jesus, the image is powerful and compelling:

> Jesus came to Bethany, where Lazarus was, who Jesus had raised from the dead. There they made him a supper; Martha served, . . . Mary took a pound of costly ointment of pure nard and anointed the feet of Jesus and wiped his feet with her hair; and the house was filled with the fragrance of the ointment. But Judas Iscariot[41] . . . said, "why was this ointment not sold for three hundred denarii and given to the poor?" . . . Jesus said, "Let her alone, let her keep it for the day of my burial. The poor you always have with you, but you do not always have me." (John 12:1-8)

The Temple was one of the most magnificent building structures in the world at the time, but it represented the ultimate symbol of religious corruption to the Way. The Saducean priesthood kowtowed to the Romans, who held the sacred robes and jeweled breastplate of the High Priest in the Antonia Fortress—only allowing them to be displayed on four of the major religious events each year.

The outer court of the Temple was the domain of the money changers, who collected the temple tax and made a profit on

---

[41] Here the fictional Judas Iscariot is inserted by the Roman writers to diminish the roles of Judas Thomas and Mary Magdalene and to confuse the facts.

exchanging foreign coins for the Hebrew shekel required to purchase sacrifices. Pigeons for the poor, and sheep and oxen for the wealthy, were available at a price, and were handed over to the priests for slaughter on the altar. The entrails were tossed on the flames of sacrifice, which burned 24 hours a day, the blood was sprinkled on the four horns of the altar, and the meat was preserved to feed the priests and their families.

Rising above the Temple—with a clear view of all the courtyards and proceedings—was the fortress where the priestly garments were stored and where the Roman soldiers monitored traffic in the Temple precincts. We have no real historical knowledge about what Jesus did during his final visit to the Temple, but we can imagine him storming the money changers, overturning their tables, and chasing them and the sacrifice merchants with a whip. Undoubtedly, his actions drew the attention of the "chief priests and the scribes" and the Roman centurions, who stormed down and seized Jesus.[42]

Jesus might have chosen to symbolically cleanse the Temple as the culmination of his mission. If his actions only offended the Saducees and Pharisees, his fate would have been determined by the Sanhedrin—the Jewish Council—and he might have been stoned to death. If, however, his riot attracted the attention of the Romans stationed in the Antonia Fortress, and if Jesus's words and violence were perceived by Pilate as seditious, there would have been no trial, no washing of hands, nor an offering to free another prisoner. No, Pilate had only to wave his hand and thousands were put to death. As a troublemaker, Jesus's penalty was a summary public execution by immediate crucifixion, the Romans' brutal way to deal with those who dared to challenge their power.[43]

---

[42] In contrast to the Synoptic Gospels, John places the cleansing of the Temple immediately prior to the crucifixion of Jesus making it more likely he was arrested by the Romans for rioting. The dating of the execution in relationship to Passover also appears to be more accurate in John than the other Gospels.

[43] As power had become increasingly concentrated in the Roman emperor during the reign of Caesar Augustus, he and his appointed officials assumed greater and more direct control of legal proceedings. Criminal law due process became imperial edict. A *praetor* no longer required an accuser or a formal charge; he could institute proceedings and impose punishments on his own initiative—particularly if a noncitizen was accused.

Jesus may not have been alone in his agony. If it is true that two others were crucified at the same time, they were other Zealots accused of insurrection instead of theft. The Greek word, *Lestai,* usually translated in the Gospels as thief or robber, also can mean revolutionary or insurrectionist. That they died together was appropriate, as the Zealots served as the militant wing of the Way of Righteousness.

Crucifixion had a despised history in Israel, which is addressed in Deuteronomy (21:23), where it is said that "one who has been hanged is accursed of God." This abhorrence is also reflected in the Dead Sea Scrolls in a commentary on the Book of Nahum:

> vengeance on the Seekers-after-Smooth-Things [Pharisees] when he hangs men up alive . . . in Israel before-time, for of the man hanged alive upon a tree it reads: "Behold I am against thee says Yahweh of hosts, and I will burn in smoke thine abundance, and thy young lions the sword shall devour. And I will cut off from the land his prey."

Whether or not the execution of Jesus took place as described in the Gospels, or as routinely practiced by the Romans, it was a brutal and agonizing death. Archeological evidence that this form of execution was used at the time of Jesus was established by the discovery of a skeleton during excavations in Jerusalem.

According to a report by the Hebrew University Medical School in Jerusalem, the cross was made of olive wood. The victim was supported on the crossbar by nails driven through his forearms near the wrist. The plaque (*titulus*) which declared the charge of his crime had been posted on the cross by a nail driven through the victim's heels. The body was twisted at the waist, so that the feet were side-by-side with one ankle flat against the cross. The legs were drawn up under the victim nearly to his buttocks.

Roman victims were usually scourged before being nailed to the crossbeam, which was then hoisted to the top of a permanent post resulting in a "T", rather than the familiar cross. Death resulted from exhaustion, heart failure, and asphyxiation, as the victim's collapse made it impossible to breath. Depending on the caprice of the executioners, the legs could be broken to accelerate collapse and death. The practice was designed to humiliate, as well as to kill the victim, and it was intended to deter the behavior that resulted in the victim's execution. Usually, the body was left to rot by the roadside and to be consumed by birds of prey and other scavengers.

With the execution of Jesus taking place within the walls of Jerusalem, the authorities may have allowed the body to be removed following death. Philo of Alexandria wrote that there were times when "people who have been crucified have been taken down and their bodies delivered to their kinfolk, . . ."

Once it was established by the soldiers that Jesus was dead—perhaps by piercing his chest with a lance—the crossbeam would be dropped to the ground and the body would have been removed for disposal. Dead bodies were dealt with in several ways at the time. The bodies of criminals were buried in common graves. For the more affluent, the body was placed in a tomb for a period until the flesh had rotted away, and the bones would be gathered and permanently stored in a stone ossuary made for the purpose. For the poor, a hole would be dug in the rocky soil, the body would be buried in the ground wrapped in a shroud, and the grave would be covered with stones.

Although the Gospels tell us that Jesus's body was interred in the large tomb of a wealthy benefactor—before Jesus physically rose from the dead, rolled aside the rock that blocked the entrance, and walked out of the tomb—the disposition of his corporeal body may have been more modest. Trusting that Jesus was a member of the Congregation of the Way at Qumran, his burial there would be much more likely.

Archeological excavations at Qumran have identified more than 1,200 graves located in six cemeteries near the ruins. Of all places where Jesus's body may have come to rest—and may possibly remain—the hallowed ground of the Way of Righteousness may be the most likely. (See Photo #11)

The Gospels contain elaborate stories about how the tomb was found empty and Jesus's subsequent physical appearance to Mary Magdalene and others; however, these stories were written decades after his death to describe and justify a physical resurrection. These

Gospels follow Paul's doctrine of sin and redemption which he preached about Jesus's resurrection. The gospel writers missed Paul's point, however, that it was a spiritual body that arose from the dead. Under Paul's convoluted reasoning—perhaps reflecting an unhealthy blending of his Gnostic instruction and his Pharisaic training—there is a difference between earthly bodies and those that ascend into heaven. It was Jesus's spiritual body that was immortal and beyond pain and suffering. For Paul—who never saw the living Jesus during his life and only experienced him during a vision or hallucination—the resurrected Jesus must have had *some* substance, otherwise he could not have been visible and speaking to Paul.

Regarding resurrection in First Corinthians, Paul seems to get it when he writes:

> What is sown is perishable, what is raised in imperishable. It is sown in dishonor; it is raised in glory. It is sown in weakness; it is raised in power. It is sown a physical body; it is raised a spiritual body. (14:42-44)

The resurrection story, later fabricated by the Gospel authors, however, is purely physical. As reported by Luke, Jesus tells his disciples, "behold my hands and my feet, that it is I myself. Handle me and see, for a spirit does not have flesh and bones as you see I have." (21:23)

Much like the virgin birth narrative at Christmas, the image of a physical resurrection at Easter has become glorified in the Roman Christian religious tradition. The concept of resurrection, however, meant something entirely different to the family of Jesus and the congregation of the Way. For them, a spiritually aware soul arises and joins the Abiding Mind, or it is reborn—if Gnosis or self-awareness has not been achieved. The corruptible body remains, always, and ultimately decays into dust.

Later, confronting the wealthy and powerful, James the Just accuses, "You have condemned, you have killed the righteous man; he does not resist you." (James 5:6) Although James counsels the brethren to be patient "until the coming of the Lord," (5:7) he makes no mention in his letter about the resurrection and postmortem visitations by Jesus. Neither does his other brother, Judas Thomas, who counsels the beloved in the Letter of Jude to "keep yourselves in the love of God; wait for the mercy of our Lord Jesus Christ until eternal life." (Jude 21)

For the Way and the Gnostic Christians, the resurrection is a spiritual awakening from the hell in which we live here on Earth—until we achieve spiritual awareness, or Gnosis. Resurrection is not something that takes place in the future; it takes place the moment we become aware of our conscious self and our connection with the Abiding Mind and the minds of others. We are then freed of bodily constraints, including the corruption of the body that necessarily follows death.

Among the books found at Nag Hammadi is *The Treatise on Resurrection* which is attributed to the "Word of Truth" received "through our "Savior, Our Lord Christ." It discusses the spiritual resurrection as being different than the corruption following death: "What then, is the resurrection? It is always the disclosure of those who have risen. . . . do not think the resurrection is an illusion. It is no illusion, but it is truth." Those inquiring "if he leaves his body behind, will be saved immediately. Let no one be given cause to doubt this. . . . indeed, the visible members which are dead shall not be saved, for (only) the living [members] which exist within them would arise." *The Treatise* says, "The thought of those who are saved shall not perish. The mind of those who have known him shall not perish."

The Salvation of Jesus

That Jesus would have chosen to offer himself as a sacrifice for others would not have been considered shameful in his culture. Indeed, just as religiously motivated suicide bombers continue to blow themselves and others up on a regular basis in the Middle East today, the voluntary choice of martyrdom had a long tradition at the time of Jesus. The concept of dying so that others might live was well-established in Mediterranean cultures, and the Judaic literature at the time of Jesus contained many stories about the suffering of righteous men for the benefit of others.

Jesus did not die for the sins of others. The gospel of the Way he followed and taught had moved beyond the repressive concept of sin and redemption under the Law to a simple spiritual life of righteousness. The members of the Way lived their lives—every day—as a demonstration of piety to the precepts of their covenant and righteousness, and as an example for all of humanity. Jesus's choice to make himself a sacrifice for the cause of righteousness, was a focus of everything the Way stood for. He willingly accepted the role of being the suffering messiah and offered his death as a sacrifice for all of humanity in the presence of the Spirit of Wisdom.

At the time of his death, Jesus was the honored teacher of his own Congregation of the Poor. His small group of followers included all the members of his family and several women. Nothing politically or militarily about the Herodian and Roman occupation of Israel was changed or improved by his short mission spent teaching the religious precepts of the Way of Righteousness, but as he said in his Parable of the Mustard Seed describing the Kingdom of God:

> It is like a grain of mustard seed, which, when sown upon the ground, is the smallest of all the seeds on earth; yet when it is sown it grows up and becomes the greatest of all shrubs, and puts forth large branches, so that the birds of the air can make nests in its shade. (Mark 4:30-32)

The small remnant of Jesus's followers at the time of his execution has now grown to more than two billion Christians, worldwide, who worship in his name, and more than 1.6 billion Muslims who worship in a religion influenced by Jesus's essential message of love and righteousness. Surely, the thoughts and mind of Jesus did not die on the cross. His Gnosis was preserved for all eternity, and—clearly sounding through all attempts to distort and misrepresent its content—the essence of his message has rung true for 2,000 years. The commandment to "Love one another" has been sorely tested by inquisitions, crusades, pogroms, and wars, but his essential mission remains as a beacon of light to guide all of humanity to the stars—and beyond in the realm of an Abiding Mind.

As we continue along the Way, we will next consider what happened to Jesus's Congregation, who were also known as the

Ebionim (the Poor) and as the Nazoreans.[44] Jesus's congregation followed the Way of Righteousness, and it continued under the leadership of James the Just for 26 years until he was murdered by the authorities and thereafter by his other brother, Simeon. Jesus's congregation remained in Jerusalem until the city was destroyed by the Romans; however, its members and others of the Way carried forth the Gospel of Yeshua and the Way, first in Judea-Israel and its surrounding regions, and then around the world.

---

[44] Named for their Nazirite leaders, Jesus, James, and Simeon.

The Remnant of the Way of Righteousness

Jesus's Congregation of the Poor, which remained in Judea after his crucifixion, did not originate a new religion. They were Jews, who continued to believe in their Judaic religion as refined by the Way of Righteousness. They did not witness a physical resurrection, nor did they believe Jesus was a God, or a son of God. For them, he had been their Righteous Teacher and the suffering Son of Man Messiah predicted by their scriptures—whose spirit had ascended to Heaven upon his death. The Poor elected James the Just, the brother of Jesus, to be their leader, and they continued to be zealous for the law and the freedom of their land.

While others left to carry the message of the Way to other nations, the Nazoreans of the Way and their warrior Sons of Light remained behind, and they suffered and died during the wars that followed.

As one of their last acts, they buried their precious books of the Way in caves near their refuge at Qumran by the Dead Sea.

JESUS'S BROTHER, JAMES THE JUST, WAS THE PRIESTLY MESSIAH

Without having been there to walk along the Way with the congregation of Jesus after his crucifixion, we cannot be certain about what occurred. If the stories in the Gospels about his physical resurrection and appearances are fables written decades later to justify a spurious belief that Jesus was God, it is difficult to trust other stories about the actions and existence of his disciples.

Conflicting stories are told in the Gospels. In Matthew, the disciples go to Galilee, where Jesus meets with them and gives them final instructions. In Luke, the disciples are told by Jesus not to go to Galilee, but to remain in Jerusalem for 40 days to receive the Holy Spirit. Acts which was written by the same author as Luke says Jesus took his disciples to Bethany, where they are told to stay in Jerusalem and to worship in the Temple.

An argument can be made that the gospel stories about the 12 evangelizing disciples were created at the same time as the resurrection fables in order to be in accord with other traditions. Just as there were 12 astrological constellations, and there were 12 tribes of Israel, there had to be 12 disciples. Confusion among the Gospels about the identities of these disciples raises further doubts about their historical reality. Paul's epistles, the earliest writings in the New Testament, do not mention the 12 disciples—only James the Just (Jacob), Cephas (Peter), and John (the priest) as being the "pillars" of the Jerusalem church. Acts acknowledges the "other eleven" only in connection with the acts of Peter and John at the time of Pentecost, and thereafter only mentions some local proselytizing by Peter, in addition to that by Jesus's brother, Joseph (Barnabas or Joses) and Paul on their trips abroad. Roman Christian tradition defines an evangelizing role for some, or all, of the disciples; however, other than Peter and John the Priest, they mostly disappear from the New Testament after Pentecost. When Peter himself mysteriously goes away in Acts 12:17 for "another place," he says, "Tell this to James and to the brethren."

Peter is supposed to appear later in Antioch involved in the conflict between Paul and Joseph over table fellowship with the

Gentiles and may, or may not, have been present at the conference with James in Jerusalem about Paul's ministry. The conference was the last mention of "Peter" in the New Testament, and his subsequently becoming the first Bishop of Rome and being crucified was likely a political fiction created later by the Pauline orthodox in Rome to justify their control over all of Christianity. There is an even chance that the character of Peter was entirely cut from whole cloth by the gospel writers who used the name of Jesus's father-Cleophas, and brother-Simeon, (who were leaders of the Way) to confuse the issue. If this is true, Saint Peter's Basilica in Rome may actually honor the biological father and brother of Jesus.

This is not to say that there may not have been a council of twelve chosen in Jerusalem to oversee the affairs of the Poor. Recall that the Way not only relied on an "Overseer," or "Master," to instruct and lead their congregation, but that he was also assisted by a "Council of the Community" consisting of twelve men and three priests, all of whom were chosen by lot. The names of the Jerusalem Council may well have included some of the disciples listed in the New Testament, and may have included one named Peter, and John the Priest. Their actual identities may have been lost in time; however, we are certain who the first bishop was.

James Becomes Bishop of Jesus's Jerusalem Congregation of the Poor

In the Gospel of Thomas, one of the Gnostic Gospels recovered at Nag Hammadi, there is a scene in which the disciples are meeting with Jesus. "The disciples asked Jesus. 'We know that you will depart from us. Who will be our leader?' Jesus said to them, 'Wherever you are, you are to go to James the Righteous, for whose sake heaven and earth came into being.'"

Outside of the New Testament, there is far more historical information about James than about Jesus. As reported by Hegesippus, James was a lifelong Nazirite like John the Baptist, who may have taken ascetic vows. Eusebius states, "Now Jacob, the brother of the Lord, who, as there were many of this name, was termed the Just by all, from the days of our Lord until now, received the government of the Community with the Apostles."[45]

> This apostle was consecrated from his mother's womb. He drank neither wine nor fermented liquors and abstained from animal food. A razor never came upon his head; he never anointed himself with oil or used a public bath.
>
> He alone, was allowed to enter the Holy Place. He never wore woolen, only linen garments. He was in the habit of entering the Temple alone, and was often to be found upon his knees and interceding for the forgiveness of the people; so that his knees became as hard as a camels . . ..
>
> And indeed, on account of his exceeding great piety, he was called the just and oblias, which signifies Justice and the People's Bulwark; as the Prophets declare concerning him.

In the Pseudo-Clementines, probably written in the third century, there are several references to James the Just. In the *Homilies*, Peter refers to him as "James, the lord and bishop of the holy Church under the Father of all . . ." And in the *Recognitions*, Peter warns, "Wherefore observe the greatest caution, that you believe no teacher, unless he brings from Jerusalem the testimonial of James the Lord's brother, or of whosoever may come after him."

Jesus's Congregation of the Poor Followed the Way

Following the execution of Jesus, it was his brother, James the Just who became bishop of Jesus's Congregation of the Poor

---

[45] The work of Dr. Eisenman as presented in his book, *James the Brother of Jesus* (and other works listed in the Sources) was a significant and valuable source of information throughout this Part, and it would be grossly incomplete without his scholarly contribution. The *Economist* said Eisenman was "Patently thorough and careful . . . ." I have placed a great deal of trust in his work, and a footnote to it would be appropriate following many of the paragraphs that follow.

(*Ebionim*), who were also known as the Nazoreans.[46] According to Eusebius in his *Ecclesiastical History*, "This same James, to whom men had accorded the surname of the Just One . . . was recorded to be the First elected to the Throne of the Bishopric of the Church in Jerusalem." The closest parallel to the office of bishop in existence at that time in Judaism was the position of the Master, or Overseer of the Congregation in the Dead Sea Scrolls, whose governing responsibilities included ordinances and judgments.

Acts (6:7) tells us that "the word of God increased; and the number of the disciples multiplied greatly in Jerusalem, and a great many of the priests were obedient to the faith." These priests were the Sons of Zadok—those members of the priesthood of the Way who resided on Mount Zion, just south of the Temple. They—and other members of the Way and its Jerusalem congregation—continued to worship at the Temple and would never have thought about abandoning their Judaic religion. For them, Jesus's mission was a confirmation and expansion of the message of the Way, rather than a replacement of their religious beliefs and expectations.

History, rather than the Gospels, supports the view that the ministry of Jesus was not originally intended by him, or his followers, to be a substitute for their Judaic religion, especially as observed by the Way. It merely fulfilled their expectations about the redemption by a suffering Son of Man messiah. History also confirms that James the Just was an actual brother of Jesus who led the Poor in Jerusalem for decades after the execution of Jesus. As such, Jesus's Congregation was the mother church, and James—as the bishop of that congregation—was the master of all those who taught the Gospel of Yeshua, including Mary Magdalene, Judas Thomas, Joseph (Barnabas or Joses), Simeon, and Paul.

Perhaps the most important ruling of James resulted from a dispute regarding the need for Gentile proselytes to accept the full requirements of the Law of Moses and the oral laws and traditions of the Jews. In perhaps the most succinct expression of

---

[46] The Greek word, "Christian," would have no meaning for the followers of Jesus in Jerusalem. They would have considered themselves to be Nazorean (which has the same basis as "Nazirite") meaning those who kept the Law or Covenant. In modern Hebrew, Christians are known as *Nozrim*, or "Keepers."

the requirements of the movement, James writes, "Therefore my judgment is that we should not trouble those of the Gentiles who turn to God, but should write to them to abstain from the pollutions of idols and from unchastity and from what is strangled and from blood." (Acts 15:19-20) Thus, the only requirement placed upon Gentile converts was that they adhere to the ancient law of Noah to respect all living things.

While membership in Jesus's Jerusalem Congregation of the Poor included Gentiles, who accepted James' minimum requirements, they were an observant Jewish assembly of the Way. They considered themselves to be faithful doers of the law in the tradition of the Zaddiks, Hasideans, the Way, and the nationalist Zealots.

Inasmuch as the essential message of Jesus transcended and blended the doctrine of the Way with Eastern and Hellenistic religious philosophies, along with the Gnosticism, the success of these evangelizing missions to other countries depended on how accurately they taught the Gospels of the Way and Jesus and resisted attempts to paganize the message in attracting foreign converts.

Paul Throws James Down the Temple Steps Breaking his Legs—James Forgives Him

After Pilate was removed from office because of his brutality, Judea was temporarily without a procurator, and the Romans were preparing for a war against the Arabs. During this interim, the Sadducees and Pharisees stepped into the power vacuum. The Sadducean House of Annas (Ananus) joined with the Pharisees under Gamaiel and began to violently persecute the Nazoreans. A young Pharisee named Saul participated in these persecutions. Many Nazoreans had to flee Jerusalem and to seek refuge and asylum at Qumran, Jericho, and other places in the Wilderness.

Recognitions, which probably drew upon lost books such as *The Preachings of Peter* and the *Ascents of Jacob*, talks about the first physical assault upon James on the Day of Atonement during the period of persecution:

Much blood is shed; there is a confused flight, in the midst of which that enemy attacked Jacob, and threw him headlong from the top of the steps; and supposing him to be dead, he cared not to inflict further violence upon him.

But our friends lifted him up, for they were both more numerous and more powerful than the others; but, from fear of God, they rather allowed themselves to be killed by an inferior force than they would kill others.

But when the evening came the priests shut up the Temple, and we returned to Jacob's [James's] house, and spent the night in prayer. Then before daylight we went down to Jericho, to the number of five thousand men.

Other than for its inclusion in Acts (7:54-60), there is no historical evidence for the story about the stoning of Stephen. There are, however, parallels between that story and the later stoning of James, which does have an historical provenance. Creating the Stephen story in Acts—which, as its climax, has Saul (Paul) watching and holding the cloaks of those throwing the stones *and* consenting to the assault—makes one wonder if the actual event in which Paul was involved was the throwing of James down the Temple stairs. An assault on James by Paul is mentioned in the Pseudo-Clementine *Recognitions*, in which Paul armed with "a strong stick" acted insanely excited and encouraged "everyone to murder," before racing off to "Damascus" the next week to make arrests.

If Paul participated in the attempted murder of James, it makes Paul's blinding attack of conscience the next week while on the way to Damascus[47] in a murderous rage to seize members of the Congregation of the Poor (and perhaps the disabled James) much more understandable. Moreover, it makes James' subsequent forgiveness of Paul and acceptance of him into the Way even more saintly than humanly imaginable.

---

[47] Rather than the modern city in Syria, Damascus in this context referred to the area east of Judah where the Osim maintained camps in the wilderness, and probably included Qumran. In Acts (9:2), Paul is instructed that if "he found any there of the Way, whether men or women, he might bring them bound to Jerusalem."

It is very likely that the temporary evacuation of the Poor to Jericho extended to the refuge at nearby Qumran, which was included by the Osim in their "Damascus." It may have been at this time during his recovery that James prepared an original composition which was later redacted into *The Protevangelion of James*. The book concludes with:

> I, James wrote this History in Jerusalem; and when the disturbance was, I retired into a desert place, until after the death of Herod. And the disturbances ceased at Jerusalem. That which remains is, that I glorify God that he had given me such wisdom to write unto you who are spiritual, and who love God: to whom (be ascribed) glory and dominion forever and ever, Amen.

The death of Herod probably refers to Herod Antipas I, who had been exiled to Gaul, where he died. These events would have allowed James and the Poor to return to Jerusalem.

During a visit to Jerusalem in 37 CE, the Roman general Vitellius became concerned that the inhabitants of Jerusalem were being provoked by the Sadducees and Pharisees against the Romans. He deposed the high priest Jonathan and appointed his brother, Theophilus.

With the removal of Jonathan as high priest and the death of Herod Antipas I, the persecution of the Nazoreans lessened, and a brief period of relative peace prevailed.

James Was The Righteous Teacher and Priestly Messiah of the Way

James returned to the Nazoreans in Jerusalem and continued to lead Jesus's Congregation of the Poor as their bishop. For 26 years, from the crucifixion of Jesus in approximately 36 CE to his own judicial murder by stoning in 62 CE, James was the last Righteous Teacher of the Way, and probably represented their expected Priestly Messiah. He strictly followed the Way, and his piety and righteousness commended him to the Poor, the Way, the Zealots, and to all the people. The oath he had taken in the Way required initiates to love Piety towards God and Righteousness towards men. The three-letter Hebrew roots, "Z-D-K" (Zaddik) apply to James as the Righteous One in leading Jesus's Congregation of the Poor *and* as the Way's Righteous Teacher at Qumran—and as their Priestly Messiah.

Jesus's family may have been Rechabites, those who disavowed material things, and earned their living as craftsmen, such as carpenters. James, a lifetime Nazirite, was a priest in the linage of the Way's Sons of Zadok, who were chosen for their piety and righteousness, instead of their membership in a priestly clan. James was believed by several orthodox Christian writers to have worn the white linen garments of a priest. He is said to have prayed for forgiveness of the sins of the whole people in the Temple's Holy of Holies on *Yom Kippur*, the Day of Atonement.

Epiphanius writes:

> To James alone it was permitted to enter the Holy of Holies once a year, because he was a Nazirite and connected to the priesthood . . . James was a distinguished member of the priesthood . . ..

The Way of Righteous Was the Predominate Practice of Judaism at the Time of Jesus

The congregation of the Way at the time of Jesus and James was large and widespread. It had accumulated an extensive library documenting its beliefs, doctrine, and practices. It was the message of the Way that Jesus taught, and which James continued with the Congregation of the Poor and Judas Thomas took to the Middle East. Jesus's teachings further refined that doctrine in his Gnostic language and symbolism, and by his sacrifice as the suffering Son of Man messiah.

The Pharisees and the Sadducees were minority sects with very few members, but because of their political and economic power, they achieved an enhanced place in history. Despite them, most of the people in Israel-Judea were inspired by and followed the rebellious Zealots and their spiritual leaders in the Way. The Way was the spiritual face of the Jewish people.

A side-by-side comparison of these three groups, the Way, the Gnostics, and the Nazoreans who survived the execution of Jesus and the destruction of the Way during the Zealot wars reveal their shared religious philosophy. Of all the books of the New Testament, the Letter of James contains language (in italics) which is most like that found in the Dead Sea Scrolls:

> Count it all joy, my brethren, when you meet various trials, for you know that the testing of your faith produces steadfastness. And let steadfastness have its full effect, that you may be *perfect and complete*, lacking in nothing. If any of you lack *wisdom*, let him ask God, who gives to all men generously and without reproaching, and it will be given him. But let him ask in faith, with no doubting, for he who doubts is like a wave of the sea that is driven and tossed by the wind. For that person must not suppose that a double-minded man, unstable in all his ways, will receive anything from the Lord." (1:1-8)

> Do not be deceived, my beloved brethren. Every good endowment and every *perfect* gift is from above, coming down from the *Father of lights* with whom there is no variation or shadow due to change. Of his own will he brought us forth by the word of *truth* that we should be a kind of *first fruits* of his creatures. (1:16-18)

> James warns, "But be *doers of the word*, and not hearers only, deceiving yourselves . . . . But he who looks into the *perfect law, the law of liberty*, and perseveres, being no hearer that forgets but a doer that acts, he shall be blessed in his doing. (1:22-25)

> James teaches, "Listen my beloved brethren. Has not God chosen those who are *poor* in the world to be rich in faith and heirs of the kingdom which he has promised to those who love him?" (2:5)

Echoing the lessons of Jesus and James, the closing psalm of the *Community Rule* (X) says, "I will pay to no man the reward of evil; I will pursue him with goodness. For judgment of all the living is with God and it is He who will render to man his reward."

Parallels to the Letter of James have also been found in the Gnostic Gospels. In *The Apocryphon of James*, Jesus takes aside James and Peter for special revelation. Included is this instruction:

> Become earnest about the word! For as to the word, its first part is faith, the second, love, the third, works; for from these comes life. For the word is like a grain of wheat: when someone has sown it, he has faith in it; and when it has sprouted, he loved it because he had seen many grains in the place of one. And when he had worked, he was saved because he had prepared it for food, and again he left some to sow. So also, can you yourselves receive the kingdom of heaven; unless you receive this through knowledge, you will not be able to find it.

Among the scrolls recovered from Cave I at the Dead Sea is a lengthy work known as *The Thanksgiving Hymns*. Although it has suffered deterioration, its translation provides several prayerful hymns like the biblical Psalms. Most scholars believe at least some of them to be the personal composition of the Last Teacher of Righteousness—who may have been James. Several allude to the experiences of the Teacher persecuted by his enemies, including the Pharisees (seekers after smooth things).

> And they, teachers of lies and seers of falsehood, have schemed against me a devilish scheme, to exchange the Law engraved on my heart by Thee for the smooth things (which they speak) to Thy people. And they withhold from the thirsty the drink of Knowledge, and assuage their thirst with vinegar, . . . (*Hymns* IV)

The Hymns offer thanks for salvation from the lot of evil:

> Thou hast upheld my soul, strengthening my loins and restoring my power; my foot has stood in the realm of

ungodliness. I have been a snare to those who rebel, but healing to those of them who repent, prudence to the simple and steadfastness to the fearful of heart.

Thanks are also given for the knowledge of the divine mysteries, "These things I know by the wisdom which comes from Thee, for Thou hast unstopped my ears to marvelous mysteries." (*Hymns* I)

Philo's account in *The Contemplative Life* (Section 80) of the banquet celebrated by the Way and Therapeutae during Pentecost may indicate the performance of these Hymns. According to Philo, when the leader finished his commentary on the scriptures, he chanted a hymn and was followed by the other brethren. Thus, these Hymns may have been composed by members of the Covenant for delivery during the annual Feast of the Renewal of the Covenant.

Philo, in *Every Virtuous Man is Free*, begs the Way and Therapeutae "to come out to us and pacify our too turbulent and troubled lives, preaching to us to substitute for our wars and slavery and unspeakable evils their gospel of peace and freedom, and an abundance of their other rich blessings."

The Judicial Murder of James by the High Priests, the Pharisees, and Herodians

In 41 CE, the Roman emperor Claudius extended the reign of Herod Agrippa I[48] to include Judea, as well as Samaria and Caesarea. For the Nazoreans and Zealots, Agrippa was a usurper to the throne of David, a foreigner, and a despised friend of Caesar. To stamp out sedition, Agrippa and the Sadducees launched a violent campaign against the Congregation of the Poor.

Agrippa suddenly died in 44 CE under suspicious circumstances, after having appeared in public wearing a robe of silver and being hailed by his pagan audience as a god. Since his son, Agrippa II was only 16 years old and was studying in Rome, a Roman procurator, Cuspius Fadus was appointed to govern Judea, Samaria, and the

---

[48] Agrippa I was the son of Aristobulus, who had been strangled to death along with his brother, Alexander, for disrespecting their father, Herod the Great.

Galilee. Public outrage followed over Fadus's order to return the high priestly robes to Roman custody in Fort Antonia and by his appointment of the high priests.

In 59 CE, when Agrippa II assumed the Herodian throne, he appointed a new high priest. This appointment was followed by class warfare between the Sadducees and the lesser priests led by James. Riots broke out with stone throwing and abusive language. The lesser priests, many of whom were Nazoreans, refused to make sacrifices on behalf of Romans and other foreigners in the Temple—including the emperor—and they occupied Mount Zion. The Sadducees retaliated by sending slaves to collect the tithes from the threshing floors, and they refused to distribute food to the poor priests. Many starved, and James rose in their defense.

In or about 60 CE, the apostle Paul returned from his final missionary journey and was confronted by a riot of zealous opponents—which probably included members of the Congregation of the Poor. Paul was taken into custody and comfortably lodged in the Herodian palace in Caesarea. James and the Nazoreans washed their hands of Paul and shunned him. Paul called for the political support of his fellow Pharisees and was acquitted by Agrippa II— his fellow Herodian.

Because of continuing disturbances, Agrippa II once again changed high priests in the hope that the newly appointed Ananus II could help restore order. Following the death of the Roman procurator Festus in 62 CE and prior to the arrival of his replacement, there was a power vacuum in the province of Judea. Taking advantage of the situation, Ananus II, the high priest, conspired to act against James and the Sons of Zadok priesthood. Ananus was probably encouraged by Agrippa because of James' opposition to Agrippa's incestuous lifestyle and his erection of pagan statues in honor of the emperor.[49]

For the Sadducean and Pharisaic leaders, and the Herodians, it was intolerable for the Nazoreans to maintain a rival priesthood,

---

[49] Ananus II was the son of Annas (Ananus) and brother-in-law of Caiaphas— who condemned Jesus in the Gospels. Ananus II was killed in Jerusalem in 68 CE while fighting against the Zealots during their revolt. Agrippa II, the last Herodian client king of the Romans, escaped from Jerusalem and died of old age in Italy.

which followed the Way of Righteousness under the leadership of James.

James was probably charged with having entered the Holy of Holies on *Yom Kippur* wearing the miter and linen of the High Priest (in opposition to the Sadducean appointee) and pronouncing the forbidden "Name" of God in his prayers for the people.

The Holy of Holies was a perfect cube-shaped room located at the very center of the Temple which was entered only once a year on the Day of Atonement, and then only by the high priest who offered incense and a blood sacrifice in atonement for the sins of the people and their priests. For James to enter and pray for the deliverance of humanity would have been considered a blasphemy by the Sadducees (and a political threat).

The verdict of the Sanhedrin was guilty, and the penalty imposed was death by stoning.

The Second Apocalypse of James found in the Gnostic Gospels talks about the judicial murder of James:

> On that day all the people and the crowd were disturbed, and they showed that they had not been persuaded. And he arose and went forth speaking in this manner. And he entered again on that same day and spoke a few hours. And I was with the priests and revealed nothing of the relationship, since all of them were saying with one voice, 'Come, let us stone the Just One.' And they arose, saying, 'Yes, let us kill this man, that he may be taken from our midst. For he will be of no use to us.

According to Hegesippus in his Memoirs, quoted by Eusebius:

> The aforesaid Scribes and Pharisees, accordingly, placed Jacob upon a wing of the Temple, and cried out to him, "O thou Just One, whom we ought all to credit, since the people are led astray after Jesus that was crucified, declare to us what is the door to Jesus that was crucified." But he answered with a loud voice, "Why do you ask me regarding Jesus the Son of Man? He is now sitting in the heavens on

the right hand of Great Power and is about to come on the clouds of Heaven."

And as many were confirmed, and gloried in the testimony of Jacob, and said, "Hosanna to the Son of David," these same priests and Pharisees said to one another, "We have done badly in affording such testimony to Jesus; but let us go and cast him down, that they may fear to believe in him." And they cried out, "Oh, oh, the Just himself is deceived," and they fulfilled that which is written in Isaiah, "Let us do away with the Just, because he is offensive to us; wherefore they shall eat the fruit of their doings."

Going up therefore, they cast down the Just One, saying to one another, "Let us stone Jacob the Just." And they began to stone him, and he did not die immediately when cast down; but turning around, he knelt, saying, "I beseech thee, O Lord God and Father, forgive them, for they know not what they do."

Thus, they were stoning him, when one of the priests of the sons of Rechab, a son of the Rechabites spoken of by Jeremiah the prophet, cried out saying, "Stop! What are you doing? The Just is praying for you." But one of them, a fuller, beat out the brains of the Just with the club he used to beat out clothes. Thus, he suffered martyrdom, and they buried him on the spot where his tombstone still remains, close to the Temple. He became a faithful witness, both to the Jews and Greeks, that Jesus is the Christ. Immediately after this, Vespasian invaded and took Judea." (Eccl. Hist. II.xxiii)

The exact year in which James was murdered is not certain; however, it was around 62 CE, at a time when Paul was in Rome awaiting his appeal to Caesar. The only historical note made of his murder is by Josephus, who refers to the fanatical high priest Ananus and his stoning of James:

So he assembled the sanhedrin of the judges, and brought before them the brother of Jesus who was called Christ, whose name was James, and some others, (or some of his companions); and when he had formed an accusation against them as breakers of the law, he delivered them to be stoned. (*Antiquities* XX:ix:1)

Who Was The Wicked Priest and the Spouter of Lies of the Scrolls?

It was not the ordinary Jewish people who murdered James (and Jesus), for the anger of the people was primarily directed against their oppressors, the Romans and Herodians, *and* their sycophants—the Sadducees and Pharisees who collaborated with them. Given the oppression the people suffered under, many, if not most of the people were members of the Way and would have considered themselves be Zealots—those who, like James and his Congregation, were zealous for the law.

Evidence regarding James's primary opponents was found among the Dead Sea Scrolls. Rather than the Oral Torah of the Pharisees, the Way chose to rely on their own interpretations of the prophets for guidance. One notable effort is the complete *Commentary on Habakkuk* recovered from Cave I. It may have been composed as late as after the death of James and before the final conquest and destruction of Judea by the Romans around 135 CE. Most scholars believe the commentary refers to a variety of earlier times, but this belief does not hold up under scrutiny. The commentary quotes sections of Habakkuk (in italics) and then provides an interpretation.

The quotation, *"But the righteous shall live by faith"* is interpreted "this concerns all those who observe the Law in the House of Judah, whom God will deliver from the House of Judgment because of their suffering and because of their faith in the Teacher of Righteousness . . . ."

And the Lord answered and said to me, 'Write down the vision and make it plain upon the tablets, that he who reads may read it speedily . . . and God told Habakkuk to write down that which would happen to the final generation, but He did not make known to him when time would come to an end. and as for that which He said, That he who reads may read it speedily: interpreted this concerns the Teacher of Righteousness, to whom God make known all the mysteries of the words of His servants the Prophets.

In opposition to the Teacher of Righteousness are two primary enemies, a Wicked Priest and a Liar. If James is the Righteous Teacher, the Wicked Priest would be his murderer, Ananus II, the Sadducean high priest: *"For the wicked encompasses the righteous . . .* The wicked is the Wicked Priest, and the righteous is the Teacher of Righteousness . . . ."

The prediction of revenge against the Wicked Priest may have been caused by the stoning of James the Just, and may be based in fact on the later assassination of Ananus II and the death of the entire House of Ananus at the hands of the Zealots and their collaborators during their first revolt.

Moreover, the arrogant man seizes wealth without halting. He widens his gullet like Hell and like Death he has never enough. All the nations are gathered to him and all the peoples are assembled to him. Will they not all of them taunt him and jeer at him saying, "Woe to him who amasses that which is not his! How long will he load himself up with pledges?" Interpreted, this concerns the Wicked Priest who was called by the name of truth when he first arose. But when he ruled over Israel his heart became proud, and he forsook God and betrayed the precepts for the sake of riches. He robbed and amassed the riches of the men of violence who rebelled against God, and he took the wealth of the peoples, heaping sinful iniquity upon himself. And he lived in the ways of abominations amidst every unclean defilement.

Shall not your oppressors suddenly arise, and your torturers awaken; and shall you not become their prey? Because you have plundered many nations, all the remnant of the peoples shall plunder you. Interpreted, this concerns the Priest who rebelled and violated the precepts of God . . . . And they inflicted horrors of evil diseases and took vengeance upon his body of flesh. And as for that which He said, *Because you have plundered many nations, all the remnant of the peoples shall plunder you*: interpreted this concerns the last Priests of Jerusalem, who shall amass money and wealth by plundering the peoples. But in the last days, their riches and booty shall be delivered into the hands of the army of the Kittim [Romans], for it is they who shall be the *remnant of the peoples."*

Woe to him who causes his neighbors to drink; who pours out his venom to make them drunk that he may gaze on their feasts! Interpreted, this concerns the Wicked Priest who pursued the Teacher of Righteousness to the house of his exile that he might confuse him with his venomous fury. And at the time appointed for rest, for the Day of Atonement, he appeared before them to confuse them, and to cause them to stumble on the Day of Fasting, their Sabbath of repose.

Because of the blood of men and the violence done to the land, to the city, and to all its inhabitants. Interpreted, this concerns the Wicked Priest whom God delivered into the hands of his enemies because of the iniquity committed against the Teacher of Righteousness and the men of his Council, that he might be humbled by means of a destroying scourge, in bitterness of soul, because he had done wickedly to His elect.

The second enemy of the Teacher of Righteousness was the Liar, or Spouter of Lies.

Behold the nations and see, marvel and be astonished; for I accomplish a deed in your days, but you will not believe it when . . . told. Interpreted, this concerns those who were unfaithful together with the Liar, in that they did not listen to the word received by the Teacher of Righteousness from the mouth of God. And it concerns the unfaithful of the New Covenant in that they have not believed in the Covenant of God and have profaned his holy name.

Woe to him who builds a city with blood and founds a town upon falsehood! Behold, it is not from the Lord of Hosts that the people shall labor for fire and the nations shall strive for naught? Interpreted, this concerns the Spouter of Lies who led many astray that he might build his city of vanity with blood and raise a congregation on deceit, causing many thereby to perform a service of vanity for the sake of its glory, and to be pregnant with works of deceit, that their labor might be for nothing and that they might be punished with fire who vilified and outraged the elect of God.

If the *Commentary on Habakkuk* is referring to James the Just as the last Teacher of Righteousness, some scholars believe the Wicked Priest must have been Ananus II. If that is the case, the Spouter of Lies must necessarily refer to Paul, who initiated the sacrament of consuming Jesus's blood and body, which was contrary to that of James and the Congregation of the Poor. If the *Commentary* refers an earlier time, there is no shortage of adversaries to be identified as Wicked Priests and Liars.

The Righteous Legacy of James Preserved the Essential Message of Jesus's Gospel

As the brother of the original proponent of "Christian" principles, as a practicing Jew who became the first Bishop of the first Christian church—whose members were predominately Jewish—and as the Righteous Teacher and Priestly Messiah of the Way, James binds all of these together into a unity of religion, philosophy, and righteous practice. While the message of the Way was refined by the genius of Jesus, it was the righteousness, piety, and steadfastness of James that provided the physical and psychic energy required to transmit the essential message through the millennia to the people of today who continue to search for meaning in their lives.

Jesus may have been the botanist who bred and planted the fertile seeds of his gospel, but it was James who lovingly tended the garden for almost three decades, tenderly nurturing the shoots, pulling the weeds, and carefully watering the plants. Although

The Remnant of the Way of Righteousness

variations were later grafted onto the mature plants, Jesus's hybrid creation has persevered. Even more so than Paul, who imposed his personal interpretation on the ministry, and Mary Magdalene, whose Gnostic views were outshouted by Paul's, it was James who held everything together and who is most responsible for the fact that today more than 3.5 billion people practice religions inspired by Jesus's essential message.

It was during these decades of James' leadership that the gospel of Jesus was first being taught, not only in Judea, but by Joseph (Barnabas or Joses) and Paul in Asia Minor and Greece, by the Gnostic followers of Mary Magdalene in Syria and Egypt, by Judas Thomas in Arabia and the Middle East, and by others in Rome and beyond. At first, the followers may have recited the lessons orally, but as we learned earlier, some began to write down the messages they conveyed. Earlier, we learned that some of these first writings were among the Dead Sea Scrolls and Gnostic Gospels, but most were lost forever during the wars that engulfed the Galilee and Judea during the century following the execution of Jesus and the destruction they caused.

Perhaps the best evidence that the New Testament Gospels were composed much later than the events described therein is their complete failure to mention any of the contemporary violence and mayhem constantly being wrought by the Romans against the Jewish people. Reading only these Gospels, one might conclude that Judeans and Galileans were peaceful people who were content to tend their crops and fish the waters of the Sea of Galilee, when in fact "the whole sea ran red with their blood," as reported by Josephus. Jesus, himself, is pictured as being able to wander around unmolested for three years as he preached against the powers that be, encouraging the people to render unto Caesar what was Caesar's and to not upset the apple cart.

We know from history that the pacific tenor of the Gospels is false and misleading. Judea in the first century was a dangerous and deadly place and time to live—both for Jesus and for James—and the people who were in revolution. The old were being slaughtered and the young sold into slavery by Herod Agrippa II or tossed to the animals during Roman games at Caesarea. (See Photo #12)

The End Times were not expected by the people—they were living them!

All the events related thus far occurred historically prior to any of the Gospels being written. It is not difficult to see how the real-life history of James influenced the story of Jesus told in those books, especially those apocalyptic portions predicting the fall of the Temple.

The traditional belief among the early historians of the Pauline Roman Catholic Church was that the destruction of Jerusalem and the Temple was because of the stoning death of James. According to Jerome, "This same Josephus records the tradition that this James was of such great Holiness and repute among the people that the downfall of Jerusalem was believed to be on account of his death."

There is a large, rather elaborate tomb carved in the eastern stone face across the Kidron Valley from the Pinnacle of the Temple which was believed by the orthodox Roman Christians to be that of James the Just. While this tradition has him buried there on the Mount of Olives, it is far more likely that James' final resting place would have been alongside Jesus in a simple unmarked grave covered with rocks in the Qumran cemetery. His humility would not have permitted anything different.

Another Brother, Simeon, Succeeds James as Bishop of Jesus's Congregation

According to Christian tradition, following the judicial murder of James in 62 CE, his and Jesus's first-cousin, Simeon (also Symenon or Simon) assumed leadership of the Congregation of the Poor in Jerusalem. Simeon reportedly was the son of (their father) Joseph's younger brother, Cleopas. For the second time, the election of Simeon kept the leadership of the Congregation of the Poor and Nazorean Way within the family of Jesus.

Eusebius reports that:

> After the martyrdom of James and the conquest of Jerusalem which immediately followed, it is said that those of the apostles and disciples of the Lord that were still

living came together from all directions with those that were related to the Lord according to the flesh (for the majority of them also were still alive) to take counsel as to who was worthy to succeed James. They all with one consent pronounced Symeon, the son of Clopas, of whom the Gospel also makes mention; to be worthy of the episcopal throne of that parish.[50]

In an account by Epiphanius, the Rechabite Priest who cries out in defense of James during his murder is identified as Simeon bar Cleophas. The Rechabites took lifetime Nazirite vows, and Epiphanius says all "Joseph's sons revered virginity and the Nazirite life-style."

Simeon is confidently reported as having survived into the next century before he too was finally arrested, tortured, and executed in the vicinity of Jerusalem by the Romans during the reign of Trajan. The date of Simeon's execution is uncertain; however, if there is one place where he may have been laid to rest, it would have been in the cemetery at Qumran alongside his brothers and the other Saints of the Way.

Simeon's father, Cleopas is reported in John (19:25) and Luke (24:18) as being present at the crucifixion of the execution of Jesus and his resurrection. This may be true, but in reality, Cleopas was most likely the true name of Joseph, the father of Jesus, James, Judas Thomas, Joseph (Joses), and Simeon. Dr. Robert Eisenman makes a convincing argument that Joseph's true name was Cleophas, and that Simeon bar Cleophas was not a cousin—but was another actual brother of Jesus who was listed along with the others in Matthew as Simon. (13:55-56)

The stoning of James occurred only a few years before the Zealots revolted and the Romans destroyed the Temple and Jerusalem. It is believed that Simeon anticipated the revolution and removed many members of the Congregation of the Poor from Jerusalem to Pella, east of the Jordan River.

---

[50] Two books that are now lost, the *Ascents of Jacob* and the *Gospel of the Hebrews* reportedly spoke of Simeon's leadership. Hegesippus also records a Simon or Symenon, son of Cleopas, as the second bishop of Jerusalem.

According to Eusebius:

> The people of the church at Jerusalem, having been commanded by a Divine oracle given by revelation to men of approved piety there before the war, removed from the city and dwelt in a certain town of Peraea called Pella. Here, those that believed in Christ, having removed from Jerusalem, as if holy men had entirely abandoned the royal city itself; the Divine justice, for their crimes against Christ and the apostles, finally overtook them, totally destroying the whole generation of those evil doers from the earth.

Josephus, the fawning Roman apologist, may have been referring to this period when he wrote in *War*:

> Those who would deceive the people and the religious frauds, under the pretense of Divine inspiration fostering innovation and change in Government, persuaded the masses to act like madmen and led them out into the desert promising them that there God would give them the tokens of freedom.

As soon as it was safe to do so, a remnant of the Nazoreans-Ebionites returned to Jerusalem and rebuilt the Congregation of the Poor there under a series of bishops, whom they chose by lot.

After the death of Simeon, there were thirteen more Jewish bishops of the Poor in Jerusalem, until the succession terminated around 133 CE during the Bar-Cochba revolt. It is not known if any were of the family of Jesus, but as we learned earlier and will see again in The Righteous Way of Islam, the descendants of Judas Thomas—another brother of Jesus—continued to play a leadership role along the eastward direction of the Way.

THE WAR OF THE SONS OF LIGHT AGAINST THE SONS OF DARKNESS

The Qumran community understood its decision to live in the desert in righteous perfection according to the Law to be a determination to walk in the light. The war between the forces of light and darkness, of good and evil, had first to be won in the lives of a faithful remnant of God's People. Then and only then would there be enough righteous warriors ready to fight on God's side in the war to reclaim the land of Israel.

They choose a disciplined manner of life, which would perfect and purify their own lives and give them the training necessary to win the final battle, but they did not consider themselves to be pacifistic and nonviolent—they were also preparing for war. The people of the Way carried swords and were prepared to defend themselves and their faith. They were the spiritual leaders of the Zealots, who composed the militant arm of the Way of Righteousness.

These militant members of the Way are initially referred to by Josephus (the turncoat historian of the period) as Zealots, but then he begins to refer to the warriors in more derogatory terms as the Sicarii—the ones who targeted Romans, Herodians, and their collaborators for assassination using their daggers. Josephus identified this "Fourth sect of Jewish Philosophy" as having been founded by Judas the Galilean (who led the revolt during the time of Jesus's childhood). The clear point he makes is that they were a part of the same movement of the Way.

Victory in the war had to be first won within the minds and hearts of the members. For those who entered the Community of the New Covenant, the war within their individual lives was fought and won by their choosing to walk in the light. The power of the spirit of light filled them and healed them as they participated in the daily life of the community—a life which included prayer, worship, study, and living in love with their brothers and sisters. Though the gift of the spirit could not be guaranteed by joining the community, it was far more likely to be granted under those circumstances than when living in the outside world, where the forces of darkness held sway.

Those forces of darkness not only included the Romans, who had brutally conquered the land, but the dark powers also incorporated the Herodians—who dominated and subjugated the people to a police state and heavy taxation. The Hasmoneans were also included—they who had once been the delight of the people during their brief reign over an independent Israel; however, the Hasmoneans had intermarried with the Herodians and degenerated into debauchery and wife swapping. Finally, the minority Sadducees and Pharisees—who openly collaborated with the Romans and Herodians—were counted among the forces of darkness.

Among the documents recovered in Cave I by the Dead Sea is the *War of the Sons of Light against the Sons of Darkness*, or *War Rule*. It develops the doctrine found in the *Community Rule*, but it is also a military manual specifying organization and strategy: "The sons of Levi, Judah, and Benjamin, the exiles in the desert, shall battle against them . . . when the exiled sons of light return from the Desert of the Peoples to camp in the Desert of Jerusalem; and after the battle they shall go up from there (to Jerusalem)." (*War Rule*, I)

The *War Rule* depicts a future war fought on behalf of all the children of God against the Romans and their Herodian vassals. The warriors of God identify themselves: "O God of Israel, who is like Thee in heaven or on earth? Who accomplishes deeds and mighty works like Thine? Who is like Thy people Israel which Thou hast chosen for Thyself from all the peoples of the lands; the people of the saints of the Covenant?" (War Rule, X)

If we accept that Jesus was a teacher and leader of the Way of Righteousness, we can have a better understanding of the conflict when Jesus says, on one hand, "Do not resist one who is evil. But if one strikes you on the right cheek, turn to him the other also;" (Matthew 5:39), contrasted to his warning: "Do not think that I have come to bring peace on earth; I have not come to bring peace, but a sword." (Matthew 10:34)

THE ZEALOT REVOLUTION AND THE ROMAN DESTRUCTION OF THE TEMPLE

The revolt which ultimately led to the fall of the Temple can be traced to an incident that occurred when the Jews were gathered in Jerusalem for Passover. A Roman soldier exposed himself to the crowd in an indecent manner, and a riot resulted in which 10,000 Jews were killed. The flames of rebellion were fanned by the Zealots and Sicarii, who cried "No Lord but God," and James the Just was no longer present to advocate for the Poor and those who were zealous for the law.

Josephus describes these times in *War*:

> There was now enkindled mutual enmity and class warfare between the High Priest on the one hand and the Priests and Leaders of the masses of Jerusalem on the other. Each of the fractions formed and collected for itself a band of the most reckless Innovators, who acted as their leaders. And when they clashed, they used abusive language and pelted each other with stones. And there was not even one person to rebuke them.

The Roman governor did his share to foment revolution by attempting to seize the Temple treasure in 66 CE and by slaying thousands of Jews who gathered in Jerusalem to protest. Zealots seized the Temple and tore down the passageway to the Antonia Fortress.

War became inevitable when the Zealots captured Masada and killed all its Roman defenders, and after they stormed the Antonia Fortress at the Temple and killed all the Roman soldiers stationed there. They then burned down the palaces of the high priest and King Herod Agrippa II *and* the Temple archives containing the loan documents created by the Pharisees. One of the Zealot leaders at Masada was Manahem, the son of Judas the Galilean, who had led the original rebellion 50 years earlier in Galilee during Jesus's childhood.

The Zealot Revolution and the Roman Destruction of the Temple

The Zealots were in command of the revolution and appointed commanders, one of whom was John the Osim.[51] Initially, at least, the Zealots were the militant arm of the Way (and the Poor). Josephus says, "they have an inviolable attachment to freedom, insisting that God alone is their only Ruler and Lord." He writes:

> They also think little of dying any kind of deaths, nor do they heed deaths of their relatives or friends, nor can any such fear make them call any man Lord.

The war raged on as the Romans began to augment their forces and to defeat the Zealots whenever they engaged in set battles. The Romans destroyed the towns and villages they captured, thousands were slaughtered and taken into slavery, and a vast horde of refugees flooded into Jerusalem. The Zealots controlled Jerusalem and executed anyone suspected of collaborating with the Romans.

Vespasian, who commanded the Roman forces, drove the Zealots from most of the Galilee and forced his way south as far as Jericho, as he cleared the Jordan valley of resistance. Qumran, being remote from the action, may have still been unscathed when Vespasian received word that Emperor Nero had been killed. Vespasian delayed his movement against Jerusalem while other Roman generals fought and killed each other to determine who would succeed Nero.

Josephus, the Zealot turncoat, met with Vespasian and predicted that he would be the next Roman emperor. As icing on the cake, Josephus also told Vespasian he was the prophesized "World Leader" messiah in fulfillment of the "Star and Scepter" prophecy of Numbers (24:17).

Divisions within the Zealots began to appear, as they extended their conquests beyond Masada into Idumea. When John of Giscala kidnapped the wife of Simon bar Giora and brought her to Jerusalem, Simon's Zealot forces surrounded the city. As John proved to be corrupt, the people opened the gates for Simon, and he occupied the city; however, John retreated onto the Temple mount.

---

[51] Another Zealot leader was Josephus, who quickly surrendered and began to collaborate with the Romans. He would go on to write the definitive history of the Jewish people and their wars.

In the meantime, Vespasian's troops declared him to be the emperor. He sailed for Rome, leaving his son, Titus, in charge of the army. Josephus remained as an advisor. Titus moved toward Jerusalem through Jericho, and Qumran was probably destroyed at this time. Zealots in the area, the Way, and the remaining Congregation of the Poor retreated to caves in the immediate area and south along the shore of the Dead Sea toward Ein Gedi and Masada.

With the civil war between the Zealots continuing within the walls of Jerusalem, the Romans surrounded the city and encircled its walls with another banked wall constructed with trees cut from the surrounding countryside. Titus sent a demand for surrender to the Zealots, and Josephus walked around the walls, calling upon the Zealots to lay down their arms, until he was hit on the head by a stone. Believing that the city belonged to God, the Zealots refused to surrender, and they killed anyone who attempted to do so.

There was no food, and people would leave the city looking for food in the valleys between the two walls. Many of these were captured, and as many as 500 a day were crucified in view of those within the city. Titus brought up siege machines, broke through the stone wall near the Temple and, denying quarter to those remaining, killed all the Zealot rebels in the city.

Jerusalem was leveled, except for the citadels of Herod's palace. These towers were left to show how great the walls had been and how powerful the Romans were—since they were the ones who had destroyed them. The Citadel still stands as the south pillar of the Jaffa Gate, and is the home of the Jerusalem Museum. (See Photo #13)

The Romans killed most of the elderly men and made slaves of almost 100,000 young people. Vespasian and Titus celebrated a grand triumph in 71 CE during which the golden seven-armed candlestick and the table of showbread from the Temple were carried in the procession through Rome.

The Arch of Titus is still standing in Rome, and the procession of the triumph can be seen carved into its inside south wall. (See Photo #14)

Even though they were outnumbered ten to one, almost a thousand Zealots continued to resist at Masada for three more years. After a gigantic earthwork ramp was built by slaves against the mountain on which Masada sits, the Romans breached the wall in 74 CE. On entering, they found that all but a few women and children had committed suicide. In his history, Josephus imagines the final speech of Eleazar (a descendant of the original Zealot Judas the Galilean) who led the Zealots at Masada. While Josephus refers to the Zealots as brigands, the speech he wrote reflects the strong influence that the Way and the Gnostics had on the Zealots . . . and on Josephus:

> Ever since primitive man began to think, the words of our ancestors and of the gods, supported by the actions and spirit of our forefathers, have constantly impressed on us that life is the calamity for man, not death. Death gives freedom to our souls and lets them depart to their own pure home where they will know nothing of any calamity; but while they are confined within a mortal body and share its miseries, in strict truth they are dead. For association of the divine with the mortal is most improper. Certainly, the soul can do a great deal even when imprisoned in the body: It makes the body its own organ of sense, moving it invisibly and impelling it in its actions further than mortal nature can reach. But when, freed from the weight that drags it down to earth and is hung about it, the soul returns to its own place, then in truth it partakes of a blessed power and an utterly unfettered strength, remaining as invisible to human eyes as God Himself. Not even while it is in the body can it be viewed; it enters undetected and departs unseen, having itself one imperishable nature, but causing a change in the body; for whatever the soul touches lives and blossoms, whatever it deserts withers and dies: such a superabundance it has of immortality.

During the excavation of Masada in 1963-1965 under the floor of the Zealot's assembly room within the fortress, Yagael Yadin discovered a kind of *genizah*, consisting of a hole in which old manuscripts were stored, rather than destroyed. (See Photo #15)

A fragment of a scroll was found which contained a line which read, "The song of the sixth Sabbath sacrifice on the ninth of the second month." Yadin was "struck by the amazing fact that this text was the same as the text of one of the scrolls discovered in Cave 4 at Qumran. That scroll was a very definite sectarian scroll which details 'songs of the Sabbath sacrifices' dealing with each Sabbath and its date."

In addition to fragments of *Psalms* and *Leviticus,* a portion of the lost original Hebrew text of the scroll *The Wisdom of Ben-Sira* (also known in the Greek translation which survived as *Ecclesiasticus*) was found. Interestingly, portions of the Hebrew version of *The Wisdom of Ben-Sira* had also been found, along with the *Damascus Rule,* in the Cairo *genizah* by Solomon Schecter in 1896. Also recovered from the ruins of Masada was a fragment of the *Book of Jubilees*, which details the special calendar maintained by the Osim.

Also found were the remains of a scroll of the *Book of Ezekiel*, which included portions from Chapter 37 containing the "standing up of the bones" prophecy which gave rise to the belief in a life after death for the Hasideans, the Pharisees, and the members of the Qumran Community.

There is little doubt that members of the Way were present with the Zealots at Masada.

The Revolt of the Last Zealot, Simeon Bar Kochba, is Crushed by the Romans

Even though Jerusalem was destroyed in 70 CE, Judea remained as a province of Rome and Herod Agrippa II continued to rule. Persisting in the incestuous behavior for which the family was infamous, he had a sexual relationship with his sister Berenice II, the widow of Herod of Chalcis (who had also been her uncle). Agrippa allied with the Romans against his own subjects and was given additional areas in the north to rule. When he died in 100 CE as the last of the Herodians, Judea ceased to exist as a state and was incorporated into the Roman province of Syria.

In 132 CE, another Zealot, Simeon bar Kochba, "the Son of the Star" (who was probably another descendant of the original Zealot,

Judas the Galilean), declared a new messianic war on Rome. Relying on the same "Star and Scepter" prophecy used by Josephus to gain favor with Vespasian, Simeon claimed he was the messiah who was expected to lead the world.

Instead of set battles, Simeon mostly relied on guerilla warfare in which the Zealots would attack from a network of underground tunnels and hidden places before disappearing. They also occupied the caves of Qumran and Ein Gedi.[52] Relying on outside volunteers, who included mercenaries and veterans, Simeon was able to defeat the Romans in several pitched battles. During the first year of his campaign, Simeon destroyed at least one Roman legion of 5,000 men, and perhaps another.

After clearing the Romans from Judea, Simeon set up a government in Jerusalem and issued copper and silver coins between 132 and 135 CE, many of which were struck over Roman coins. These celebrated the freedom of Jerusalem and were stamped with a star in celebration of Simeon as the Son of the Star.

Hadrian, the Roman emperor organized a massive invasion army in Syria consisting of 20 legions, with more than 80,000 soldiers. When he struck, the Romans crushed all resistance, killed more than 500,000 Jews and left nothing behind but scorched earth. Fifty walled towns and almost 1,000 villages were leveled. Simeon barricaded himself and his remaining Zealot fighters in the fortress of Betar.[53] After a three-year siege, the Romans forced entry in 135 CE and killed all inhabitants, including Bar Kokhba. There would be no Jewish government in Israel for almost 2,000 years.

---

[52] During the search for additional Dead Sea Scrolls in the early 1950s, several documents, some of which may have been personally written by Bar Kochba, were found in a cave.

[53] Beitar Illit (modern Gush Etzion) is located 6.2 miles southwest of Jerusalem in the Judean Mountains of the West Bank.

THE RIGHTEOUS REMNANT CLINGS TO JERUSALEM

According to Epiphanius, those of the Poor who returned from Pella after Jerusalem and the Temple were destroyed built a small church on Zion. It was still there in 131 CE, when the emperor Hadrian, started building the new city of Aelia Capitolina on the ruins of Jerusalem as a colony for his Roman legionaries. Construction was disrupted in the following year by the Zealot War. Justin Martyr relates that the Nazoreans were persecuted because they would not accept Bar Cochba as their messiah.

Dedicated to Jupiter and named in honor of Hadrian, Aelia Capitolina was completed once the Zealots were defeated. Enraged by the revolution, Hadrian renamed Judea as Syria Palaestina, forbade circumcision, and denied entrance of any Jews into the city limits upon pain of death. The ban continued for six hundred years until the Muslim conquest in the seventh century.[54]

When an exemption was made for Christians in the fourth century, a new church could be built in the city. It did not have any Jewish members or any of the Poor—it was a Gentile church under a Gentile bishop in the Roman Christian tradition.

Nothing remained of the righteous remnant of the Way and their Congregation of the Poor—those who had seen themselves as preparing the Way for the final fulfillment of the promised Kingdom of God.

---

[54] The Samaritans had continued to thrive during the Jesus era, but their temple was destroyed along with everything else by the Romans following the Bar Kochba Revolt. They rebuilt their temple on Mount Gerizim and remained in the land until they were wiped out by the Christian Byzantine Empire, and their religious practice was outlawed. A remnant remains in Israel today.

HIDING THE SCROLLS OF THE WAY IN THE CAVES BY THE DEAD SEA

According to coin evidence found during the excavation of Qumran, the peak period of occupancy came just prior to the destruction of Jerusalem in 70 CE. Coins were found, however, that indicate that Qumran was occupied as late as 135 CE.

At some point during this period, members of the righteous remnant of the Way, the Congregation of the Poor, and the Zealots deposited the books of their extensive library in caves located in the bluffs overlooking the Dead Sea. The majority were probably deposited in the vast Cave 4 which had been carved out of the soft stone, and other books were stored in Cave I. It appears that all the scrolls were carefully wrapped in linen cloth and placed in large earthen jars. The jar caps were then sealed with tar, and they were secreted in their secure hiding place.

Those who reverently hid the scrolls in the caves surely expected they would be able to return and reclaim their written treasures, but they were slaughtered by the Romans. There the books remained until some of them came into the hands of the third century Christian theologian Origen, who was compiling an edition of various Greek versions of the Old Testament called the Hexapla. He said he "hunted them out of their hiding places" near Jericho "and brought them to light."

Another reference to a discovery of manuscripts in a cave is given by the tenth century Karaite Al-Qirqisani. In the second chapter of his history of Jewish sects, just after speaking of the Sadducees, he says, "Thereupon appeared the teaching of a sect called Magharians; they were called so because their books were found in a cave (*maghara*)." The Magharians were said to have used the same calendar found in the Osim's *Book of Jubilees*.

The scrolls are also mentioned in a letter written at the same time by a diplomat at the court of the caliph of Cordova to the King of the Khazars. Writing about the Babylonian conquest of Judah in 586 BCE, the writer believed that was the period when the Jews "buried in a cave the books of the law and the holy writings, and on this account, they prayed in the cave."

The Remnant of the Way of Righteousness

> And because of the books, they taught their sons to pray in the cave evening and morning until the times were prolonged, and in the multitude of days they forgot and did not know concerning the cave why they were accustomed to pray within it, but carried on the custom of their fathers without knowing why. But at the end of many days there arose a certain Jew, and he sought to know why: And he came to the cave and found it full of books and brought them out from there. And from that day until now they set their faces and learn the law. Thus, our fathers have told us as the men of old heard, and these matters are ancient.

Another earlier reference to the hidden scrolls is found in letter dated sometime shortly before 805 CE, by Timotheus, Patriarch of Seleucia to another ecclesiastic:

> We learned from trustworthy Jews who were being instructed . . . in the Christian faith that 10 years ago, near Jericho, some books were found in a cave. . .. The dog of an Arab hunter followed an animal into a cave and didn't return. The Arab went in after it and found a small cave in which there were many books. The Arab went to Jerusalem and told the Jews there who came out in large numbers and found books of the Old Testament and other books in Hebrew characters. As the person who told this story to me was a learned man . . . I asked him about the many references in the New Testament which are referred to as originating in the Old Testament, but which cannot be found there . . . He said; they exist and can be found in the books from the cave . . .[55]

The remaining undiscovered scrolls remained hidden until another Arab boy searching for his lost goat found them in 1945.

---

[55] Probably, it was during one of these earlier discoveries that most of the scrolls originally stored in the Cave 4 library were found and removed. When Cave 4 was excavated following the most recent discovery of hidden scrolls in 1947, only fragments of more than 900 manuscripts were sifted from the thick layer of dust on the floor of the cave.

Along with the Gnostic Gospels, which had been unburied under equally fortuitous circumstances a year earlier, the sudden revelation of these ancient documents at this precise moment in human evolution—just as we are now striving to travel beyond Earth—may be a modern miracle.

Some people fear the science fiction fantasy of conquest from outer space; however, if we can learn from the discovery of these documents and succeed in flying from our terrestrial nest, it is more likely we will encounter a peaceful philosophy similar to Jesus's injunction to love one another. As our progeny travel throughout the starry heaven searching for warm water planets where life and creativity can prosper, they will tell the story about how our awakening of consciousness came from literary treasures long buried in the sand and caves.

With the death and destruction of the Way and their Congregation of the Poor, the Way divided into several paths, each carrying differing messages about the Way around the world. Those of you—wherever you may be found—who read these words may question which path to follow, and what you will discover upon arrival.

The Parting of the Way of Righteousness

Following the executions of Jesus, James, and Simeon, the teachings of the Way of Righteousness in the West came be divided between Mary Magdalene's Gnostics and Paul's Roman Catholic Church, and their ministries coincided with the creation of Rabbinic Judaism by the Pharisees.

THE GNOSTIC WAY OF MARY MAGDALENE

Outside of Judea, the primary form of Christianity practiced during the first centuries following the executions of Jesus and James was Gnostic. Particularly in Egypt and Syria, most Christian bishops were Gnostic. As with the Congregation of the Poor in Jerusalem, these Gnostic congregations did not believe in the divinity of Jesus.

Although Paul may have had some differences about whether Jesus was the Son of God, underlying what he actually said (in those epistles personally attributed to him) were some of the Gnostic lessons he learned during his three-year indoctrination with the Way following his conversion on the road to Damascus. There was another difference: The Gnostic congregations considered Mary Magdalene, the companion of Jesus, to have been the most honored and trusted of his disciples.

In the New Testament we learn that Mary Magdalene may have been the sister of Martha and Lazarus of the town of Bethany; that Mary anointed Jesus as the Messiah; and that she was the first to whom Jesus appeared following his resurrection. Beyond that, there is no other mention in the Bible; however, with the revelation of the Gnostic Gospels and other ancient manuscripts, there is much to learn about this amazing woman and why she was so beloved by Jesus.

During and following the Zealot revolutions of the first and second centuries, many of the Nazorean, or Poor members of the Way, fled Judea. Some escaped east into Jordan or northeast into Syria, but many emigrated to Egypt, swelling the population of Alexandria until it was one-third Jewish. It is from this last group that the books found at Nag Hammadi can most likely be traced.

Radiocarbon testing of the papyrus used to thicken the leather bindings of the Gnostic Gospels produced a finding of 350-400 CE. These codices are Coptic[56] translations of more ancient manuscripts believed to have been written no later than 120-150 CE. Indeed, the *Gospel of Thomas* contains sayings that predate the New Testament

---

[56] Reflecting centuries of Greek rule, Coptic is a later stage of the Egyptian language, which was primarily written with a Greek alphabet.

Gospels and may have been a source for their creation. There is a strong likelihood that *Thomas* and some of the other books found at Nag Hammadi accurately convey the words of Jesus.[57]

The Egyptian congregation primarily followed the Gnostic principles of the Way and was the progeny of those who immigrated to Egypt following the destruction of Jerusalem. One of the oldest texts found at Nag Hammadi, the *Apocalypse of Adam*, in which Gnosticism is transmitted to Seth by Adam on his deathbed as his last will and testament was written at the same time as the last of the Dead Sea Scrolls, during or shortly after the lives of James and Simeon.

Mary Magdalene, Jesus's Favorite Disciple, Was the Apostle to the Apostles

One of the great slanders of Roman Christianity is that Mary Magdalene was a prostitute. The story erroneously associated with her as a prostitute is inserted at John 7:53-8, which is omitted in some translations, or it is inserted as Luke 21:38 in others. The fable relates to a woman being caught in adultery and who was to be stoned in accordance with the Law of Moses. When asked about this by the Pharisees, Jesus told them, "Let him who is without sin among you be the first to throw a stone at her." After all her accusers had slunk away, Jesus told the woman, "Neither do I condemn you; go, and do not sin again."[58]

Luke goes further than the other gospels in diminishing the role of Mary by saying she was driven by demonic spirits (8:2), and he omits her name from wherever it was included by Mark. In the other gospels, Mary is listed as one of the women who followed Jesus and who was present at his crucifixion.

---

[57] Dr. James M. Robinson (1924-2016) chaired the committee of biblical scholars that translated the Gnostic Gospels into English. He also edited the photographs of the Dead Sea Scrolls that were published in 1991. *The Nag Hammadi Library* is the standard English translation of the Gnostic Gospels and was invaluable in the preparation of this book.

[58] In 1969, the Vatican finally admitted its error in labeling Mary Magdalene as a prostitute, and in 2016, Pope Francis elevated her saint's day on July 22 to a "major feast" on the same liturgical level as the other apostles.

All evidence available to us, including the high regard in which she was held by Jesus and others, indicates that she was a chaste woman who dedicated herself to Jesus during his lifetime and to the ministry of his gospel after his death.[59] The proof of her elevated status has been found in a number of the books discovered at Nag Hammadi.

The Gospel of Philip tells us, "There were three who always walked with the Lord: Mary his mother, and her sister, and Magdalene, the one who was called his companion." *Philip* later identifies Mary with Divine Wisdom, "As for the Wisdom who is called 'the barren,' she is the mother of the angels. And the companion of the Savior is Mary Magdalene. But Christ loved her more than all the disciples and used to kiss her often on her mouth. The rest of the disciples were offended by it and expressed disapproval. They said to him, 'Why do you love her more than all of us?' the Savior answered and said to them, 'Why do I not love you like her?'"

Less we misunderstand the nature of the kiss, *Philip* teaches:

> Those who are begotten by him cry out from that place to the perfect man because they are nourished on the promise concerning the heavenly place . . . from the mouth, because if the word has gone out from that place it would be nourished from the mouth and it would become perfect. For it is by a kiss that the perfect conceive and give birth. For this reason, we also kiss one another. We receive conception from the grace which is in each other.

The wisdom book of *Pistis Sophia*[60] records a problem that Peter had with the status of Mary. He complains to Jesus that she is usurping Peter's rightful place by dominating the conversation, and

---

[59] A storyline of several recent popular books and films has Jesus and Mary married with children. Although some of this work substantiates the elevated role of Mary in the ministry of Jesus, there is no real evidence they were ever married or had children. More likely, as a Rechabite Nazarite, Jesus had taken vows of chastity, and Mary accepted a similar role for herself as one of his most devoted disciples.

[60] The *Pistis Sophia* is a Gnostic text discovered in 1773 and was not included in the Nag Hammadi library.

he urges Jesus to silence her. Peter is scolded by Jesus, but Mary later confides her intimidation to Jesus because, "Peter makes me hesitate; I am afraid of him, because he hates the female race." Jesus encouraged her, saying that whoever the Spirit inspires is divinely ordained to speak, whether man or woman.

The Gospel of Thomas concludes with Peter saying, "Let Mary leave us, for women are not worthy of Life." Jesus answered, "I myself shall lead her in order to make her male, so that she too may become a living spirit resembling you males. For every woman who will make herself male will enter the Kingdom of Heaven."

An understanding of what Jesus meant by changing Mary into a male can be found earlier where Jesus saw nursing babies and said, "These infants being suckled are like those who enter the Kingdom." When asked by the disciples, "Shall we then, as children, enter the Kingdom?" Jesus replied:

> When you make the two one, and when you make the inside like the outside and the outside like the inside, and the above like the below, and when you make the male and the female one and the same, so that the male not be male nor the female female; and when you fashion eyes in place of an eye, and a hand in place of a hand, and a foot in place of a foot, and a likeness in place of a likeness; then will you enter [the Kingdom].

In *The Dialogue of the Savior*, Mary, along with Thomas and Matthew, are selected to be shown "the whole of heaven and earth." Her response to Jesus's instruction was marveled at, "This word she spoke as a woman who knew the All." Later Jesus says, "When the Father established the world for himself, he left behind many things from the Mother of the All."[61]

---

[61] The Magdalen College, at Oxford University, is named for the Magdalen Manuscript, written by the Archbishop of Mayence, Rabanus Maurus (776-856 CE). It reports that Mary Magdalene is buried at Aix in France where her latter ministry took place. Several different churches in France claim to hold her relics. She was known as the *apostola apostolorum*, "Apostle to the Apostles."

The Mission of Mary Magdalene

The gospel of the Way, as taught by Jesus, allowed one's own conscience to be the guide as a self-aware doer of the law, rather than a blind obeyer of the law—or seeking excuses for noncompliance. The Gnostic Spirit of Wisdom taught by Mary is the guide of conscience. Mary's gospel was one of motherly unconditional love and understanding, rather than a judgmental fatherly one of repeated sin and forgiveness, as created by Paul.

Although its first six pages are missing, enough remains of *The Gospel of Mary* to learn some of the secret teachings Jesus provided to his disciples.[62]

In the gospel, Peter asks, "What is the sin of the world?" And, Jesus answers:

> There is no sin, but it is you who make sin when you do the things that are like the nature of adultery, which is called "sin." That is why the Good came into your midst, to the essence of every nature, in order to restore it to its root. . . . Matter gave birth to a passion that has no equal, which proceeded from (something) contrary to nature. Then there arises a disturbance in the whole body. That is why I said to you, "be of good courage," and if you are discouraged (be) encouraged in the presence of the different forms of nature. He who has ears to hear, let him hear.

Upon completing his lessons, Jesus says,

> Peace be with you. Receive my peace to yourselves. Beware that no one lead you astray, saying, "Lo here!" or "Lo there!" For the Son of Man is within you. Follow after him! Those who seek him will find him. Go then and preach the gospel of the kingdom. Do not lay down any rules beyond what I appointed for you, and do not give a law like the lawgiver lest you be constrained by it. When he had said this, he departed.

---

[62] *The Gospel of Mary* is one of a few Gnostic Gospels revealed before the Nag Hammadi discoveries. It was included with several others in a leather-bound codex and was sold on the antiquities market in Cairo in 1896.

But they were grieved. They wept greatly, saying, "How shall we go to the Gentiles and preach the gospel of the kingdom of the Son of Man? If they did not spare him, how will they spare us?" Then Mary stood up, greeted them all, and said to her brethren "Do not weep and do not grieve nor be irresolute, for his grace will be entirely with you and will protect you. But rather let us praise his greatness, for he has prepared us (and) made us into men." When Mary said this, she turned their hearts to the Good, and they began to discuss the words of the Savior.

Peter said to Mary, "Sister, we know that the Savior loved you more than the rest of women. Tell us the words of the Savior which you remember—which you know (but) we do not nor have we heard them." Mary answered and said, "What is hidden from you I will proclaim to you." And she began to speak to them these words: "I," she said, "I saw the Lord in a vision, and I said to him, 'Lord, I saw you today in a vision.' He answered and said to me, 'Blessed are you, that you did not waver at the sight of me. For where the mind is, there is the treasure.' I said to him, 'Lord, now does he who sees the vision see it through the soul or through the spirit?' The Savior answered and said, 'He does not see through the soul nor through the spirit, but the mind which is between the two—that is what sees the vision . . .'" (The next three pages are missing.)

The gospel resumes with Mary telling about a journey of the soul through the levels of heaven as it encounters the forms of darkness, desire, ignorance, excitement of death, flesh, the foolish wisdom of flesh, and finally wrathful wisdom. When asked from whence it comes, the soul answers:

What binds me has been slain, and what turns me about has been overcome, and my desire has been ended, and ignorance has died. In a world I was released from a world, and in a type from a heavenly type, and from the fetter of oblivion which is transient. From this time on will I attain to the rest of the time, of the season, of the aeon, in silence.

When Mary had said this, she fell silent, since it was to this point that the Savior had spoken with her. But Andrew answered and said to the brethren, "Say what you wish to say about what she has said. I at least do not believe that the Savior said this. For certainly these teachings are strange ideas." Peter answered and spoke concerning these same things. He questioned them about the Savior: "Did he really speak privately with a woman (and) not openly to us? Are we to turn around and all listen to her? Did he prefer her to us?"

Then Mary wept and said to Peter, "My brother Peter, what do you think? Do you think that I thought this up myself in my heart, or that I am lying about the Savior?" Levi answered and said to Peter, "Peter, you have always been hot-tempered. Now I see you contending against the woman like the adversaries. But if the Savior made her worthy, who are you indeed to reject her? Surely the Savior knows her very well. That is why he loved her more than us. Rather let us be ashamed and put on the perfect man, and separate as he commanded us and preach the gospel, not laying down any other rule or other law beyond what the Savior said." . . . and they began to go forth to proclaim and to preach.

Sophia's Spirit of Wisdom is the True Holy Spirit

Proverbs (3:19) records that "The LORD by wisdom founded the earth; by understanding he established the heavens; by his knowledge the deeps broke forth, and the clouds drop down the dew." Continuing to speak of wisdom, Proverbs (8:22) says, "The LORD created me at the beginning of his work, the first of his acts of old." Throughout the Bible, references to wisdom are feminine.

In the *Wisdom of Sirach*, a book favored by the Way and Zealots, we find that Wisdom came from the mouth of God; she is God's word, breath, Spirit; as the spirit/wind that hovered over the waters of creation and as mist/steam that covered the earth at the beginning; she is universal, everywhere. (24:1-27)

Some Gnostics identified God as a Trinity consisting of Father, Mother, and Son, in which the Mother is equated to the Holy Spirit. As described by the *Apocryphon of John* "... (She is) ... the image of the invisible, virginal, perfect spirit ... She became the Mother of everything, for she existed before them all, the mother-father..."

Writing in *The Gnostic Gospels*, Elaine Pagels draws on the Gnostic Gospels and skillfully develops the concept of Wisdom as being the source of the feminine Holy Spirit:[63]

> In addition to the eternal, mystical Silence and the Holy Spirit, certain Gnostics suggest a third characterization of the divine Mother: as Wisdom. Here the Greek feminine term for "wisdom," *sophia*, translates a Hebrew feminine term, *hokhmah*. Early interpreters had pondered the meaning of certain Biblical passages—for example, the saying in *Proverbs* that "God made the world in Wisdom." Could Wisdom be the feminine power in which God's creation was "conceived"? According to one teacher, the double meaning of the term conception—physical and intellectual—suggested the possibility: "The image of thought [*ennoia*] is feminine, since ... [it] is a power of conception."

In some respects, Sophia served as the goddess of wisdom for the Gnostics, but she also became synonymous with the Holy Spirit. Hagia Sophia, the magnificent Eastern Orthodox cathedral in Constantinople, was named in her honor.

The Pauline sect, however, abandoned the feminine aspects of the Holy Spirit when they conceived a masculine Trinity, consisting

---

[63] Dr. Elaine Pagels was a member of the scholarly committee that translated the Nag Hammadi Library into English. Her work in *The Gnostic Gospels* is heavily relied on throughout this chapter, and virtually every paragraph deserves a footnote to her book.
The New York Times referred to Dr. Pagels's work as "The first major and eminently readable book on Gnosticism ..." *The New Yorker* called it "An intellectually elegant, concise study ..." TIME placed *The Gnostic Gospels* among the 100 best and most influential nonfiction books written in English during the twentieth century. The reader interested in Gnosticism would do well to start with her book—I did.

of the Father, the Son, and the Holy Spirit. Being indivisible, the Spirit was neutered or made masculine. As Origen would write, "With regard to the Holy Spirit it is not yet clearly known whether *he* is to be thought of as begotten or unbegotten, or as being *himself* a Son of God or not, but these are matters which we must investigate to the best of our power from holy scripture." (The distressing masculine pronouns are emphasized.)

By changing the feminine Spirit of Wisdom into the masculine Holy Spirit, the Roman Christian Church destroyed the very soul of the Gospel of Jesus it professed to teach. How much different would the world be today if the Spirit of Wisdom had been guiding the decisions of conscience for the past 1,700 years, instead of being buried in the graveyard of Paul's victims?

Gnosticism is the Heart of the Nag Hammadi Codices

Gnosticism is derived in part from Zoroastrianism—which had an influence on post-exile writings in the Old Testament and, even more so, on the religious philosophy of the Way. In accusing the Indian Brahmins of heresy, the orthodox Pauline writer Hippolytus provides an insight about Gnosis and how it may have influenced the Way (and Jesus):

> they say God is light, not like the light one sees, nor like the sun nor fire, but to them God is discourse, not that which finds expression in articulate sounds, but that of knowledge (Gnosis) through which the secret mysteries of nature are perceived by the wise.

If one is to grasp the essential mission of Jesus, especially as it is expressed in Gnostic Christianity, one must have a sound understanding of Gnosticism. A basic outline was presented in an earlier chapter (a quick review of which would aid comprehension), but perhaps we should dig a bit deeper in the subject before looking at the Nag Hammadi documents for their Gnostic content.

Writing around 150 CE, the Gnostic teacher, Theodotus, said that a Gnostic is one who has learned "who we were, and what we have become; where we were . . . Whither we are hastening; from what we are being released; what birth is, and what is rebirth."

Monoimus, another Gnostic teacher, says: "Abandon the search for God and the creation and other matters of a similar sort. Look for him by taking yourself as the starting point. Learn who it is within you who makes everything his own and says, 'My God, my mind, my thoughts, my soul, my body.' Learn the sources of sorrow, joy, love, hate . . . If you carefully investigate these matters, you will find him in *yourself*."

Orthodox Jews and Christians believe they are entirely separate from the God that created them. For the Gnostics, however, there is no separation, and learning to know oneself *is* learning to know God. For them, Jesus did not come to save them from sin; he came to educate and inform them—to lead them to spiritual awareness. Once one achieves Gnosis, Jesus is no longer their spirit guide, he and God and the adept are all one in the same.

Orthodox Roman Christians believe that Jesus is the physical Son of God; he is their God and personal savior, but he is forever remote. As we see in the Gnostic *Gospel of Thomas*, Jesus tells Thomas that they both had the same origin.

> Jesus said, "I am not your master. Because you have drunk, you have become drunk from the bubbling stream which I have measured out. . .. He who will drink from my mouth will become as I am: I myself shall become he, and the things that are hidden will be revealed to him."

Of all the books in the New Testament, the Gospel of John is closest in content of thought to the Gnostic Gospels, and it serves as a literary bridge between the Gnostic Gospels and the Dead Sea Scrolls to which it is also similar. In John (14:4-7) where, following the Last Supper, Jesus is providing his final instruction to his disciples and is speaking of his Father's house where he is going to prepare a place for his disciples. Jesus says, "and you know the way where I am going." His brother, Judas Thomas responds, "Lord, we do not know where you are going; how can we know the way?" And Jesus answers, "I am the way, and the truth, and the life; no one comes to the Father, but by me. If you had known me, you would have known my Father also; henceforth you knew him and have seen him."

Borderline heretical because of its Gnostic content, John was accepted by the orthodox Paulines because an inference can be drawn from it that the only salvation is through the Roman Christian Church. To the contrary, the Gnostic Gospels teach that the path to salvation is through one's own mind and the learned ability to identify the correct way through self-knowledge. In the *Dialogue of the Savior*, when the disciples ask Jesus about the path to salvation, his answer is, "the place which you can reach, stand there!" In the *Gospel of Thomas*, Jesus again refers to the path when asked how to get there saying, "there is light within a man of light, and it lights up the whole world. If he does not shine, he is darkness."

Following Paul's Pharisaic influence, the Roman Christians believe that sin is one of the things that separates God from humanity. The Greek term used in the New Testament for sin, *hamartia*, comes from the sport of archery; literally, it means "missing the mark." Paul taught that we suffer distress because we fail to achieve our moral goals: "all have sinned and fall short of the glory of God" (Romans 3:23).

Gnostics, however, believe it is ignorance, not sin, that causes human suffering. Personal insight is valued by both Gnostics and psychotherapists, and few psychiatrists would disagree with the following saying attributed to Jesus in the *Gospel of Thomas*.

> If you bring forth what is within you, what you bring forth will save you. If you do not bring forth what is within you, what you do not bring forth will destroy you. . . .. Recognize what is before your eyes, and what is hidden will be revealed to you.

In the *Gospel of Truth*, "Ignorance . . . brought about anguish and terror. And the anguish grew solid like a fog, so that no one was able to see." A failure to have self-awareness is described in the *Gospel of Truth* as a nightmare in which there is "terror and confusion and instability and doubt and division." The failure leaves one dwelling in a "deficiency" consisting of ignorance.

As with someone's ignorance, when he comes to have knowledge, his ignorance vanishes by itself; as the darkness vanishes when light appears, so also the deficiency vanishes in the fulfillment.

Common sense tells us that the maintenance of ignorance is self-destructive, which the *Dialogue of the Savior* confirms:

If one does not [understand] how the fire came to be, he will burn in it, because he does not know his root. If one does not first understand the water, he does not know anything . . . .. If one does not understand how the wind that blows came to be, he will run with it. If one does not understand how the body that he wears came to be, he will perish with it . . . .. Whoever does not understand how he came will not understand how he will go . . . ..

The *Gospel of Thomas* cautions, however, that self-discovery can provoke anxiety.

Jesus said, "Let him who seeks continue seeking until he finds. When he finds, he will become troubled. When he becomes troubled, he will be astonished, and he will rule over all things."

Gnostics believe that "the lamp of the body is the mind," which the *Dialogue of the Savior* attributes to Jesus. The Gnostic Gospels contain the *Teachings* by Silvanus, who says, "Bring in your guide and your teacher. The mind is the guide, but reason is the teacher. . . .. Live according to your mind . . . Acquire strength, for the mind is strong . . . Enlighten your mind . . . Light the lamp within you."

In the *Gospel of Thomas*, Jesus ridiculed those who think the "Kingdom of God" literally exists:

If those who lead you say to you, "Look, the Kingdom is in the sky," then the birds will arrive there before you. If they say to you, "It is in the sea." then the fish will precede you. Rather, the Kingdom is inside of you, and it is outside of you. When you come to know yourselves, then you will be known, and you will realize that you are the sons of the living Father. But if you will not know yourselves, then you dwell in poverty, and it is you who are that poverty.

A similar lesson is taught by Jesus in Luke (17:20-21), "The Kingdom of God is not coming with signs to be observed; nor will they say, 'Lo, here it is!' or 'There!' for behold, the kingdom of God is in the midst of you."

In *The Gospel of Thomas,* Jesus asks his disciples who he is like in comparison to others.

Thomas says to Him, "Master, my mouth is wholly incapable of saying whom you are like." Jesus said, "I am not your master. Because you have drunk, you have become intoxicated from the bubbling stream which I have measured out."

Later in *Thomas*, Jesus says, "He who will drink from My mouth will become like Me. I myself shall become he, and the things that are hidden will be revealed to him."

For the Gnostics, the mission of Jesus was a place to begin their search for self-awareness, not the end. They believed the search was endless and would take them beyond what they had received from Jesus. Responding to attacks by the orthodox Paulines, the Gnostics wrote the *Apocalypse of Peter* in which those who "name themselves bishop, and deacon, as if they had received their authority from God" are "waterless canals."

Jesus's Resurrection: Spirit or Physical Body?

In traditional Judaism at the time of Jesus, the Sadducees did not believe in a resurrection. For them, and the Pharisees, only Moses had been taken up into Heaven to be with God upon his death. In addition, the Way believed that Enoch had also achieved the same status. As for the rest of humanity, the Pharisees and the Way relied on a passage in Ezekiel (37:1-14) to imagine a way for the faithful to be resurrected at some point in the future following their death.

> The hand of the LORD was upon me, and he brought me out by the Spirit of the LORD and set me down in the midst of the valley; it was full of bones. And he led me round among them; and behold, there were very many upon the valley; and lo, they were very dry. And he said to me "Son of man, can these bones live?" And I answered, "O Lord GOD, thou knowest." Again, he said to me, "Prophesy to these bones, and say to them, O dry bones, hear the word of the LORD. Thus, says the Lord GOD to these bones: Behold, I will cause breath to enter you, and you shall live.

James and his Congregation of the Poor did not believe that Jesus was God, or the Son of God, or that he was physically resurrected from the dead. They thought that, in the manner of Moses and Enoch, Jesus may have ascended into Heaven to be with God when he died, and they accepted that they could experience his spiritual presence. For those of his followers who had achieved Gnosis, the ascension of Jesus was a spiritual union with an Abiding Mind.

As we learned during the earlier discussion of the resurrection of Jesus following his crucifixion, the concept of a physical, bodily resurrection by the Roman Christians arose from their misunderstanding of Paul's twisted logic on the subject. As a Pharisee, Paul shared a generalized belief in Ezekiel's "standing up of the bones" prophecy; however, he was also certain he had experienced the spirit of Jesus during his blinding attack of conscience. His hallucination was so real that he believed it must have had a substance, but as he wrote in First Corinthians (14:42-44), "What is sown is perishable, what is raised is imperishable. . .. It is sown a physical body; it is raised a spiritual body."

The Gnostics accepted the spiritual resurrection of Jesus as a symbol which they experienced through visions and dreams, and they relied on Jesus as a spirit guide in their search for illumination and self-awareness.

Reflecting upon the fact it was Mary Magdalen, rather than Peter, to whom Jesus first appeared following his execution, the *Gospel of Mary* reports on her question to Jesus during a vision: "How does he who sees the vision see it? [Through] the soul, [or] through the spirit?" Jesus told her that it was through the mind.

In the *Treatise on Resurrection*, a Gnostic teacher says, "Do not suppose that resurrection is an apparition," but that "It is . . . the revealing of what truly exists . . . and a migration into newness." The teacher in the *Treatise* says one can be "resurrected from the dead" and asks, "Are you—the real you—mere corruption? . . . Why do you not examine your own self, and see that you have arisen?"

The primary difference between the Gnostics and Roman Christians is that Paul's followers continue to wait for the Second Coming of Jesus, but for those who achieve Gnosis, he never left their side.

What If Jesus's God Was a Mother?

In the beginning, there was only the Mother Goddess who was worshipped for her gift of life and the comfort she provided against the harshness of existence. Found at Gravettian sites (c. 27,000-20,000 BCE) scattered from Siberia to Western Europe are prehistoric Venuses, which are small statuettes of motherly women with large breasts and torsos. Becoming Earth Mother, her worship continued with the growth and expansion of the agricultural societies of the Neolithic period. Goddesses are depicted as a woman seated on a throne and flanked by two lions, or with a single lion draped across her lap. Then war was born! Male gods replaced women, and it was men who were depicted as having tamed the wild animals. Women were relegated to a secondary status as consorts of the male gods in virtually every culture.

With the religious reforms of Kings Hezekiah and Josiah, YAHWEH, the God of Israel was divorced from his consort Asherah and forced to live a bachelor existence without a Divine female companion. In exclusively masculine terms, God is the king, lord, and father throughout the Bible, and the absence of any feminine symbolism for Him carried over from Judaism into Christianity and Islam. Although the Roman Christians initially accepted women in leadership role in the early church, they are no longer allowed to serve in the priesthood, and, while Catholics revere Mary as the mother of Jesus and call her the Mother of God, they do not consider her to be a God.

The Gnostics often used sexual symbolism to describe God as embracing both male and female attributes. Some describe the Mother as part of a divine couple, and others pray to the Mother as "the mystical, eternal Silence."

The *Great Announcement* told how creation resulted from, "a great power, the Mind of the Universe, which manages all things, and is a male . . . the other . . . a great Intelligence . . . is a female which produces all things." The union was "discovered to be duality . . . This is Mind in Intelligence, and these are separable from one another, and yet are one, found in a state of duality."

Some Gnostics thought God was masculofeminine; others did not believe the Divine was either male or female; and others used alternative terms depending on which trait was being emphasized.

Found among the Gnostic Gospels is the powerful feminist poem *Thunder, Perfect Mind*:

> I am the first and the last. I am the honored one and the scorned one. I am the whore, and the holy one. I am the wife and the virgin. I am [the mother] and the daughter. . . . I am she whose wedding is great, and I have not taken a husband. . . . I am knowledge, and ignorance. . . . I am foolish, and I am wise. . . . I am godless, and I am one whose God is great.

Is God Really Jealous, or is That Just Another Fable?

The first of the Ten Commandments in Exodus is: "You shall have no other gods before me. The commandment is immediately followed by a dire threat of punishment for its violation, "you shall not bow down to them or serve them; for I the LORD your God am a jealous God, visiting the iniquity of the fathers upon the children to the third and fourth generation of those who hate me, ..." (20:3)[64]

The Gnostics said that God believed he had created everything all by himself; however, it was because Wisdom, his Mother, "infused him with energy" and indoctrinated him with her own ideas. The

---

[64] The Ten Commandments are an overlay of law imposed by the Mosaic priesthood over Abraham's more ancient covenant of peace and righteousness.

third century theologian, Hippolytus wrote that the Gnostics believed God "was even ignorant of his own Mother."

God speaks in the *Apocryphon of John* saying "'I am a jealous God, and there is no other God beside me.' But by announcing this he indicated to the angels . . . that another God does exist; for if there were no other one, of whom would he be jealous? . . . Then the mother began to be distressed."

According to Irenaeus, Gnostics believed, "The creator, becoming arrogant in spirit, boasted himself over all those things that were below him, and exclaimed, 'I am father, and God, and above me there is no one.' But his mother, hearing him speak thus, cried out against him, 'Do not lie, Ialdabaoth . . .'"[65]

In the *Hypostasis of the Archons*, God is chastised by his mother and her daughter when, "he became arrogant, saying, 'It is I who am God, and there is no other apart from me.' . . . And a voice came forth from above the realm of absolute power, saying, 'You are wrong, Samael' [which means, 'god of the blind']. And he said, 'If any other thing exists before me, let it appear to me!' And immediately, Sophia ("Wisdom") stretched forth her finger, and introduced light into matter, and she followed it down into the region of Chaos. . . . And he again said to his offspring, 'It is I who am the God of All.' And Life, the daughter of Wisdom, cried out; she said to him, 'You are wrong, Saklas!'"[66]

The Gnostic teacher Justinus is reported to have described the Lord's shock, terror and anxiety "when he discovered that he was not the God of the universe." Gradually God's shock gave way to wonder, and finally he came to welcome what Wisdom had taught him. Justinus concludes, "This is the meaning of the saying, 'The fear of the Lord is the beginning of Wisdom.'"

The Roman Christians Gain Political Power and Destroy Gnosticism

One difference between the congregations founded by Paul in Asia Minor, Greece, and Italy was that those who walked in the

---

[65] Ialdabaoth is the name of the archon who created Earth and the Garden of Eden.
[66] Saklas is an assistant angel.

footsteps of Paul were aggressively proselytizing and dogmatic, whereas the Gnostic congregations in Syria and Egypt were more content to let individuals find their own way, with intellectual and spiritual guidance. Although the Gnostics did not seek to impose their views on the Roman Christians, the insecure orthodox were challenged and offended by the alternative views of the Gnostics and sought to eliminate their influence on the Pauline faithful.

Writing in Second Timothy, Paul (or one of his followers) repudiates the Gnostics:

> Do your best to present yourself to God as one approved, a workman who has no need to be ashamed, rightly handling the word of truth. Avoid such godless chatter; for it will lead people into more and more ungodliness, and their talk will eat its way like gangrene. Among them are Hymenaeus and Philetus, who have swerved from the truth by holding that the resurrection is past already. They are upsetting the faith of some. But God's firm foundation stands, bearing this seal: The Lord knows those who are his, and, "Let everyone who names the name of the Lord depart from iniquity." (2:15-19)

Responding to the Roman Christians, the author of the *Apocalypse of Peter* has Jesus saying,

> They will cleave to the name of a dead man, thinking that they will become pure. But they will become greatly defiled and they will fall into a name of error and into the hand of an evil, cunning man and a manifold dogma, and they will be ruled heretically. For some of them will blaspheme the truth and proclaim evil teaching. And they will say evil things against each other. . . .. But many others, who oppose the truth and are the messengers of error, will set up their error and their law against these pure thoughts of mine, as looking out from one [perspective], thinking that good and evil are from one [source]. They do business in my word. . . .. And there shall be others of those who are outside our number who name themselves bishop and deacons,

as if they have received their authority from God. They bend themselves under the judgment of the leaders. These people are dry canals.

When Constantine the Great became the emperor in 313 CE, he sought to unify the Roman Empire by becoming the patron of the Pauline Church headquartered in Rome and by empowering it to enforce its orthodox views against those who dissented. Seeking unity in his realm, his motivation was more political than spiritual. Recognizing Christianity alongside Sol Invictus, Constantine declared Sunday to be an official day of rest. He granted imperial favors to the Roman Christians, including the right to hold public office. As emperor, he established a precedent for subsequent rulers to help the Church enforce its orthodox dogma against dissenters, including the Gnostics.

Constantine died in 337 BC, having received a Christian baptism on his death bed by a distant relative, the Arian Bishop of Nicomedia. At that point in time, most bishops in the Eastern Church were Arian (Gnostics). The Roman Christians later declared Arianism—in which Jesus was believed to be a wholly mortal and great teacher—to be a heresy, and thousands were slaughtered for their beliefs.

The Legacy of Gnosticism

As we page through the Gnostic Gospels that miraculously appeared in Egypt in 1945, we are filled with a sense of what might have been. How different the last 2,000 years would have been had Mary's Gnostic message prevailed and Paul's heresy forgotten. The inquisitions, crusades, pogroms, holocausts, and intellectual suppression could have been avoided. Instead of living a life burdened by the cycle of sin and forgiveness—with the abominations of original sin and purgatory—we could have experienced centuries of joy in living a life guided by reason, righteousness, and the Spirit of Wisdom. What more can be said? It's too late to start over, but not too late to learn from our mistakes.

Saving the Gnostic Codices by Burying Them in a Large Sealed Jar

In 367 CE, Athanasius, the powerful Roman Christian Archbishop of Alexandria, wrote an Easter letter that condemned heretics and their "apocryphal books." Many of the books in the Nag Hammadi Library came to be at risk for official suppression. Fortunately, one or several of the monks at the nearby monastery hid their precious manuscripts to avoid destruction. They placed 13 codices bound in leather, containing at least 52 tractates (books), in a large sealed jar, which they buried at the bottom of a nearby cliff. They probably hoped to return for the books when less dangerous circumstances prevailed. There, however, the books remained until being discovered in 1945 by an Egyptian Muslim farmer digging for nitrates to fertilize his fields.

The recovered Gnostic Gospels are only a small sample of all those destroyed by the Roman Christians. None of these books were included in the New Testament—even though they could surely have helped illuminate many questions asked there but left unanswered. By the time the canon of the New Testament was finalized, any femininity in the nature of God had been eliminated; the role of Mary Magdalen as Jesus's most honored disciple was slandered and minimized; the Spirit of Wisdom was banished, and the masculine Trinity of God the Father, God the Son, and a neutered Holy Spirit was enshrined. The death and physical resurrection of Jesus Christ became an indisputable article of faith, the denial of which carried the death penalty.

With the destruction of the Gnostic Gospels, the world lost much of what was gentle, feminine, insightful, and forgiving from the gospels of Jesus and his Way of Righteousness for almost 1,700 years. Christianity became dogmatic, paternalistic, bureaucratic, and accusatory. This led to original sin, indulgences, inquisitions, crusades, pogroms, and genocides from which humanity is still reeling. Nonetheless—even through the dark ages that descended upon the world—the essential Gospel of Jesus shined through the distortions that obscured and diluted its message, and it remains today as a beacon of light for the future. But, before we get there, we must first traverse the diverging paths trod by Paul and the Rabbinic Jews, the wayward of the Way.

JESUS SENT HIS BROTHER, JOSEPH, AS THE MESSENGER TO THE GENTILES

The list of Jesus's brothers in Mark (6:3) and Matthew (13:55-56) includes one named Joses, and Acts (4:36) relates an inspirational story about how a "Levite from Cyprus" named Joseph (Greek *Joses*) sold a field and donated the proceeds to the apostles. Joseph was then surnamed Barnabas (Aramaic for son of the prophet, or consolation, or encouragement). It is very likely that Barnabas was another brother of Jesus who was personally involved in the Way and his ministry. Only Joses (Joseph) among the brothers listed in Matthew (13:55-56) is missing from the historical apostolic dynasty of Mary's sons: Jesus, James, Judas, and Simeon, who were leaders of the Way. There is a strong likelihood that Joses, Joseph, and Barnabas are one in the same person, the youngest brother of Jesus.

In the same manner that the Pauline authors of the gospels substituted Thomas for Judas, and made him a traitor to Jesus, the writers took away Joseph's name and reassigned it to his father, Cleopas, and then dubbed the younger brother with a diminutive, Joses. They then created a fictional background based on Cyprus, the headquarters of Joseph's mission as a messenger of the Way to the Gentiles.

Mary named each of her five sons for the heroes of her people, Joshua, Jacob, Simeon and Judas Maccabee, and Jacob's eleventh and favorite son, Joseph.

Following Paul's three-year initiation into the Way, Joseph spoke on his behalf in obtaining James's authorization for Paul to undertake a mission to his hometown in Asia Minor to teach the Word of Righteousness. Subsequently, James placed Paul under Joseph's supervision for an extended mission to the Gentiles—until they had a dispute about doctrine. Most likely, Paul's preaching to the Gentiles was increasingly deviating from that he initially learned from the Way at Qumran, and Joseph, unable to control Paul, was unwilling to further sanction Paul's heresy. Paul was acting as a Pharisee and was peddling a false interpretation of righteousness.

Little is known about the mission of Joseph once he and Paul split up. He is thereafter ignored in Acts, and although Catholic tradition has Barnabas as a martyred saint, there is little support for the alternative forms of torture he was supposed to have endured. It is said that his remains were buried with the Book of Matthew, which he wrote, in a tomb in Egypt. Joseph is the patron saint of Cyprus and his body is believed to been recovered and reinterred at the Monastery of Saint Barnabas in Cyprus.[67]

Joseph Was a Righteous Lay Minister of the Way in the Order of Melchizedek

Not only was Joseph thought to have been the original author of Matthew (in Hebrew), many believe that he also wrote The Letter to the Hebrews (in Greek). Because of its Gnostic content, Hebrews barely made it into the very back of the canon of the New Testament, and then only because a forged postscript made it appear that Paul was the author. This was easily disproven by modern textual analysis; however, the interesting thing is that Hebrews contributes a blend of Gnosticism and the righteous gospel of the Way with the ministry of the Order of Melchizedek.

Another possible writing by Joseph is the *General Epistle of Barnabas,* which is included in the Pseudepigrapha, and which almost made it into the New Testament. The book was cited by Clemens Alexandrinus, Origen, Eusebius, and Jerome, and other ancient fathers of the Church as authoritative, and the *Codex Sinaiticus* included *Barnabas* after Revelations. For some unknown reason *Barnabas* was omitted from the New Testament (perhaps simply because Revelations concludes with a dire warning about adding to the book, making for a more dramatic literary ending to the New Testament).

The language of *Barnabas* is that of the Way and is like James, Hebrews, and the Dead Sea Scrolls.

For God will judge the world without respect of persons: and everyone shall receive according to his works. If a

---

[67] The monastery and Icon museum are located between Tuzla and Salamis in the northern region of Cyprus.

man shall be good, his righteousness shall go before him; if wicked, the reward of his wickedness shall follow him. (*Barnabas* 4:13-14)

And therefore, the Scripture again speaks concerning our ears, that God has circumcised them, together with our hearts. For thus saith the Lord by the holy prophets: By the hearing of the ear they obeyed me. (8:1)

Barnabas offers a Gnostic blessing, "And may God, the Lord of all the world give you wisdom, knowledge, counsel, and understanding of his judgments in patience." (15:12)

The Letter to the Hebrews of the New Testament is an intellectual exercise generally supportive of the theory that Jesus was the Son of God, but uniquely as the perfect and eternal high priest of the Order of Melchizedek.[68] In Genesis (14:17-24), Melchizedek was the righteous king of Salem (Jerusalem), who, as "the priest of the most high God" blessed and welcomed Abraham to Canaan with bread and wine. The meaning of the name is "my king is righteousness."[69] More basically, the priesthood could have been called the Order of Righteousness.

The Son of God described by Joseph in Hebrews is in line with that of the Way in that Jesus ascended spiritually into communion with God at his death in the same manner as Moses. Joseph called Jesus the "apostle and high priest of our confession" (3:1) appointed by God, "Thou art a priest forever, after the order of Melchizedek."

An understanding of the priesthood as a higher level of Gnostic insights is expressed:

About this we have much to say which is hard to explain, since you have become dull of hearing. For though by this

---

[68] Here Joseph may be referring to the alternative priesthood of the Osim, the Sons of Zadok, which has the same meaning of righteousness as the Sons of Melchizedek.

[69] The Mormon Church of Jesus Christ of Latter-Day Saints anoints its adult male laity as priests in the Order of Melchizedek. Although it originated from the spurious writings of its founder, the LDS church generally pursues a doctrine of righteousness.

time you ought to be teachers, you need someone to teach you again the first principles of God's word. You need milk, not solid food; for everyone who lives on milk is unskilled in the word of righteousness, for he is a child. But solid food is for the mature, for those who have their faculties trained by practice to distinguish good from evil. (5:11-14)

Joseph supports the position of James in terms of justification, saying "let us consider how to stir up one another to love and good works . . . ." (10:24):

Though we speak thus, yet in your case, beloved, we feel sure of better things that belong to salvation. For God is not so unjust as to overlook your work and the love you showed for his sake in serving the saints, as you still do. (6:9-10)

Joseph defines faith in his Letter:

Now faith is the assurance of things hoped for, the conviction of things not seen. For by it the men of old received divine approval. By faith we understand that the world was created by the word of God, so that what is seen was made out of things which do not appear. . ... (11:1-3)

By faith Enoch was taken up so that he should not see death; and he was not found because God had taken him. Now before he was taken, he was attested as having pleased God. And without faith it is impossible to please him. . ... By faith Noah . . . became an heir of the righteousness which comes by faith. (11:5-7)

Like the language of *The Thanksgiving Hymns* of the Way, Joseph talks about prayer in his Letter to the Hebrews.

Through him [Jesus] then let us continually offer up a sacrifice of praise to God, that is, the fruit of lips that acknowledge his name. Do not neglect to do good and to share what you have, for such sacrifices are pleasing to God. (13:15)

Joseph concluded his Letter with a brief statement of Christian duty that has its roots in the Way of Righteousness:

> Let brotherly love continue. Do not neglect to show hospitality to strangers, for thereby some have entertained angels unawares. Remember those who are in prison, as though in prison with them; and those who are ill-treated, since you also are in the body. Let marriage be held in honor among all and let the marriage bed be undefiled; for God will judge the immoral and adulterous. Keep your life free from love of money and be content with what you have; for he has said, "I will never fail you nor forsake you." (13:1-5)

There is no evidence that Joseph was considered a messiah of the Way, but he was certainly a minister of Jesus's Order of Melchizedek—which is open to everyone who chooses to lead a life of righteousness.

The Legacy of Joseph

Of all the members of Jesus's family, Joseph was the most prolific writer and the least acknowledged. If it is in fact true that Joseph wrote the original Book of Matthew, the book of *Barnabas*, and the Letter to the Hebrews, then we must seriously consider if he may have contributed to or wrote the Book of John. Unlike the first three gospels in both facts and theology, John attempts to unify the Gnosticism of Mary Magdalene with the teachings of the Way of Righteousness.

It is easy to imagine Joseph, as the youngest of Jesus's brothers being given the task of keeping the headstrong Paul in line—and failing. Joseph warned near the conclusion of Hebrews, "Do not be led away by diverse and strange teachings" (13:9), but the Gentiles still ended up with the Roman Christianity of Paul, instead of the Way of Righteousness. We next concern ourselves with how this came to be.

PAUL, THE PHARISEE, GOES OFF THE PATH AND CREATES HIS OWN RELIGION

The form of Christianity observed by billions of believers around the world today is not the same as that taught by Jesus's brothers or by his most honored disciple following his crucifixion. To the contrary, Roman Christianity primarily resulted from the ministry of a most unlikely preacher—one who never met Jesus, except in ecstatic visions. The hallucinatory religion established by Paul is significantly different from the gospel taught by Jesus and others who followed him during and after his lifetime. To learn how Roman Christianity came into existence, we must first understand the background, mindset, and motivation of the man who created it.

Who Was Saul, The Man Who Became Known as Paul?

Paul was born as Saul in the city of Tarsus, which was in the province of Cilicia in Asia Minor (Turkey). Tarsus had been a nest of pirates until they were subdued by Pompey, and Vespasian later incorporated Cilicia into a province governed by a Roman proconsul at the time of Jesus.

Paul's father may have been a tentmaker who died and left his wife, Priscilla, a widow. It was her second marriage, however, that provided Paul's family with money, status, political connections, and Roman citizenship. Paul referred to this family in Romans (16:13), where he sends greetings to "Rufus, eminent in the Lord, also his mother and mine." Rufus Pudens was of a Roman senatorial family, and he and Paul apparently had the same mother. Other greetings to those of "the household of Caesar" (Philippians 4:22) connects Paul with imperial insiders.

Paul also reveals in Romans (16:10-11) that he may have been related in some manner to the Herodians. In closing, he wrote, "Greet my kinsman Herodion." (the littlest Herod) As we learned earlier from the complicated Herodian genealogy, the "littlest Herod" was probably Aristobulus, who was the child of the incestuous marriage of Herod of Chalcis and his niece, Bernice.[70]

In Rome, Aristobulus managed to gain favor with the emperor Claudius, who awarded him the title of "friend" and appointed him King of Lower Armenia (which may have included Tarsus). As we will see later in Paul's story, these and other influential connections would serve Paul well when he came into violent conflict with James and the Congregation of the Way in Jerusalem and was arrested by the Romans for rioting.

Paul's privileged status gave him the ability to speak both Greek and Latin, and provided him with the wealth to travel to Jerusalem as a student to study under Gamaliel I, the son of Hillel, the great leader of the Pharisees.[71] Paul must have been of some means—as residence, support, and tuition in Jerusalem to study under the famous leader of the Pharisees and *Nasi* of the Sanhedrin would be as relatively expensive at the time of Jesus as it would be today.

Paul arrived in Jerusalem during the political and religious strife that followed the crucifixion of Jesus—at a time when James the Just and Jesus's Congregation of the Poor were being violently persecuted by the Sadducean and Pharisaic leaders. Paul quickly became personally involved in physically attacking Jesus's family and congregants.

The Pharisaic assault on the Day of Atonement resulted in James being thrown down the Temple steps and breaking his legs. This historical event was replaced in Acts (7:58-60, 8:1) with the fable of Stephen's stoning, during which Paul passively guarded the cloaks of those who threw the stones and encouraged their violence. It was

---

[70] Bernice was the daughter of her husband's brother, Herod Agrippa I. Appallingly, following the death of her husband-uncle, Bernice then engaged in an incestuous affair with her own brother, Herod Agrippa II—the last Herodian king of Judea, who conspired in the judicial murder of James the Just and hosted and acquitted Paul.

[71] Acts (5:33) relates that Gamaliel ordered the apostles to be beaten and charged to "not to speak in the name of Jesus."

Paul who—acting with the zeal of Phineas[72] to cleanse the Temple of those who rejected the oral Torah of the Pharisees—personally assaulted James with a club forcing him down the Temple stairs.

Apparently, Paul was unmarried, and there is no record of his physical appearance in the New Testament; however, he was described in *The Acts of Paul and Thecla* (1:7), which reported Paul's arrival at Lystra.

> At length they saw a man coming (namely Paul), of a low stature, bald (or shaved) on the head, crooked thighs, handsome legs, hollow-eyed; had a crooked nose; full of grace; for sometimes he appeared as a man, sometimes he had the countenance of an angel.

Paul may have suffered from a health problem, such as stuttering, or an emotional disease as he relates in Galatians (4:13-14) while identifying himself with Jesus, "you know it was because of a bodily ailment that I preached the gospel to you at first; and though my condition was a trial to you, you did not scorn or despise me, but *received me as an angel of God, as Christ Jesus.*" (emphasis added) In Second Corinthians (12:7) Paul once again identifies himself with Jesus in discussing his disabilities.

> And to keep me from being too elated by the abundance of revelations, a thorn was given me in the flesh, a messenger of Satan, to harass me, to keep me from being too elated. Three times I besought the Lord about this, that it should leave me; but he said to me, "My grace is sufficient for you, for my power is made perfect in weakness." I will all the more gladly boast of my weaknesses, that the power of Christ may rest upon me.

One does not have to be trained in psychology to conclude from

---

[72] Numbers (25:6-8) tells about how Phineas, the grandson of Aaron, speared a Midianite woman who had entered the camp of the Israelites *and* the man who had dared to bring her into the midst of Moses' congregation. For his "zeal," Moses awarded perpetual priesthood to Phineas and his family. Moses then ordered the genocide of the Midianite people.

reading the epistles of Paul that he was petty, jealous, vindictive, vain, insecure, egoistic, truth challenged, and quite possibly schizophrenic. Throughout his letters, he talks about dreams, visions, and hearing voices. He says things like, "I must boast" and "I am not at all inferior to these superlative apostles." (1 Corinthians 12:1&11) Paul constantly swears oaths, such as the one in Galatians (1:20), "In what I am writing to you, before God, I do not lie." Jesus condemned the practice of swearing as being evil:

> But I say to you, Do not swear at all, either by heaven, for it is the throne of God, or by the earth, for it is his footstool, or by Jerusalem, for it is the city of the great King. And do not swear by your head, for you cannot make one hair white or black. Let what you say be simply "Yes or No"; anything more that this comes from evil. (Matthew 5:34-37)

This has been a snapshot of the troubled, but highly capable and overweeningly ambitious, man who experienced a hallucinatory revelation that convinced him that he was the spiritual reincarnation of Jesus with a new mission to preach the gospel of Jesus—as he, a trained Pharisee, was free to interpret and revise.

Paul Sees the Light and Converts to the Way

After Paul allegedly aided and abetted in the murder of Stephen, Acts (8:1-3) reports:

> And on that day a great persecution arose against the church in Jerusalem; and they were all scattered throughout the region of Judea and Samaria, except the apostles. . .. But Saul laid waste the church, and entering house after house, he dragged off men and women and committed them to prison.

While many of the Nazoreans were forced to flee to Pella, James and others were probably gathered with the Congregation of the Way at Qumran, which was a part of the wilderness area referred to by the Way as "Damascus."

According to Acts (9:1-19):

> But Saul, still breathing threats and murder against the disciples of the Lord, went to the high priest and asked him for letters to the synagogues at Damascus, so that if he found any belonging to the Way, men or women, he might bring them bound to Jerusalem. Now as he journeyed, he approached Damascus, and suddenly a light from heaven flashed about him. And he fell to the ground and heard a voice saying to him, "Saul, Saul, why do you persecute me?" And he said, "Who are you, Lord?" And he said, "I am Jesus, whom you are persecuting; but rise and enter the city, and you will be told what you are to do.

With the hindsight of 2,000 years and, hopefully, a better grasp of psychological issues and their role in behavior, we must accept that Paul was probably under extraordinary emotional pressure as he ran about in a manic frenzy participating in religious rioting, attempting murder, arresting and imprisoning men and women, and racing down the road to shackle those whose only crime was to have a different opinion about religion.

Given all of this—possibly combined with a hot sun and dehydration—it is not difficult to imagine that Paul, an emotionally tortured man, suffered an attack of conscience and a psychic break. Somewhere inside of himself, he must have known that, irrespective of his zeal for the Pharisaic cause, he was violating Abraham's Covenant of Righteousness, the basic tenet of Moses's Commandments, and human decency. Or, perhaps it was simple schizophrenia, untreated by modern medication, that caused him to hear a voice he didn't recognize. The only thing we know for sure is that he claimed to have experienced a vision that day on the road to Damascus which diverted him to a different path. That and his future visions, *and* his overwhelming ambition, led him to create his own unique brand of Christianity—as we know it today.

Luke, Paul's biographer, continues the story in Acts with Paul being found by Ananias, a Nazorean, who said, "Brother Saul, the Lord Jesus who appeared to you on the road by which you came, has sent me that you may regain your sight and be filled with the Holy

Spirit. And immediately something like scales fell from his eyes and he regained his sight. Then he rose and was baptized and took food and was strengthened." (9:17)

Paul spent several days with the disciples in Damascus during which time he proclaimed Jesus in the synagogues saying, "He is the Son of God." Luke writing in Acts tells us that shortly thereafter Paul went to Jerusalem and attempted to join the disciples, who were justifiably fearful of him. According to Paul's own testimony in *Galatians* (1:16-18), however, he did not immediately return to Jerusalem. He first went into Arabia and then returned to the wilderness of Damascus where he remained for three years.

There is no indication in the New Testament as to what Paul did during those missing years. Given what reportedly occurred at the end of that period; however, the most likely scenario is that he petitioned to join the Way (whose probation lasted for three years and whose exile homeland was called Damascus). While it is possible that all members of the Way did not join Jesus's congregation or accept him as their long-anticipated suffering messiah, most of the Way certainly did—and their belief system was at the heart of the gospel taught by Jesus.

We can easily imagine that Paul was forced to endure the life of a novitiate of the Way in the desert until such time as he repented of the violence he had committed against James and the Poor in Jerusalem, completed his indoctrination, and was baptized into the congregation.

Continuing the story as told by Paul in Galatians (1:18), "Then after three years I went up to Jerusalem to visit Cephas [Peter] and remained with him for fifteen days. But I saw none of the apostles except James the Lord's brother." Paul then swears an oath before God that he is not lying.

Accepting Paul's version as related by him in Galatians, one must have a genuine appreciation of the great forgiveness demonstrated by James—who may have been crippled by having his legs broken in the Pharisaic riot led by Paul. Paul apparently received the blessing of James, the bishop of the Congregation of the Poor allowing Paul to preach the gospel of Jesus—in his own hometown of Tarsus in Turkey.

Paul, the Wayward Missionary

The parallel story related by Luke in Acts omits the missing three years but provides more detail about what happened when Paul returned to Jerusalem following his exile at Qumran. The "disciples" remained afraid of him when he attempted to become a missionary, but Paul was supported by Jesus's brother, Joseph (Barnabas), who spoke on his behalf before the "apostles." According to the story in Acts (9:28-30), when Paul attempted to preach in Jerusalem, there were those who wanted to kill him, so the brethren "brought him down to Caesarea, and sent him off to Tarsus."

James Sends Paul on a Mission to His Hometown to Teach the Gospel of Jesus

In Galatians (1:21), Paul said he "went into the regions of Syria and Cilicia" (his home town of Tarsus), as he was "still not known by sight to the churches of Christ in Judea," to preach "the faith he once tried to destroy."

Other followers of Jesus were evangelizing in the areas of Phoenicia, Cyprus, and Antioch, and they were converting both Jews and Gentiles to the Way. James dispatched his brother Joseph to Antioch to oversee the mission in that region and to supervise Paul. It was in Antioch that—for the first time—the congregants came to be known as Christians, after the translation of the Hebrew word, *messiah* into the Greek word *Christos*. Throughout his later epistles, Paul refers to Jesus and Christ interchangeably as though both were names. These events probably took place in the early 40s.

Joseph summoned Paul to accompany him, and they preached together for several years. They returned to Jerusalem to transport relief to the Poor in Jerusalem, who were suffering from a drought. Their visit to Jerusalem probably occurred around 44-46 CE and coincided with the death of Herod Agrippa I.

Regarding the visit, Paul commences to make the kind of disparaging remarks about the Jerusalem apostles that would come to characterize his epistles, "And from those who were reputed to be something (what they were makes no difference to me; God shows no partiality)—those, I say, who were of repute added nothing to me;..." (Galatians 2:6-10)

Paul goes on to say that "James and Cephas [Peter] and John, who were reputed to be pillars, gave to me and Barnabas the right hand of fellowship, that we should go to the Gentiles and they to the circumcised; only they would have us remember the poor, which very thing I was eager to do." (2:9)

Paul, Supervised by Jesus's Younger Brother, Joseph, Gets an Expanded Territory

Returning to Antioch, Joseph and Paul commenced a missionary journey that would take them by land and sea. They first sailed to Cyprus, where "Saul" took the Roman name of "Paul." They then journeyed into Asia Minor visiting Pamphylia, Pisidia, and Galatia, before returning to Antioch. They established congregations at a number of locations "saying that through many tribulations we must enter the kingdom of God. And when they had appointed elders for them in every church, with prayer and fasting, they committed them to the Lord in whom they believed." (Acts 14:22-23)

When Joseph and Paul returned to Antioch, they were confronted with some men who "came down from Judea and were teaching the brethren, 'Unless you are circumcised according to the custom of Moses, you cannot be saved.' And when Paul and Barnabas had no small dissension and debate with them, Paul and Barnabas and some of the others were appointed to go up to Jerusalem to the apostles and the elders about this question." (Acts 15:1:2)

Another account is provided by Paul in Galatians (2:11): "But when Cephas [Peter] came to Antioch I opposed him to his face, because he stood condemned. For before certain men came from James, he ate with the Gentiles; but when they came, he drew back and separated himself, fearing the circumcision party." Addressing his Gentile audience, Paul spoke disrespectfully about James and Jesus's Congregation of the Poor.

The members of the Congregation in Jerusalem were predominately Jewish, with its Gentile members considered to be "strangers within the gate," or "God fearers." The difference had both political and religious implications. A male Gentile convert to Judaism had to undergo circumcision and agree to accept the Mosaic law, including ordinances relating to food. Once accepted, the convert gained the full benefits of being a Jew, including those accorded to the Jews by the Romans as a nation instead of a religion.[73] Those Gentiles who only stepped through the "gate" did not achieve those benefits.

James and the Nazoreans did not have any problem with Paul preaching to and converting the Gentiles within the area of his assigned mission, but they did not accept that the Jews he converted were no longer required to abide by the tenets of their Jewish religion—while retaining the political and cultural benefits. Moreover, Paul continued to proselytize in Jewish synagogues to both Jews and Gentile "strangers within the gate," contrary to his agreement with James. Many, if not most, synagogues at this time were organized by local rabbis in their own homes and allowing an outsider into their home was an intimate experience, especially if the visiting preacher offended their guests.

In Jerusalem, James the Just listened to the arguments of both sides and rendered his decision:

> Therefore, my judgment is that we should not trouble those of the Gentiles who turn to God but should write to them to abstain from the pollutions of idols and from unchastity and from what is strangled and from blood. (Acts 15:19)

James confirmed his verdict in a letter he wrote which he sent to the Antioch-Edessa congregation.

> For it has seemed good to the Holy Spirit and to us to lay upon you no greater burden than these necessary things: that you abstain from what has been sacrificed to idols and from blood and from what is strangled and from

---

[73] Julius Caesar and Augustus had granted special privileges to Jews in Rome, and in 41 CE, the emperor Claudius issued a decree establishing the religious and civil rights of the Jews, especially in Alexandria. There was resentment of these special rights in Antioch leading to disturbances.

unchastity. If you keep yourselves from these, you will do well. Farewell. (Acts 15:28-29)

Acts says that the letter was carried by "Judas called Barsabbas . . . ." The surname of Barsabbas has had several interpretations, including "son of conversion" and "son of an oath." When we later review the mission of Judas Thomas to the East, we will discover that Antioch was within his assigned sphere of influence.

There is a good chance that James sent his brother, Judas Thomas to ensure that James's ruling was properly transmitted and explained. The fact that this Judas was subsequently identified in Acts as a "prophet" makes it even more likely that it was Judas Thomas whom the Roman Christian gospel authors were endeavoring to write out of history.[74]

Paul Splits With Joseph and Goes Off on His Own Path

After they returned to Antioch, Joseph and Paul had a "sharp contention" that caused them to go their separate ways. Paul planned to return to central Asia Minor and visit the congregations they had founded there, and Joseph returned to Cyprus.

Their dispute may have related to doctrine. As we will see below, the gospel that Paul was preaching to the Gentiles was increasingly deviating from that he was taught by the Way, and Joseph undoubtedly objected. Paul, leaving Joseph and all other restraint behind, goes off completely on his own track. Accompanied by Silas, one of his own disciples, Paul commenced a new mission into Asia Minor. Although his agreement with James was that he would only preach to the Gentiles, Paul's practice was to commence his missionary work in local Jewish synagogues wooing away the Gentile "strangers within the gate" who attended services without being fully converted to Judaism.

Paul arrived in Lystra in Asia Minor where he encountered a convert named Timothy, whose mother was Jewish and whose father

---

[74] In other contexts, Judas Thomas may have also been called Addai, Thaddaeus, and Theudas.

was a Greek. Paul wanted Timothy to accompany him, and although James had ruled that it was no longer necessary—Paul personally "circumcised him because of the Jews that were in those places, for they all knew that his father was a Greek." (Acts 16:1-3)

Paul and Timothy visited the Pauline congregations in the region of Phrygia and Galatia, and they may have been accompanied by Paul's personal biographer, Luke,[75] as this portion of Acts is written in the first person. Their mission continued through Asia Minor until a vision appeared to Paul in which a man of "Macedonia" told him to "Come over to Macedonia and help us."

Joseph's problem with Paul may have related to more than doctrine, as Paul imposed extraordinary authority and rigid discipline over his congregations. He demanded their adherence to his gospel and their financial support of his efforts. In his increasing isolation, Paul was now making it clear that his ordination came directly from Jesus and God in his visions and that neither he, nor his congregations were answerable to any other authority—including James and Jesus's Congregation of the Poor—whom he begins to curse. According to Paul, he and his converts enjoyed a special relationship with Jesus as the anointed Christ, which the members of Jesus's own congregation could not experience.

It was to "the churches of Galatia" that Paul addressed his Letter to the Galatians, which was probably written later while he was in Macedonia or Greece. In it, Paul chastises the Galatians for quickly deserting him and "turning to a different gospel—not that there is another gospel, but there are some who trouble you and want to pervert the gospel of Christ. . .. If anyone is preaching to you a gospel contrary to that which you received, let him be accursed." (1:6-9)

Throughout Paul's letter, he rejects those (James and the Congregation of the Poor) who teach justification by works claiming, "the gospel which was preached by me is not man's gospel. For I did not receive it from man, nor was I taught it, but it came through a revelation of Jesus Christ." (1:11-12)

---

[75] Luke's true name may have been Lucius of Cyrene, one of the founders of the congregation in Antioch.

It appears Paul had deviated even further from the Way and was pursuing his own visionary appointment as an apostle, which he changes from Jesus to God Himself. Paul channels the prophet Jeremiah when he boasts:

> I advanced in Judaism beyond many of my own age among my people, so extremely zealous was I for the traditions of my fathers. But when he who set me apart before I was born, and called me through his grace, was pleased to reveal his Son to me, in order that I might preach him among the Gentiles, I did not confer with flesh and blood, nor did I go up to Jerusalem to those who were apostles before me, . . . (1:14-17)

While there may have been a hint of Gnosticism in Paul's assertion that he and Jesus had merged, it appears he said this to increase his political authority rather than to reveal his self-awareness: "I have been crucified with Christ; it is no longer I who live, but Christ who lives in me; and the life I now live in the flesh I live by faith in the Son of God, . . ." (2:19-20)

Paul charges that all who received circumcision were "severed from Christ," and he completely misrepresents James' earlier ruling on the subject, as he accuses others of desiring "to have you circumcised that they may glory in your flesh." (6:13) Claiming to have a "new creation," Paul once again closes with his self-identification with Jesus, "the world has been crucified to me, and I to the world." Paul is advocating that Jews must abandon their religion if they are to accept the gospel of Jesus.

Acts (16:9) relates that Paul received a vision during the night in which a man of Macedonia invited him to come help them. It appears that the invitation was physically delivered and that funds may have been provided for his travel and upkeep. In any case, Paul diverts his mission toward Macedonia where the missionary party traveled through Neapolis and on to Philippi—"the leading city of the district of Macedonia, and a Roman colony."

Paul founded a Pauline congregation in Philippi to which he later addressed his letter to the Philippians. In it, Paul immediately condemns those "who preach Christ from envy and rivalry . . . out of partisanship . . . thinking to afflict me . . ." (1:15-17)

Paul concludes his letter with his appreciation for financial support, an issue that will reappear throughout his ministry, "Yet it was kind of you to share my trouble . . . in giving and receiving . . . Not that I seek the gift; but I seek the fruit which increases to your credit. . . having received . . . the gifts you sent, a fragrant offering, a sacrifice acceptable and pleasing to God." (4:14-18)

Paul and his followers then visited Lydia and passed on through Amphipolis and Apollonia to Thessalonica, where there was a synagogue. Paul preached there for three weeks and converted some of the Jews, "a great many of the devout Greeks, and not a few of the leading women." Paul was denounced and had to flee after being confronted by a crowd. His accusers pursued him, and Paul escaped by boat to Athens.

Paul arrived in Athens and began to preach in the Jewish synagogues and was invited to address the people at the Areopagus.[76] Although most of the Greeks mocked Paul and his teaching of the resurrection, some were converted and formed a Pauline congregation in the city.

Traveling next to Corinth, Paul met a Jewish couple named Aquila and Priscilla—recently arrived after having been expelled with all other Jews from Rome by Emperor Claudius—who invited him to stay in their home. He remained for one-and-a-half years and organized a Pauline congregation. Paul was accused and brought to trial before the Roman proconsul, Gallio—who found that the matter was religious, not civil, and ordered Paul released.[77]

While staying in Corinth, Paul wrote one of his first epistles to the Thessalonians. Contrary to later letters, Paul does not yet question James' doctrine of justification by works, and he includes references

---

[76] The Areopagus is a large outcropping of rock located northwest of the Acropolis—which had functioned in earlier times as a court where criminal cases were tried.

[77] Paul's arrival in Corinth can be dated around 50-51 CE, as that was the year that emperor Claudius, who had earlier granted special privileges, expelled all Jews from Rome. In addition, an inscription found at Delphi establishes Gallio's one-year term as proconsul as beginning in the spring of 51 or 52 CE.

that are clearly Gnostic and reflecting influences of the Way. He says, "For you are all sons of light and sons of the day; we are not of the night or of darkness . . . let us . . . put on the breastplate of faith and love, and for a helmet the hope of salvation." (1 Thessalonians 5:5-8)

Paul continues, "Do not quench the Spirit, do not despise prophesying, but test everything; hold fast what is good, abstain from every form of evil." (5:19-21)

In his letter to the Thessalonians, Paul introduces the novel concept of the living also being lifted into heaven with the dead which will become known as the "rapture."

> For this we declare to you by the word of the Lord, that we who are alive, who are left until the coming of the Lord, shall not precede those who have fallen asleep. For the Lord himself will descend from heaven with a cry of command, with the archangel's call, and with the sound of the trumpet of God. And the dead in Christ will rise first; then we who are alive, who are left, shall be caught up together with them in the clouds to meet the Lord in the air; and so we shall always be with the Lord.

Paul concludes with a denial that his ministry was motivated by "greed" and bragged about "how holy and righteous and blameless was our behavior to you believers; . . ." (2:5-9)

Paul took Aquila and Priscilla with him when he returned by sea to Syria. Paul then departed for Ephesus, where he established a base for his ministry in the area, before traveling to Antioch and the region of Galatia to check on his congregations. (Acts (18:18-23)

When Paul returned to Ephesus, he learned that Apollos, an eloquent and educated Jew from Alexandria had passed through on his way to Corinth to teach the gospel of Jesus. Paul encountered some followers of Apollos and learned that they baptized with water and the washing of the body. They were not acquainted with Paul's version of the baptism of the Holy Spirit in the name of Jesus. Paul rented a hall in Ephesus and preached there for two more years. (Acts 18:25-28)

It was during this period that Paul wrote his first Letter to the Corinthians who had come under the influence of the knowledgeable and well-spoken Apollos. Paul addresses himself to the "quarreling among" the congregation, where some say they "belong to Paul" and others to Apollos, that he "planted" and Apollos "watered." For the first time in his epistles, Paul's attack is not on the "circumcision party" and its justification by works, but upon the Gnostic teaching brought from Alexandria by Apollos. Paul says he was not sent by Christ to teach with "eloquent wisdom" and asks:

> Has not God made foolish the wisdom of the world? For since, in the wisdom of God, the world did not know God through wisdom, it pleased God through the folly of what we preach to save those who believe. For Jews demand signs and Greeks seek wisdom, but we preach Christ crucified, a stumbling-block to Jews and folly to Gentiles, . . . (1 Corinthians 1:20-23)

Paul said he "did not come proclaiming to you the testimony of God in lofty words or wisdom . . . that your faith might not rest in the wisdom of men but in the power of God." (2:1-5)

Although Paul does not directly disparage Apollo's message, he does elevate his own: "For though you have countless guides in Christ, you do not have many fathers. For I became your father in Christ Jesus through the gospel."

Seeking to exercise control over every practice, Paul dictates to his congregations:

> Is it proper for a woman to pray to God with her head uncovered? Does not nature itself teach you that for a man to wear long hair is degrading to him, but if a woman has long hair, it is her pride? . . . If anyone is disposed to be contentious, we recognize no other practice, nor do the churches of God." (11:13-16)

> As in all the churches of the saints, the women should keep silence in the churches. For they are not permitted to speak, but should be subordinate, as even the law says. If there is

anything they desire to know, let them ask their husbands at home. For it is shameful for a woman to speak in church. . .. [What] I am writing to you is a command of the Lord. (14:33-37)

One wonders what Mary Magdalene, who was still ministering to her own "churches of the saints," would have had to say to Paul's misogynistic diatribe about women? What would Jesus have thought?

Making a strong demand to the Corinthians for financial support, Paul proclaims:

This is my defense to those who would examine me. Do we not have the right to our food and drink? . . . Or is it only Barnabas and I who have no right to refrain from working for a living? Who serves as a soldier at his own expense? Who plants a vineyard without eating any of its fruit? Who tends a flock without getting some milk? . . . If we have sown spiritual good among you, is it too much if we reap your material benefits? If others share this rightful claim upon you, do not we still more? . . . In the same way, the Lord commanded that those who proclaim the gospel should get their living by the gospel. (9:5-14)

Emperor Claudius died in 54 CE, and his edict expelling Jews from Rome ended. Aquila and Priscilla probably left Ephesus and returned to Rome at this time, adding their presence to the Pauline converts who were gathering there.

Responding to local challenges to his leadership, Paul undertook a quick maintenance tour of his congregations in Macedonia and Greece. It may have been when Paul was en route to Corinth that he wrote his second Letter to the Corinthians, in which he becomes even more strident in his thinly disguised attacks on the leadership of James and the ministry of Apollo.

For if someone comes and preaches another Jesus than the one we preached, or if you receive a different spirit from the one you received, or if you accept a different gospel from the one you accepted, you submit to it readily enough.

I think that I am not in the least inferior to these superlative apostles. (2 Corinthians 11:4-5)

And what I do I will continue to do, in order to undermine the claim of those who would like to claim that in their boasted mission they work on the same terms as we do. For such men are false apostles, deceitful workmen, disguising themselves as apostles of Christ. And no wonder, for even Satan disguises himself as an angel of light. So, it is not strange if his servants also disguise themselves as servants of righteousness. Their end will correspond to their deeds. (11:12-15)

It was while staying in Corinth during this period that Paul sent his most important epistle (from a theological standpoint) to the Romans. Paul soon resolved to press on to Jerusalem and ultimately to Rome. Paul visited his congregation in Philippi and departed by ship. He returned to Caesarea in Judea by way of Asia Minor and Tyre, where he was warned against returning to Jerusalem. Luke may have been with Paul during this period, as this portion of Acts is written in the first person.

The Core of Truth in the Convoluted, Confusing, and Conflicted Gospel of Paul

To understand the religious doctrine taught by Paul during his ministry, we should probably start with the essential element that has allowed it to persevere for 2,000 years. While Paul may have altered and reversed other lessons he learned during his years with the Way and from James and the Congregation of the Poor, he held true to the most basic part of the Gospel of Jesus—Love. Paul expresses in it most simply in Galatians (4:14): "For the whole law is fulfilled in one word, 'You shall love your neighbor as yourself.'"

Perhaps the most poetic words Paul ever wrote were about love—words that have been repeated by ministers during countless marriages over the centuries:

Love is patient and kind; love is not jealous or boastful; it is not arrogant or rude. Love does not insist on its own way; it is not irritable or resentful; it does not rejoice at wrong but rejoices in the right. Love bears all things, believes all things, hopes all things, endures all things.

When I was a child, I spoke like a child, I thought like a child, I reasoned like a child; when I became a man, I gave up childish ways. For now, we see in a mirror dimly, but then face to face. Now I know in part; then I shall understand fully, even as I have been fully understood. So, faith, hope, love abide, these three; but the greatest of these is love. (1 Corinthians 13:4-13)

It was in other foundational areas, however—such as the divinity of Jesus, the physical resurrection, and justification by faith—where Paul diverged entirely from the Way of Jesus and diverted onto his own path. Even more so than James and the Congregation of the Poor in Jerusalem, Paul created his own religion based on the covenant prophesized by Jeremiah (31:31):

Behold the days are coming, says the Lord, when I will make a new covenant with the house of Israel and the house of Judah, not like the covenant I made with their fathers when I took them by the hand to bring them out of the land of Egypt. My covenant which they broke, though I was their husband, says the Lord. But this is the covenant which I will make with the house of Israel after those days, says the Lord: I will put My Law within them, and I will write it upon their hearts; and I will be their God, and they shall be My people . . . for I will forgive their iniquity, and I will remember their sin no more.

Perhaps the greatest failure of Paul's ministry of the Way was his smooth and easy Pharisaic view of righteousness. Living the spirit of the law, rather than its letter, in a loving and righteous manner was the essence of the Way. Paul changed that and said, "He who through faith is righteous shall live." In doing so, he condemned his followers to a spiritual death.

Was Paul Influenced by Gnosticism?

Perhaps reflecting the Gnostic elements of his education about the Way at Qumran following his conversion, Paul wrote in First Corinthians:

> Yet among the mature we do impart wisdom, although it is not a wisdom of this age or of the rulers of this age, who are doomed to pass away. But we impart a secret and hidden wisdom of God, which God decreed before the ages for our glorification. (2:6),

At least initially, Paul demonstrated some Gnostic insights, and he often begins a discussion with a certain spiritualism before using it as a springboard for the imposition of his own convoluted dogma. In addition, he uses some of the visionary imagery of Gnosticism—which is intended to be understood allegorically—to substantiate his apostolic leadership.

Paul talks about being taken up into the "third heaven" in Second Corinthians (12:3) where he "heard things that cannot be told, which man may not utter." In religious cosmology, the Third Heaven is the abode of God. If meant literally, Paul is equating himself with the angels as being in the presence of God; however, it is Jesus who God "raised . . . from the dead and made him sit at his right hand in the heavenly places." (Ephesians 1:20) Paul continually makes the case that God accomplished immeasurably great power in Jesus, which power has been transferred to Paul as his only apostle with the authority to translate what Jesus (and God) really meant to say.

Paul, the Pharisee, Creates the Quick and Easy Justification by Faith

We earlier reviewed the dispute between James and Paul about whether justification should be based on works or faith, and we saw in his Letter to the Romans how Paul started with James's view and then legalistically twisted it to arrive at a diametrically opposite conclusion. It is understandable why Paul would seek to preach a gospel that was easier for his Gentile audiences to adopt and follow. He was after all trained as a Pharisee. Would Jesus have agreed with Paul's version of justification? Highly unlikely. Jesus (as was James, Simeon, and Joseph) was a Doer of the Law, and for them, the Law was pure and simple. They believed in the two primary commandments of the Torah, to love God and to love others.

Jesus's teaching was that of the original Hasidean: *Hesed* (Piety to God) and *Zaddik* (Righteousness to fellow man)—the Way of Light. To them, the "Law" did not include the thousands and thousands of nitpicking words in the Oral Torah that had been erected by the Pharisees as a "fence around the Law"—which only they could interpret.[78] Paul was being entirely deceptive when he repeatedly hammered away about having to follow the entire "Law," when he was referring to the Oral Torah of the Pharisees—which was totally rejected by Jesus, James, and the Way of Righteousness.

From Paul's view as a Pharisee (who had created the massive body of oral law), it was impossible to fulfill every demand the law might impose. Paul taught that those (Jews) who were under the (expansive) law were cursed and were, therefore, condemned to sin. His using the Pharisaic view of the law as an argument was a shibboleth which ignored the far narrower view of the law expressed by Jesus, James, the Poor, and the Way of Righteousness. The followers of the Way lived simple lives of poverty and conscience. They knew exactly what was required to fulfill their vows of righteousness—they did not need the law or anyone to explain what it required, or how they could avoid it.

By making faith the standard for justification and salvation, Paul made a new religion out of whole cloth. By replacing his own Pharisee standard of living within the written and oral law with a continuing cycle of sin and forgiveness, Paul did away with the need for an active conscience and self-examination. By eliminating the Spirit of Wisdom from his religion, he smothered the soul of the Gospel of

---

[78] The Pharisees' oral Torah is known as *halakha*, which means a law which is not directly drawn from the Bible and which may follow the "traditions of the fathers" or "the elders." Its plural is *halakhot*, and the Osim made a word play when describing the Pharisees as *dorshe halaqot*, meaning "seekers after smooth things." This uncomplimentary label uses the root word, *halaqot* to mean lies or falsehoods.

the Way of Righteousness. In making simple faith the standard, he misuses a brief quotation from Habakkuk, "The just person shall live by faith." Incongruously, it was the Way's *Commentary on Habakkuk* that seemingly condemns Paul as the "Spouter of Lies."

Paul, Who Never Met Jesus in Person, Creates the Theory of a Physical Resurrection to Justify His Apostleship

The physical resurrection was discussed in the chapter following Jesus's crucifixion, and the primary question remaining is why Paul saw fit to preach something that was so contrary to the beliefs of the Way and Jesus's Congregation of the Poor from which he had a commission? Paul himself, in First Corinthians (15:44), makes the distinction between the spiritual and the physical body. Paul's vision of the physical resurrection most likely had to do with the fact that Paul did not personally know and follow Jesus during his lifetime. If Paul's vision of Jesus was to be accepted as his authority to be an apostle, it had to be as powerful as possible. A purely spiritual appearance, vision, or dream would not be enough—many people experienced them. Adding to the confusion, Paul made an argument about the resurrection of Jesus using this epitome of circular reasoning:

> Now if Christ is preached as raised from the dead, how can some of you say that there is no resurrection of the dead? But if there is no resurrection of the dead, then Christ has not been raised; if Christ has not been raised, then our preaching is in vain and your faith is in vain. We are even found to be misrepresenting God, because we testified of God that he raised Christ, whom he did not raise if it is true that the dead are not raised. For if the dead are not raised then Christ has not been raised. If Christ has not been raised, your faith is futile, and you are still in your sins. (1 Corinthians 15:12-17)

As wise as Jesus must have been, even he may have scratched his head over Paul's convoluted reasoning. Here, perhaps, is the seed from which the psychologically harmful concept of original

Paul, the Pharisee, Goes Off the Path and Creates His Own Religion

sin sprouted and the theory that only through faith in Jesus and his bodily resurrection can sins be forgiven.

Paul was a Pharisee, who started with a belief in a resurrection of the dead at the end of time when Israel would be restored to its former glory. At that glorious moment, all those who had remained true to God and the Law in life would be bodily raised up from Sheol (Greek *Hades*) the place of darkness where all of the dead rested, irrespective of the good or evil they did during their lives. This is the "standing up of the bones" prophesized by Ezekiel," whereupon the righteous would share in the Age to Come.

The Pharisees did not believe, however, that anybody immediately went to Heaven upon death, no matter how righteous he or she might have been in life. The novel belief by modern Christians that good people automatically get to go to Heaven upon death has evolved from their faith in the bodily resurrection of Jesus as taught by Paul. The corollary, of course is that those people who were bad during their lives must spend the remainder of eternity in Hades, or Hell as we call it today.[79]

Because Jesus died by the "cursed" crucifixion and would have otherwise been denied resurrection at the end of time, Paul had to figure out a way to make it acceptable. Therefore, Jesus chose the most shameful death for the forgiveness of our sins. His resurrection paid the price for all Christians who believe in the bodily resurrection of Jesus, and accept him as their personal savior, to join him in Heaven after death. Catholics might have to tarry for a time in Purgatory, but all believing Christians get a free ticket—no matter how often or egregiously they sin—if they continue to earnestly pray for forgiveness.

Christians are freed from the Law and its burdens; however, they are not free to entertain any doubts about the divinity of Jesus or his bodily resurrection. Today, to hear the sermons preached at Christian funerals, every believer immediately passes through the "Pearly Gates" to be with Jesus.

---

[79] Images of the tortures to be endured eternally in a burning hell primarily derives from literary—rather than biblical—sources, such as Dante's *Inferno*. The mention of hell in Mark (9:44) is based on Paul's unique "either or" view of heaven and hell, where one goes immediately after death depending on whether one has accepted Jesus Christ as his or her personal savior.

The orthodox Pauline authors of the New Testament Gospels converted Paul's spiritual resurrection into a physical one and ruled that doctrine to be the only acceptable one. All other beliefs became a heresy. Their reason for doing so was purely political. Since Jesus appeared only to their apostles, including Paul, the orthodox relied on this "fact" to justify their authority to rule over all congregations of the Roman Catholic Church and to decide all theological issues. For them, Peter and Paul created the Church; Peter preached a physical resurrection, and he was the first bishop of the congregation in Rome, thereby creating a lineage of popes that continues to this day; and the preaching of Paul superseded the teaching of Jesus. The Gnostics, however, begged to differ.

Was Jesus the Son of God, or Was His a Spiritual Ascension?

In Judaism at the time of Jesus, only Moses and Enoch had been taken into heaven to be with God. Given their faith in Jesus as the suffering Son of Man Messiah, the Congregation of the Poor may have shared a belief that Jesus ascended into heaven in the same manner. They did not, however, believe that he physically rose from the dead and shared supper with his followers, no matter what the later Pauline Gospels would say.

While the Nazoreans probably accepted that Jesus had been the expected Son of Man Messiah who suffered for the redemption of humanity, they would never have considered him to have been the "Son of God," or in any way Divine. Paul, however, following his vision and conversion, immediately began to proclaim that Jesus was the "Son of God." In Philippians, he introduces the godhood of Jesus as a concept that cannot be understood without the crucifixion:

> Have this in mind among yourselves, which you have in Christ Jesus, who though he was in the form of God, did not count equality with God a thing to be grasped, but emptied himself, taking the form of a servant, being born in the likeness of men. And being found in human form he humbled himself and became obedient unto death, even death on a cross. (2:5-8)

Paul, Who Missed Out on The Last Supper, Creates The Blood Covenant of the Eucharist

There is also the matter of the Last Supper. Inasmuch as the New Testament Gospels were written well after his epistles, the sacrament of consuming Jesus's blood and body undoubtedly originated with Paul. At least it appears he took credit for introducing it.

> For I received from the Lord what I also delivered to you, that the Lord Jesus on the night when he was betrayed took bread, and when he had given thanks, he broke it, and said, "This is my body which is broken for you. Do this in remembrance of me." In the same way also the cup, after supper, saying, "this cup is the new covenant in my blood. Do this, as often as you drink it, in remembrance of me. For as often as you eat this bread and drink the cup, you proclaim the Lord's death until he comes. (1 Corinthians 11:23-26)

The writers of the Way at Qumran were probably referring to Paul, whom they referred to as the Spouter of Lies, when they condemned his "Unrighteousness" and ridiculed his building a "Worthless City upon blood and erecting an Assembly upon Lying, for the sake of (his) Glory, tiring out Many with a Worthless Service and instructing them in works of Lying, . . ."

Given the revulsion that Jesus and the Way would have had for drinking the blood of living things—relating it to the spirit of the animal—it is unimaginable that Jesus would have ever initiated such a sacrament, or that it would have been practiced by James and the Congregation of the Poor. To the contrary, the sacrament was created by Paul so his Gentile congregations could compete with other mystery cults in the Roman world at the time in which such rituals were common. Particularly among the Greeks, the ritualistic pouring out of wine and breaking of bread was a common ritual, and the cult of Dionysus (god of the vine) was prevalent at the time and in the areas where Paul preached. For the Gentiles to whom Paul addressed his ministry, "Christianity" was just another of the many mystery cults that appeared in their midst, and Paul had to make it as competitive, familiar, and interesting as possible, if he was to attract followers.

Paul's Baptism of the Holy Spirit Eliminates the Wisdom of Sophia From His Religion

Another innovation of Paul was the baptism of the Holy Spirit. Entirely abandoning the Way-Gnostic concept that equated the Spirit with Wisdom, Sophia, femininity, and knowledge, Paul created a baptism by a neutered Holy Spirit as the Breath of God to unite his congregations.

> For just as the body is one and has many members, and all the members of the body, though many, are one body, so it is with Christ. For by one Spirit we were all baptized into one body—Jews or Greeks, slaves or free—and all were made to drink of one Spirit. (1 Corinthians 12:12)

Paul's baptism resembled that experienced by initiates into the pagan cults of the time, and it was through this baptism that converts were reborn into a new mystery group in which they would have a new life. Acting through the Holy Spirit, everyone—slave or free—would have the opportunity to play differing roles in the congregation:

> To one is given through the Spirit the utterance of wisdom, and to another the utterance of knowledge according to the same Spirit, to another faith by the same Spirit, to another gifts of healing by the one Spirit, to another the working of miracles, to another prophecy, to another the ability to distinguish between spirits, to another various kinds of tongues, to another the interpretation of tongues. (1 Corinthians 12:8)

Luke's later depiction in Acts of the Holy Spirit descending upon the followers of Jesus shortly after his crucifixion was undoubtedly influenced by Paul's imagination of it during his ministry. For Paul, the question was: Did Jesus personally appear to Paul during his hallucination on the road to Damascus, or was it the Holy Spirit?

Paul's Dispute With James Created Christian Anti-Semitism

Paul's derision of the "circumcision party" and other comments about the Congregation of the Poor were probably politically or dogmatically motivated, but they also may represent a form of self-hatred of himself as a former Pharisee, who participated in the acts he later accused the "Jews" of doing. Writing to one of his congregations, Paul says,

> For you, brethren, become imitators of the churches of God in Christ Jesus which are in Judea; for you suffered the same things from your own countrymen as they did from the Jews, who killed both the Lord Jesus and the prophets, and drove us out, and displeased God and oppose all men by hindering us from speaking to the Gentiles that they may be saved—so as always to fill up the measure of their sins. But God's wrath has come upon them at last! (1 Thessalonians 1:14-16)

Statements such as this undoubtedly influenced the writers of the Gospels who created stories that made it appear that the Jews were united in their opposition to Jesus and that they forced Pilate to crucify Jesus. The Jews rejected the stone that "has become the cornerstone." Although the Way and Jesus certainly opposed Pharisaic doctrine, the woes of Pharisaic hypocrisy expressed by the gospel writers in Matthew (23) are over the top.

Writing at the time of Constantine, Eusebius said, "The Divine Justice for their crimes against Christ and his Apostles finally overtook them, totally destroying the whole generation of these evildoers from the earth . . . Such was the vengeance that followed the guilt and Impiety of the Jews against the Christ of God."

The anti-Semitic element of Roman Christianity that says "the Jews killed Jesus" led to inquisitions, exiles, pogroms, and other untold suffering over the millennia, and finally, as an element, to the Holocaust of European Jewry during the twentieth century.

Paul's Unique Theory of Salvation and Forgiveness of Sin Eases Access into Heaven

The appeal of Paul's smooth path to salvation has been supplemented over the millennia by the faithful being able to identify with Paul as a fellow sinner. If Paul could do all the terrible things he admitted to and still be saved, so can modern sinners. All one must do is to earnestly pray for forgiveness each night, before getting up the next day to start sinning all over again—if one's faith remains intact. Thus, one is guaranteed entrance into Heaven following death, should one die before they awaken. Of course, it helps if one gives generously whenever the collection plate is passed through the congregation. Given everything we have learned, it would not be difficult to imagine Paul as a televangelist today attracting thousands to his ministry—and counseling the president about political matters.

In summary, Paul's gospel was deceptively simple: We're all sinners; Jesus, as God, came down to Earth in human form to die a shameful death on the cross as a sacrifice for our sins; and everyone who believes this fable as a matter of faith (irrespective of works) will be forgiven and saved by the Holy Spirit and will join Jesus in Heaven following death. Paul's theology is not simple, however, as it has confused, misled, distorted, and obscured the true mission of Jesus for 2,000 years. Fortunately, the essential message of love taught by Jesus continued to shine through the centuries of darkness until our lifetime when the miraculous revelation of books from the ancient past provides a better understanding of the ministry of Jesus.

What Ever Happened to Paul?

Arriving in Jerusalem during the summer of 56 CE, Paul was confronted with the fact that the Congregation of the Poor had expanded substantially under the leadership of James *and* that its members were angry that Paul continued to preach his own religion in synagogues and to proselytize Jews as well as Gentiles in violation of his agreement and mission.

Paul agreed to accompany four men who were under vows into the Temple and to pay for all of them to shave their heads and to purify themselves for seven days in the presence of God, before he presented himself openly in the city. Paul was, however, recognized in the Temple and was mistakenly thought to have brought a Gentile into the prohibited area. A riot ensued and the crowd was beating Paul when Roman soldiers from the Antonia Tower intervened and rescued him. (Acts 21:26)

Paul was shackled and was being prepared for questioning by scourging (whipping), when he asked, "Is it lawful for you to scourge a man who is a Roman citizen and uncondemned?" Paul was delivered over to the Jewish Sanhedrin for examination. Knowing that the Sanhedrin was composed of both Sadducees and Pharisees, Paul abandoned Jesus and cried out, "Brethren, I am a Pharisee, a son of Pharisees; with respect to the hope and the resurrection of the dead I am on trial."

As the resurrection was a basic tenet of the Pharisees—that was rejected by the Sadducees—Paul was able to divide the group. The Pharisees, under his former teacher, Gamaliel, said that they found nothing wrong, and Paul was returned to Roman custody. According to Paul, he had a vision that night: "the Lord stood by him and said, 'Take courage, for as you have testified about me at Jerusalem, so you must bear witness also at Rome.'"

Hearing the following day that there was a plot underway to kill Paul, his nephew (the son of his sister) intervened and Paul was moved to Caesarea.[80] The high priest Ananias traveled there to file charges against Paul as a "pestilent fellow, an agitator among all the Jews throughout the world, and a ringleader of the sect of the Nazarenes." Paul defended himself to the Roman procurator Felix, and his case was continued.

Although Paul lived under comfortable conditions in the palace of Herod Agrippa II in Caesarea for nearly two years, he was totally disowned by the Nazoreans. While James may have originally

---

[80] The nephew is believed to have been Julius Archelaus, who was the son of Paul's sister, Cypros—who may have been married to Helcias, the Temple Treasurer. Cypros is a Herodian name, having been that of the mother of Herod the Great. If this is true, it explains the easy access enjoyed by Paul's relatives to the Roman authorities *and* the comfortable way he was subsequently hosted by the Romans.

The Parting of the Way of Righteousness

forgiven Paul for the personal violence done to him, as the bishop of the Congregation of the Poor, James did nothing to defend Paul. Apparently, he could not approve of Paul's heretical ministry and his renewed alliance with the Pharisees, Herodians, and Romans.

A new procurator named Porcius Festus arrived in 59 CE and went up to Jerusalem. The Sadducean leaders requested that Festus return Paul to the city to face his accusers. When asked if he were willing to go, Paul replied "I am standing before Caesar's tribunal, where I ought to be tried . . . I appeal to Caesar." (Acts 25:10-11) Paul's decision may have also been based on his desire to visit his growing group of friends and converts in Rome.

While Paul was waiting for transportation to Rome, Herod Agrippa II arrived at Caesarea with his sister-consort Berenice II.[81] (It was Agrippa who would latter conspire in the judicial murder of James the Just.) After listening to Paul, Agrippa found that, "The man has done nothing to deserve death or imprisonment." Although he could have been released, Paul chose to argue his case before a friendly emperor rather than to confront the followers of Jesus in Jerusalem and Judea who despised him and his heretical doctrines.

Paul embarked to Rome in the summer of 60 CE. An attempt was made to winter at Crete, but was frustrated by a storm, and the boat carrying him was shipwrecked on Malta. After three months, another passing boat from Alexandria picked up the company and conveyed it to the Italian port of Puteoli, where Paul's group continued to Rome by road.

While waiting another two years for the emperor to hear his appeal, Paul was permitted to occupy his own comfortable rented apartment. It was probably at this time that Paul struck up a correspondence with Annaeus Seneca, Nero's teacher and advisor.[82] Although not included in the New Testament, *The Epistles of Paul the Apostle to Seneca, with Seneca's to Paul*, was believed to be authoritative by some early Church leaders. Seneca writes Paul that he had shared Paul's letters with Nero, who was "extremely pleased with

---

[81] The ever resourceful and sensual Bernice would soon become Titus's mistress, while he commanded the Roman army in defeating the Zealot revolution.

[82] Nero forced Seneca to commit suicide in 65 CE.

the sentiments of your Epistles." Paul may have been encouraged to convert Seneca and Nero by Poppaea, Nero's wife, who was reportedly a supporter.[83]

The New Testament does not tell us what happened with Paul's case, as Acts abruptly ends with: "And he lived there two whole years at his own expense, and welcomed all who came to him, preaching the kingdom of God and teaching about the Lord Jesus Christ quite openly and unhindered." (28:30) It is almost as if the editors of the New Testament decided that what followed should not be revealed and simply cut the scroll at that point.

Thus, Paul goes missing from Acts around 62 CE, which is a critical year, because it is at or near this time that James is murdered in Jerusalem. We have no way of knowing whether Paul remained in Rome or if he ever returned to Jerusalem, but the situation in both cities soon became very violent.

A great fire broke out in Rome in 64 CE that burned for nine days, destroying much of the city. Some Romans blamed Nero for the fire, and (according to Tacitus) "to get rid of the report, Nero fastened the guilt and inflicted the most exquisite tortures on a class hated for their abominations, called Chrestians by the populace." It was during this period of persecution that Pauline tradition holds that Peter was crucified and Paul was beheaded in Rome.

In 66 CE, the Zealots—who were closely connected to the Way and the Nazoreans—revolted in Judea after thousands of Jews were slaughtered while protesting the confiscation of Temple treasure by the Roman procurator and the imposition of a special tribute by Nero to pay for his rebuilding of Rome. Nero dispatched General Vespasian with four legions of Roman soldiers to put down the revolution; however, Nero died in 68 CE and several emperor candidates died in fighting for his succession. Vespasian won out and became emperor in 69 CE, and Roman troops under his son Titus were finally able to take Jerusalem in 70 CE. The fortress at Masada, however, was not subdued until 74 CE.

---

[83] Poppaea died after complications from a miscarriage of pregnancy, which may have resulted from her being kicked in the abdomen by Nero during an argument.

The Parting of the Way of Righteousness

Did Paul suffer under Nero's persecution? As a Herodian and friend of Nero's household, Paul probably escaped. If so, what was he doing during these missing years when the war raged in Judea? There are orthodox Pauline traditions that have Paul peacefully preaching in Spain and England and establishing congregations there for several more years before returning to Rome and being beheaded by Nero. If this is true, why aren't these voyages reported by Luke, his biographer, in Acts?

Peter's story is likewise mysterious, and there is a great likelihood that Peter never traveled to Rome. The actual truth about the fate of Peter and Paul may never be known; however, the Roman Catholic Church *was* established in Rome in their names, and the consequences of that fact are a matter of history. It was during the following period that the Rome congregation accommodated to Roman rule and began to assert authority over all other congregations in matters of doctrine and practice. All of this contradicted the events taking place contemporaneously in Judea and Jerusalem, where other followers of Jesus and the Way were fighting for their lives and freedom against Roman tyranny.

Paul's ruling in Romans regarding the respect he insisted be shown to governing authorities resulted in his congregation in Rome receiving favored treatment, while the members of the Way in Jerusalem were being slaughtered by Roman troops.

> Let every person be subject to the government authorities. For there is no authority except from God, and those that exist have been instituted by God. Therefore, he who resists the authorities resists what God has appointed, and those who resist will incur judgment. For rulers are not a terror to good conduct, but to bad. Would you have no fear of him who is in authority? Then do what is good, and you will receive his approval, for he is God's servant for your good. But if you do wrong, be afraid, for he does not bear the sword in vain; he is the servant of God to execute his wrath on the wrong doer. Therefore, one must be subject, not only to avoid God's wrath but also for the sake of conscience. For the same reason you also pay taxes,

for the authorities are ministers of God, attending to this very thing. Pay all of them their dues, taxes to whom taxes are due, revenue to whom revenue is due, respect to whom respect is due, honor to whom honor is due. (13:1-4)

By this injunction, Paul—the Herodian and Roman collaborator par excellence—married the religion he created to secular rule. This theological-political coupling influenced the later writing of the Gospels and established a special relationship between the Pauline Christian Church and ruling authorities for the next 2,000 years.

The Paulines "Fix the Books" and Create the Gospels

With the destruction of Jerusalem and the Temple, the dispersion of the Way of Righteousness, and the final defeat of the last Zealots in 135 CE, the composition of Christian congregations, which were once predominately Jewish and Gnostic—particularly in Egypt and Syria—became increasingly Gentile, until the point when Jews were no longer included or welcomed. Paul's analogy in Romans (11:18-23) of new "Christians" being grafted onto the tree of Judaism resulted in the branch growing into a larger tree, which stunted the original in its shadow. In Galatians, Paul said it was the members of his congregations who were the true Children of Abraham: "So you see that it is men of faith who are the sons of Abraham."[84] (3:7)

It was in Rome and during the immediate aftermath of the destruction of Jerusalem and the Temple in 70 CE that work commenced to implement Paul's doctrine for Gentile Christianity. Among the first requirements was the preparation of proselytizing documents to be copied and disbursed to other congregations around the Mediterranean. Rome became the headquarters that attracted the most literate of those who had been converted to Roman Christianity.

There is no evidence that Paul was still around, but an unknown author, or group of authors, working with a variety of sources,

---

[84] It is very likely that because of Claudius's earlier decree expelling all Jews from Rome and because of its very large slave population, the Rome congregation had a much higher percentage of Gentiles to begin with.

began to fabricate what would ultimately be known as the Gospel of Mark. Paul's traveling companion and biographer, Luke may have been present and may have contributed some material, including that he had accumulated to prepare Acts. Luke may also have provided copies of Paul's letters and other writings containing Paul's theology.

We saw earlier how Jeremiah and a few writers and editors were able to assemble a revised Torah from a group of disparate writings in a very short period. Remembering that there were hundreds of thousands of books contained in the Alexandria library and that Rome was the literate center of a vast empire in which numerous authors wrote a wide variety of literature in the Greek and Roman languages, it is not difficult to imagine how an author, or group of authors were able to "fix the books" and quickly draft the rather short and somewhat vacuous gospel stories about the ministry of Paul. In some respects, had things turned out differently, the fictional collection could have been titled, "The Travels and Perils of Paul."

It is generally believed that the author of Luke later copied much of Mark in preparing his own version of the Gospels, along with Acts sometime during the next two decades. The Gospels do not directly include the destruction of Jerusalem and the Temple inasmuch as the Gospels are limited to the ministry and life of Jesus; however, Mark does allude to the devastation (13:1) when Jesus prophesizes about the Temple, "Do you see these great buildings? There will not be left here one stone upon another, that will not be thrown down." The "little apocalypse" that immediately follows probably refers to the Zealot war. Acts does not mention the destruction of the Temple because its timeline abruptly ends in 62 CE—while Paul was still in Rome awaiting his appeal.

There is another possibility. Since the Gospel of Matthew was the only one deemed authoritative by the followers of Judas Thomas, who carried the Gospel of the Way to the Middle East, and because it was traditionally attributed to Jesus's younger brother, Joseph (Barnabas), Matthew may have started as a basic document written in Hebrew that was translated into Greek by Mark and later added to and revised by the Pauline authors to conform with their other gospels. The placement of Matthew as the first of the gospels also provides some evidence of its priority.

Josephus was present at, and described in detail, Titus's triumph in celebration of the defeat of the Zealots in Judea. Also, among the crowd watching the spectacle in Rome may have been those who had gathered to create the Gospels. Writing in Greek for Greek-speaking congregations in the East, these writers must have coexisted uneasily among their Latin-speaking neighbors in a nation that had just fought a bloody war against the writers' religious compatriots in Judea. It was their task to create parables and stories to convey Paul's ministry in a manner that ordinary people could understand and which the authorities would not find objectionable. In doing so, they not only had to keep Paul's theology foremost, but to also adhere to his injunction about respecting and cooperating with the Roman authorities. That they did their job well can be seen in the three Synoptic Gospels that have been successfully relied upon by Church leaders and their partners in government for 2,000 years.

Is it any wonder that all three of the Synoptic Gospels identically include Jesus's answer to the trick question about whether Jews should pay taxes to the Romans, "Render therefore unto Caesar the things which are Caesar's; and unto God the things that are God's"? (Matthew 22:15-22, Mark 12:13-17, and Luke 20:20-26)

Side-by-side comparison demonstrates that similar sections of Luke and Matthew appear in the same sequence only when they also agree with Mark. These are not large books—Mark contains only 44 pages—and the composition would not have been extraordinarily difficult. There was an abundance of written creative fiction in circulation at the time. It was demonstrated more than 100 years ago that the author of Mark used an artificial construct to tie the episodes together. Today, most religious scholars have concluded that the Gospel stories were written to present a theological philosophy, rather than to document actual historical events. And, the theology presented in these Gospels is overwhelmingly that of Paul—rather than that of Jesus, James, Simeon, Joseph, and the Congregation of the Poor, or the Way.

In addition to accommodating the Romans, the Gospels also had to minimize the role of Jesus's family in his ministry. We have seen that all four of Jesus's brothers apparently carried on the ministry of the Way after his crucifixion—which ministry was contrary to that taught by Paul. Moreover, Jesus's brothers, mother, father, and at least one sister were present at his execution and burial. Their threat to the authority of Paul and his gospel could not be allowed. Thus, Mark (3:33-35) has Jesus ignoring his mother and brothers and saying, "'Who are my mother and my brothers?' And looking around on those who sat about him, he said, 'Here are my mother and my brothers! Whoever does the will of God is my brother, and sister, and mother.'" This same statement is also included in Matthew (12:50) and Luke (8:21).

The predominate roles of brothers James and Simeon as leaders of the Way and Jesus's Congregation of the Poor is hardly mentioned in the gospels, and the leading roles of Judas Thomas and Joseph are eliminated and their names and roles were changed to confuse what little participation they are allowed.

Although the Gospel of John also derived some of the same episodes as the Synoptic Gospels from Mark, it was created for another purpose. It presented a theological approach to the Pauline doctrine, perhaps one with more appeal to eastern Gnostics. Instead of Rome, the Gospel was believed to be written between 90-110 CE at Ephesus, a city in Asia Minor where Paul had been rejected by the Christian congregation. John may have been written by a single author, but it had several subsequent editors. Given the location of its composition as being one associated in the past with members from the Congregation of the Poor, the Way, and Gnostic influences, the book may very well have been prepared to mend differences.

Long seen as separate from the three Synoptic Gospels and more difficult to compare, the Gospel of John and the Johannine epistles have found new life with the discovery of the Gnostic Gospels and the Dead Sea Scrolls. Perhaps more so than any other book in the New Testament (except for the Letter of James) John contains language almost identical with materials of the Way found at Qumran.

In the *Community Rule* the Congregation is urged to practice or to do the truth. Jesus is reported in John (3:21) to have said, "But he who does what is true comes to the light, that it may be clearly seen that his deeds have been wrought in God." Words from the *Community Rule*, "Truth abhors the works of falsehood, and falsehood hates all the ways of truth. And their struggle is fierce for they do not walk together," compares closely with those of Jesus:

> And this is the judgment, that the light has come into the world, and men loved darkness rather than light, because their deeds were evil. For everyone who does evil hates the light, and does not come to the light, lest his deeds should be exposed. But he who does what is true comes to the light, that it may be clearly seen that his deeds have been wrought in God. (John 3:19-21)

In the *Community Rule*, members of the Congregation are called "witnesses of the truth." In John (5:33), Jesus says, "You sent me to John, and he has borne witness to the truth" and in (18:37), he says, "You say that I am a king. For this I was born, and for this I have come into the world, to bear witness to the truth."

It is, however, in the battle between the forces of light and darkness that the closest parallels can be identified. "The light is with you a little longer. Walk while you have the light, lest the darkness overtake you; he who walks in darkness does not know where he goes. While you have the light, believe in the light, that you may become sons of light." (John 12:35-36) "The light shines in the darkness, and the darkness has not overcome it." (1:5) Jesus said, "I am the light of the world; he who follows me will not walk in darkness but will have the light of life." (8:12)

The First Letter of John also discusses the light of God brought by Jesus:

> this is the message we have heard from him and proclaim to you, that God is light and in him there is no darkness at all. If we say we have fellowship with him while we walk in darkness, we lie and do not live according to the truth, but if we walk in the light, as he is in the light, we have fellowship with one another, and the blood of Jesus his Son cleanses us from all sin. (1:5-7)

> He who says he is in the light and hates his brother is in the darkness still. He who loves his brother abides in the light,

and in it there is no cause for stumbling. But he who hates his brother is in the darkness and walks in the darkness, and does not know where he is going, because the darkness has blinded his eyes. (2:9-11)

The closing psalm of the *Community Rule* includes an amazing parallel in language, "All things come to pass by His knowledge; He establishes all things by His design and without Him nothing is done." John says, "all things were made through him, and without him was not anything made that was made." (1:3)

Another use of language in which John has been distinguished from the Synoptic Gospels is its introduction of the *logos*, which means word or reason. John begins with, "In the beginning was the Word (*logos*), and the Word was with God, and the Word was God." *Logos* was the term used by some Greek philosophers for a governing principle in the universe. Philo, the Jewish philosopher who lived and wrote in Alexandria during the time of Jesus—and who is associated with the Way—often identifies *logos* with Plato's world of ideas. God first created the ideal world, and this served as a blueprint for the visible world. This theory fitted in well with the passages of Scripture which represent God as creating the world by the command of a word.

In many ways, The Gospel of John serves as a latticework connecting the Roman New Testament, the Dead Sea Scrolls of the Way, and the Nag Hammadi library of the Gnostics. Just as John's book is closer in content to the books of the Osim than the Synoptic Gospels, it is also closest in content to the Gnostic Gospels.

Creation of the Roman Catholic Church in the Name of Peter and Paul

In the beginning, it was Paul's innovation of the Eucharist that attracted new Gentile converts, many of whom were without the means to gain entrance and to practice in other mystery cults; however, the communal meal enjoyed by his congregations was not restricted to consuming a symbolic wafer on Sunday morning. Initially, and perhaps drawing on the practices of the Way and the

Congregation of the Poor, the congregations would meet in secret for a potluck of meals, which they called an *agape*, or Love Feast, from a Greek word meaning "brotherly love." Rumors that the Christians ate the flesh and blood of their leader may have been the abominations mentioned by Tacitus.[85]

Just as the Way held everything in common, the Pauline congregations shared their possessions and cared for their own, particularly the widows and orphans. In Rome, the congregation began to meet secretly in the catacombs originally dug beneath the city for the burial of the dead. Tourists can still view paintings in the catacombs depicting their meals and Christian images. Jesus is not depicted on the cross, but as the gentle shepherd of his flock. The fish is the most frequent image along with the Greek word for fish, *ichthys*. The secret meaning of its letters was *Iesos Christo Theou Yios Soter*, "Jesus Christ, Son of God, Savior."

Women enjoyed a high degree of equality in the ministry of Jesus. Indeed, we have seen how he considered Mary Magdalene to be his most honored disciple. Even Paul initially said, "there is neither male nor female; for you are all one in Christ Jesus" (Galatians 3:28), before imposing doctrinal limitations on the role of women in his congregations. One of the earliest differences, however, between the Pauline congregations and the Gnostic congregations was the role of women serving in leadership roles.

Irenaeus, who served as a Roman Christian bishop in Gaul in the latter part of the second century complained about women being attracted to the Gnostic view that Grace, Wisdom, and Silence were feminine elements of the Divine. Irenaeus condemns a Gnostic initiation that blesses prophesying by women: "Behold, Grace has come upon you; open your mouth, and prophesy." The Gnostics also allowed women to act as priests in celebrating the Eucharist and to pass the cup.

Writing at or near the same time, Tertullian, an early Christian author, was outraged by Gnostic practices involving women: "These

---

[85] Two cults having monotheistic and ethical elements that coexisted at the time probably influenced the Paulines. There was Sol Invictus' halo and his birthday of December 25th, and the religion of Mithras, the Persian god, (worshipped as the protector of the empire) was celebrated with a sacrificial meal involving a ritual of bread and wine.

heretical women—how audacious they are! They have no modesty; they are bold enough to teach, to engage in argument, to enact exorcisms, to undertake cures, and, it may be, even to baptize!"

It was in the areas of marriage, divorce, sex, and procreation where the Roman Christians began to intrude into the lives (and bedrooms) of their congregants. Written into the Gospel of Matthew were words attributed to Jesus, "whoever divorces his wife, except for unchastity, and marries another, commits adultery." (19:9) Regarding celibacy, Jesus reportedly said, "there are eunuchs who have made themselves eunuchs for the sake of the kingdom of heaven. He who is able to receive this, let him receive it." (19:12)

The relationship passages were probably written to support the position taken by the unmarried Paul on the issue of marriage and celibacy when he was preaching that the end was near and that "sudden destruction" would "come like a thief in the night." Because of "the impending distress" and that "the appointed time has grown very short," Paul advises against marriage. Those already married should live as though they were single. (1 Corinthians 7:25-40) He advises that "it is well . . . to remain single as I do." (7:8) Fortunately, Christians have continued to marry and produce children for the past 2,000 years.

Early on, the debate about the carnal sins of Adam and Eve raged within the Roman Church. Should Christians live strictly ascetic lives, like Jesus and Paul, or should they live as others did in their societies? Was sex invented by Satan to tempt men and women to disobey the commandments of God? In answering these questions, the Church Fathers adopted very narrow conservative views that have dominated Christianity for the past 2,000 years. Marriage became a "sacred image," but it was not as good as celibacy. Christians should strive to suppress all sexual desire. Adultery, homosexuality, and abortion became sinful, and today a Church ruled by unmarried and childless old men denies birth control to women and forces women to bear and raise children without public or Church assistance.

Initially, the Pauline congregations were administered by lay ministers and deacons, most of whom were married. They were overseen by bishops, who were required to be married. All of this began to change with the Council of Elvira in 305 CE, which adopted canons requiring those who attended the Christian altars to abstain from having sex with their wives. Another canon in 352 CE denied the priesthood to women and denied them the right to serve as deacons. In 401 CE, higher ranked priests such as bishops were forced to separate from their wives, and finally in 1073, Pope Gregory VII forbade marriage altogether and imposed celibacy on all priests. This ruling, as much as any other, has contributed to the current scandals about pedophile priests, as the Catholic priesthood struggles to cope with the reality of human sexuality.

These celibate priests came to administer sacraments in a religion that idealized the perpetual virginity of Mary, Jesus's mother (whom the Gospel writers had mostly written out of their stories about Jesus). It was not until the fifth century that Mary was proclaimed to be the "God-bearer," or "Mother of God." According to this new doctrine, Mary was a virgin when God conceived Jesus within her, and she remained a virgin throughout her life, never having more children. In many respects Mary became the Mother Goddess, even while she was denied her sexuality and Divinity.

Mary was unequalled as a heavenly mediator, and her miraculous appearances resulted in shrines around the world and her adoption as Our Lady of Guadalupe in Mexico. The Church's official dogma began to change with the Second Vatican Council in the 1960s. Since Jesus was deemed the primary mediator between humanity and heaven, the Church ruled that the veneration of Mary should serve as a secondary aid for the adoration of Jesus. Her role was to be the "Mediatrix," and the Madonna was enshrined in a position below her son.

The Paulines, neither Protestant nor Catholic, have ever acknowledged the true greatness of Mary as the mother of five of the most remarkable men in the history of religion, Jesus, James, Simeon, Judas, and Joseph, who each followed the Way of his mother and father.

Because, in the Roman Catholic view, Mary was conceived with an immaculate soul and was sinless in the conception and delivery of Jesus, he was free from original sin; however, the rest of humanity must bear its mark. The dogma of original sin resulted from Paul tying the sins of Adam and Eve to his concept of justification by faith: "Therefore as sin came into the world through one man and death through sin, and so death spread to all men because all men sinned—sin indeed was in the world before the law was given, . . ." (Romans 5:12)

By Paul's pharisaical interpretation, justification by faith in the death and resurrection of Jesus provides the grace of a "free gift" in the forgiveness of many trespasses. (5:15-27) From this came the concept of "original sin," which questioned whether Adam's sin was the source of human sinfulness and whether all humans participate in his sin and share his guilt. The debate raged for centuries, with Augustine concluding that all souls either go to heaven or hell, and that original sin condemns unbaptized babies to hell. A council in 529 CE endorsed Augustine's view—but not completely. The question would become one of the issues in the Protestant Reformation whereby Martin Luther asserted that *everyone* inherits the guilt of Adam at conception. The Catholic Church still teaches that "As a result of original sin, human nature is weakened in its powers, subject to ignorance, suffering and the domination of death, and inclined to sin."

Recognizing that every Christian might not die in a state of total grace, the Church invented the concept of purgatory. Neither heaven nor hell, purgatory is something like the Judaic Sheol, where the dead rested until their bones were to be stood up during the end times. Purgatory is a place where one goes temporarily to be purified before entering heaven, while working off punishment for any remaining sins. It helps if someone else continues to pray for the deceased's salvation. Limbo is similar, but different because it is imagined as the "edge of hell" where unbaptized infants suffering from original sin can rest without having to endure the torment of hell.

Pauline Christians may or may not have been willing to die for these and other doctrinal beliefs, but they did in fact die in great numbers for their refusal to worship Roman gods—including Roman emperors who became gods. A refusal to sacrifice to the emperors or the empire's gods warranted the death penalty, and thousands of Christians eagerly suffered martyrdom for this reason. Rather than gods, the Christians came to view the emperors as demons. Tertullian wrote, "The more we are mown down by you, the more we multiply: the blood of Christians is seed!" The word *martyr*, in Greek, means "witness," and for Christians, it meant they were dying as witnesses to their faith in Jesus.

Angry that their disrespect of the emperors and Roman gods undermined imperial authority and fearing the spread of their inflammatory views to their domestic slaves and foreign subject nations, the Roman authorities persecuted the early Christians.

This willingness, indeed, desire, of these early Christians to die for their faith gave rise to a cult of saints that granted the highest honors to those who died a violent death by torture. Many of these martyrs became venerated as saints of the Church—who were deemed to have possessed an exceptional degree of holiness or likeness to God. Under Catholic doctrine, everyone who makes it to heaven becomes a saint, but a "Saint" is a person who has been officially canonized or declared by the Pope to be a Saint and a holder of the "Keys of the Kingdom of Heaven" by the grace of God.

While pagans were (and are) looked down upon by Christians because of their worship of multiple gods, the number of Catholic Saints rapidly surpassed all known pagan gods. There are now as many as 10,000 Saints of the Roman Catholic Church, each having his or her own special day and each having the power (or key) to intercede on behalf of those who pray to them.

The Rome-based empire suffered through a succession of weak and ineffective emperors during the third century, as the empire deteriorated and became divided into east and west regions of imperial authority. The empire recovered some strength and energy under Aurelian near the end of the second century and under Diocletian in the beginning of the third century; however, the priority of Rome as the center of the empire was not to be long lasting.

These stronger emperors improved the stability of Rome, but a series of civil wars in the early fourth century resulted in Constantine (the Great) becoming emperor of a unified empire. Politically, he established a "New Rome" in Byzantium, which he renamed Constantinople, and the imperial gravity shifted to the east. While Rome may have become an imperial backwater, its bishop gained new and greater powers under Constantine. Tracing their lineage back to "Saint Peter," from whom they drew their authority, the bishops of Rome came to be considered as the head, or pope (Latin *papa*) of the Roman Catholic Church.

Just prior to the pivotal battle in 312 CE that secured his empire, Constantine experienced a visionary dream in which he was advised "to mark the heavenly sign of God on the shields of his soldiers." Believed to have been the Chi Rio symbol representing the first two letters of the Greek spelling of the word *Christos* or Christ, the symbol was minted on coins and on a helmet worn by Constantine as depicted on a commemorative medallion. Nonetheless, to officially honor his victory, Constantine offered sacrifices to several gods, and the triumphal arch he constructed did not contain any Christian symbols.

Initially, Constantine ordered a complete freedom of religion throughout the empire. His government ceased the persecution of Christians and legalized the observance of Christianity—along with all other religions in the empire. Subsequent edicts returned property that had been seized and provided other relief. Constantine provided financial support to the Church and granted privileges to its clergy. Acting under the influence of his mother, Helen, Constantine constructed the Church of the Holy Sepulcher in Jerusalem and the original Saint Peter's Basilica in Rome.

In 331 CE, Constantine ordered 50 copies of what would ultimately become the New Testament to be delivered to the Roman Christian congregation in Constantinople. Although efforts had been underway for some time to create a list of approved documents to be read to congregations, it took Constantine's order to concentrate work on the creation of an official canon. By 383 CE, final decisions were made about what was to be included and what was to be left out (none of the Gnostic Gospels made the cut). Such decisions were as much political as religious, as the emperor had to ensure the Christian doctrine he accepted became that of all his subjects.

Constantine received a Christian baptism just before his death. It was not, however, performed by a Roman Christian bishop, but by a Gnostic Christian bishop who denied the divinity of Jesus. Even so, the Paulines continued to gain power to the detriment of the more numerous Gnostic congregations.

The full shift of this power was demonstrated in 380 CE when emperor Theodosius issued an imperial command dictating a belief in Christianity:

> It is Our Will that all the peoples We rule shall practice that religion which the divine Peter the Apostle transmitted to the Romans. We shall believe in the single Deity of the Father, the Son, and the Holy Spirit, under the concept of equal majesty and of the Holy Trinity.
>
> We command that those persons who follow this rule shall embrace the name of Catholic Christians. The rest, however, whom We adjudge demented and insane, shall sustain the infamy of heretical dogmas, their meeting places shall not receive the name of churches, and they shall be smitten, first, by divine vengeance and secondly by the retribution of Our own initiative, which We shall assume in accordance with divine judgment.

Thereafter, pagans (or Gnostics) could not hold public office; pagan sacrifices were prohibited, and pagan temples were destroyed or were converted to Christian churches. Baptized Christians who relapsed into paganism were subject to execution.

Paul's church became the one and only Christian church, and there was no salvation outside of that church. Only those who belonged to his church were "straight thinking," or orthodox. The Roman Church became universal, or "Catholic." All other beliefs and churches were deemed to be heretical and were suppressed and prosecuted criminally.

Bishops were empowered to rule over their communities "as God rules in heaven." They became master, judge, and lord over their congregations with the power to judge and discipline their "laity." They held the power of life or death, and there was no appeal. Religious heresy equated to treason against the state.

With recognition and imperial support came power, and the Church was not loath to exercise that power *vis-à-vis* the political power that created it. Art and buildings began to show Jesus and the emperor as equals, or in some cases with Jesus in the superior position. Politically, the Church bishop was supposed to be obedient to the emperor, but an incident in 390 CE between Bishop Ambrose and Emperor Theodosius switched the eminence. After the emperor ordered the brutal slaughter of more than 5,000 people as a collective punishment, Ambrose withheld Holy Communion from Theodosius until he did public penance for the crime. Theodosius had to publicly remove his royal robe on several occasions and plead for a pardon before receiving the sacrament. Withholding communion and the threat of excommunication allowed the religious power to became co-equal with the secular.

The power of the Roman Catholic Church reached an epitome with the crowning of Charlemagne as emperor by Pope Leo III on Christmas day 800 CE, creating the Holy Roman Empire in Europe. The empire was based on the concept that the emperor inherited his supreme power from the Roman emperors, but the crown was placed on his head by the Pope. The battles to challenge and to sustain the empire would rage across Europe for centuries, as the continent was plunged into five centuries of Dark Ages. During this time, extraordinarily horrendous crimes were committed by the Church and by those acting at its bidding—all in the name of Jesus, the Prince of Peace.

Disputes over matters as serious as the priority of the Roman Pope as the head of all Christian churches and as minor as to the use of leavened or unleavened bread for the Eucharist, led to the Great Schism in 1054 between the Roman Catholic churches and the Eastern Orthodox churches. Although there have been attempts to heal the differences, the division remains to this day.

The Destruction of Heresy by the Murderous Inquisitions

The word heresy comes from the Greek *hairesis* meaning "choice," and those who chose to belong to factions other than Roman Christianity became known as *haereticunt hominem*. Whether or not it was written by Paul, his letter to Titus advocates the shunning of those who disagreed with his dogma: "But avoid stupid controversies, genealogies, dissentions, and quarrels over the law, for they are unprofitable and futile. As for a man who is *haereticunt hominem*, after admonishing him once or twice, have nothing to do with him." (3:10-11) Unfortunately for thousands of factious people, shunning was insufficient to control the spread of heretical beliefs. For them, the consequence was torture and painful death.

With the destruction of their books, the orthodox Paulines succeeded in reducing Gnostic influence, but the righteous gospel of the Way and Jesus taught by Mary Magdalene managed to survive throughout the Dark Ages despite the most violent acts by the Roman Catholic Church. Believing that God was neither male nor female, but represented an Abiding Mind; that Jesus was a great, but human, prophet and Righteous Teacher, who achieved Gnosis at his death; and that the Holy Spirit was a masculinization of the feminine Spirit of Wisdom, the Gnostics continued to flourish in spite of the violence done to them by the Roman Church. The expression of alternative views took different forms over the centuries, but the Church's response was uniformly violent.

One of the first major challenges to orthodoxy came from the teachings of Mani, who was born in Baghdad in 214 CE into a Persian royal family. Mani was initiated into Gnosticism and began to write a series of books in which he claimed superior knowledge of the teachings of Jesus, which he combined with Zoroaster and Buddha. Illustrating the battles between light and darkness, Mani believed in "an illuminated elect," and taught that Jesus was divine only by virtue of his enlightenment. For his thinking, Mani was flayed to death and decapitated in 276 CE, and his body was publicly displayed as a warning to others who might stray from the orthodox path.

The predominance of women in several groups also attracted the ire of the Church. The Collyridians had a feminine priesthood and worshipped the Virgin Mary. They were popular in the fourth century until being assimilated into the Church, as it began to officially adopt the Cult of Mary. Attracted by the prophecy and teachings of Montanus (a Christian living in west-central Turkey toward the end of the first century) two women, Maximilla and Priscilla claimed the same prophetic gifts. The Christian-believing group became popular for its prophecies, but it also allowed women to serve as priests and bishops. Despite orthodox opposition, the Montanists were able to spread as far west as Spain and to maintain influence until at least the ninth century.

Perhaps the most widespread and difficult to defeat heresy was that resulting from the teaching of an Alexandria presbyter named Arius. His simple message was that there was only one supreme God, and that Jesus was not his son. Arianism was essentially the same as that taught by James and the Congregation of the Way. Although condemned by the Roman Church, Arianism was favored by Constantine, and it was an Arian bishop who baptized him. The heresy became so widespread that during the fourth century practically every bishopric was either Arian or vacant. The Goths, Ostrogoths, Vandals, and Visigoths were all Arian. Under the Visigoths, Arianism became the dominant form of Christianity in Spain and Southern France.

A form of Gnosticism that ultimately attracted violent suppression was that originating with the lessons of a wealthy fourth century teacher named Priscillian of Avila. A layman, his ministry combined Judaism and Gnostic Manichaeism. The Sabbath was observed on Saturday; the congregations denied the Trinity, and used some of the Gnostic Gospels, including the *Acts of Thomas*. In 386 CE, Priscillian and several his disciples were accused of sorcery, and they were among the first heretics to be executed by secular authorities at the request of the Roman Church. Even so, Priscillianism continued to smolder for centuries as thousands of Cathars and Albigensians were tortured and killed by the Church for entertaining similar views.

The greatest threat to the Roman Church came in the thirteenth century when some of its own ascetic priests in southern France began to teach a form of dualism that contrasted the evil Old Testament God with the good God of the New Testament. The good God was the God of Love and was entirely pure spirit, while the old God created a material world that was intrinsically evil.

Known as Cathars or Albigensians, they referred to themselves as Good Christians, and they repudiated the monotheistic doctrine of the Roman Catholic Church. Recognizing the feminine principle in religion, their ministers and leaders were of both sexes. They were tolerant of all religions, and they honored philosophy and the pursuit of knowledge and wisdom. The Good Christians considered Jesus to have been an honored prophet who died for the principle of love, but they denied that he was the Son of God. Most lived a simple life of devotion and just wanted to be left alone.

When missionary attempts by Church authorities failed, the Pope dispatched an army of 30,000 northern European knights and soldiers into southern France. Known as the Albigensian Crusade, the war lasted for 40 years. In an area that was one of the most sophisticated and advanced in the world at the time, an entire people were slaughtered, and their cities and towns were burned and leveled. Writing to Pope Innocent III, Arnaud Amalric, his legate and inquisitor said, "neither age nor sex nor status was spared." To a soldier who was worried about accidentally killing orthodox Catholics instead of heretics, Amalric reportedly said, "kill them all; God will sort it out later."

The Albigensian Crusade introduced the new monastic order of the Dominicans, who would become known for their violence done in the name of Jesus and the Catholic Church. The mission of the "Hounds of the Lord" was to root out and destroy heresy. The effort became known as the Inquisition, which was based on the Roman judicial process known as the *inquisitio*. The Inquisition did not initially have authority over Jews but was primarily concerned with the heretical behavior of Christians. Once convicted, the sentences ranged from having to wear a cross to being burned at the stake. The purpose of the Inquisition was to terrorize people to warn them "away from the evils they would commit." No place in Europe—which remained under the domination of the Holy Roman Empire—was to be spared.

Once the Muslims were expelled from the areas they had occupied in Portugal and Spain, an Inquisition was instituted to sort out those who should remain, or become, Roman Catholic—including former Jews. When a violent pogrom killed hundreds of Jews in Seville, thousands of Jews converted to Catholicism as a means of survival. These *conversos* became subject to the Inquisition because their conversion was deemed to have been voluntary. In 1492—the year Columbus discovered the Americas—Spain expelled all unconverted Jews and began to prosecute as heretics those converted Jews who continued to secretly practice their faith. Once Spain took control of large portions of the Americas, it administered its new land through inquisition tribunals.

Many Jews had escaped into Portugal, but they too became subject to a new Inquisition instituted there in 1515. The primary target was the converted and exiled Jews. Among the punishments was the *auto-da-fé*, in which heretics (or those who had been forcibly converted and secretly practiced their original faith) were burned at the stake. As time passed, the Inquisition came to monitor every aspect of Portugal's society, and ultimately as many as 2,000 people were burned to death.[86]

With the launching of the Protestant Reformation in 1517 by Martin Luther and its spreading popularity in Northern Europe, the Church was no longer able to effectively prosecute heresy in its inquisitorial tribunals. In 1542, Pope Paul III established the Congregation of the Holy Office of the Inquisition as a permanent body to maintain and defend the Catholic faith by examining and exposing false doctrines.[87]

With Protestantism becoming the leading form of Christianity within entire countries, the Church was limited in its ability to torture and murder religious opponents through the Inquisition. As an alternative, the Church resorted to even more deadly wars with the Protestant nations: The Thirty Years War in Germany between Catholics and Protestants killed 8,000,000 people, and the French Wars of Religion fought by Catholics and Huguenots killed 3,000,000.

The Inquisition was abolished in Portugal in 1821 and in the Americas by 1825. After untold thousands suffered and died during the Inquisition for their religious beliefs, Pope John Paul II apologized

---

[86] As a more practical and lucrative punishment, the properties of wealthy *marranos* were also confiscated by the Church.

[87] The most famous case prosecuted by the Congregation was that of Galileo Galilei in 1633 which forced him, upon threat of torture and death, to renounce his scientific conclusion that the earth circled the sun. The Congregation continues to exist to this day; renamed as the Congregation for the Doctrine of the Faith, it exercised indirect control over the suppressed Dead Sea Scrolls until they were published in 1991.

in 2000 for "errors committed in the service of the truth through recourse to non-evangelical methods." These centuries of religious violence have left their mark on a world still suffering from perpetual war, much of which is based on religious differences.

The Inquisition and the religious wars of the seventeenth century were manifestations of the internal violence the Church was willing to inflict on its own people to defend its Pauline doctrine. The Crusades launched by the Church promoted violence against people in other countries because of their different religious beliefs.

The Repeated Failure of the Christian Crusades Against the People of Palestine

An enormously complicated set of geopolitical issues resulted in a request from the Byzantine Emperor Alexios I to Pope Urban II in 1095 for military assistance against the encroachment of Islamic Turks in Anatolia *and* in Urban's decision to launch a religious crusade in response. Alexios probably expected some mercenary reinforcements under his own command, but what he got was an invasion by a motley army of poor Christians who streamed eastward in hope of fame, fortune, forgiveness, and adventure. The People's Crusade surged through Germany, slaughtering the Jews it encountered, until it stumbled into an ambush at Nicaea, from which only a few survived.

A more traditional army of knights was organized in France and Germany leading to a force of almost 100,000, which marched eastward until it arrived in Byzantium. Many of the noblemen pledged allegiance to Alexios, and after some initial reverses, the army was able to take Antioch, Aleppo, Edessa, and finally Jerusalem in 1099. Not since the Romans leveled the city in 70 CE had so much blood flowed. One account said the "slaughter was so great that our men waded in blood up to their ankles." Christians had been allowed to leave before the final assault, but almost all the Muslim defenders were killed, along with many Jews—some of whom were burned in their synagogues. Having fulfilled their vows, most of the knights returned home, leaving a few hundred in control of the Crusader Kingdom of Jerusalem.

The subsequent retaking of Aleppo and Edessa by the Muslims resulted in the Second Crusade in 1147, led by King Louis VII of France and King Conrad III of Germany. Once again, this crusade resulted in the widespread deaths of Jews along the route in Germany amid claims the Jews were not contributing financially to the rescue of the Holy Land. The crusade strengthened the force holding Jerusalem but was insufficient to roll back advances being made by Saladin—who had become the leader of the Muslim forces. In 1186, the crusaders organized the largest army yet deployed to the Middle East, but it was soundly defeated at the Battle of Hattin, in the Galilee.

As a devoted Muslim, Saladin observed the Koran's rule that Muslims must cooperate if a truce is offered. He gave the crusaders the choice of leaving Palestine or remaining in peace under Islamic rule. Most Christians departed, and Jerusalem fell shortly thereafter.

The Third Crusade organized in 1189 became stalemated by Saladin at Acre, until the Muslim siege was lifted by the arrival of King Richard the Lionheart of England. Richard's attempts to retake Jerusalem were unsuccessful; however, a truce allowed Christians access to the holy sites in the City. Following the death of Saladin in 1193, a German crusader army seized Sidon and Beirut, but failed to reach Jerusalem.

A Fourth Crusade set out in 1200, primarily from France, but was diverted to the Christian city of Constantinople, which was conquered twice. The second time, the army killed many of the city's Christian citizens and looted its churches. It never came close to the Holy Land.

A disastrous attempt to recapture Palestine occurred in 1212 when two groups consisting of thousands of children and young people set out from France and Germany to the Middle East. Collectively known as the Children's Crusade, neither group was able to travel out of Europe and as many as two-thirds died of starvation and illnesses.

The Fifth Crusade pursued an alternative strategy of invading Palestine by first conquering Egypt. The army was primarily organized under the kings of Austria and Hungary and were later joined by a mixed army from Germany and the Low Lands. Invading in the direction of Cairo in 1221, the combined army was defeated and forced to surrender. Consequently, however, an armistice was agreed upon, resulting in a temporary peace between Europe and the Islamic world.

A sputtering Sixth Crusade accomplished little militarily, but ensuing diplomacy permitted the Kingdom of Jerusalem to regain some control over the City for fifteen years. After Jerusalem was recaptured by the Muslims, a Seventh Crusade led by French King Louis IX was initially successful in defeating an Egyptian army, but he was captured in 1250 during a battle in which his army was destroyed. Louis was ransomed and retreated to Acre, where attempts at another invasion failed. He returned to France and attempted to organize a subsequent crusade in 1270, but this, the Eighth Crusade, also failed.

Europe had grown tired of the crusades, and possession of Jerusalem no longer seemed as important as the internal battles within the Holy Roman Empire. The Muslims became better organized and developed improved tactics—which made invasions more difficult and easier to defeat. The last of the Crusader states fell by the end of the thirteenth century.

The several military orders created during the crusades included the Knights Templar, who fought wearing a white mantle with a red cross. As the crusades ended and the occupied lands were lost, the Templars—who had gained wealth and power—defeated and occupied Rhodes and Malta. Having become a political and military threat, however, many of the Templars were arrested and burned at the stake in France in 1307. The order was officially dissolved by a papal order in 1312.

After eight major crusades and the expenditure of an enormous fortune, an estimated 1.7 million people paid with their lives in the series of futile attempts to seize the Holy Land. The Muslims would hold Palestine until the twentieth century, when the returning Jews were able to evict many native Palestinians and to create the Jewish state of Israel.

The Pauline Protestant Reformation of the Pauline Catholic Church

A crisis arose in the Roman Catholic Church in 1378 when the cardinals elected Urban VI as Pope. He immediately proved to be a violent bad choice, and the cardinals experienced buyer's remorse. They removed themselves to Avignon in France and elected a different pope, Clement VII. The religious problem became political as the countries (and peoples) of Europe divided on which pope they would recognize. The religious and political turmoil continued when both popes died, and successors were elected. The matter was finally resolved by the Council of Constance, after a third antipope was elected. Two popes resigned, a third was excommunicated, and the cardinals elected a new pope in 1414. The result, however, was not approved by all the crowned heads of Europe, and political unrest in the Holy Roman Empire continued.

Arising out of the Papal Schism was an increased public concern over, and attention to Church practices (language of mass and composition of communion) and corruption (the sale of indulgences). Recall that purgatory was invented by the Church as a place where dead people rested until their sins could be sufficiently redeemed to allow them entrance into heaven. The Church had made it easier for people to escape from purgatory by offering indulgences as a form of insurance to shorten their time there. Indulgences had been offered to the crusaders, or as a reward for other good works; however, it was when Pope Sixtus IV placed them on the market for cash that protests arose.

The same Council of Constance that resolved the triple-pope issue also condemned Jan Hus, a priest and master at Charles University in Prague, for agitating for a married priesthood and against purgatory and indulgences. He was burned at the stake, and the body of another protester was exhumed and burned.

The ecclesiastical turmoil finally boiled to the surface when a German priest and professor named Martin Luther wrote and circulated his *Ninety-Five Theses on the Power and Efficacy of Indulgences* to stimulate academic discussion of the issue. In the new age of the printing press, Luther was a prolific writer issuing pamphlets on a wide variety of complaints, which were quickly reproduced and circulated. Luther refused to renounce his writings upon the demand of Pope Leo X in 1520 and was excommunicated. He was also branded an outlaw by the Holy Roman Emperor Maximilian I.

Luther was joined in his protest movement by John Calvin, another writer, and they began to establish a network of agreement with others across a wide area of Europe. In addition to the sale of indulgences, causes of concern included matters that went to the heart of the Catholic Church: authority of the pope, ecclesiastical law, excommunication, the buying and selling of clerical offices, the involvement of secular rulers in religious matters, and the cozy relationship between the hierarchy of the Church and the crowned heads of state.

The protest movement, which became known as Protestantism, was not a protest of the Pauline dogma on which the Church was built, but upon the way the Church administered the church, performed the sacraments, and interpreted the scriptures. The Church relied on the authority of the apostolic priesthood; a lineage of men ordained by bishops in an unbroken succession from Peter. The reforming churches relied on the authority of the scriptures and taught that the Bible is the only source of God's revelation. Both Catholics and Protestants, however, rejected the position of James and the Way of Righteousness regarding justification. Indeed, Luther went even further than the Catholics. He taught that salvation was not earned by good deeds (including those performed for indulgences) but are a gift of God's grace through the believer's faith in Jesus Christ as the redeemer from sin. Luther insisted that justification was based on faith *alone*, without the contribution of *any* works of the Law. Although Luther wrote that "reason is the greatest enemy that faith has," he also said that enlightened human reason "furthers and advances" faith.

Those who most closely adopted Luther's teachings (including the catechisms he wrote, his translation of the Bible, and the supervisory church body he created) were known as Lutherans and became one of the largest groups in the emerging Protestant movement. Lutheranism was primarily centered in Germany, Scandinavia, and the Low Countries. Luther wrote negatively about Jews, and later in life, he condemned Judaism, saying that the homes and synagogues of Jews should be destroyed, their property seized, and their freedoms limited. This was the subject of his last sermon three days before his death. Although rejected by most Lutherans, the effect of his writings on the later emergence of Nazism in the area where Lutheranism was the strongest cannot be overlooked.

With the organizational efforts of John Calvin, Protestantism became an evangelizing movement with missionaries spreading the message of reform over a wide area and baptizing converts. The popularity of the Huguenots in France led to the religious wars in that country, and as more and more countries became predominately Protestant, disputes among nations over their religious views led to the Thirty Years War that devastated Europe.

Although Henry VIII divorced his crown and religion from the Roman Catholic Church, the resulting Church of England failed to satisfy the demands of reformers. The Puritans objected to the Catholic forms of ritual that remained in the Anglican Church and wanted it to more closely resemble the European Protestant churches. The Puritans emigrated to America and established the colony of Massachusetts, and other religious-based colonies followed. All but one, Maryland, were Protestant.

The Peace of Westphalia that officially ended the European wars of religion in 1648 also marked the close of the Protestant Reformation. Thereafter, nations aligned themselves for or against others based on issues other than religion.

Of the religions that continue to practice Pauline Christianity, Roman Catholicism is the largest with 1.2 billion members, and it is followed by Eastern Orthodoxy with approximately 225-300 million members. Protestantism now attracts between 800 and 900 million believers; however, they are spread out through as many as 30,000 denominations.

Protestantism is united in its belief in the supremacy of scripture over tradition, of faith over works, and of the laity over a priesthood. Collectively, most also believe in an evangelical Protestantism that seeks to unite every person with Jesus Christ as a personal savior from sin and death.

Except for a few Christian congregations that profess Gnostic principles, all Christian churches and congregations continue to base their authority on the words of the Pauline writer attributed to Jesus that close the Book of Matthew.

> All authority in heaven and on earth has been given to me. Go therefore and make disciples of all nations, baptizing them in the name of the Father and of the Son and of

the Holy Spirit, teaching them to observe all that I have commanded you; and lo, I am with you always, to the close of the age. (28:18-20)

Fundamentalism is Driving Pauline Christianity Even Further From The Way

As Protestantism became widespread around the world, and its congregations became a substantial part of the societies and states that hosted them, they became increasingly liberal in their interpretation of the scriptures they relied on. Confronting and accommodating to science—such as the age of the universe discovered by physicists and astronomers, plate tectonics uncovered by geographers and geologists, and the role of natural selection in the evolution of life established by biologists and chemists—many, if not most, Christian congregations entered the mainstream and reinterpreted their theology to meet the reality of human existence. They adjusted their theological thinking to conclude that for God, a day might last billions of years in the creation of the heavens and earth, and that the miracles and parables of Jesus must be viewed allegorically if one is to properly understand the more profound truths he was teaching. Through all the upheavals of the modern age, Christianity continued to offer a comforting ethical system that met the needs of most, but not all their congregants.

Inasmuch as Protestantism is scriptural based, there came forward those who rejected, not only science, but their own observations and life experiences as well. For these "fundamentalists," the scriptures were inerrant and literal, and alternative interpretations were heretical. As Protestantism is an evangelical religion, these fundamentalists responded to the call to indoctrinate others with their ultraconservative views.

Commencing in the late nineteenth and early twentieth centuries, English and American Protestant fundamentalists began to unite in their rejection of theological liberalism and cultural modernism. Following the publication of writings defining the orthodoxy now claimed by fundamentalists, the movement began to organize new congregations, denominations, and national and international associations. They saw themselves as militants doing battle for the fundamentals of Christianity.

It is not, however, an either-or situation between the fundamentalists and modernists—as there are many conservative individuals and groups who see the fundamentalists as being too extreme to represent their more intellectual approach. These less militant fundamentalists tend to refer to themselves as evangelicals.

Published in 1910, a subsidized distribution of more than three million copies of *The Fundamentals*, a 12-volume study, established the core beliefs of fundamentalists: the inerrancy of the Bible; the literal nature of biblical accounts; the virgin birth of Jesus; the bodily resurrection and physical appearances of Jesus; and the atonement of Jesus on the cross for the sins of everyone.

The fundamentalist attack on modernism was organized in several missionary training schools, evangelical seminaries, and bible colleges established in the United States. These schools primarily taught students—many of whom lacked standard academic qualifications—using a curriculum primarily devoted to an intense study of the Bible. These specialized schools produced thousands of graduates who were called to the ministries of existing congregations, or who organized their own churches.

These bible schools also teach an anti-evolution approach to scientific discoveries which they package as "creation science," in which they attack the scientific principles of natural selection. Relying on an explanation of creation called "intelligent design, or cause," its proponents argue that the complexity of life proves that it could have only been created by God. Its opponents label the theory as pseudoscience because it lacks empirical support and does not provide a testable hypothesis.

Fundamentalist efforts to compel the teaching of intelligent design alongside science in public school classrooms generally have been unsuccessful. The courts have uniformly ruled that teaching intelligent design would be unconstitutional, as it is a religious belief, rather than science.

When the United States Republican Party executed its plan under presidential candidate Ronald Reagan to entice the "silent majority" of primarily white, working-class and southern voters into an alliance to vote against their own interests in favor of corporate-sponsored candidates, the Party deliberately embraced the fundamentalists and courted their preachers. In what became known as the "Christian Right," televangelists and other "Moral Majority" leaders uniformly used their pulpits to endorse right-wing candidates. Following his election, Reagan asked, "Can we begin our crusade joined together in a moment of silent prayer?" Since that time, the fundamentalists have overwhelmingly voted for Republican candidates such as George W. Bush and, more recently, Donald Trump.

The Republican's "God Strategy" has paid off, and today, the political power of the fundamentalists continues to grow as they increasingly seek to impose their minority religious views on others in a new religious-political alignment. The Gospels, which were originally written by the Paulines to facilitate a similar relationship with their Roman oppressors, serves to justify those who read the words as the "gospel truth."

Christian Terrorism is as Deadly as Islamic Terrorism

The past half century in the United States has seen an infiltration of extreme right-wing groups by a radical religious ideology known as Christian Identity. The combination of religious fervor and bigotry has resulted in hate crimes that included bombings, shootings, and other acts of terrorism. Claiming descent from the "Lost Tribes of Israel," the groups appeal to those who believe the White Race and the United States have a special place in God's plan for humanity. Virulently anti-Semitic, the groups claim that Jews are false Israelites and are children of Satan. Contending that God's creations prior to Adam and Eve were "mud people" without souls, they believe that only "Adamic" White People are descended from the couple in the Garden of Eden. Christian Identity holds that non-whites cannot achieve salvation, and they will either be exterminated or enslaved to serve the White race in the Heavenly Kingdom on Earth under the rule of Jesus Christ.

Organized groups included the New Christian Crusade Church, the Christian Defense League, Posse Comitatus, the Committee of the States, and the Church of Jesus Christ Christian—which became the Aryan Nations. Members of Christian Identity were involved in a series of armed robberies committed by a terrorist group known as The Order. The Phineas Priesthood is based on the acts of the zealous Phineas who killed a fellow Israelite and the Midianite woman for "race mixing." Members of the group were convicted for having committed bombings and bank robberies.

A recent study conducted by the Georgia State University examined terrorist attacks in the United States over a five-year period. It found that while Muslims had carried out only 11 of the 89 reported attacks, those received 44 percent of the media coverage. Another study by the Nation Institute examined 201 terrorist incidents between 2008 and 2016 and found that 115 of the cases were committed by right-wing extremists, including white supremacists, militias, and "sovereign citizens."

Federal law enforcement authorities notified President Trump in August 2017 that white supremacist groups were committing more attacks than any other domestic extremist group. Supremacists "were responsible for 49 homicides in 26 attacks from 2000 to 2016.

It is the matter of abortion and women's freedom of choice, however, that drives religious fanatics to commit crimes of violence on behalf of the unborn. These anti-abortion zealots are considered by the U.S. Department of Justice to be a terrorist threat, as most of the violence is concentrated in the United States.

Claiming a defense of justifiable homicide, there have been at least eleven murders committed in the U.S. since 1990 against abortion providers. In addition, there have been 173 arson fires set and 41 bombs exploded at providing clinics since 1977. During the same period, according to the National Abortion Federation, there have been 17 attempted murders, 383 death threats, 153 assaults, 373 physical invasions, and three kidnappings. Many of these offenses were directed at facilities operated by Planned Parenthood.

Although many of these crimes were committed by individuals acting alone, organizations such as the Army of God, Bible Missionary Fellowship, and priests of the Catholic Church have claimed responsibility and have offered moral support to individuals. Other anti-abortion groups have denounced such violence.

The Fraudulent Legacy of Paul

Fundamentalists, who are relentlessly seeking to recreate the United States (and other governments) as a "Christian Nation," can find encouragement in the words of Paul, who is quoted in First Corinthians as saying:

> For though I am free from all men, I have made myself a slave to all, that I might win the more. To the Jews I became as a Jew, in order to win Jews; to those under the law I became as one under the law—that I might win those under the law. To those outside the law I became as one outside the law—that I might win those outside the law. To the weak I became weak, that I might win the weak. I have become all things to all men, that I might by all means save some. I do it all for the sake of the gospel, that I may share in its blessings.
>
> Do you not know that in a race all the runners compete, but only one receives the prize? So, run that you may obtain it. Every athlete exercises self-control in all things. They do it to receive a perishable wreath, but we are imperishable. Well, I do not run aimlessly, I do not box as one beating the air; but I pommel my body and subdue it, lest after preaching to others I myself should be disqualified. (9:19-27)

Paul's "zero sum" strategy of winning at all costs is thoroughly modern, and we can see its success today in that billions of people adhere to the religion he created, and they continue to deprecate and attack the beliefs of others who dare to disagree with them.

Paul, quite simply, lost his way, and the flock he created has wandered far afield over the centuries. His version of Christianity silenced Sophia, the voice of Wisdom—which is the true equation of the Holy Spirit. By his easy justification by faith, Paul destroyed the heart of the Way—the joy of living a life of simple righteousness. In making a God out of Jesus, Paul misplaced the soul of Jesus, and the time has come to make him whole. Paul and his strays need to return to the Way.

Even with all its defects, Pauline Christianity has served billions of people for the past 2,000 years as an ethical guide. Inherited from and inspired by the Jews (against whom Paul and his gospel writers turned), Christianity has also served to initiate and perpetuate some of the darkest ages in human history, including the rabid anti-Semitism that resulted in the industrialized slaughter of millions of Jews during a world war that cost humanity the lives of more than 80 million people.

All of this—both the positive and the negative—can be laid at the feet of Paul the Pharisee, as he too must exist in a purgatory until such time as he learns from his errors and achieves self-awareness. We are no longer limited by the words written by Paul, and those attributed to Jesus in the gospels created to support Paul's ministry; we now have the illuminating words of others who were spiritually inspired to write at or near the same time. Whether or not we take advantage of the opportunities presented by these words is up to us. It is time to forgive and to go forward along the Way of Jesus and his family to a righteous and spiritual life based on wisdom.

THE WAY OF RABBINIC JUDAISM

Following the judicial murder of James the Just—and during the time when the Temple was destroyed and up to the final defeat of the Zealot revolutions—there were three primary divisions among the Jews in Judea: the Sadducees, the Pharisees, and the largest component composed of the Way, the Congregation of the Poor, and the Zealots. All these groups traced their Judaic roots to the Covenant of Abraham and the Ten Commandments, and all but the Sadducees shared a common heritage in the Way of the Hasideans and Zaddiks.

Alone among the groups, the Pharisees had memorized an extensive Oral Torah, which they handed down, generation to generation, along with the accumulated layers of commentary and interpretation. The Pharisees separated from others in the Way over how to respond to Hellenization under the Syrian Greeks. The Pharisees were content with the spiritual and religious autonomy allowed by the Syrians—while the Zaddiks, Maccabees, and the Way revolted to defend their political and religious independence.

The Pharisees came to see themselves as having been set aside from the ordinary people, whom they believed were mostly incapable of living a pure life. Equipped with their Oral Torah, the Pharisees became a teaching and lawyering sect, whose primary influence was in the synagogues that came into existence during and after the Babylonian Exile. They perceived their knowledge of the Law as a mark of their higher culture, and their ability to interpret and mitigate the harsher aspects of Mosaic law as an intellectual and spiritual gift for the common people who had to live under the Law.

The Pharisees pursued a politically pragmatic philosophy of "going along to get along" and transferred their allegiance to the Romans once the Syrian Greeks were defeated. The Pharisees considered the Sadducees and the Way to be political and religious opponents, and during the original Roman invasion led by Pompey, it was the Pharisees who cut down the lower priests of the Way in the Temple as they carried out their duties.

In their collaboration with the Romans and Herodians, the leadership of the Sadducees and Pharisees had isolated themselves from most of the Jewish people. Once the Temple fell in 70 CE and Jerusalem was leveled, the Sadducees disappeared from history, but the Pharisees were able to forge a new accommodation with the Romans, allowing them to remain in Judea outside of Jerusalem.

The Romans laid waste the cities and towns of Judea-Palestine in 135 CE following the Bar Kokhba revolt, and they slaughtered tens of thousands of Jews, many, if not most of whom followed the Way, and the Romans carried off most of the young people as slaves. Unaffected by all of this, the Pharisees, who were protected by the Romans, reduced their Oral Torah to writing—thus creating the canon of Rabbinic Judaism.

With the elimination of competition from the Zealots, the Way, and the Congregation of the Poor—only the Pharisees were left in Judea. As the Pauline Christian congregations became exclusively composed of Gentiles, the Rabbinic Jews became the only survivors of Judaism, *except* for those who migrated to the Middle East and were led by Judas Thomas and those led by Mary Magdalene in the West.

In many ways, Rabbinic Judaism and Roman Christianity are flip sides of the same coin in that they both diverged from the Way, and the canons of both were influenced by the Pharisees. Paul the Pharisee created his own easy-going, politically collaborative brand of Christianity—which became the canon of the New Testament, and the politically cooperative Rabbinic Jews created the written Mishnah and the Talmud—which documented their oral canon.

The Jews continued to wait for their Messiah to save them, and although their Messiah had already appeared for the Christians, they themselves awaited his "second coming." These two surviving Pharisaic-based religions became adversaries. Paul created the blood libel that the "Jews had murdered Jesus," and the Rabbinic Jews created the slander that Jesus's mother, Mary was an adulteress who had conceived Jesus with a Roman soldier named Pantera.

Among the oldest surviving writings by the Rabbinic Jews is the *Seder Olam Rabbah,* compiled in 160 CE, which established the date of creation as 3761 BCE. Thus, the secular year 2020 is the Jewish year 5781. In the seventeenth century, a Christian archbishop calculated an earlier date for creation as having taken place on October 23,

4004 BCE. As the days and years continue to flow by, the time may be drawing near when the Roman Christians and Rabbinic Jews—who share a religious heritage and an ever-shrinking Earth—will find common ground in their beliefs.

Escape From Jerusalem and Accommodation With the Romans

In 68 CE, just before the final destruction of Jerusalem, one of the graduates of Hillel's academy in Jerusalem, Johanan Ben Zakkai, managed to escape from the city by concealing himself in a coffin and having himself lowered by rope over the city wall. Obtaining an audience with Vespasian shortly before he was proclaimed emperor by his army, Ben Zakkai confirmed the prediction of Josephus that Vespasian was the fulfillment of the prophesy of Numbers (24:17), *"a star shall come forth out of Jacob, and a scepter shall rise out of Israel."*

After he also predicted that the Temple would soon be destroyed, Ben Zakkai negotiated an agreement with Vespasian which provided Roman protection for the reestablishment of the Hillel academy in the village of Yavne (Jabneh).[88] Moreover, the religious privileges previously afforded by the Romans to the Jerusalem Temple were transferred to the academy.

As the Temple was being leveled in 70 CE, Ben Zakkai began to transform the Hillel academy into a Jewish religious center complete with a Sanhedrin. Serving as its Nasi (president), Ben Zakkai secured a consensus by the Sanhedrin to replace the animal sacrifices previously performed at the Temple with prayers.[89] He promulgated numerous decrees establishing and modifying Jewish practices, as necessary, to conform with changing conditions as the nation lurched from the destruction of Jerusalem towards the elimination of Judea during the coming Bar Kochba revolt. The Levite priesthood ceased to exist, and its survivors no longer played a role in the religion.

---

[88] Located inland between Tel Aviv and Ashdod, the modern town of Yavne was built on the site of the Arab village Yibna, which was depopulated during the Palestinian Nakba exodus in 1948.

[89] The Sadducees no longer played any role in the Sanhedrin, which had become exclusively Pharisaic.

Another concession obtained from Vespasian was the survival of Hillel's descendants. Following Ben Zakkai's death in 90 CE, he was succeeded as Nasi by Gamaliel II, the great-grandson of Hillel. Gamaliel was recognized by the Romans as a spokesman for all Jews, and he traveled to Rome to lobby emperor Domitian for imperial protection during the period when Domitian was persecuting the Christians.

Ben Zakkai and his successors as Nasi of the Sanhedrin were called Rabban (our master), while those who were ordained as an authority in the Jewish Law became known as Rabbis (my master). The Romans recognized the Nasi as the political patriarch of the region, yet his political powers were limited.

Gamaliel dictated requirements for Jewish life, such as the frequency of prayer, a requirement of marriage and monogamy, and dietary regulations. Unifying all these laws was an absolute belief in a single, indivisible God, who provided both the written and oral law—the obedience of which governs who will and will not be resurrected at the end of time.

The rulings of the Nasi and the Sanhedrin were enforced by banning those who disobeyed from participating in the activities of the community and synagogues. Those who persisted were excommunicated. Among the rulings was the excommunication, as heretics, of all Jews who professed a belief that Jesus had been a messiah. Moreover, *all* Jews were required to abide by both Mosaic *and* rabbinic precepts on pain of excommunication. With the authority of these rulings and documentation of the oral Torah, Rabbinic Judaism became the only remaining form of Judaism. Any followers of the Way or Zealots who refused to follow rabbinic rulings were no longer considered to be Jews.

The Pharisees Write Down Their Oral Torah and Create Rabbinic Judaism

Following the original thinking of Hillel, the Oral Torah was interpreted through logic to arrive at reasonable conclusions that did not violate the letter of the Law; however, Rabbi Akiba held that there was not a superfluous letter in the law—each one of which had a special meaning. As the body of oral law grew to the point where transmittal by memorization was becoming impossible, Rabbi Akiba devised a system of written organization by which materials were grouped with sixty headings under six major topics.

At the beginning of his revolt in 132 CE, the rabbis at Yavne proclaimed that Bar Kochba (rather than Vespasian) was the expected messiah in fulfillment of the Star Prophecy. When the revolt was violently suppressed, Rabbi Akiba was killed by the Romans for failing to withdraw from teaching the Torah. Although there was a period during which religious services had to be held in secret, there was an unbroken chain of ordination maintained of qualified rabbis to teach the Law.

The Oral Torah, which was known as the *Halakah*, was collected and written into the *Mishnah* (study) during this period. Originally intended as the approved collection of Halakah for study, the Mishnah came to be regarded as an authoritative canon of beliefs. Even though the Temple had been destroyed, the Mishnah contained detailed instructions for the utopia when it would be restored, and a high priest and king would once again rule Israel.

At the same time, the canon of scriptures was settled as the Masoretic Text (Old Testament). Some of the books that were excluded, including the *Books of Maccabees* and the *Wisdom of Solomon*, were preserved by the Roman Christian Church and became known as the Apocrypha. Both the Mishnah and the Masoretic Text became the subject of further study, discussion, and interpretation—which came to be known as the *Gemara* (also meaning study). The leading rabbi of the third century in Palestine was Johannan ben Napaha who edited the Mishnah and Gemara and devised a systematic organization which was called the Palestinian Talmud.

In 425 CE, the Romans abolished the office of the Jewish patriarch in Palestine, and the Sanhedrin ceased to exist. For more than three centuries, the Palestinian rabbis had trained and ordained new generations of rabbis and had provided the leadership for Judaism throughout the Diaspora. Several of these students had returned to the homeland of Hillel in Iraq and formed their own academies there to study the Mishnah and Palestinian Talmud. Through the quality of their study and writings, these new centers of learning in Babylon assumed the leadership of Rabbinic Judaism. A vast Gemara evolved around the Mishnah, which was once again edited and compiled into what became known as the Babylonian Talmud, or more simply The Talmud (doctrine, to learn). The leadership of the Babylonian rabbis continued for centuries—even after the Muslim conquest. The only real change was the adoption of Arabic, in lieu of Aramaic, as the language of Jewish scholarship.

The Golden Age of Judaism Under Islam

The Judaic religion provided the spiritual foundation for Islam—which recognized and honored Jews and Christians as "People of the Book." The Quran considered there to be a community of faith among monotheists. As such, Jews were not only *not* persecuted under Islamic rule, but they and their religion were honored. As the Muslim conquest swept across Africa and into Spain, Jewish centers of learning were established in its wake.

Primary among these centers was one in Tunisia at Kairawan, which was established by Babylonian rabbis. Those who studied and worked in Kairawan became known as Karaites, who began to display a daring independence in thought and in their interpretations of the Torah and Talmud. Their influence spread to the Spanish Jews who had been oppressed by the Christian Goths but were freed by the Islamic conquest.

The Spanish rabbis went ever further than the Karaites in their attempts to determine exactly what the biblical writers intended. Casting aside existing rabbinic interpretations that varied from their own conclusions, they went so far as to suggest that David could not have written all the Psalms, and that the Book of Isaiah may have been added to by an author other than Isaiah. Most daring was the idea that Moses may not have personally transcribed every word of God in the Pentateuch.

Although their status ebbed and flowed during different periods, Jewish life under Muslim rule in Spain prospered in a generally tolerant society. Overall, Jews were much better off than they were in other areas of Europe under Christian rulers, and many Jews immigrated to Spain from other areas. The Jews prospered economically, culturally, and intellectually, creating major works in mathematics, science, medicine, poetry, and philosophy. They were also engaged in translating the extensive Arabic literature into Romance languages, and Greek and Hebrew texts into Arabic.

Spain was ruled by a Muslim Caliphate, which began to disintegrate after 1000 CE, and the land was invaded by Berber Islamic fundamentalists from Morocco known as the Almoravids, and later by the even more puritanical Almohades. These purist Muslims forcibly converted Jews, and there was a massacre of thousands of Jews in Granada in 1066. Following the Christian Reconquista of Spain in 1085, the position of Jews in Spain and Portugal became increasingly precarious, until they were finally expelled from both countries in 1492 and 1496.

Maimonides Restores Gnosticism to Judaism

Historically known as Maimonides, Rabbi Moshe ben Maimon (1135 or 1138-1204) was born in Cordoba during the golden age of Jewish culture in Spain. He was trained as a physician but wrote widely on science and philosophy. His first work was the *Commentary on the Mishnah*, which he followed with a comprehensive 14-volume revision of the entire body of rabbinic law known as the *Mishneh Torah* or *The Repetition of the Torah*. In doing so, he ignored the prophetic visions and imagined the Messiah as a great political leader who would liberate the Jewish people and restore their nation in Palestine.

Maimonides did not dispense with the Law, but he did not believe that a faithful adherence was the goal. For him, obeying the commandments was basic training for achieving perfection through a contemplation of the truth. An understanding of philosophy—in addition to a knowledge of scripture—was required for an intellectual aristocracy to achieve the capacity to fully realize the existence of God.

Just as a simple adherence to the commandments was all that was required for most, Maimonides also believed that the concept of the resurrection was enough for ordinary people. There is a form of spiritual immortality, however, that is limited to those who achieve intellectual awareness. Almost fully expressing the Gnostic principle of equating God with an Abiding Mind, Maimonides talked about a permanent reunion of the soul with the "Active Intellect."

Were it not for the Muslims and Jews, the works of the Greek philosophers might have been lost to humanity during the Christian Dark Ages. These books were translated by the Muslims into Arabic, which became available to Jewish intellectuals. They in turn translated the classics into Latin, which ultimately allowed their introduction into medieval Europe.

The Kabbalah, Spinoza, Luria, and Mendelssohn Rationalize Judaism

From ancient times it was understood that there were different levels of interpreting the Torah—from the direct through the allegorical to the secret, or inner esoteric meanings. The secrets of the Torah were transmitted orally only to the most spiritually mature students.

Attributed to the Patriarch Abraham, the *Sefer Yetzirah*, or *Book of Formation* may be dated as early as the second century CE. It offers a foundation for understanding the secret wisdom of the Jews. The Jewish philosopher Philo, who was associated with the Way or Righteousness at the time of Jesus, is believed to have contributed to this wisdom.

Emerging around the time of Maimonides—and perhaps in reaction to his rationalism—the study of these secrets became more mainstream in a form known as the Kabbalah (tradition), which is related to Gnosticism. Believed to have been authored by Moses de Leon but attributed to a famous rabbi teacher from the Palestinian period, the *Sefer ha-Zohar* or *Book of Splendor* appeared in the thirteenth century. Obviously inspired by genius (or divine guidance), the *Zohar* was enriched by scriptural interpretations, parables, and myths.

Appearing at, or near, the same time was the *Bahir*, consisting of fragmentary pages, which may have been derived from even older works. The Bahir refers to the pleroma, which the Gnostics believed to be the dwelling place of their God (an Abiding Mind). In addition, there is language about a cosmic tree of life that parallels references to the All discussed in the Gnostic *Gospel of Truth* and *Book of Thomas*.

God is known to the Kabbalists as *En Sof*, or the Infinite, and is unknowable. God is, however, revealed to humans through ten intermediary spiritual powers known as sefiroths, which include Wisdom and Mercy. As people aspire toward God through contemplation and purification, they are illuminated by and attracted to the divine light. Upward progress depends on righteousness and piety, while sinfulness interferes with the light. In a reflection of Persian dualism (or the Way's war between light and darkness) the sefiroths arrange themselves on the sides of good or evil. For the Kabbalahists, the Messiah is a cosmic figure, rather than a political liberator.

Where Maimonides had sought a rational understanding of the commandments, the Kabbalists searched for spiritual understanding through imagination and poetry. For the next four hundred years, kabbalistic ideas and study had a profound effect on Rabbinic Judaism. Modern Kabbalists believe the *Zohar* is a bridge between our consciousness and our inner transformative powers—which allows us to disconnect from the material world and to achieve self-awareness. We are entering an age of revelation in which a new level of consciousness is coming into being.

Baruch Spinoza (Espinosa) was born in 1632 into a Portuguese Marrano family which had been forcibly converted to Christianity but reverted to Judaism. Spinoza was raised and educated in the Amsterdam Jewish community, but he was placed under a ban of heresy when he questioned the nature of God and whether Moses wrote the Pentateuch.

Spinoza associated with rationalists and other dissident Christian groups and became more outspoken in his heretical beliefs—stating that the Law was not given by God and was no longer binding on Jews. For Spinoza, the state should be secular and separate from religion. He believed in a philosophy of tolerance and benevolence and lived a simple life as a glass lens grinder and instrument maker. Spinoza enjoyed a wide correspondence with the leading intellectuals of the period but was reluctant to publish his views openly. In 1663, however, he published *Descartes' Principles of Philosophy*, his only philosophical work during his lifetime.

Spinoza died in 1677 at age 44 due to lung disease. His major works, including *Ethics*, were all published posthumously. Spinoza argued that God exists but is abstract and impersonal. He regarded the universe as a living manifestation of God, but one that has no relationship with humanity. God is neither loving, nor responsive to prayers. Reflecting a Gnostic point of view, however, the mind and spirit of humans are as much a part of God as the land and sea. As a matter of personal philosophy, individuals should free themselves from outward ambition and inner emotional distress by addressing the universe as it exists. Spinoza defined the ultimate achievement as the knowledge of God—which requires rationality and reasoning by the mind. He considered the goal to be an "intellectual love of God."

Although Jewish reformers in the future would agree that Spinoza's philosophy was a complete break with the past, and that the scriptures and halakha were not handed down by God, they would nonetheless strive—more than Spinoza did—to remain within Jewish tradition.

The last few surviving Rabbinic Jews in Palestine had been killed by the crusaders, but following the Turkish conquest in the sixteenth century, a small group returned and established a center of Jewish mysticism in the town of Safed in the northern Galilee, which is the most elevated city in Israel. The group was led by an Egyptian Jew named **Isaac Luria**, who died at a young age. The secrets he taught were intended to redeem the world from evil and to restore the nation of Israel.

Luria believed that the light from En Sof, the Infinite God, had become intermingled with darkness, and that good and evil had become twisted in disorder. He sought to separate the light from the dark and to unite the pure light in perfect righteousness, allowing for the appearance of the Messiah. Like elements of Gnosticism, Luria taught that human lifetimes may be too short to achieve separation, requiring reincarnation to allow souls to be reborn in new bodies. The righteous are reborn as saints, while the evil become beasts. Since the task of separating light from darkness is so great, Luria taught that God joins multiple souls together in a composite, more powerful reincarnated body.

Luria's group was not large, but its influence, especially in its Messianic aspects, spread beyond Palestine. One person influenced by the message was Sabbatai Zevi, who was born in Turkey in 1626. Some Kabbalahists had calculated that 1648 would be the year that the Messiah would appear, and the massive pogroms being suffered by Jews in Poland at the time provided the period of dark tribulation thought necessary for his appearance and deliverance. Believing himself to be the anticipated Messiah, Zevi attracted a large group of followers and publicly proclaimed in 1665 that he was the Messiah. Thousands sold their belongings to join him in a triumphant return to Palestine, but Zevi was arrested and imprisoned by the Turkish authorities while en route. Given the choice between Islam and death, Zevi became a Muslim and was provided a comfortable pension. Many of his faithful followers believed Zevi had accepted the impurity of Islam in order to facilitate the separation of light and darkness, and some followed their Messiah and adopted Islam while waiting. Zevi died in 1676; however a dedicated small group of followers, known as the Dönmeh (Turkish "converts"), continue to follow his teachings.

Educated by his rabbi—who introduced him to the philosophy of Maimonides—**Moses Mendelssohn** was born in Germany in 1729. Learning multiple languages, Mendelssohn delved into contemporary philosophies and mathematics. Winning a prize for an essay on the application of mathematical proofs to metaphysics, Mendelssohn became well known and was acquainted with Immanuel Kant and other philosophers. In 1767, he published *Phaedo,* or *On the Immortality of Souls*, which quickly became a best seller and was translated into other languages. In later life, Mendelssohn wrote about the freedom of religion from the state, and the freedom of individual Jews to deviate from Jewish tradition. He believed the basic principles of Rabbinic Judaism were all rational concepts; however, the commandment that "Thou shalt believe" was not included in the Law.

Thus, the stage was set for the reforms to come.

Jewish Accommodation Failed to Prevent Pogroms, Ghettos, and Political Oppression

After the First Crusade and the slaughter of Jews along its campaign trail through Germany and following other anti-Jewish riots that occurred in Europe during the Middle Ages, many European Jews migrated to Poland. They were welcomed by a generally tolerant regime which took advantage of their knowledge and industry. Poland (then united with Lithuania) primarily consisted of a landlord class of nobles and their peasants, and the Jews were able to form a thriving middle class, promoting the commercial interests of the nation.

The Magdeburg Law guaranteed the rights and privileges of Jews, and subsequent laws and charters granted religious freedom and the right to engage in trade and travel. The Roman Catholic Church encouraged persecution of the Jews by local authorities, while the national government protected them and their industries. Although there were blood libels issued against the Jews by the Catholics, and local pogroms caused death and destruction, the population of Polish Jews continually increased because the conditions in the rest of Europe were so much worse.

By the end of the fifteenth century, the Jews had been expelled from Spain and Portugal. These expulsions, along with an exodus from Germany, Austria, and Hungary increased the Jewish population in Poland to the point where it contained most of the Jews in the world. Throughout the sixteenth and into the seventeenth centuries, the Polish-Lithuanian Commonwealth was a "heaven for the Jews" and was the spiritual center of Rabbinic Judaism.

Everything changed in 1648 with the Cossack uprising in the Ukraine (which was then a part of Poland), followed by an invasion from Sweden in 1655. The anger of the Cossacks was directed at the Polish nobility; however, since the Jews were perceived as being allied with the nobility, as many as 100,000 Jews were massacred in the pogroms that took place between 1648 and 1657. Some stability was regained with the defeat of the Swedes, but by the second half of the eighteenth century, Poland was overrun by an alliance of Russia, Austria, and Prussia, and its lands and people divided among the three. All Jews in the Russian sector were required to relocate into the Pale of Settlement formed in 1791 by Catherine the Great. Hundreds of pogroms, involving thousands of deaths, took place in the Pale and continued into the twentieth century.

Simultaneous with these events in Poland, Jews were being forced into ghettos in Germany, Austria, and Italy. The ghettos were walled off; Jews had to retreat inside each night; and they were locked inside on all Christian holidays. On leaving the ghettos, Jews had to wear yellow badges and suffer other forms of humiliation. Laws prohibited Jews from engaging in certain occupations, and limitations were placed on the number of Jewish marriages.

The grandson of Catherine the Great, Nicholas, became Tsar of Russia in 1826 and commenced a relentless campaign to convert all Jews to Christianity. Jewish dress was violently suppressed, and Nicholas used compulsory military service to sever young Jewish men from their families by stationing them in remote places for 25 years. Those who were baptized were promoted, and those who refused were brutalized. Even little boys were seized for military service and kept until past middle age, when most returned home to embrace a barely remembered Judaic faith.

While Nicholas's son, Alexander II attempted some reforms and freed the Russian serfs, his assassination in 1881 promoted a wave of violence against Jews. Pogroms were planned by the military and local police to intimidate and eliminate Jews. The government enacted the "May Laws" to make Jewish life in Russia economically and physically impossible. Procurator Pobedonostev, a government official, acknowledged the purpose: "One-third of the Jews will emigrate, one-third will be baptized, and one-third will starve." Other countries followed suit.

The Spiritual and Joyous Revival of Hasidic Judaism

Based on the same Hebrew root word for piety (*Hesed*) that named the Hasideans of the second century BCE, the modern Hasidic movement arose in the seventeenth century among the Jews of the Poland-Lithuanian commonwealth, particularly in the Ukraine. Inflamed by the appearance of Sabbatai Zevi, the Turkish Messiah, popular interest in the Lurianic Kabbalah was fueled by the availability of inexpensive printed pamphlets allowing the secret teachings to be openly discussed. Coexistent with the numerous Christian revivals taking place around the world, the Jewish people were ready to consider a simpler and more spiritual religion than that offered by traditional Rabbinic Judaism.

Hasidism was founded in 1726 by a folk healer named Israel ben Eliezer, who, at age 36, announced a heavenly calling to be a great kabbalist and miracle worker. Ben Eliezer taught that God was present in everything in the material world, including food, and that, instead of abstinence, one could achieve communion with God through eating. He believed the worship of God should be enjoyed through fervent and vigorous prayer—which would provide openings for the divine light to shine into the material world. The worship of God should be accompanied by humility, enthusiasm, and joy. Music and dancing encouraged a frenzy of cheerful devotion.

Upon Ben Eliezer's death in 1760, the small elite group of disciples with whom he shared the most mystic secrets provided the impetus to the Hasidic movement. Several books were quickly published defining the Hasidic teachings, and new congregations or "courts" were organized across Eastern Europe. Hasidism protested the narrow intellectualism and hair-splitting of the Talmud. By openly practicing the simple principles of Kabbalism, ordinary people had greater freedom to worship as they chose and to experience the godly light. The groups not only provided welfare support but offered educational and recreational opportunities as well.

The movement came to enshrine the leaders of its courts with the honorific title of *Tzaddiq* (The Righteous One) and taught that the Tzaddiq connected the people of his court with the spiritual realm. He became much more than a leader who guided his flock and shared large communal meals with them, the Tzaddiq channeled prosperity and happiness from heaven—which his congregants could experience through obedience and physical contact. Study of the Torah and Talmud was expanded to include the teachings of the Tzaddiq, whose every word and act took on a profound meaning.

Although the movement began to suffer from superstition and scandals, and membership began a steady decline after a half-century of rapid growth, Hasidism continues to offer an original and enjoyable way to engage in Judaic practices. The total number of Hasidim today approaches a half million adherents, most of whom live in New York City and Israel. Although there are some more liberal congregations, the Hasidim mostly represent the Ultra-Orthodox positions of Rabbinic Judaism and support conservative political policies in the State of Israel.

Reformation, Liberalization, and Reconstruction of Rabbinic Judaism

As German Jews entered the nineteenth century, many shared a widespread disillusion with the ability of their faith to cope with the society they lived in. Their religion had become moribund and uninspiring, and some Jews were allowing their children to be baptized and to be raised as Christians. While they had achieved some economic and cultural security, Jews were not accepted into the general society, and they were barred from the civil service and certain professions.

Among those who were concerned about the discrimination, a reform movement arose to redefine Jewish culture and religious practices to make them more suitable for the modern society they lived in. Reflecting the ongoing European Enlightenment, there was a search for the essence of Jewish beliefs—a belief in God, a commitment to ethical and moral practices, and the hunger for human freedom. A group of educators and intellectuals established a reformed Temple in Hamburg. They introduced a new prayer book that questioned the authority of the Oral Torah, and they were denounced as heretics by the Orthodox. A group of "Friends of Reform" circulated a statement of beliefs in 1843 which challenged the Talmud and messianic beliefs and declared that Judaism is "capable of unlimited development."

Leopold Zunz was the first professing Jew to graduate from the University of Berlin. After obtaining a doctorate degree, he founded the Academy of Judaic Studies. In his book, *The Devotional Addresses of the Jews*, Zunz demanded justice for the Jews. Although his book was suppressed by the Prussian government, Zunz continued to encourage Jews to overcome the stigma of cultural inferiority by engaging in a vigorous study of their creative intellectual history and society. The number of Jewish scholars expanded rapidly and works of Jewish literature and history increased in circulation.

Expanding beyond the Talmud, the scholars examined the secular history of the Jews and documented the influence of that history on other cultures. While acknowledging that the Scriptures and Talmud were valuable records of the evolution of Jewish thought, the intellectual honesty and scientific discoveries of the reformers caused them to seek an end to a religious belief in miracles. Reformers insisted that Judaism be allowed to transform itself from its earlier, more primitive forms to embrace the reality of the modern world. Dr. Abraham Geiger, who is the founder of Reform Judaism, encouraged Jews to abandon their hope for a future Messiah and to work for universal righteousness and peace.

The first Jewish congregation in North America—The Spanish and Portuguese Synagogue—was formed in New Amsterdam (New York City) in 1654.[90] Pursuing the freedoms established by the new nation that emerged in the following century, immigrating Jews established congregations throughout the United States and translated their Torah and prayer books into English. Identifying with democracy, these congregations were receptive to the reformers who arrived with them, especially Rabbi Isaac M. Wise. He considered the U.S. Constitution to be "Mosaism in action," and taught that the nation was founded on Jewish ideas. America needed a reformed Judaism that was freed from an obsolete past and prepared to demonstrate its rational and humane basis.

Wise was instrumental in the establishment of the Union of American Hebrew Congregations in 1873 by Reform Judaism groups—and the Hebrew Union College two years later. Among the changes wrought by the reformers were equal rights for women, instrumental music, confirmation of boys and girls, and family pews. Wise also introduced Sabbath Eve services on Friday nights in lieu of Saturday morning worship.

In response to a countermovement against reform launched by the Orthodox, a rabbinical conference in 1885 attempted to define the principles of reform. Among these were a recognition that— while the concept of God in Judaism continues as an achievement of the human mind—many of the primitive elements in the Bible reflected the thinking of the ancient age and must be discarded. They rejected a belief in heaven and hell, and they rejected the resurrection of the body, while upholding the doctrine of spiritual immortality.

Today, Reform Judaism is the major Jewish denomination in America. It endorses the evolving nature of Judaism, ethics over

---

[90] Congregation Shearith Israel is still active on West 70th Street in New York City.

ceremony, and a belief in continuous revelation. Recognizing the autonomy and free will of every individual, reformers do not believe that Jewish Law is binding, and they embrace progressive values and personal spirituality. While the reform movement continues to be centered in North America, reform congregations can be found in nations around the world.

Jews who agree that reform is necessary but are unwilling to go as far as the reformers constitute Conservative Judaism. They want to *conserve* some of the theology and rituals eliminated by Reform Judaism. Their motto is "tradition and change," in that they remain bound to observe ritual law but agree that its interpretation and application can evolve with study and time in conjunction with modern circumstances.

Arising out of the Conservative Judaism in the early twentieth century, Reconstructionist Judaism was founded in the United States upon the philosophy of Rabbi Mordecai Kaplan (1881-1983). It offers the greatest theological diversity of all modern forms of Judaism. The Reconstructionists view the body of Jewish Law as a valuable cultural heritage, but do not believe it to be binding. Although they have their own rabbinical college and ordain their own rabbis, each synagogue congregation engages in communal decision-making based upon education and modern principles. The Reconstructionists recognize that Jews have a duty to question the past and study the present to identify individual paths to the nature of God. They do so with a recognition that Judaism is as much a civilization, as a religion—as they share a love of Jewish culture, morality, and philosophy. The Reconstructionists emphasize the service of righteousness.

Zionism, Nationalism, the Holocaust, and the Palestine Settlement

The religious anti-Semitism fostered by Paul's blood libel continued to run deep into the nineteenth century, and was characterized by the seizure of a Jewish child in 1858 by Catholic Church authorities in Bologna, Italy because he had been secretly baptized by his nurse making him irrevocably a Catholic. Despite public outrage, the Pope became Edgardo Mortara's substitute father—who raised the boy as a Catholic to become a priest. The event was instrumental in the later reduction of the Papal States in Italy to the current tiny Vatican City in Rome.

As anti-Semitism took on modern aspects, it was transformed from a religious slander into a racial bias among those who believed that nations should be racially homogeneous. These bigots who believed Jews to be incurably alien and parasitic were easily exploited by politicians who sought justification for discriminatory laws and scapegoats for governmental failures.

The Dreyfus Affair arose in 1894 with the fraudulent conviction of a Jewish army officer for treason, and France was divided by the refusal of anti-Semitic French military officers to acknowledge the false conviction. Writing about the case, a Jewish journalist, Theodor Herzl wrote a pamphlet titled *The Jewish State* which argued that the problem with anti-Semitism could not be solved until it was recognized that Jews are a nation instead of a religion. Only with a homeland—guaranteed by treaties—could Jews free themselves from prejudice by economically and physically withdrawing from the places where they suffer from discrimination. Herzl became a spokesperson for the worldwide movement that came to be known as Zionism.

Opposition to Herzl's proposal came from Reform Jews who had given up on the hope of ever returning to Israel, in favor of full integration into the nations, particularly in America—where they were free to live openly as Jews and to practice their religion. Others condemned Zionism as a secular campaign for political autonomy which was incompatible with Rabbinic Judaism.

Overcoming opposition, a World Zionist Congress was held in 1897 in Basel, Switzerland. The purpose of the Congress was "to establish for the Jewish people a publicly and legally assured home in Palestine." The Jewish Nation Fund was established in 1901 to purchase land in Palestine to be cultivated by the Jewish people who emigrated there.

Among the leading supporters of Zionism were European socialists who agreed that the Jewish problem could only be solved by the creation of a Jewish state, but who additionally believed that the nation could only be successful if it was modeled on socialist principles.

Herzl died in 1904 at age 44, as the movement he started slowly gained support in a world preparing itself for war. The War to End all Wars provided the political backing necessary that ultimately led to the nation of Israel. In gratitude for the chemical researches of Dr. Chaim Weitzman—which allowed England to produce enough gunpowder to defeat Germany—the British government issued the Balfour Declaration in 1917 that supported the creation of a Jewish National Home in Palestine. England emerged from the war with a League of Nations mandate to rule Palestine, that had been relinquished by Turkey (which had chosen the losing side of the war).

The Balfour Declaration was ratified by the allied powers, including the United States, and plans were made for the eventual independence of the country—which was primarily populated by Palestinian Muslims. The Jewish population began to expand rapidly as immigrants moved in, bought land, and went to work. Among the settler's first endeavors was the foundation of the Hebrew University in Jerusalem in 1918.

Founded on the socialistic principles of many of the settlers, collectives known as kibbutz were established on land purchased by the Jewish National Fund. These colonies were politically and economically independent and were governed by their members. Other than for personal items, everything was owned in common, including the incomes of those working outside of their kibbutz. Labor groups established the General Labor Foundation representing most Jewish workers in the country to provide health and retirement benefits.

This is where Jewish matters stood when Hitler came to power in Germany and implemented the racist program that ultimately resulted in the deaths of more than 80 million people during World War II, including six million Jews (men, women, and children) who were systematically murdered by industrial means as a matter of government policy. All of the books every written in the history of the world would be insufficient to adequately describe the full extent of the horror of these events, but the consequences—for the purpose of this book—resulted in the exodus of the Jewish survivors from Europe to Palestine, their terrorist rebellion against its British mandate, their war against the indigenous Palestinian people and their Arab neighbors, and their creation of the State of Israel in 1948.

Upon its creation, Israel assumed the laws that were in place under the English occupation, including the English common and martial law, and a state of emergency that continues to this day.[91] In addition, the law earlier inherited by the British from the Ottoman Empire allowed family matters such as marriage, divorce, and inheritance to be handled according to the religious law of the affected individuals. For Jews, these matters came to be administered by the Chief Rabbinate of Israel, consisting of a Council and the two Chief Rabbis (one Sephardic and one Ashkenazi). The Chief Rabbinate and the Chief Rabbis oversee the Rabbinical Courts. In addition, the Ministry of Religious Services, a cabinet position, provides budgets for religious councils and facilities and grants financial assistance to yeshivas and for the construction of synagogues. These administrative functions are predominately Orthodox, primarily representing the interests of the 15-20 percent of Israelis who identify themselves as Orthodox or Ultra-Orthodox. The Rabbinate does not, however, religiously represent the half of all Israelis who are secular, or the 35 percent who consider themselves to be non-denominationally religious—even though the Rabbinate decides the most intimate and personal matters affecting their daily lives.

Given the parliamentary system of government inherited from England, the minority religious parties in Israel also possess the pragmatic political power to help form governments, and consequently they demand and often receive the cabinet portfolios relating to the citizenship, residency, visas, and local governments.

Jewish Terrorism Creates the State of Israel

The flow of Jewish immigration into Palestine between the First and Second World Wars resulted in a volatile social and political

---

[91] Israel has yet to create a written constitution to guarantee the rights of all its citizens, including the native Palestinians.

confrontation between the resident Palestinians and the immigrant Jews, who settled on land purchased from the Palestinians by the Jewish National Fund.

Resentment of the Palestinians about the growing Jewish population and political power resulted in riots in 1921 and 1929. The Labor Foundation, which was gaining political power, established the self-defense force that later became the *Haganah*. Although outlawed by the English—who failed to control the riots—the Haganah assumed the defense of Jewish settlers.

Responding to the growth of Jewish militancy and armed underground organizations, the English government circulated a White Paper in 1939 which proposed increased restrictions on Jewish immigration and land purchases. It declared an intention to establish the independence of Palestine—with a majority Palestinian population—within ten years.

There was a reduction of Jewish militancy against the English mandate of Palestine during World War II; however, rumors of the genocide of European Jewry resulted in a renewal of Zionistic efforts to facilitate illegal immigration and to establish a Jewish nation in Palestine.

The armed Jewish insurrection resumed after the war and supported the influx of Holocaust survivors. The Haganah, which had originated as a defense force, united with the Irgun and Lehi (Stern Gang) terrorist groups to form the Jewish Resistance Movement.[92] The insurgency engaged in an armed rebellion to undermine and terminate the British occupation and mandate. Its terrorist activities included political assassinations, bombings, kidnappings, and armed attacks on British military and police forces within Palestine. The insurrection also included external terrorist acts, including multiple bombings, against British targets in Europe.

In April 1947, England surrendered and referred all political

---

[92] Two men who would later serve as prime ministers of Israel were active members of these terrorist gangs: Menachem Begin was the head of the Irgun, which bombed the King David Hotel, killing 91 guests, and Yitzhak Shamir was a leader of the Stern Gang, who personally ordered the assassination of the Middle East representative of the United Nations, who was supervising the truce of 1948.

issues regarding Palestine to the United Nations—which recommended the partition of Palestine into Jewish and Palestinian states. The British Mandate ended on May 15, 1948, and the State of Israel was declared by the Jewish inhabitants of Palestine.

During and following the War of Independence against the Palestinian people and the adjoining Arab nations—which ended with an armistice in 1949—more than 700,000 Palestinians were either forced from their homes or fled the violence, and more than 400 Palestinian villages were depopulated in the Palestinian exodus known as the *Nakba*.

The State of Israel ended up with approximately one-third more territory that it had been allocated by the United Nation partition plan, including the Negev, Galilee and Jezreel Valleys, West Jerusalem and the coastal plain. The Palestinian state was never established; Gaza was occupied by Egypt and the West Bank by Jordan. These surrounding areas, and the Golan Heights, were conquered by Israel during the Six Day War in 1967 and remain under Israeli military occupation in defiance of international law.

The Legacy of Rabbinic Judaism

The purpose of this book is not to discuss the status of Israel today, whether it illegally occupies Palestinian land, if it engages in apartheid regarding its own Palestinian citizens, if its government exhibits elements of fascism, or whether it is a democracy or theocracy, but rather the goal has been to trace the origin and development of Rabbinic Judaism, the religion of some of the Israeli people and the racial, social, and familial self-identification of most of them.

At the time around 200 BCE when the Pharisees were first identified as members of the Hasidean-Zaddik movement that came to be known as the Way of Righteousness, Judaism was the only law- and ethics-based religion in the world resting on the exercise of free will. At that point, Judaism had already matured from its primitive roots to include enlightened elements from the eastern religions it encountered during the Babylonian Exile. Judaism asserted its independence from an occupying force—even as it absorbed Greek philosophies from the Syrians and Egyptians.

It was upon the righteousness foundation of the Way (which it also shares with Roman Christianity and Islam—as we will see in the following part) that Rabbinic Judaism was constructed, and which allowed it to survive and evolve throughout the past 2,000 years. All of this as its adherents have been exposed to the most inhuman discrimination and tortures ever imagined. The righteousness influences of the Way allowed the Jewish people to preserve the core of their collective being. They were able to absorb, replicate, improve upon, and to share what they encountered along the Way, as well as the unique and valuable creations they contributed to the human store of knowledge, wisdom, art, music, and literature.

Throughout the toil and tribulations endured over 2,000 years, an irresistible spirit of joy has characterized Judaism. It is expressed in the Jewish toast to life, *L'Chaim*, and from which there is much for everyone to learn. In addition to knowledge, wisdom, and peace, there must be joy in life. A wise saying holds that "in time to come, everyone will have to account for all the good things God created which he refused to enjoy."

The Jewish people have always sought to be free and independent. Limited, always, by the small number of those who ascribe to their faith, the Jews repeatedly have been forced for thousands of years to accommodate to a series of superior secular powers in order to survive. The Jews made a spiritual and intellectual contribution to these political powers, which ultimately turned on their Jewish supporters.

Today, having suffered through thousands of years of discrimination and violence, and the Nazi Holocaust, the Israeli people of the State of Israel may be exhibiting the behavior of their oppressors in creating an apartheid, fascist government that denies the rights and freedom of its indigenous Palestinian and Samaritan citizens. The racial ancestry of the Palestinian, Samaritan, Druze, and Jewish people in the land are one and the same under Abraham's ancient Covenant of Righteousness, and all have an equal moral right to its possession and governance. That said, there is no doubt that Israel—possessed of nuclear weapons—will never surrender the political and social dominance of its Jewish citizens. Before that occurs, the Israelis will take the entirety of humanity down with them.

Israel remains in a state of war against its Muslim neighbors in the Middle East; however, throughout the years the Jews lived in peace within the Islamic Empires, they were treated with respect. It has been Israel's seizure of land from their Muslim neighbors that has caused primary difficulties.

Although there are Orthodox and Ultra-Orthodox Jews who sincerely believe every word in the Torah is inerrantly true, most fair-minded Jews could accept that God is not a being outside of our material world and mind, but is in fact a composite universal consciousness, consisting of everything ever imagined and created. An understanding and acceptance of this Gnostic view of an Abiding Mind is what will ultimately allow all paths of the Way to merge together. On that day, Rabbinic Judaism—having faithfully preserved its spiritual foundation over the millennia—will have earned a large share of the glory.

The Righteous Way of Islam

Following the death of Jesus—and as James and Simeon led Jesus's Congregation of the Poor in Jerusalem—their brother, Judas Thomas, took the message of the Way of Righteousness to the East, where the Way ultimately became Righteous Islam.

Influenced by the stories of the Way he heard from his Christian-Jewish relatives, Muhammad had a Gnostic experience and recited the message he heard in his mind to others. He attracted followers, who became known as Muslims into a new religion known as Islam. Muhammad was the reformist leader of the Way of Islam and the last prophet of Abraham's God.

JUDAS THOMAS WAS THE MESSENGER OF THE WAY TO THE EAST

The New Testament recites the Roman Christian fable about Thomas, the doubting disciple who refused to believe in the resurrection of Jesus until he could see him with his own eyes. According to the Gospel of John (20:24-29), "Now Thomas, one of the twelve, called the Twin, was not with them when Jesus came. So, the other disciples told him, 'We have seen the Lord.' But he said to them, 'Unless I see in his hands the print of the nails, and place my hand in his side, I will not believe.'"

In Roman Christian churches all over the world, the sermons on the Sunday following Easter are usually dedicated to contrasting Thomas's lack of faith with that of the faithful believers. For Jesus said to Thomas after he had seen Jesus and declared him Lord and God, "Have you believed because you have seen me? Blessed are those who have not seen and yet believe."

The Roman authors not only eliminated the true role of Judas Thomas from the their Gospels, just as they did James, Simeon, Joseph (Barnabas or Joses), and Mary Magdalene, but they used his name for the fictional character of Judas Iscariot, the betrayer of Jesus. These literary fictions may have been designed to cast doubt on Judas, as they confusingly refer to him as Thomas. The historical role of Judas Thomas—as the true twin brother of Jesus—is presented more fully in the Gnostic Gospels and other sources suppressed by the Roman Christians. Most amazingly, with the revelations of the Dead Sea Scrolls, it can now be established that, in addition to Jesus and James, Judas may have been one of the three expected messiahs of the Way of Righteousness.

Jesus's Twin Brother, Judas Thomas, Was the Third Messiah of the Way

The Gospel of John refers to Judas as Thomas Didymus. Both words mean twin: Thomas is derived from the Aramaic or Syrian *Toma* and Didymus is from the Greek *Didymos*. According to the

Gospel of Thomas found at Nag Hammadi, he is identified as Judas Thomas. The *Acts of Thomas* also calls him Judas Thomas. There, it is said that when Jesus appears to a young man, "he saw the Lord Jesus in the likeness of the Apostle Judas Thomas . . . The Lord said to him: 'I am not Judas who is also Thomas; I am his brother.'"

The *Pistis Sophia*, a Gnostic Gospel discovered in 1773, establishes the priority of Judas Thomas in terms of doctrine. In *Pistis Sophia,* Mary Magdalene says:

> Now at this time, my Lord, hear, so that I speak openly, for thou hast said to us "He who has ears to hear, let him hear:" Concerning the word which thou didst say to Philip: "Thou and Thomas and Matthew are the three to whom it has been given . . . to write every word of the Kingdom of the Light, and to bear witness to them;" hear now that I give the interpretation of these words. It is this which thy light-power once prophesied through Moses: "Through two and three witnesses everything will be established. The three witnesses are Philip and Thomas and Matthew."[93] (1:43)

We have previously recognized the probability that Jesus saw himself, and was viewed by the Way, as the suffering Son of Man Messiah who had been expecting to sacrifice himself for the salvation of humanity. Moreover, we considered the strong likelihood that his brother, James the Just was viewed by the congregation as their Righteous Teacher and expected priestly messiah. Both Jesus and James, as well as their brother, Simeon lived their lives under Nazarite vows, which meant, among other things, that they never married or begat children. Joseph (Barnabas or Joses), as a lay priest of the Sons of Zadok in the Order of Melchizedek had taken the gospel of the Way to the Gentiles. The question is whether Judas Thomas was the Davidic Messiah expected by the Way?

The *Testament of Judah* speaks of Judea following the return from the exile and goes on to describe the attributes of the expected kingly messiah:

---

[93] As we've learned, the original Book of Matthew may have been written in Hebrew by Jesus's younger brother, Joseph (Barnabas or Joses), as well as The Letter to the Hebrews.

And after these things shall a star arise to you from Jacob in peace. And a man shall arise from my seed, like the sun of righteousness. Walking with the sons of men in meekness and righteousness; And no sin shall be found in him. And the heavens shall be opened unto him, to pour out the spirit, even the blessing of the Holy Father; and He shall pour out the spirit of grace upon you; And ye shall be unto Him sons in truth, and ye shall walk in His commandments first and last. Then shall the scepter of my kingdom shine forth; and from your root shall arise a stem; and from it shall grow a rod of righteousness to the Gentiles, to judge and to save all that call upon the Lord . . . . And ye shall be the people of the Lord and have one tongue; and there shall be there no spirit of deceit of Beliar, for he shall be cast into the fire forever. (4:20-30)

From the *Testament of Benjamin*, the youngest of Jacob's sons, there comes a description of the third combined messiah, who by his work and word will enlighten the Gentiles:

And there shall arise in the latter days one beloved of the Lord, of the tribe of Judah and Levi, a doer of His good pleasure in his mouth, with new knowledge enlightening the Gentiles . . . . And he shall be inscribed in the holy books, both his work and his word, and he shall be a chosen one of God forever. (2:26-28)

Even though the Way of Righteousness determined that the kingly messiah did not have to be of the royal linage of David, the question about whether Judas and his children were of this linage became a matter of concern to the Romans during the time following their destruction of Jerusalem and Judea-Israel.

We do know that Judas Thomas fathered children. His descendants became known in history as the *Desposyni* (The Master's People), and they were known to maintain private records of their lineage. According to Eusebius, ". . . there still survived of the Lord's family the grandsons of Jude, who was said to be his brother, humanly speaking. These were informed against as being of David's line and brought . . . before Domitian Caesar . . . . Domitian asked them whether they were descendants from David, and they admitted it." Eusebius also reports that the Desposyni survived to become leaders of various Christian churches, according to a strict dynastic succession. He traces them to the time of Emperor Trajan (98-117 CE). Even if it were not true that Judas was of the royal lineage of King David, the Romans believed it to be true. That is a fact.

The Jesuit historian Malachi Martin reports that Pope Sylvester met personally in 318 CE with eight descendants of Judas Thomas. The Desposyni demanded (1) that the confirmation of Christian bishops of Jerusalem, Antioch, Ephesus, and Alexandria be revoked, (2) that these be conferred on the Desposyni, and (3) that Roman Christian churches "resume" sending money to the Desposyni Church in Jerusalem. Sylvester turned them down, stating the Mother Church was now Rome, and Rome had the authority to appoint its own bishops.

As we examine Judas Thomas's mission to the East, we can see that the Way of Righteousness he taught created a spiritual foundation which was a unique blending of Judaism and Christianity. It appears his ministry inspired spiritual kingdoms throughout the Middle East, specifically within Arabia, that lasted for hundreds of years, and which ultimately contributed to the creation of Islam. If this is true, Judas's role could also fulfill the prediction of the third kingly messiah by the Way.

Judas's Message to the East Was the Only Branch of the Way That Survived

At the time Judas undertook his mission to expose the Way of Righteousness to those who lived to the east of Judea-Israel, he took with him the only surviving element of Judaism that existed following the destructive wars of the Zealots. Except for the tiny sect of the Pharisees, which collaborated, the Romans killed and enslaved all the "Jews" in the nation. As the slaughter began, the fact and face of Judaism in the nation was one and the same as the Way of Righteousness, and their militant wing—the Zealots.

Once Judas and his family, the survivors of the Way, and the

Congregation of the Poor migrated east, Judea-Israel was emptied of everyone who practiced the enlightened Judaism of the Way and the Zealots. There remained only those who allied themselves with the Romans. Moreover, once Paul subverted Joseph's (Barnabas's) mission to the Gentiles, and his Roman Christian followers destroyed the Gnostic Church of Mary Magdalene, the *only* survivors of the Way of Righteousness left in the world were to be found in the East among the followers of Judas Thomas.

Eusebius, the Roman church historian who wrote in the fourth century, described Judas Thomas's mission as being to the East. Reportedly, he evangelized among the Parthians, who occupied the region from the Tigris-Euphrates basin up through what is now Iran. (*History* 3:1) Judas Thomas is also believed to have evangelized the Medians in Iraq.

A similar tradition exists among a sect of Syrian Christians, who call themselves, "Christians of St. Thomas." According to them, they were converted by Thomas, who later died in India.

In the *Acts of Thomas*, an apocryphal work dating from the third century, Thomas's mission takes him into India. There, tradition identifies seven cities in which he established Judaic congregations that professed a belief in the ministry of Jesus and the Way. Reports dating to the late second century specifies Christian tribes in India who claimed to have been converted by Thomas and to have the books to prove it.

Thomas is believed to have died in Mylapore, India in 72 CE after being pierced with lances. If this true, Judas may have been a Zealot of the Way, who died with his sword in his hand, defending his faith and family.

Nestorian Christians built a church over his traditional burial place in the tenth century. Records in the sixteenth century demonstrate that the site was revered by Hindus and Muslims, as well as Christians. The tomb was maintained by the Muslims, who kept a lamp burning. When the Portuguese came to power in the area, they built the San Thome Basilica upon the tomb in 1522. That building was subsequently replaced by the Santhome Cathedral Basilica, which was completed in 1896. It still stands.

Syrian-descended Christian communities in India—among the oldest anywhere—claim Thomas as their founder; it is a church of the highest social caste, using Syriac as a liturgy, but with Nestorian elements.

Although Indian Christians believe Thomas's relics are still in India, the Roman Catholic Church says that his bones were moved to Edessa (now Urfa in Turkey) in 232 CE.[94] Following the recapture of Edessa from the crusaders by the Muslim Turks in 1144, the shrine to Thomas was destroyed; however, according to Church tradition, his relics were saved and transported to the West where they were enshrined in the Cathedral of Saint Thomas the Apostle in Ortona, on the east coast of Italy.[95]

Jesus's Congregation of the Poor and The Way Leave Judea-Israel

As we have seen, the Way of the Zaddik, Hassideans, and the Way of Righteousness evolved to have other names, including the Congregation, Saints, and the Poor. As the religious philosophy of the Way culminated in the mission of Jesus in Jerusalem, his followers became known as the Congregation of the Poor, or as the Nazoreans. Following the destruction of the Temple and Jerusalem in 70 CE, those members of the Congregation who were able to escape to the east became known in history as the Nazoreans and Ebionites (which means the Poor).

The Ebionites were Jews who followed the Way and who recognized Jesus as the suffering Son of Man Messiah who sacrificed

---

[94] Edessa was the capital city of King Abgar. From ancient times the Mediterranean world had made a cult of the Dioscuri, the Divine Twins. Under the names of Castor and Pollux, these twins had played an extremely important role in the formation and evolution of Greek mythical thought. Romulus and Remus were revered as the pair from whom the foundations of Rome derived. Edessa was a center of the twin cult, worshipping the pair under the names of Momin and Aziz. This pair may have been supplanted by Jesus and Judas Thomas in mythology—if not in fact.

[95] Thomas' relics are believed to still be there, except for his skull, which may have come to rest in the Monastery of Saint John the Theologian on the Greek Island of Patmos.

his life for the salvation of humanity. The Ebionites supported the ruling by James regarding justification by works, instead of faith; however, the Mosaic law they followed did not include the oral Torah of the Pharisees, or the succeeding Rabbinic Judaism. The Ebionites were militantly hostile towards Paul—as a false apostle—and the heretical theology he created.

Around 200 CE, Irenaeus, Bishop of Lyons, issued his *Adversus Haereses,* a violent and dogmatic attack on the prevalent heresies of the time. In the book, he condemns the Ebionites:

> Those who are called Ebionites agree that the world was made by God; but . . . .. They use the Gospel according to Matthew only, and repudiate the Apostle Paul, maintaining that he was an apostate from the law. As to the prophetical writings, they endeavor to expound them in a somewhat singular manner: they practice circumcision, persevere in the observance of those customs which are enjoined by the law, and are so Judaic in their style of life, that they even adore Jerusalem as if it were the house of God. (Book I, Chapter 26)

Irenaeus rages on about the Ebionites:

> Vain also are the Ebionites, who do not receive by faith into their soul the union of God and man, but who remain in the old leaven of [the natural] birth, and who do not choose to understand that the Holy Ghost came upon Mary, and the power of the Most High did overshadow her. (Book V, Chapter 1)

As seen in the earlier quotation from the *Acts of Thomas*, the Ebionites did not accept the Roman masculine or neutered definition of the Holy Spirit. They followed the teachings of Mary Magdalene and the Gnostics, who viewed Sophia and the Spirit of Wisdom as being feminine.

Another extra-biblical source that provides information about the Ebionites is the Clementine literature, which is a religious romance that appeared in early Church histories. The *Clementines* contain a narrative of discourses allegedly involving Pope Clement I, James the Just, and the Apostle Peter. They were written before 325 CE, as they are mentioned by Eusebius in his *Ecclesiastical History* (III,xxxviii). The Clementine writings survive intact in both Greek and Latin editions.

The Clementines contains an Ebionite treatise that questions whether Jesus is "the eternal Christ" in discussing his ministry and role as a savior. This material is like that found in Joseph's Letter to the Hebrews about his mission to the Gentiles. In the Clementine story, Clement hears Joseph (Barnabas or Joses) speak and follows him to Jerusalem.

There is also a close correlation of the Ebionites with the *Ascents of James*, a lost work referred to by Epiphanius of Salamis in another attack on the Ebionites. He complained that the Ebionites esteemed James, the brother of Jesus, and denigrated Paul as a "certain hostile person." The *Ascents* is written from a Jewish Christian perspective in which Jesus is presented as a prophet in the lineage of Moses who was sent by God to complete the work of Moses by abolishing sacrifices to redeem Israel.

The Clementine *Recognitions* (IV:34-5) calls Paul "the enemy" and identifies his justification by faith as a heresy. Paul was a false apostle and an apostate from the Judaism of the Ebionites. The *Recognitions* argues that Peter never in fact accepted Paul's theology, and quotes Peter as issuing a warning against any authority other that of James. It maintains that James was the rightful heir of Jesus.

The Way of Righteousness That Judas Thomas Showed to the Middle East

We have no direct record of the gospel taught by Judas Thomas, but from a review of the documentary evidence, we can determine that his mission was a continuation of the Way or Righteousness as taught by Jesus, James, and Mary Magdalene. Following the Spirit of Wisdom ministry of Mary Magdalene, the *Acts of Thomas* recognizes the Holy Spirit as feminine:

> Twin brother of Christ, Apostle of the Most High and fellow initiate into the hidden words of Christ, who dost

receive his secret sayings . . . Come Holy Spirit, the Holy Dove that bearest the twin young. Come, Hidden Mother.

The Roman authors eliminated most references to Jesus's brothers from the Gospels and Acts; however, the Roman editors who later compiled the canon of the New Testament in the fourth century were likely forced to include the authoritative letters of James and Judas—although they did so at the very end, along with Joseph's Letter to the Hebrews and first and second John, where their importance was minimized.

As was previously discussed in the Remnant of the Way, the Letter of James most accurately represents the dogma of the Way of Righteousness and its Congregation of the Poor established by Jesus, during the almost three decades following the crucifixion of Jesus—when James was the head of the congregation. James not only taught that faith without works is dead, but some of James's language closely reflected that of the Way and the Dead Sea Scrolls. Using Qumran imagery of the "Crown of Glory," James wrote: "Blessed is the man who endures trial, for when he has stood the test, he will receive the crown of life which God has promised to those who love him." (1:12)

Using Way, Gnostic, *and* Kabbalistic imagery, James writes:

> Do not be deceived, my beloved brethren. Every good endowment and every perfect gift is from above, coming down from the Father of lights with whom there is no variation or shadow due to change. Of his own will he brought us forth by the word of truth that we should be a kind of first fruits of his creatures. (1:16-17)

In words similar to those we will soon find in the Noble Quran, James describes: "Religion that is pure and undefiled before God and the Father is this: to visit orphans and widows in their affliction and to keep oneself unstained from the world."(1:27)

Continuing to present Gnostic lessons, James teaches:

> But the wisdom from above is first pure, then peaceable, gently, open to reason, full of mercy and good fruits,

without uncertainty or insincerity. And the harvest of righteousness is sown in peace by those who make peace. (3:17-18)

The only direct evidence of the gospel taught by Judas Thomas is found at the very end of the New Testament. The Letter of Jude is the last book before Revelations. Judas identifies himself as, "Jude, a servant of Jesus Christ and a brother of James, To those who are called, beloved in God the Father and kept for Jesus Christ." The letter begins with the purpose of writing for, ". . . admission has been secretly gained by some who long ago were designated for this condemnation, ungodly persons who pervert the grace of our God into licentiousness and deny our only Master and Lord, Jesus Christ."

These opponents are not identified by name or sect, but may have been directed at Paul and his deviate ministry:

Yet in like manner these men in their dreamings defile the flesh, reject authority, and revile the glorious ones. . . . But these men revile whatever they do not understand, and by those things that they know by instinct as irrational animals do, they are destroyed. Woe to them! (8-10)

The opponents are described using words like writings found in the Dead Sea Scrolls and the Letter of James, including rain-making imagery.

These are blemishes on your love feasts, as they boldly carouse together, looking after themselves, waterless clouds, carried along by winds; fruitless trees in late autumn, twice dead, uprooted; wild waves of the sea, casting up the foam of their own shame; wandering stars for whom the nether gloom of darkness has been reserved forever. (12-13)

Judas goes on to quote Enoch, a hero of the Way and whose book was excluded from the biblical canon, "'Behold, the Lord came with his holy myriads, to execute judgment on all.'" Continuing (to refer to Paul), Judas says, "These are grumblers, malcontents, following their own passions, loud-mouthed boasters, flattering people to gain advantage." (14-16)

The faithful are encouraged by Judas to, "build yourselves up on your most holy faith; pray in the Holy Spirit; keep yourselves in the love of God; wait for the mercy of our Lord Jesus Christ unto eternal life. And convince some, who doubt; save some, by snatching them out of the fire; on some have mercy with fear, hating even the garment spotted by the flesh." (20-23)

The late Hebrew University professor Schlomo Pines (1908-1990) discovered a collection of Arabic manuscripts in Istanbul in 1960 that he dated from the tenth century. Included were quotes from an earlier fifth or sixth century text, which the Arab writer ascribes to "*al-nasara*"—the Nazoreans. That earlier text is believed to have been written originally in Syriac and may have been found at a Christian monastery in Khuzistan.

The Nazorean text appears to reflect a tradition of Jewish law dating, without a break, back to the original Nazorean group under the leadership of Jesus's brother, Simeon, who fled Jerusalem just prior to the Roman invasion in 66 CE. In it, Jesus is stated to be a man—not a god—and any suggestion of his divinity is rejected. Paul is castigated and his followers are said to "have abandoned the religion of Christ and turned towards the religious doctrines of the Romans." The New Testament Gospels are dismissed as unreliable, second-hand accounts which contain only "something—but little—of the sayings, the precepts of Christ and information concerning him." The document goes on to say that the Nazoreans were still in existence and were the elite among Christians.

These Arabic documents were written soon after the life and prophecy of Muhammad, which we will shortly consider regarding its relationship to the Way—as it existed in Arabia at the time.

The Kingdoms of The Way in Syria, Ethiopia, and Arabia

Even though Judas may have been killed and originally buried in India, evidence demonstrates that his descendants continued as a Davidic lineage for many generations. During the centuries following the life of Judas Thomas, several Jewish and Christian Kingdoms were established in the Middle East. Given the fact that the eastern migration of Judaism and "Christianity" were one and the same as the Way of Righteousness, we can surmise that these kingdoms reflected the core doctrine of the Way: Living a life of righteousness in the Spirit of Wisdom.

The first Christian monarch was King Abgar of Edessa (now Urfa in Turkey), whose kingdom extended into Syria. Possibly as the result of Ebionite influences, some of the Jews of Edessa accepted the gospel of the Way and Jesus around the middle of the second century. The form of their Christianity observed in Edessa was Gnostic. One of their members wrote an allegorical account entitled the *Odes of Solomon* about the self-transfiguration of the Soul resulting from the search for the Pearl of Knowledge. The Gnostic Christian writing was probably composed in the second century by a Syrian Jew.

Another Syrian Christian kingdom was established by Zenobia, who was born around 241 CE in Palmyra, the daughter of one of the Roman generals governing the city. Zenobia is the form of the name used by Latin and Greek historians; the Aramaic form is Bat-Zabba, daughter of Zabba, and to Arabic writers she is known as al-Zabba. Her rise to political importance was a result of her marriage to the Roman senator and self-proclaimed king of Palmyra, Septimius Odaenathus. Odaenathus was regarded as the savior of the East when in the 260s he repulsed a Persian invasion. He was murdered soon after this, and his son by Zenobia, Vaballathus (Aramaic Wahballath) became king of Palmyra. Third century Syria was a melting pot of religions, and Christian doctrine was hotly debated. Zenobia, as a Jewish proselyte with Christian beliefs, supported these religions during the reign of her son.

The Himyarite Kingdom was established in the area of Yemen on the southwest tip of the Arabian Peninsula around 110 BCE and lasted until the sixth century CE. Commencing around 380 CE, the dynasty converted to a form of Judaism that was associated with the Christian Kingdom of Ethiopia across the narrow Red Sea. The Himyarites dominated Arabia throughout these centuries and controlled the trade of ivory from Africa and other products with the Roman Empire.

The influence of the Himyarite Kingdom on the events which follow in Arabia cannot be overly stressed. During the centuries between the lives of Jesus and his brothers and that of Muhammad, the predominate religion in the area of Mecca, where Muhammad lived, was that of the Way of Righteousness.

The Kingdom of Aksum in northern Ethiopia was established around 100 CE and lasted for more than 800 years. Its power extended as far north as Egypt in Africa and across the Red Sea into the Arabia Peninsula through its domination of the Himyarite Kingdom. The ruling dynasty converted to Christianity in 325 CE and was the first state to use the cross on its coinage. At one point, the Aksum installed a Christian viceroy to watch over the Himyarite Kingdom and extended the Christian faith into Arabia.

As the Davidic Messiah of the Way, it appears that Judas Thomas shared the word of righteousness in the Middle East. That blending of Judaism and Gnostic Christianity persisted for more than five centuries as the essential religion of Arabia, and the Way was in fact the spiritual inspiration of Islam. If it is also true that all other branches of the Way were destroyed by the Roman Christians, then the Muslims of Islam are the only living representatives of the Way, who have a direct connection with Jesus, through his brother, Judas Thomas.

THE LAND, PEOPLE, AND RELIGION OF SEVENTH CENTURY ARABIA

During the five centuries following the fall of the Temple in Jerusalem and the forced migration of the Ebionites to the East, the missionary plantings of Judas Thomas established deep roots in the land of Arabia and beyond. A unique brand of Judaism that accepted Jesus as having been the messiah and teaching his message of love and salvation, the Ebionites coexisted with their Arab neighbors in a harsh land governed by tribal rules and ancient pagan rites.

Primarily consisting of arid deserts and volcanic mountains, these surface features have existed for eons but float on a massive sea of petrochemicals deposited more than 400 million years ago when the Arabian Peninsula was connected to Africa and was underwater before being split away and uplifted by the Red Sea Rift and subsequent tectonic events. Fourteen hundred years ago, the land was desolate and largely uninhabited except for areas along the coasts of the Red Sea on the west and the Persian Gulf on the east, and at scattered oases in the interior. At that time, Arabia shared long borders with Syria on the northwest and Iraq on the northeast. Yemen was situated in the southwest corner of the peninsula across the Red Sea from the land of Abyssinia (Ethiopia). The two cities now known as Mecca and Medina are located inland and approximately halfway along the east coast of the Red Sea.

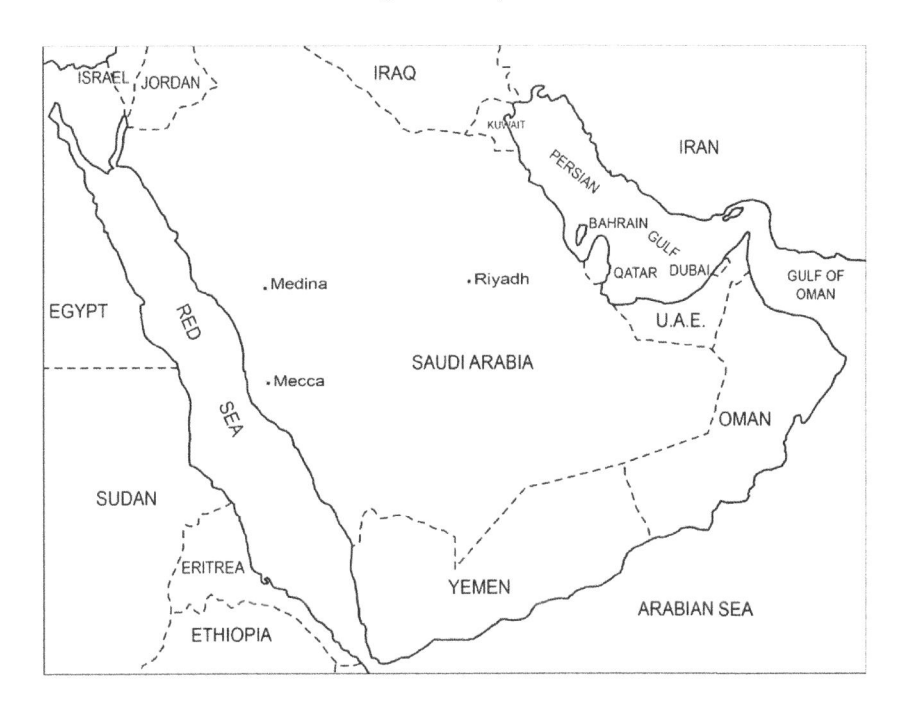

Ancient trade routes existed across the peninsula between Africa and Iraq and between the Persian Gulf and the Red Sea, and at various times and places local civilizations arose and declined. The most significant of these was that of the Nabataeans in the extreme northwest, who expanded from their capital city of Petra (located southeast of Jerusalem). The Nabataeans controlled trade routes that passed through Petra and the Arabian desert oases and became wealthy from the tribute they collected from mercantile caravans. The Nabataeans were defeated by the Romans, and later converted to Christianity during the Byzantine era.

The Arabians were of Semitic origin and shared the same racial background as the Jews, Samaritans, Syrians, and Assyrians.[96] They were organized by familial tribes in both the towns and deserts, and were led by men selected for strength and adherence to the code of

---

[96] The name of the inhabitants of the Arabian Peninsula first appears in writing as the *Aribi* in cuneiform on the Kurkh stela created by the Assyrian king Shalmaneser III in 853 BCE to commemorate the battle of Qarqar in northern Syria. The Arabs contributed a cavalry consisting of 1,000 camels in their alliance with King Ahab of Israel against the Assyrian invasion.

tribal conduct.[97] Order was maintained by force and blood feuds, where the death of a tribal member was immediately balanced by killing the murderer, or a member of his family. Women and slaves had no rights and were the property of the men who controlled them. Infanticide was common, especially female babies who had little value, and men could have as many wives as they could support.

Literacy was little valued in the society; however, poets were honored. Songs glorified tribal victories in which God, or gods, played little part. Poets would recite or sing their verses, which would be memorized by listeners and repeated. Because of their abilities, poets were thought to have magical powers and to be possessed by superhuman spirits known as *jinns*. Their ability to curse enemies and to inspire warriors was valued by the Arabs.

The Arabs practiced an Abrahamic religion based on the combination of Judaic and Christian influences expressed by the Way of Righteousness, with elements of paganism. On one hand they worshipped the supreme god al-Llah (Allah), the High One, at an ancient shrine known as the Kaaba in the city of Mecca. The Kaaba contained the horns of the ram believed to have been Abraham's substitute sacrifice for his Arabic son, Ishmael, and images of Jesus and his mother, Mary.[98]

Most Arabs believed that Allah was the same god as the Hebrew god Yahweh. In addition, the Arabs also paid homage to lesser gods, including the numerous subordinate gods, or tribal totems that surrounded the Kaaba, and three other nearby shrines that were dedicated to the daughters of Allah.

---

[97] The *muruwah* honored the virtues of bravery, hospitality, justice, and a commitment to the tribe's well-being.
[98] The Kaaba is a cube-shaped building of ancient construction featuring a football-sized black stone, believed to be a meteorite, set into its eastern wall. The Arabs believed the Kaaba was established by Adam, rebuilt by Noah after the Great Flood, and rediscovered by Abraham while visiting his firstborn son, Ishmael. The Kaaba was mentioned by Ptolemy as early as the third century BCE, when Mecca was known as Macoraba. In the seventh century, the Kaaba was a roofless, walled enclosure constructed of stones containing the most important effigies, including those of Abraham, Jesus, and Mary. The word cube may be derived from the Arabic *Kaaba*.

Everything within a 20-mile radius surrounding the Kaaba was a sacred sanctuary. This provided protection to pilgrims who would journey to Mecca each autumn in a pilgrimage known as the Dhu al-Hijja, or the *hajj*. In a ceremony dating back many centuries, the pilgrims would circle the Kaaba seven times and perform other rituals to their favorite tribal gods in the surrounding area.

Because it was home to the Kaaba and its surrounding sanctuary zone, Mecca thrived in the seventh century as a place of religious pilgrimages and, because of that fact, as a major center of commerce. Mecca was a resupply depot and trading post located just off of the main north-south caravan route between the Red Sea ports of Yemen and the population centers of Damascus in Syria and on to Bagdad in Iraq. With tribal feuds stayed at the sanctuary border, there was safe access to a market in products that included silver, the precious myrrh and frankincense, cloth, clothing, blankets, leather, harnesses, saddles, meat, and camel butter.

The leading tribe of Mecca was the Quraysh, who had originally immigrated from Yemen. They were successful merchants who were the "Keeper of the Keys" to the Kaaba and had the responsibility of guarding it. They also supplied the homespun seamless linen cloths worn by the pilgrims during *hajj*. In addition, the Quraysh managed a large outdoor carnival and bazaar each year outside of the city in conjunction with the *hajj*, which sold a wide variety of products, including date wine and fermented mare's milk. Some of these caravan merchants were so successful that they owned houses and properties in Egypt, Gaza, Syria, Palestine, and Iraq. There they would spend time at the end of their trading journeys and would connect with other trade routes, such as the "Silk Road" to China.

It was at this point in the history of Arabia, in or about 570 CE, that Muhammad[99] was born in Mecca to the Banu Hashim clan of the prominent tribe of Quraysh. His clan had the honor of selling water to the pilgrims who did *hajj*.[100]

---

[99] Muhammad's full birth name is Abū al-Qāsim Muhammad ibn 'Abd Allāh ibn 'Abd al-Muttalib ibn Hāshim.

[100] For the benefit of the pilgrims, Muhammad's grandfather, Abd al-Muttalib excavated a freshwater spring feeding the Zamzam well adjacent to the Kaaba.

MUHAMMAD, THE RELUCTANT MESSENGER OF GOD

The first written biographies of Muhammad were not completed until several hundred years after his death, and the details of his life before he became a prophet are unknown; however, the first 25 years of his life seem to have been relatively uneventful. His father died before he was born in 570 CE, and he was raised by a Bedouin wet nurse in the desert for his first five years. Muhammad, from a young age, watered and grazed the goats and camels on which life depended, and guarded them at night against wolves and hyenas. The desert was a place where death lurked behind every rock, and the spirits of *jinns* flitted about.[101]

Muhammad's mother died a year after he was returned to her, and two years later his paternal grandfather died. The orphaned boy was taken in and raised by the new clan leader, abu-Talib—one of his father's nine brothers. Muhammad was conditioned as a wrestler and trained to fight with the sword and bow.[102]

Literacy was not widely experienced at Mecca, and tradition tells us that Muhammad was unlettered; however, it is highly likely that Muhammad was literate in the languages of trade. He had been trained by his uncle to be a merchant and accompanied him on trading caravans from an early age. Muhammad soon became his uncle's trusted lieutenant and began to lead caravans on his own into Syria and Iraq. At night he might have chanted the ancient incantation, "Tonight I take refuge in the lord of this valley of the *jinn* from any evil that may lie here."

---

[101] Jenns (also djinns or genies) were supernatural creatures in Arabic mythology believed to be a mixture of fire and smoke. Jenns possessed free will and could be benevolent or evil.

[102] Relying on oral histories, the first comprehensive biography of Muhammad was not written down until the *Sira* was completed in the eighth century by Muhammad Ibn Ishaq—which became the primary resource for all subsequent biographies. Over time, there came to be differences between the earliest records and subsequent elaborated traditions. Ibn Ishaq, himself often said "Only God knows which is true."

Muhammad, the Reluctant Messenger of God

Growing into manhood, Muhammad presented an inconspicuous physical appearance—not too tall or too short, nor too dark or too light, but he did have a thick chest and broad shoulders. He had a noble Arab nose, long black hair plaited behind his ears, thick brown beard, wide-set brown eyes, and a calm, luminous, and empathetic look about him. He was a serious, grave, and dignified man, who spoke Arabic with a Bedouin accent. The common trade language of the Middle East was Aramaic, which Muhammad undoubtedly spoke. This enabled him to understand and memorize the biblical and apocryphal stories told in that language by the Jews and Christians he regularly encountered in his travels.

Muhammad's wealthy and twice-widowed distant cousin, Khadija bint Khuwaylid, contracted with him to lead a caravan on her behalf to Syria. During the trip, which took place in 595, a Syrian Christian monk saw Muhammad resting in the shade of a tree and predicted that he was a prophet.[103] Upon hearing about the prophecy, Khadija consulted her cousin (one of the Quraysh who had converted to Christianity) about the prediction. Reportedly, he said, "If this is true, Khadija, verily Muhammad is the prophet of this people!"

Khadija was 15 years older and much wealthier than the 25-year-old Muhammad when she proposed to him. They were married, and he would have no other wives during her lifetime. Muhammad and Khadija seemed to have enjoyed true love and mutual respect throughout their 24-year monogamous marriage. She birthed five children—one son who died and four daughters who lived. In addition, Muhammad adopted a slave boy named Zayd ibn Harith, and he raised a nephew named Ali, who was the son of the tribal leader who had cared for him.

Muhammad became a successful commercial trader and was well respected as an arbitrator of disputes. He was called al-Amin (faithful and trustworthy) and al-Sadiz (truthful). Despite the family's prosperity, they lived frugally, and he shared his wealth with the poor. His sandals were worn, and his homespun robe was threadbare.

---

[103] Syria was a part of the Christian Byzantine Empire.

Muhammad Learned About The Way of Righteousness From His Relatives

Significant populations of foreign Jews and Christians had settled in Arabia, and many Arabs had converted to these religions. They were generally respected by the Arabs as "People of the Book" because of their devotion to their scriptures. Most likely, these Christians and Jews were descendants of the Ebionite members of the Way of Righteousness, as there is evidence that Christian Arabs contributed to the development of written Arabic poetry, which in turn contributed loan words that were used in the Quran.

The Abrahamic religion of the Arabs was associated with the Christianity-Judaism of the Way, as practiced in the region. The Arabs were aware of the role Abraham played in the Jewish and Christian religions, and through his slave wife, Hagar, as the father of Ishmael and the ancestral Arabs. The Arabic association with the Way influenced worship at the Kaaba, but there remained a longing by some Arabs for a religion based on their own unique scripture in their own language. They yearned for their own messenger, or prophet.

Arabs were also aware of Arabic translations of the Gospel of John done by Arab Christians of the Syriac Church which spoke about a "Comforter," or "Counselor" being sent by Jesus. (14:16) The translation of this Greek word *Paraclete* into Arabic was Munahhema, which was close in pronunciation to Muhammad. An alternative translation resulted in the Arabic word Ahmad, which along with Muhammad, means "praised one."

The expectations of neighboring Jewish tribes for the appearance of a prophet were raised by a prominent rabbi. He proclaimed, "His time has come" and warned "he will be sent to shed blood and to take captive the women and children of those who oppose him. Let not that keep you back from him."

Among the Quraysh of Mecca were a few men who decided to stop worshipping idols and to explore the true religion of Abraham, their patriarch. Some of them converted to Christianity, but they all became *hanifs*—those who acknowledged one god and none other. Many *hanifs* were ascetics who practiced solitary mediation.

From history, we know that some of Muhammad's relatives were *hanifs*, and there is a good likelihood that the religion they observed was one very closely related to the Way of Righteousness brought to the East by the mission of Judas Thomas. Arabia at the time of Muhammad was not a particularly literate society; however, it was one with a very rich oral tradition in which stories were recited in a highly poetic fashion, that encouraged them to be memorized and repeated. We cannot possibly know the content of the conversations Muhammad had with his relatives of the Way; however, we do know that he either was, or he became a person who lived a life of piety and righteousness.

Muhammad may not have been an openly professing *hanif*, but each year during the month of Ramadan, he would retreat to a cave on Mount Hira for spiritual reflection, and to distribute food and money to the poor in the area. In Judaism, one does not have to be a Jew in order to be considered a Zaddik. From everything we know, Muhammad was a righteous man.

Muhammad Kept His First Gnostic Experience a Secret, Except From His Wife

Muhammad was in the cave in the year 610 when he experienced a revelation, he believed came from the angel Gabriel, who commanded him to "recite"! Initially refusing, Muhammad was overwhelmed and began to repeat the first words of his revelation:

> Recite in the name of your Lord who created, created man from clots of blood.
>
> Recite! Your Lord is the Most Bountiful One, who by the pen taught man what he did not know. (Sura 96)[104]

Despairing that he may have been hallucinating, or had become possessed by a *jinn*, Muhammad was terrified. He left the cave and

---

[104] All quotations from the Noble Quran are from the Penguin Classics edition as translated by N. J. Dawood.

began to climb higher on the mountain in order to throw himself from the heights. He experienced another vision:

> When I was midway on the mountain, I heard a voice from heaven saying: "O Muhammad! thou art the apostle of God and I am Gabriel." I raised my head towards heaven to see who was speaking, and lo, Gabriel in the form of a man with feet astride the horizon . . .. I stood gazing at him, moving neither backward nor forward; then I began to turn my face away from him, but towards whatever region of the sky I looked, I saw him as before.

In an altogether human reaction, Muhammad shared his experience and apprehensions with the one he trusted the most—the one to whom he had been married for 15 years. His wife, Khadija, soothed Muhammad's fears, telling him he was a kind and caring man and that Allah would not act arbitrarily. She consulted her Christian cousin, Waraqa, a leader of the *hanifs*. He reassured her that what had appeared to Muhammad was the same as had spoken to Moses, and that Muhammad was a messenger—the long awaited "prophet of his people." The advice he sent to Muhammad was to "be of a strong heart."

Muhammad spent the next two years in prayer and reflection. He abandoned his business and began to spend more time in the mountains. We cannot possibly at this remote time identify, psychologically and precisely, what occurred within Muhammad's mind as he fasted and meditated in silence and isolation on the meaning of what he was seeing and hearing within his own mind. The best evidence that he sincerely experienced visions—that had a valid ethical and righteous relevance to his people—is his very reluctance to express them openly. If Muhammad were intentionally making up the verses he recited, he would join a long line of pseudo prophets and self-professed messiahs who had presented themselves as the oracles of God over the millennia.

We must also give Muhammad credit for being the emotionally and psychologically healthy person he was when he became a prophet. Although there is no evidence he ever learned to write, Muhammad was undoubtedly fluent in at least one other language than Arabic, and he must have been able to read and understand the legal and trade documents used in his business. We must also give Muhammad credit for having the ability, common among his people, to listen carefully and to memorize the words of songs, poems, and stories recited by others.

We know Muhammad was exposed to the Abrahamic narrative of the Old Testament through the *hanifs*—some of whom were members of his family.[105] Moreover, it is also a fact that both Judaism and Christianity—a blending of the two in the mission of Judas Thomas—had been widespread within his society for centuries, along with their stories and books.

Yemen—from where the Quraysh of Mecca emigrated—became a Jewish kingdom known as the Sabeans around 380. They extended their power throughout much of the Arabian Peninsula and worshipped the Judaic God, which they called *Rahman* (the Merciful). The Jewish kingdom was defeated in 523 by Christian Ethiopians aligned with the Orthodox Roman Christian Byzantines.

We must acknowledge that the final product of Muhammad's lifetime of revelations was a massive, religiously and politically powerful instrument of social change, *and* that such a change occurred. That fact, alone, is evidence of a superior, well-informed, and disciplined mind—one motivated by righteous intentions.

When Muhammad died 23 years after his first revelations, the tribes of Arabia were united. They would go on to dominate the known world from Spain to Indonesia, and from the sub-Sahara in Africa to Afghanistan. Islam became a world religion, and the Muslims were a dominate force in that world. Muhammad's Noble Quran remains as a literary masterpiece that guides the daily conduct of more than 1.5 billion Muslims and affects the lives and future of everyone on Earth.

Looking back through biblical history at the long line of visionary Abrahamic prophets, from Moses—through Ezekiel, Elijah, Isaiah, and Daniel—to Malachi, we have to recognize that each of them was gifted with the wisdom and inspiration to speak about the political

---

[105] Early historical sources mention contact between a youthful Muhammad and one of the *hanifs*, known as Zayd, during which Muhammad is reprimanded for worshipping idols and taught about the one god of Abraham.

and religious issues of their time. Each prophet was also imbued with the knowledge and practices of the religion about which he prophesized. So, too, was Muhammad—the last of this long lineage of prophets. But he was more: along with Moses, who delivered the Torah, and Jesus, who "brought the Gospels," Muhammad was a *Rasul Allah*, a "Messenger of God."

The Spiritual Insights of Muhammad

Initially, we are told that Muhammad experienced visual revelations he had difficulty finding the words to express, but with time and reflection, the words more easily came to him. All we know for certain is that the verbal recitations resumed. Among the first words that came to him were these recited in the sura of the *Daylight*, or *Morning*:

> By the light of day, and by the fall of night, your Lord has not forsaken you, Muhammad, nor does He abhor you. The life to come holds a richer prize for you than this present life. You shall be gratified with what your Lord will give you. Did He not find you an orphan and give you shelter? Did He not find you in error and guide you? Did He not find you poor and enrich you? Therefore, do not wrong the orphan, nor chide away the beggar. But proclaim the goodness of your Lord.

With growing confidence, Muhammad began to recite about the matters he received in revelation—which became the suras of the Quran (archaic Koran). The Noble Quran (*al-Qur'an* "Recitation") is the collection of Muhammad's revelations. There are approximately 6,200 verses organized into 114 *suras*.[106]

Jesus taught that the first and great law was, "You shall love the Lord your God with all your heart, and with all your soul, and with all your mind." More succinctly, Muhammad proclaimed, "Your God is one God. There is no god but Him."

---

[106] In Arabic, the word for verse is *aya*, or sign. The word *sura* (or *surah*) designates a chapter containing verses.

At first, Muhammad's revelations were short, poetic observations about the material world and those who shared it with him. With time—as the role of Muhammad expanded from being a prophet to becoming a political and military leader—the verses became more detailed and specifically referred to contemporaneous events. In all these matters, the suras of the Quran were signs from God intended to guide and direct the actions and beliefs of the faithful.

Muhammad began to warn the people around him about the dangers of the lives they were following. Particularly, he addressed those of his own class of merchants, who had become obsessed with the accumulation of wealth and were failing to care for the poor, weak, and disadvantaged of their society. Muhammad, as a prophet, was there to warn his fellows about that conduct and how it would be judged by Allah. Muhammad was a reformer.

The earliest lessons in the Quran reinforced the ancient Arabic code that requires people to care for the less fortunate and those who visit their home or camp. Muhammad taught that it was wrong to selfishly build up wealth and to fail to distribute the benefits of society to all its members. For him, Allah had created the world for the good of everyone—not just for a privileged few who were able to take advantage of it.

In lessons very similar to those found in the biblical Letter of James to his Congregation of the Poor (and carried to the East by Judas Thomas), the basic religious duties imposed on the faithful by the Quran were to assist others in need, reject cheating and the love of wealth, remain chaste, and to stop killing the baby girls.

Repeatedly, many of the verses of the Quran make clear that righteousness and justification are demonstrated by works—and not by faith—as taught by Jesus, James, and the Way of Righteousness.[107] The sura on *Alms* says:

> Have you thought of him that denies the Last Judgment? It is he who turns away the orphan and does not urge others

---

[107] The giving of alms is one of the five pillars of *Islam*. The others are bearing witness to "There is no god but God, and Muhammad is his messenger;" praying five times a day; fasting during the month of Ramadan; and doing *hajj* to the Kaaba in Mecca at least once during a lifetime.

to feed the poor. Woe to those who pray but are heedless in their prayer, who make a show of piety and give no alms to the destitute.

Woven through the verses of the Quran is imagery that strongly resonates with the Gnostic symbolism of the Way, such as these words in the *Light*:

Allah is the light of the heavens and the earth. His light may be compared to a niche that enshrines a lamp, the lamp within a crystal of star-like brilliance. It is lit from a blessed olive tree neither eastern nor western. Its very oil would almost shine forth, though no fire touched it. Light upon light; Allah guides to His light whom He will. (Sura 24)

Verses in the Quran even express Gnostic spiritual concerns about the environment, such as these in *The Sun* and *Ya Sin* suras:

By the sun and his midday brightness; by the moon, which rises after him; by the day, which reveals his splendor; by the night, which veils him! By the heaven and Him that built it; by the earth and Him that spread it; by the soul and Him that molded it and inspired it with knowledge of sin and piety; blessed shall be the man who has kept it pure, and ruined he that has corrupted it! (Sura 91)

Let the once-dead earth be a sign to them. We gave it life, and from it produced grain for their sustenance. We planted it with the palm and the vine and watered it with gushing springs, so that men might feed on its fruit. It was not their hands that made all this. Should they not give thanks? (Sura 36)

The First Muslim Converts Surrender to Allah

Muhammad continued to show respect for the Kaaba and the traditional worship there and very slowly began to reveal his revelations to his friends and family members. How the revelations were verbalized was poetic, in that the suras were recited as a rhyming prose known as *saj* (which has the meaning of "cooing," or pleasing to the ear). Most listeners were mesmerized by hearing the words of Allah in their own musical language; they no longer had to be envious of the Christians and Jews and their books. They had their own Messenger!

Recitations remained a private matter, and those who met to offer prayers to Allah in the morning and evening consisted of a very small, but devoted group known as Muhammad's Companions. In addition to his wife, four daughters, his 13-year-old nephew, his adopted son, and several cousins, the wives of other relatives joined in the prayers. A key outside convert was Muhammad's friend, Abu Bakr. He became a Muslim leader and attracted many converts from other tribes—who were primarily young, poor, and marginalized, including slaves.[108] Another significant convert was a wealthy member of the Quraysh tribe from Taif named Uthman ibn Affan, who married Muhammad's daughter Ruqayya.[109]

Although they did not challenge the traditional religion, the sight of the Muslims kneeling with their forehead on the ground and buttocks in the air—in abject surrender to Allah—offended the prideful sensibilities of other members of the Qurayshi tribe. The group also upset the status quo by embarrassing the powerful merchants about their wealth and their failure to properly care for the poor and disadvantaged. Muhammad's group was soon forced to meet in the wadis outside of Mecca for their prayer services. Collectively, the Muslims were known as the *umma* (the entire community of Muslims united by their surrender to Allah).

It was important to Muhammad to recreate—within his ministry—the proper balance between its adherents and Allah. He demanded that people physically prostrate themselves in surrendering themselves to Allah. Initially, they faced in the direction of Jerusalem

---

[108] Abu Bakr became Muhammad's father-in-law and a most trusted companion and advisor. Following Muhammad's death, Abu Bakr the Truthful became the first Muslim Caliph—until his own death two years later.

[109] Uthman was one of the four *banifs* who had first converted to Christianity. He became a faithful disciple of Muhammad and was elected to be the Third Caliph following Muhammad's death.

during prayers twice a day. The requirement of these devotional prayers became one of the five pillars of Islam.

The name of the religion that arose from the revelations of Muhammad is Islam, which means "submission to the will of Allah." Converts became known as Muslims, an Arabic word that means "one who submits" (to Allah).[110] By submitting, Muslims committed themselves to compassion and generosity and to creating a caring and responsible spirit within themselves. Muhammad referred to his followers as the people of Paradise.

Much like Gnostics, Muslims were encouraged to follow the signs of the Quran in transfiguring their lives from selfish ignorance and chaos into a generous consciousness of order and wellbeing. Among all the creatures on Earth, only humans have the inherent intellectual freedom to voluntarily chose to submit to Allah's will and to confirm their lives to the orderliness and beauty of Allah's creations. Unlike the "original sin" of the Christians, the Islamic world is essentially good. Verses such as these contain Gnostic and Way imagery:

> In the creation of the heavens and the earth; in the alternation of night and day; in the ships that sail the ocean with cargoes beneficial to man; in the water which Allah sends down from the sky and with which He revives the dead earth, dispersing over it all manner of beasts; in the movements of the winds, and in the clouds that are driven between earth and sky: surely in these there are signs for rational men. (Sura 2:164)

Suppression by the Authorities and Banning of the *Umma*

The beginning of the Quran focuses on the requirement that one believes in Allah, prays often, and asks for forgiveness of sins. Later, in an expansion of Judaic-Christian imagery, the Quran

---

[110] A convert formally accepted Islam by simply reciting the declaration of faith known as the *shahada*, "There is no god but Allah, and Muhammad is his prophet."

discusses the judgment of Allah, the resurrection of the dead, the torments of hell, and the blessings of Paradise. Once Muhammad began to openly proclaim his revelations in public at the Kaaba, it was the innovation of an individual last judgment that began to pose issues of acceptance by the people of Mecca.

Traditionally, clan members were encouraged to accumulate the wealth that allowed them to provide for the welfare of other clan members. Muhammad's revelations changed all of that. On the day of judgment, their wealth and that of their clan would be of no avail. Instead, every "soul will stand alone" and will be personally judged by whether he had shared—rather than hoarded—his wealth with *all* the orphans and the poor. Much as Jesus, James, and the Way taught, only righteous deeds produce the favorable judgment of Allah.

Muhammad's merchant peers might have scoffed about a resurrection of the bones from the desert sand and the afterlife in Paradise, but it was the requirement to worship Allah and no other gods that provoked the most resistance. Muhammad's neighbors failed to see the harm in continuing to honor their tribal totems and the daughters of Allah as they had in the past—especially when the worship was connected to the wealth that the *hajj* pilgrims brought to the city. When Muhammad forbad the worship of Allah's daughters, many of converted fell away, and the outside attacks increased.

Perhaps fearful of offending the Bedouins tribes who worshipped Allah at the Kaaba and at the nearby shrines to his daughters, *and* the loss of their business trade, the city leaders offered Muhammad increased commercial opportunities and a favorable marriage to cease his prophecies, but he refused. They then declared Muhammad to be an enemy of the Arab people—because the worship of the daughters of Allah was a duty binding on all Arabs. Muhammad was attacking the "Ways of the Fathers," and they accused him of being an atheist and a danger to their society.

Although threatened, Muhammad's uncle, abu Talib continued to support and protect him. His opponents, however, intensified their efforts to break up the Muslims, who were concentrated in the smaller Hashim and al-Muttalib clans. The two largest clans signed a proclamation prohibiting anybody from intermarrying or

The Righteous Way of Islam

trading with the two lesser clans, cutting them off from food and necessities.[111]

The ban lasted for two years until four Quraysh, who were related to the shunned clans, spoke out against it at the Kaaba and produced the proclamation, which had been eaten by worms.

Muhammad's wife of 24 years, Khadija, and Abu Tilid, the uncle who had raised him, died shortly after the ban was lifted in 619 CE—in what became known as the "Year of the Sorrow." The new leader of the Hashim clan withdrew his support of Muhammad, and people began to ridicule him in the streets. He would nonviolently sit silently by the Kaaba while being berated, and stones would be thrown at him if he attempted to recite.

Life for the Muslims was becoming untenable in Mecca. With the loss of clan support, Muhammad's life was placed in danger, since there was no longer a reciprocal threat of blood revenge for his murder.

At the carnival that year held in conjunction with the *hajj*, the word spread about Muhammad's prophecy and the threats being made against him. He became the most talked about man in Arabia, yet he continued to seek silence and meditation during which the revelations would flow. Muhammad recited the new suras to all who would listen, and his *umma* (entire community) of Muslims continued to grow.

---

[111] In what became known as the First Hijra, a group of Muslims and their families, including Uthman and Muhammad's daughter, Ruqayya, emigrated across the Red Sea to Ethiopia, where they were placed under the protection of the large Ethiopian Orthodox Christian Empire, known as the Aksumites which extended into Sudan, Egypt, and Yemen.

MUHAMMAD, THE RIGHTEOUS REFORMER

Following the deaths of his wife and uncle, and the loss of clan protection, Muhammad struck the nadir of his ministry. Unsure if things could get worse, but refusing to give up, Muhammad set out to find a way to lead his Muslim *umma* out of danger.

Muhammad left Mecca and traveled to Taif, a city in which one of the daughters of Allah was worshipped. He contacted three brothers there and asked them to accept Islam and to provide protection to him and the new religion. They refused, and their slaves chased Muhammad through the streets throwing stones at him. Hiding in an orchard outside the city, Muhammad prayed for a revelation using words that could have been spoken by a Gnostic or a follower of the Way:

> O Allah, to Thee I complain of my weakness, little resource, and lowliness before men. O Most Merciful, thou art the Lord of the weak and Thou art my Lord. To whom wilt Thou confide me? To one afar who will misuse me? Or to an enemy to whom Thou hast given power over me. I take refuge in the light of Thy countenance by which the darkness is illuminated, and the things of this world and the next are rightly ordered, lest Thy anger descend upon me or Thy wrath light upon me. It is for Thee to be satisfied until Thou art well-pleased. There is no power and no might save in Thee.

Returning to Mecca, Muhammad found temporary protection with the Mawfal clan, which had not supported the ban. He fell asleep one night after he had been praying alongside the Kaaba and experienced a different kind of vision. Muhammad was awakened by the angel Gabriel and placed on a flying horse, which carried them through the night to the Temple Mount in Jerusalem. There, they were greeted by a host of prophets, including Moses, Abraham, Jesus, and others. After praying together, they offered Muhammad three goblets containing water, milk, and wine. He chose the milk in moderation between asceticism and indulgence.

In an adventure replete with well-established Gnostic and Way elements, Muhammad and Gabriel were led to a ladder which extended up to the heavens.[112] They began to climb up through the levels toward the Throne of God and met a different prophet in each of the seven heavens, beginning with Adam and followed by Jesus, John the Baptist, Joseph, Enoch, Aaron and Moses, and finally Abraham in the Seventh Heaven on the threshold of the Devine Sphere.

There is only a slight reference to the Night Journey in the Quran (Sura 17), "Glory be to God, who made his servant go by night from the sacred house to the far house, that we might show him some of our signs." Muhammad's first biographer, ibn-Ishaq says, "I have heard it said that the messenger used to say, 'My eyes sleep while my heart is awake.' Only Allah knows how revelation came and what he saw." Speaking years after Muhammad's death, his youngest wife, Aisha said, "The messenger's body remained where it was, but Allah removed his spirit by night."

The idea of seven heavens originated in ancient Iraq and may have been derived from the magical properties of the number seven[113] and Babylonian astronomy. In Second Corinthians (12:2-4) Paul claims to have been caught up to the third heaven in Paradise. In the *Second Book of Enoch*, Enoch describes his travels through the seven heavens on his way to meet God. Although the *Book of Enoch* was not included in the canon of the Old Testament, it has been validated by copies found among the scrolls of the Way at Qumran. *Enoch* is quoted by Judas Thomas in The Letter of Jude (1:14) and is mentioned by Muhammad in his revelations as Idris—who was described as trustworthy and exalted to a high station.

From this point forward, Muhammad transitions from being a messenger of God to becoming a social and political reformer of his people.

---

[112] During Jacob's dream about God as described in Genesis (28:10-17), he saw a ladder connecting Earth to Heaven which was used by the angels of God to ascend and descend.

[113] Asked to name a number between one and ten, most people will pick seven. Moreover, one divided by seven produces an amazing little decimal number, 0.142857142857 etc., which can be used to calculate close approximations of *Pi* and the Golden Proportion.

Driven Out of Mecca, Muhammad Removes His Congregation to Medina

Muhammad returned to Earth determined that prayers must be offered more frequently during each day, and he redoubled his efforts to find a place where the Muslims could exercise their religion in peace. In 620 CE, he encountered six Arabs from the agricultural oasis of Yathrib (Medina) who were on *hajj* in Mecca.[114] He shared his revelations and troubles with them, and they told him about the conflicts among the Arab and Jewish tribes in Yathrib, who had engaged in internecine violence for the last century. Thinking that Muhammad's arbitration abilities and his mission might be a solution for their own problems, the six readily surrendered to God and became Muslims. They said, "no tribe is so divided by hatred and rancor as they. Perhaps God will unite them through you." They agreed to invite the members of their tribes to join the religion and promised to report back the next year during *hajj*.

During the year, Muhammad married an older widow named Sawdah, and he contracted for a future marriage with Aisha, the six-year-old daughter of his best friend, Abu Bakr.

The six converts from Medina returned during the *hajj* of 621 CE and brought seven others with them. Acknowledging their success, Muhammad dispatched a seasoned Muslim who had just returned from Abyssinia to accompany them to Medina in order to teach them the Quran. The religion quickly spread to many of the families in Medina.

There were three main Jewish tribes in Medina, who named the oasis-valley from their Aramaic word *medinta,* for "the city." To improve relations with the Jews, Muhammad proclaimed a new Muslim service on Friday afternoons to coincide with the beginning

---

[114] Yathrib was a series of villages and tribal forts located in a fertile, eight-mile-long, spring-fed valley two hundred miles north of Mecca. The primary product was its date crop from the numerous trees in the valley that was prized throughout Arabia.

The Righteous Way of Islam

of the Jewish Sabbath.[115] He ordered the Muslims to fast on Yom Kippur, the Jewish Day of Atonement, and to change the direction of their prayers toward Jerusalem. He encouraged the Muslim men to marry Jewish women—as he did—and he included many of the Jewish dietary and purity laws in his revelations.

The *hajj* of 622 CE was wildly successful with 73 Muslim men and two women from the leading families in Medina making the pilgrimage to Mecca. They "pledged ourselves to war in complete obedience to the apostle, in weal or woe, in ease and hardship and evil circumstances; that we would not wrong anyone; that we would speak the truth at all times; and that in God's service we would fear the censure of none." The pledge was necessary because Muhammad was planning to make another Muslim *hijra* from Mecca to Medina and to place his *umma* under the protection of tribes to which they were not blood related. These Medina tribes became known as the "Ansar, the Helpers of the Prophet and his Companions."[116]

The Muslim families began to slip away to Medina until only Muhammad, Ali, and Abu Bakr were left. Hearing that a conspiracy to murder Muhammad was underway, he and Abu escaped to a nearby cave, while Ali remained behind in Muhammad's bed pretending to be him. When they discovered him missing, the Quraysh offered a reward of 100 milk camels for his return—dead or alive.

Muhammad and Abu Bakr made their way to Medina, and Muhammad signed the Constitution of Medina establishing an alliance with all eight of the tribes—as long as they did not cooperate with Mecca.[117] Muhammad was designated as the sole arbitrator of disputes and war leader, and he was recognized as the Messenger

---

[115] The majority of the Jews in Medina were not immigrants from Israel but were Arab converts. They spoke an Arabic-Aramaic language called *ratan* and were unlikely to be fully observant Jews, being more like the Arabic *hanifs* in their monotheism. Almost certainly, they were spiritually descended from those who followed Judas Thomas's Way of Righteousness.

[116] The Islamic calendar dates from 622 CE, the year of the *Hijra* to Medina, because this was the year that action was taken to fulfill the prophecies of Muhammad. During most of 2019, the current Islamic year is 1440.

[117] Shortly after arriving in Medina, Muhammad and Abu Bakr's nine-year-old Aisha were married, but she remained with her parents until she reached puberty.

of God. The constitution recognized "those who are in federation" with the Muslims as one community, or *umma*. The word would come to define the entire congregation of believers, wherever they might be located.

Muhammad purchased land and built a mosque where all could pray.[118] Most of the Arabs and some of the Jews of Medina converted to Islam, and a *muezzin* was appointed to summon people to prayer five times a day by crying:

> al-Llahu Akbar! I bear witness that there is no god but Allah, I bear witness that Muhammad is the apostle of God. Come to prayer. Come to prayer. Come to divine service. Come to divine service. *al-Llahu Akbar, al-Llahu Akbar.* There is no god but Allah.

Muhammad encouraged the believers who came with him from Mecca to adopt a "brother" from among the helpers of Medina in order to strengthen bonds between the two communities. As his own "brother," Muhammad selected his nephew Ali, whom he had raised as a son.

Muhammad's Respect for the Way of Righteousness and Its Books

Despite Muhammad's attempts to maintain good relations with the Jewish tribes, they resisted Islam, and most refused to accept Muhammad as a true prophet. Other Jews were intrigued; however, and they educated Muhammad about Jewish history and the conflicts with Christianity. This dichotomy is reflected in the Quran, where Muhammad takes different sides of the issues between the two faiths. At times he exalts Jesus as a prophet above the Jews, but he also ridicules the idea that Allah was the father of Jesus. The Quran is, however, generally supportive of both Christianity and Judaism:

> Be courteous when you argue with the People of the Book, except with those among them who do evil. Say, "We believe

---

[118] The mosque was a palm-frond covered structure in the middle of a mud-brick enclosure, with sleeping sheds along the wall for Muhammad and his wives.

in what has been revealed to us and which was revealed to you. Our God and your God is one. To Him we surrender ourselves." (Sura 29)

As Muhammad learned more about the history of the Old Testament, he realized that Abraham had preexisted Moses and Jesus—both of whom had introduced innovations into the ancient covenant of Abraham, the father of Ishmael and the Arabs. Abraham—the first *Muslim* to surrender to God—replaced Moses as Muhammad's favorite prophet.[119] He explains in *The Imrans*:

> Abraham was neither Jew nor Christian. He was an upright man, one who had surrendered himself to Allah. He was no idolater. Surely the men who are nearest to Abraham are those who follow him, this Prophet, and the true believers. Allah is the guardian of the faithful. Some of the People of the Book wish to mislead you; but they mislead none but themselves, though they may not perceive it. (Sura 3)

The ancient Arab tradition was that the Kaaba had been built by Abraham and Ishmael, and Muhammad expanded on this story with revelations which have Abraham and Ishmael praying together for God to send a prophet to the Arabs—who would bring them their own Book.

For Muhammad, the religions of Judaism and Christianity, as well as eastern Zoroastrianism, were perfectly valid religions. He simply saw his prophecies, and the religion they produced, as a continuation and reform of these earlier versions of the worship of the one Allah.

As political and security relations with the Jews of Medina continued to deteriorate, Muhammad made a break with the Jews in a very creative manner. He received a revelation one day during prayers in the mosque, and he suddenly ordered the congregation

---

[119] The prophets discussed in Muhammad's revelations are primarily the ones related by Christians and Jews in their oral stories he would have heard during his travels. Most of the minor prophets found in the Old Testament are never mentioned.

to reverse the direction of their prayers from Jerusalem and to offer their supplication toward Mecca.

From this point forward, the role of Muhammad begins to change more forcefully from that of the prophet of the Muslims, toward becoming their political reformer and military leader. His revelations more directly concern themselves with political conditions and the enactment of practices, legislation, and strategy to create a righteous society.

Jihad: Violently Creating a Just and Peaceful Society

Given the harsh life of their existence, there was deep within the Arab consciousness a demand for justice. The blood feuds and the allowable alternatives to blood revenge provided a means of exacting justice and avoiding further violence. The Muslims were offended by the manner in which they and their prophet, Muhammad, had been treated by the Quraysh of Mecca, and as their welcome in Medina wore thin, they sought ways to improve their situation.

At this stage, the revelations of Muhammad began to urge Muslims to engage in a *jihad* (striving or struggling), which is usually translated as a "Holy War;" however, the word has a deeper and more profound meaning for Muslims. While a *jihad* may entail violence and bloodshed, it also requires a moral and spiritual commitment—along the path of Allah—to create a just and righteous society.

Muhammad and His Muslims Become Desert Pirates to Survive

While a violent struggle may be necessary to protect and defend themselves and their mosques from attack, a Muslim victory would only occur if the battle were being fought for a righteous cause. Initially, Muhammad did not envision an all-out war; he only wanted to exact revenge against the Quraysh and secure the means of survival.

Practiced primarily by Bedouin tribes, the *razzia*, or raid, was a swift, narrowly focused attack to secure loaded camels or goods. It was designed to avoid bloodshed *and* the resulting blood feud and vengeance. The Muslims adopted this tactic in a series of successful guerrilla raids on passing caravans.

A major assault at the Well of Badr near the Red Sea was planned by the Muslims in 624 CE on a large, 2,000-camel Quraysh caravan returning from Damascus in Syria loaded with trade goods for Mecca. The raid failed, however, and Muhammad was forced into a battle with the caravan's armed guards and a relief force of 1,000 fighters from Mecca. Outnumbered three to one, the Muslims rallied and killed 44 men and took many prisoners, while only losing 15 men. In many of these battles, Ali was the standard-bearer, fighting alongside of Muhammad.

The normal Arab practice at the time—once blood was shed in battle—was to kill all the men and enslave the women and children; however, Muhammad received a revelation that the prisoners were to be ransomed. He ordered that the Quraysh prisoners be treated with respect and given enough food and lodging. This was followed by revelations that prisoners must not be harmed and should be treated as members of the captor's family. If no ransom could be obtained, prisoners were to be allowed to work to earn their own release, and captors were informed that freeing their prisoners was a righteous act.

The Muslim attacks against caravans aroused opposition against them at Medina, especially among the Jewish tribes who feared repercussions. The Quraysh organized an attack on Medina and secretly met with the leader of one of the Jewish tribes. The raid destroyed crops and date palm trees and killed two of the Helpers. Another of the Jewish tribes began to make overtures to the Quraysh and was forced by the Muslims to leave Medina, and subsequently yet another Jewish tribe was forced from Medina when it plotted to kill Muhammad.

Following a successful raid by the Muslims on a caravan at the Well of Qarada, an attack force of 3,000 fighters left Mecca and were joined by the warriors of two Bedouin tribes. Muhammad resisted with a force of 700 men and was defeated. He was knocked unconscious and was carried to a nearby grove where he recovered.[120]

---

[120] One of his warriors named Umar rallied to Muhammad and organized a defense ring around him. Muhammad later married one of Umar's daughters. Following the death of Muhammad, Umar served as the Second Caliph after Abu Bakr.

Thinking him dead, the attacking force left the battlefield and returned to Mecca.[121]

Muhammad's daughter, Ruqayyah died at this time and her husband, Uthman, married another of Muhammad's daughters named Umm Kulthum. In addition, Muhammad's nephew, Ali, married his youngest daughter, Fatima. Muhammad also married the young widowed daughter of Umar named Hafsah. All these marriages sealed important relationships. Muhammad later married another widow, Zaynab bint Kuzaymah, who was not long-lived. Muhammad then married Hind bint al-Mughira, the widow of one of his cousins. Most controversially, Muhammad also married another cousin—the divorced wife of his adopted son, Zayd.[122]

These multiple marriages created dissension within Muhammad's family that lasts until this day. On one side was his daughter Fatima and her husband (Muhammad's nephew), Ali—who were opposed by his youngest wife, Aisha and the some of the other in-laws. None of his marriages after his first wife produced children, and following the death of Muhammad, it was the followers of Fatima and Ali and their descendants who would become the Shia. Aisha, Uthman, and Umar would become leaders of the Sunnis.[123]

Muhammad led an attack in January 627 CE that captured 2,000 camels, 5,000 sheep and goats, and 200 women—the most beautiful of whom Muhammad would marry, once he convinced her to convert to Islam, instead of posting a ransom.

The Qurayshi organized an army of 10,000 to attack the Muslim force of 3,000 fighters in Medina. A siege resulted during which

---

[121] Severely concussed, Muhammad suffered from headaches for the rest of his life—which may have contributed to his death five years later.

[122] When Muhammad received a revelation that it would not be incestuous for him to marry his son's divorced wife, who also happened to be his cousin—because the son was adopted, his youngest wife Aisha, quipped, "truly thy Lord makes haste to do thy bidding."

[123] As there were more women than men, the Quran allowed men up to four wives, if the husband was able to care for them and to treat them equally. It was thought better to have multiple wives than unmarried girls and widows to be exploited. Muhammad, however, received a special revelation that allowed him—as the leader of the *umma*—to have as many wives as he wished. Allah informed him that "This privilege is yours alone, given to no other believer."

the Qurayshi communicated with the last remaining Jewish tribe for supplies and for an entrance into the city. The attack and siege were called off by the Qurayshi when the weather suddenly turned cold and rainy with a high wind, but the battle wasn't over. The Muslims attacked the collaborating Jewish tribe in their fort and demanded an unconditional surrender. After 25 days, the Jews opened their gates and surrendered. Seven hundred Jewish men were beheaded, and their wives and children were sold into slavery.

Muhammad's Victorious Return to Mecca

By 626 CE, Muhammad was the most powerful man in Arabia. He had defeated or deflected everything thrown at him and his Muslim fighters. His ruthlessness in destroying the Jewish tribe that threatened his position in Medina put the fear of God in the hearts of those who opposed him and steel in the spines of those who supported him. Muhammad began to build a fighting confederacy with several Bedouin tribes, some of whom became Muslims. He also sought to make peace with other Jewish tribes in the region.

Muhammad received a vision in 628, seeing himself with a shaved head and white cloth of a pilgrim standing at the Kaaba holding a key in his hand. He announced that he was going to do *hajj* and 1,000 Muslims joined him. They gathered 70 camels for sacrifice at the Kaaba and the unarmed group set off. A troop of 200 Qurayshi cavalry fighters stopped him at the 20-mile sanctuary limit and refused him entrance. He negotiated a 10-year treaty with the Quraysh in which he agreed not to enter that year, but that he would return the next, and the Quraysh would vacate the city. Before returning to Medina, the Muslims shaved their heads, sacrificed the camels, and performed the rites of pilgrimage at the boundary where they had stopped.

In 629, Muhammad, accompanied by 2,600 Muslims, led the pilgrimage to Mecca riding his favorite camel. Upon arrival, he kissed the Black Stone and began to circle the Kaaba followed by his fellow pilgrims. After the agreed upon three-day truce, the Medina party left in peace.

Muhammad, the Righteous Reformer

Muhammad continued to solidify his control over Arabia by attacking a Jewish town at Khaybar, which had supported the Quraysh during the siege of Medina. The town surrendered and accepted Muslim protection in exchange for half of its date crop each year. Another Jewish tribe at Fadak also surrendered on the same terms.

Muhammad married the young, widowed daughter of one of the Jewish tribal chiefs to confirm the agreement. Even though he had many wives at this time, Muhammad then married yet another widow in a politically important marriage—the daughter of Abu Sufyan, the leader of the Quraysh in Mecca. In addition, al-Muqawqis, the ruler of Egypt, sent Muhammad a young Egyptian slave girl—a Coptic Christian named Maryam, or Mariya—to be his concubine. He grew fond of her and she bore him a son named Ibrahim, who died in infancy.

Aisha retained a special place among his wives, as she was young, devoted, and intelligent. When he was absent from Medina, he instructed people to consult her about religious matters. More than a hundred traditions were later attributed to Aisha, as having been given directly to her by Muhammad. Following Muhammad's death, Aisha later led a Sunni revolt against Ali during his caliphate.

At this point, a revelation called the Verses of Choice gave all of his wives the choice to leave or remain in their marriages to Muhammad. All chose to remain and were designated by the Quran as the "Mothers of the Faithful." They agreed not to remarry following the death of Muhammad in order to maintain unity of the *umma*.[124]

After the Quraysh supported an attack on a town in the Muslim confederacy in violation of the peace agreement, Muhammad had the excuse to attack Mecca. The leader of the Quraysh, Abu Sufyan (now Muhammad's father-in-law) came to Medina and reached an agreement to personally provide protection to any Meccan who wished to surrender when the Muslims entered the city.

---

[124] The privacy of Muhammad's wives was protected by a muslin curtain in their rooms, which later became a thin shawl as a matter of status. No other women wore veils at that time—their lives were far too difficult for that later innovation.

There was little resistance when Muhammad's army of 10,000 fighters arrived at Mecca. Abu Sufyan met with Muhammad outside of the city and accepted Islam by reciting the *Shahada*.[125] Muhammad erected his red tent near the Kaaba and circled it seven times on his camel before ordering the smashing of the surrounding idols. All images were removed from inside the Kaaba, except for frescos of Jesus and Mary. A general amnesty was issued, and all who sought forgiveness were forgiven. Muhammad entrusted Ali with the responsibility to ensure that the conquest of the city was as bloodless as possible and to destroy the idols.

Muhammad then turned his attention to the towns where the shrines to the daughters of Allah still existed. A major battle was fought outside of Taif in which the Muslim forces prevailed. All the shrines were destroyed.

Over the next two years, Muhammad consolidated his control over most of Arabia when other tribes recognized that he had become too powerful to oppose. As they joined the Muslim confederacy and many of their members converted to Islam, the tribal system broke down, as the uniting Muslim *umma* became established.

In 630, Muhammad led an army of 30,000 to Tubuk located in the far northwest corner of the Arabian Peninsula on the border of the Byzantium Empire. The show of force resulted in agreements with local leaders, including the Christian king of Eilat, who paid tribute to the Muslims—along with other Jewish settlements in what is now Jordan.

As the Arabs began to look beyond Arabia for lands to conquer, the Muslims revisited the justification of *jihad*. Inasmuch as there is only one Allah, the entire world should be united in His worship. The Muslims came to consider *jihad* as a duty to impose a divinely inspired, just society on the remainder of the world. Their House of Islam was a sacred area where the will of Allah had been accepted, and the rest of the world was the House of War which had to be forced to surrender to Allah. This theology worked as a political,

---

[125] Abu Sufyan's son, Muawiya, became one of Muhammad's scribes and later served as the first Muslim governor of Syria after its conquest. Following the assassination of Ali, the Fourth Caliph, Muawiya gained control over the entire Arab-Muslim empire and founded the Sunni Umayyad dynasty in Damascus.

religious, and military strategy for the next hundred years as the Arab Conquest swept across Africa to Spain and the Middle East to Afghanistan. Once the geopolitical situation became static; however, the Muslims reached accommodations with the other nations that better served their economic and diplomatic interests, rather than continual war and conquest.

With his final campaign to the north, Muhammad was effectively the political and military leader of Arabia, as well as the religious head of the Muslim *umma*. He returned to Medina and continued to consolidate the religion, and the nation of its origin.

MUHAMMAD'S DEATH AND SUCCESSION

In 632, Muhammad traveled from Medina to Mecca for *hajj*. That year, for the first time, the Pilgrimage of Fulfillment was limited to Muslims, to merge the ancient religion of the Arabs into Islam. Arriving outside of Mecca, Muhammad spoke the traditional words, "Here I am at your service, O Allah," and began to lead his followers in the ancient rituals, but with a new emphasis.

At Mount Arafat, a rocky hill 12 miles southeast of Mecca, Muhammad preached his Farewell Sermon to the *hajj* pilgrims. He urged them to abandon blood revenge and tribal differences, to treat women kindly, and to deal justly with each other. He said, "Know that every Muslim is a Muslim's brother, and that the Muslims are brethren. It is only lawful to take from a brother what he gives you willingly, so wrong not yourselves." Muhammad stressed that no one should be forced to convert, and that Christians and Jews were to be treated with respect. "If they embrace *Islam* of their own accord, they are among the faithful with the same privileges and obligations, but if they hold fast to their tradition, they are not to be seduced from it."

From that moment forward, most Arabians considered themselves to be part of the Islamic *umma* first and foremost, rather than as members of their tribal families.

On their way home from Mecca, Muhammad stopped the caravan and gathered the pilgrims for prayers. Muhammad then took Ali by the hand and told his followers, "He of whom I am the master, of him Ali is also the master."

Returning to Medina, the 62-year-old Muhammad began to experience weakness, fevers, and severe headaches and collapsed. He was carried to Aisha's hut where he rested with his head in her lap. He asked her to dispose of his last personal possessions—seven coins. On June 8, 632, after nine days of illness, Muhammad died in the arms of Aisha. Abu Bakr informed the faithful in the mosque telling them, "O men, if anyone worships Muhammad, Muhammad is dead; if anyone worships Allah, Allah is alive, immortal!"[126]

---

[126] Images of Muhammad and his worship are prohibited in Islam.

Muhammad's Death and Succession

Muhammad was buried in the dirt floor where he died in Aisha's house, the location of the current Mosque of the Prophet.

Abu Bakr had begun to lead the prayers during Muhammad's illness, and following his death was chosen—with the support of his daughter, Aisha—to be the first Caliph (Arabic, *khalifa*, "successor").[127] He led the Muslims for the next two years until his own death.

Acting as directed by Muhammad prior to his death, the 30-year-old Ali wrote down a complete version of the Quran during this period, and as Islam spread beyond Arabia, he helped to establish the foundations of the religion and the Islamic Empire. Thereafter, the Noble Quran went through several additions and revisions.

The Sunni and Shia Split Apart Over Succession—Never to Reunite

The descendants of Muhammad believed that Ali ibn Abi Talib had been designated by Muhammad as his successor during the last return to Medina when he declared Ali to be "the Master." Moreover, as the male heir of Muhammad, husband of his only living child, Fatima, and father of Muhammad's only grandsons, the lineal descendants believed Ali was the logical choice to succeed Abu Bakr. Their expectations were, however, disappointed.

The Second Caliph was Umar, another father-in-law of Muhammad, and the Third Caliph was Uthman, a son-in-law of Muhammad.

The older Uthman was selected over the youthful Ali. Calling himself the Successor to God, Uthman proved to be an incompetent and corrupt leader. A rebellion arose throughout the Caliphate, and he was killed in his home in Medina when he refused to abdicate.[128]

Ali was elected the Fourth Caliph in 656, but refused to use the

---

[127] Abu Bakr considered his position as Caliph to be secular, rather than religious. He was the first among equals and subject to the collective deliberations of the *umma*.

[128] The primary accomplishment of Uthman was the organization of a uniform, approved version of the Noble Quran in 650.

The Righteous Way of Islam

title, preferring to be known as the Commander of the Faithful. To maintain peace, Ali announced a general amnesty and declined to act against the rebels who had killed Uthman. Even though she detested Uthman, and her own brother was involved in killing him, Aisha used the amnesty to oppose having Ali, or any other descendant successor, as Caliph. She led a rebellion against Ali in the Battle of the Camel later that year outside of Basra, Iraq. Alisha's group was defeated, and she was escorted back to Medina.

As a successor to Muhammad, Ali believed the leader of the *umma* should be chosen because of his righteousness and piety, instead of his being a familial descendant or tribal representative.[129] Ali saw his task as making life easier for the poor and disadvantaged and to ensure they were treated justly. In a sermon, he said, "A virtuous man is recognized by the good that is said about him and the praises which God has destined him to receive from others."

Following a rebellion that divided Islam into two camps, Ali was attacked in 661 with a poisoned sword while prostrate at prayer in Kufa, Iraq and died two days later. His Shia[130] followers selected his son Al-Hasan ibn Ali to be the Fifth Caliph, and their Second Imam—Ali having been the First. A civil war with the Sunnis[131] resulted, which was resolved with the abdication of Hasan six months later.

In 661, Muawiyah bin Abi-Sufyan (the son of the converted Quraysh leader) was the first non-family member to become Caliph. Muawiyah succeeded in transforming the Caliph into a monarch and the *umma* into his kingdom. He spent the next 20 years expanding his Islamic kingdom. Muawiyah was succeeded by his son, Yazid, who had fought a key battle with Hasan's brother, the Third Imam Husayn ibn Ali in 680 near Karbala in Iraq.[132] Husayn was killed and beheaded in the battle, and the schism between the Sunni and

---

[129] Ali's position in this matter resembles that of Jesus, James, and Judas Thomas's Way of Righteousness.
[130] The *shiat Ali*, or the "followers of Ali" became the Shia.
[131] The name Sunni comes from the word *sunnah*, referring to the exemplary behavior of Muhammad and a compilation of his traditions beyond the Quran.
[132] These locations in Iraq continue to be places of violent confrontations between the Shias and Sunnis.

Muhammad's Death and Succession

Shia became permanent. The Shia were primarily centered in Iran and Iraq, while the Sunnis predominated in all other areas under the Umayyad Dynasty established by Muawiyah.

When Muawiyah transformed the Caliphate into a secular monarchy, religious matters became the exclusive domain of the *Ulama* (Arabic "the learned ones."). The *Ulama* became the guardians of Islamic law, and they were able to block the Caliphs from dictating religious matters or legal results. Composed of legal scholars, the *Ulama* continues to have the authority in Islam to interpret the Quran and the *sunnah*.

In addition to his recitations in the Quran, there were numerous stories told by those who personally knew Muhammad about his rulings, conversations, actions, or habits during his daily life. These traditions are collectively known as Muhammad's *sunnah*, and the stories are known as known as *hadith*. The most authoritative of these stories were those reported by his youngest wife, Aisha. These hadith were accumulated in several different collections, most prominently the separate ones of the Sunni and the Shia. The hadith are secondary to the Quran in matters of Islamic jurisprudence and theology, but they can be useful in determining matters where the Quran is silent.

Even though the Caliphate no longer exists, the *Ulama* continues to exert its authority over religious matters in both the Sunni and Shia traditions. The purpose of the *Ulama* is to guide believers on the straight path to Allah, and their most effective tool is a comprehensive and binding code of conduct called the *Sharia*. The Sharia affects every aspect of Muslim life because it is the basis for judging all actions as being either good or bad.

Islam became permanently divided with the Sunnis convinced that the manner of choosing the successors of Muhammad should be guided by the Quran and result from an election by the entire *umma*.

The Shias discount the legitimacy of the first three "in-law" Caliphs and believe that Ali had been divinely inspired—as was Muhammad—and that his descendants through Fatima are the only legitimate leaders of Islam. The couple had four children, including two sons, Hasan and Husayn, whom Muhammad called "the leaders

The Righteous Way of Islam

of the youth of Jannah" (Heaven). Shias also believe spiritual and prophetic qualities have been granted by God to the familial descendants of Muhammad through Ali, the First Imam, and other Imams in his lineage.[133]

The only lineal descendant to survive the massacre at Karbala was Husayn's son, Ali, who was also known as Zayn al-Abadin. After being held as a prisoner in Damascus for years, he returned to Karbala, where he was succeeded by his son, Muhammad al-Baqir in 712, and whose son, Ja'far as-Sadiq became Imam upon his death. Ja'far established the primary school of law for the Shias, which differs from the Sunnis's with its own set of hadith (which includes stories of the Imams in addition to those of Muhammad).

The Jafari school uses *ijtihad*, or reasoning, as a source of Shi'ite jurisprudence, which holds that "whatever is ordered by reason, is also ordered by religion." Those who practice ijtihad are known as the *mujtahid*, and the ones who achieve the very highest plane of scholarship are known as the *ayatollahs* ("the sign of Allah"). The modern democratic theocracy in Iran is led by an Ayatollah.

Although the leadership question would divide the Muslims, it did not slow the military advance of the Arabs. Within 100 years, the Arabs had conquered a 4,000-mile arc from Spain across North Africa and through the Middle East to Afghanistan. The conquest was not particularly religious, in that the defeated people were not required to convert or to observe the Muslim religion. In fact, there was a period around 700 during which people were not allowed to convert. Subsequently, the religion of Islam became established in most of the conquered areas as a matter of choice by those who lived there.

The Umayyad Dynasty lasted from 661 to 750, when it was succeeded by the Abassid Dynasty—who claimed descent from one of Muhammad's uncles. They moved the capital to Baghdad, where they were rejected by the Shias. Although the dynasty lasted until the eleventh century, they became figureheads, rather than political or religious leaders. There were other dynasties in Spain, Egypt, and

---

[133] A Shite Imam is believed to be the living spirit of Muhammad and, as such, possesses a spiritual authority that places him above any secular ruler.

Syria, and the last Caliphate was organized by the Ottoman Turks. A Sunni dynasty ruled in Istanbul from 1453 to 1924. Today, Islam is a religion within most of the countries of the world, and except for Iran, it does not exercise control over the government of the land in which its adherents practice their religion.[134]

---

[134] Iran was captured from Arab caliphs in 1501 by radical Shi'ites led by a precocious 14-year-old sheikh and Sufi Grand Master named Ismail I. He became the first *Shah* (king) of the Safavid Empire and declared Shi'ism ("Twelver") as the state religion. The Safavid Empire was the last of the great Persian empires, remaining in power until the eighteenth century. Following the revolution in 1979 against Muhammad Reza Pahlavi, the last Shah of Iran, the Ayatollah Ruhollah Khomeini created a modern Shi'ite theocracy—The Islamic Republic of Iran.

ISLAMIC MYSTICISM, THE MAHDI, SUFISM, AND THE DRUZE

Unlike Christianity, which receives much of its validation from the miracles believed to have been performed by Jesus during his ministry,[135] there are no miracles in Islam—except for the Quran itself. Muhammad could not have spoken any clearer when he recited:

> They ask: "Why no sign been given him by his Lord?" Say: "Signs are in the hands of Allah. My mission is only to give plain warnings."
>
> It is not enough for them that We have revealed to you the Book for their instruction. Surely in this there is a blessing and an admonition to true believers. (Sura 29)

Also contrary to Roman Christianity—in which Jesus is depicted and worshipped as being one with God—Islam prohibits the worship of Muhammad or the display of his image.

Today, more than 1,500 years removed from the creation of the Quran, we continue to be amazed at the power of the words it contains. Even now—when revelations are primarily those resulting from science—we are in awe of the ability of Muhammad to have recited words that have had more effect on the world than those of almost any other human who ever walked upon it. With more than 1.6 billion people worshipping in the religion resulting from those words, Muhammad is exceeded only by Jesus, who has more than 3.5 billion worshippers. Of course, we have seen that the Jesus presently worshipped by most is a gross distortion of the humanly figure who preached in Israel 2,000 years ago.

This is not so with Muhammad; his words were preserved at or near the time they were delivered. There is little doubt about what he said, but we must ask what do the words mean in the bright light of today's knowledge—which is equally without doubt? In other words,

---

[135] Jesus allegedly said, "If I am not doing the works [miracles] of my Father, then do not believe me; but if I do them, even though you do not believe me, believe the works, that you may know and understand that the Father is in me and I am in the Father." (John 10:34-38)

it is a fact that Muhammad spoke these words, but it is equally factual that some of what he said simply cannot be true in the spotlight of reality.

Muhammad spoke eloquently and poetically about Noah, Abraham, and Moses and the acts they performed, including their creation of the Arab people and their native religion. We saw earlier, however, that it is impossible that these events took place as recited, and it is improbable that these prophets ever existed as human figures.

Muhammad relied on the biblical stories told by the Jews and Christians he encountered in life to discover—as a Gnostic experience within his own mind—the meaning of these stories in relationship to the society in which he lived. This is not to say that Muhammad did not himself believe that the words he recited were those of Allah speaking within his mind. Certainly, he did—Muhammad was a good and wise man, righteous in his deeds and pious in his worship of the Allah he believed in. He would not have lied about this.

Muhammad himself instructed his followers about the importance of purification and prayer to allow a divine response while awake in the form of "an inclination of the heart," or just before sleep, when it would come as a dream. He encouraged Muslims to achieve the spiritual and self-awareness of Gnosis.

Today, one does not have to be a neuroscientist or psychiatrist to understand that the voices everyone hears in his or her head are the normal activities of a mind produced by a healthy brain with two hemispheres talking to one another—as they help us to navigate through life and to confront and solve the difficulties it presents. We not only hear our favorite songs, but we can also hear the sweet voice of our lovers and the sounds of the ocean without having them present.

It cannot be a blasphemy to respectfully suggest that Muhammad really believed in the visions he saw, and that he truly repeated the thoughts and words produced by his mind to explain the visions he saw—and that he took effective action regarding the words he recited. Since the words were righteously inspired and were intended to do good in the world in which he lived and to benefit the people within it, the words and the actions they produced not only have validity, but they are indeed prophetic.

Islam is primarily a religion of words and not images. The Quran's prohibition of idolatry led to an absolute proscription of images of Allah, Muhammad, and his family, as well as the depiction of all humans and other animals. There are no saints. It is in words and in their meaning that the images of Islam appear.

The Christian-Judaism that Muhammad encountered was undoubtedly influenced by the Gnosticism of the Way of Righteousness that existed in the areas of Syria and Arabia during the hundreds of years after the death of Jesus and prior to the life of Muhammad. How could it have not been? These are the very kind of stories that would been told and repeated. The Judaism he encountered was certainly influenced by the Zoroastrianism the Jews were exposed to during the Babylonian Exile, and which was incorporated into the theology of the Way by the Zaddik and Osim, and brought to the East by the mission of Judas Thomas and others. So, it is a valid question to ask, again, what do these words mean today?

> Allah is the light of the heavens and the earth. His light may be compared to a niche that enshrines a lamp, the lamp within a crystal of star-like brilliance. It is lit from a blessed olive tree neither eastern nor western. Its very oil would almost shine forth, though no fire touched it. Light upon light; Allah guides to His light whom He will. (Sura 24)

We can readily imagine that these words were found in the Gnostic Gospels or the Kabala, but in the context of Islam, what do they mean? At least to the Shia, the words mean that Muhammad passed along secret knowledge to Imam Ali. The Jafari School teaches that just as the sacred oil shines without being touched by fire, so divine knowledge issues from the mouth of the Imam, "even if Muhammad had not spoken it."

Muslims Expect the Imminent Return of the Mahdi (Guide)

The Shia, far more than the orthodox Sunni, believe in the "Mahdi." The word, which means "one who guides divinely," was used as an honorific title for Muhammad and Ali, and for some of their descendants, particularly the Seventh and the Twelfth Imams. There is a belief among some of the Shias—the Seveners and the Twelvers—that one or the other Imam has been concealed by Allah since their deaths and that one or the other of the "Hidden Imams" will return on the Day of Judgment to restore order on the earth. There is no mention of the Mahdi in the Quran; however, he appears in both the Shia and the Sunni hadiths as the redeemer of Islam who will appear at the end of time to create a perfect and righteous Islamic society.

The Shia also have a belief in a spiritual realm which connects humans and God. In their profession of faith, the Shia say, "There is no god but Allah, Muhammad is Allah's Messenger, and Ali is Allah's Executor." The Shia believe that their Imams were created from eternal light and that they possess secret esoteric knowledge which is handed down from Imam to Imam as a mystical transfer of consciousness. While the straight-forward words of the Quran exist to guide all Muslims, the secret messages contained within those words come from a place beyond human comprehension. Many of these beliefs are virtually indistinguishable from Gnosticism.

Sufism, the Soul of Islam

Although held by many to be indefinable, Sufi (*Tasawwuf*) is usually referred to as "Islamic mysticism." It is the ancient practice of reducing one's self to insignificance in order to become one with Allah—who, or which, incorporates everything in the universe. Islamic scholars consider Sufism to be the inner or esoteric dimension of Islam.

Islamic Sufism arose during the first centuries of the Islamic empire in response to the excessive luxury and indulgences enjoyed by the caliphs and other Muslim administrators in the lands they conquered. Rejecting this worldliness, the Sufis—who likely included Gnostic followers of the Way who converted to Islam—created a system of worship in both the Sunni and Shia traditions to seek a personal and profound love of God through asceticism, meditation, and piety.

Considered by many to be the second most influential Muslim leader after Muhammad, Al-Ghazali was born in 1058 in Iran and became a greatly honored educational leader in Baghdad. Seeking an intimate knowledge of Allah, Al-Ghazali abandoned his comfortable position in 1095 for a life of poverty and meditation. He made a lengthy pilgrimage to Mecca, Medina, and Jerusalem before returning to Iraq. Al-Ghazali lived in seclusion, practiced and taught Sufism, and published more than 70 books on Islamic philosophy and Sufism. The most significant of these is *The Revivification of the Religious Sciences* in which he argues that the practice of Sufi devotion is the only way to fully comply with Quranic requirements. His exceptional and inspired work encouraged the *Ulama* authorities to tolerate Sufism as an acceptable Islamic practice.

Two centuries later, al-Arabi, who is one of the greatest Sufi poets and philosophers, created a broad body of literature that allowed Sufism to be recognized beyond Islam. His emphasis was on seeking metaphysical knowledge to become the "Perfect Man." As he wrote in the *Bozels of Wisdom*, "When you know yourself, your 'I'ness vanishes and you know that you and God are one and the same." Sufism contributed to the spread of Islam—as it presented an admirable aspect of spirituality in contradiction to the stifling *Ulama*, which al-Arabi condemned as contributing to the decline of Islamic civilization.

Sufism continues to be practiced by both Sunnis and Shias, and both agree that the connection between Muhammad and the practice of Sufism is through Ali. Muhammad said, "I am the city of knowledge and Ali is its gate."

While most Muslims see themselves as coming close to Allah (and Paradise) following death and the Last Judgment, Sufis believe it is possible to experience the divine presence during life. Sufis transcend the laws and theology of Islam, and they use its practice to personally become one with Allah. These outward trappings of Islam are replaced in the soul with pure love—once a Sufi achieves enlightenment.

The Sufis do not believe that the Divine can be fathomed with human reason, and its membership declined with the advent of the Muslim Modernists of the nineteenth century. Moreover, the dramatic increase in the power of Islamic fundamentalism has suppressed the practice of Sufism, especially in Saudi Arabia where it is outlawed altogether. Interestingly, the Ayatollah Khomeini—who led the Iranian revolution leading to a conservative Shi'ite theocracy in Iran in 1979—was a devoted Sufi during his university years.

The Independent and Unitarian Druze

Although the group arose within Islam in the eleventh century, resulted from the teachings of Islamic leaders, and is in Muslim countries, the Druze faith is no longer considered to be a part of Islam. With as many as one million adherents, the Druze is a highly esoteric Unitarian religion that combines the Old Testament, the Quran, the philosophies of Aristotle, Socrates and Plato, along with Christianity, Gnosticism, and the works of other religions and philosophies into a six-volume canon in the Arabic language known as the *Epistles of Wisdom*.

The Druze do not have a clergy; however, about ten percent of its most knowledgeable members known as the "enlightened" are initiated into the Druze holy books and attend special religious meetings. The "noninitiated" body of the faithful are not allowed access to the books or the meetings but do adhere to a strict code of moral and ethical behavior.

The Druze call themselves the *Muhwahhidun*, or the Unitarians, and they believe in absolute monotheism. They are also the "Sons of Beneficence," who help others.

For the Druze, Allah is the whole of existence and has no attributes apart from His essence. Upon death, reincarnation occurs instantly, with the soul moving into another Druze body. Once the soul is released after multiple reincarnations, it rejoins the Cosmic Mind and achieves consummate joy. For the Druze, Hell represents the failure to achieve life's goal of becoming a just person.

ISLAM, TODAY AND TOMORROW

Of the 1.6 billion Muslims in the world today, only 20 percent live in Arabic-speaking countries. Sunnis constitute 85 to 90 percent of all Muslims worldwide, and there is a mixture of Sunni and Shia Muslims in every country. Iran, Iraq, Azerbaijan, and Bahrain are predominately Shi'ite nations, while Pakistan and India also have large Shi'ite populations.

Social and political upheaval in most of the Muslim nations during the past century have had a substantial impact on their populations and on the rest of the world. The combination of politics and religion has been a volatile mix since the birth of Islam, and today, it has explosively become one of its identifying features.

Political Islam

By the beginning of the twentieth century, most of the countries with Muslim populations were dominated by the European powers—or the Turkish Ottoman Empire. The defeat of the Turks in World War I, and the dissolution of their empire, allowed European domination of Muslim nations to became complete. Although the primary purpose of imperialism was the exploitation of the minerals, products, and economies of the subject people, the European nations justified their domination of Muslim nations as a mandate to civilize the countries and to convert their subjects to Roman Christianity.

The seminal event in the political and religious rebellions against imperialism that characterized the twentieth century occurred earlier in 1857 with the mutiny of Muslim soldiers in Lahore, India against the governing East India Company. Their complaint was the constant proselytization by their British Christian commanding officer and the deliberate contamination of rifle cartridges with beef and pig fat—which they refused to touch. Their rebellion spread throughout India, resulting in mass arrests and beatings, thousands of deaths, and the massacre of 500 Muslim soldiers who had surrendered.

An influential group of educated Muslim Modernists believed that the iron grip of the Islamic *Ulama* had stifled Muslim scientific and economic advancement by forbidding discourse about Islamic law and scripture. The Modernists believed that the adoption of European values, including education and the rule of law, would be the path to independence—leading to the rebirth of a liberalized Islam in which everyone would be free to interpret and understand the Quran and *sunnah* for themselves. They envisioned a united Pan-Islamic community, including Sunnis, Shias, and Sufis of all Muslim nations.

Two groups disagreed with the Modernists for different reasons. The secular nationalists believed the Modernists' religious ideology interfered with their goal of economic and political independence—obtained by armed rebellion if necessary. The archconservatives of the Islamic purity movement opposed all religious liberalization and innovations.

Reconciling these groups was the lesson of an Egyptian Sufi teacher named Hasan al-Banna who taught that "Islam is the answer." Creating a socialist movement to improve the wellbeing of the disadvantaged faithful, al-Banna named his group the Society of Muslim Brothers, or the "Muslim Brotherhood." Beginning in 1928 and quickly spreading across the Middle East, the Brotherhood's version of Islamic socialism sought to improve the poverty of the people and to empower them politically in opposing their autocratic Arab monarchies, their European overlords, *and* Zionist infiltration into Palestine. Its charter declared:

Allah is our objective.

The Prophet is our example.

The Quran is our law.

The Jihad is our life.

Martyrdom is our goal.

For al-Banna and the Brotherhood, Islam was superior to all other religious, political, cultural, and social systems because it combined all these elements into one universal structure. Its application, however, required an Islamic government that cared for all members of its society. Al-Banna was silenced by his assassination in 1949 by the Egyptian government, but his martyrdom led to increased membership and political power of the Brotherhood. The movement encouraged the revolt of the Free Officers Corps under the leadership of Colonel Gamal Abd al-Nasser—who promised to implement the Brotherhood's social agenda in Egypt.

After first outlawing all political organizations—other than the Brotherhood—Nasser then sought to demolish the Brotherhood in 1953 by imprisoning its members and executing its leaders. Nasser's efforts to secularize the government and to extend his version of nationalization into other Middle East countries led some members of the Brotherhood to conclude that providing for social welfare was insufficient—only force could prevail.

One of the Egyptian prisoners, Sayyid Qutb wrote in 1964, "Those who have usurped the authority of Allah and [who] are oppressing Allah's creatures are not going to give up their power merely through preaching." He believed that "setting up the kingdom of Allah on Earth, and eliminating the kingdom of man, means taking power from the hands of its human usurpers and restoring it to Allah alone." In Qutb's ideology of "Islamism," the only ruler would be Allah, the only law would be the *Sharia*, and the society would be defined only by Islamic values.[136] He was hanged for treason in 1965, and many members of the Brotherhood sought sanctuary in Saudi Arabia.

Islamic Fundamentalism

An alliance between a puritanical Muslim preacher named Abd al-Wahhab and an ambitious Arabian sheikh named Muhammad bin Saud in 1744 resulted in the establishment of the most fundamental

---

[136] Islamism can be defined as the desire to impose Islam and Islamic law on human society by political means. The term jihadism has the same objective, but allows for the use of force, in addition to political means.

and regressive form of Islam ever practiced on a major scale.[137] The agreement by which Saud became the political leader of the Muslim community and al-Wahhab became its religious leader allowed the two to expand their power from Saud's tiny Emirate of Diriyah at a desert oasis to encompass all of modern Saudi Arabia.

The uncompromising and austere practice of Islam which Saud and al-Wahhab imposed on Saudi Arabia has prevailed for more than 250 years. All the tombs of Muhammad, his family, and his companions were destroyed, and their veneration was outlawed along with the celebration of Muhammad's birthday. Under Wahhabism men must grow beards and women must be secluded. Women who appear in public must wear veils or burkas and be accompanied by a male relative. Women only recently achieved the right to vote and to drive. Hands are chopped off for theft, and people are publicly beheaded for murder and other offenses, such as political protest, blasphemy, sorcery, and witchcraft, at the rate of more than three per week.

With the establishment of the Kingdom of Saudi Arabia as an absolute monarchy in 1932, the discovery of the massive petroleum resources beneath its surface, and the establishment of the Arabian American Oil Company (ARAMCO) to extract and sell the oil, the Saudi monarchy became extraordinarily wealthy.

One of the Five Pillars of Islam is the giving of alms and—in addition to daily giving by everyone—wealthy Muslims are expected to pay an annual "Zakat" of 2.5 percent of their wealth beyond their essential needs.[138] In the case of the Saudi royalty, the Zakat has amounted to hundreds of billions of dollars over the years.

The Saudis not only financed the battles against secular nationalism throughout the Middle East, but they also funded Wahabbi mosques, elementary schools, universities, charities, cultural centers, and missionary work in other countries to extend

---

[137] Fundamentalism is a Christian term denoting those who maintain the literal Divine origin and inerrancy of the Bible. It is used here only because its use in other religions has become commonplace. Critics have suggested alternative terms such as puritanical or Islamic revivalism.

[138] In Saudi Arabia, the Zakat is mandatory and is collected by the state. Its percentage can amount to as much as 15 percent.

their fundamentalist ideals throughout the Muslim world. Since the Saudis also control the sacred sites of Mecca and Medina, they have also expended billions in improvements and facilitating the annual *hajj* pilgrimages. Politically, the funding and influencing of radical Islamic political groups has facilitated the infiltration of Islamic fundamentalism into all other Muslim nations, and its effects are being felt around the world.

The Radicalization of Islam and the Terror it Has Produced

Although U.S. President Donald Trump—who criticized Hillary Clinton for not using the term, "Radical Islamic Terror" during the 2016 presidential campaign—has now stopped using the term, the subject of radical Islam and its use of terror as a political and religious weapon has become a fact of the twenty-first century. For our purposes here, "radical Islam" implies an individual and societal acceptance of the use of violence, including terrorism and martyrdom, as a political tool.

The term, radical Islam, first appeared in the news media in connection with the Iranian Revolution of 1979 and Ayatollah Khomeini's role in establishing the Islamic Republic of Iran. The term was also used to describe Iran's funding of the Shia-Hezbollah party in Lebanon to encourage its opposition to the Israeli occupation of Southern Lebanon. The issue of radical Islam was first raised in the United States during the 1984 presidential election, when it was identified as a threat to American interests.

Prior to that time, the Palestine Liberation Organization had relied on an armed struggle in its resistance to Israel, but it had been primarily viewed as a means of establishing a secular Palestinian state. With the birth of the Islamic Jihad movement in Palestine, radical Islam supported the effort to establish an Islamic Palestinian state. Following the First Intifada in Israel, Hamas was established in 1987 as a Sunni-Islamic fundamentalist organization to operate social services and to provide military opposition to the Israeli occupation of Gaza and the West Bank. The latter two groups are offshoots of the Muslim Brotherhood.

Spending the billions contributed by the Saudis, the Wahhabis established their radically conservative Islamic schools and cultural centers in Muslim nations, and "radical Islam" soon followed. By the 1980s, its presence was reported in Algeria, Libya, Syria, and Egypt, and then around the world in Indonesia, Malaysia, Thailand, and the Philippines.

Especially in Afghanistan and Pakistan, the *madrasas* (schools) funded by the Wahhabis were often located in backward, rural areas where there was no other access to education or intellectual stimulation for young people. With a medieval mindset, the teachers in these schools taught a brand of ultraconservative and uncompromising Islam that encouraged their students to follow the path of jihad to achieve some meaning in their lives. Given the poverty of the student's existence, other alternatives were unimaginable and unattainable.

It was from these schools in the Pashtun regions of Afghanistan and Pakistan that the group known as the *Mujahideen* ("striving" or "struggling") emerged to fight against the occupation of Afghanistan by the Soviet Union between 1979 and 1989. Secretly supported by the United States Central Intelligence Agency in cooperation with the Saudi government, the Mujahedeen eventually forced the Soviets to withdraw.

In the subsequent civil war among the Mujahideen fighting for power in Afghanistan, the *Taliban* (students of Islam), who were organized by a mullah named Mohammed Omar, prevailed, with the overt assistance of the Pakistan military. The Taliban established the Islamic Emirate of Afghanistan in 1996 and imposed a strict interpretation of Islamic law—which devastated the countryside and starved and brutalized its people.

Working with the United States and Saudi Arabia during the war against the Soviets was a highly placed Saudi named Osama bin Laden, the son of a Saudi billionaire builder. Bin Laden joined the Mujahideen in 1979 and funneled money, arms, and Arab fighters into Afghanistan. Near the end of the Soviet War, he organized *al-Qaeda* ("the base") as a multi-national network consisting of Islamic extremists and Salafist jihadists to resist Western influences in Saudi Arabia and throughout the Muslim world.

Motivated by a conviction that a Christian-Jewish alliance is determined to destroy Islam, al-Qaeda ignores all secular laws in favor of a strict interpretation of Islamic law—which they believe sanctions the killing of non-combatants and liberal Muslims (whom they view as heretics) in their war against the West. Primary funding of al-Qaeda came from Islamic charities and other private donors amounting to millions of dollars each year.

After being expelled from Saudi Arabia and later from Sudan, bin Laden found a sanctuary in Afghanistan under Taliban protection in 1996. Following the 1993 bombing in the World Trade Center garage and the 1998 bombings of U.S. embassies in Tanzania and Kenya by al-Qaeda, bin Laden was designated a "most wanted" criminal fugitive by the Americans. But it was with the al-Qaeda attacks using hijacked commercial airliners in the United States on September 11, 2001 that international terrorist warfare truly arrived. Most of the suicide hijackers were from Saudi Arabia, but others were from Lebanon, the United Arab Emirates, and Egypt. Saudi Arabia may not have directly funded the attack, but others connected with its government, including intelligence agents, provided financial and social assistance to the hijackers. A $25 million reward was immediately offered for the capture of bin Laden, but it was not until 2011 that the U.S. military located and killed him in his sanctuary in Pakistan.[139]

Following the 9/11 attacks, President Bush—who had been personally bailed out financially during his earlier business failures by the bin Laden family—said, "this great nation of many religions understands, our war is not against Islam, or against [the] faith practiced by the Muslim people. Our war is a war against evil." That said, Bush formulated the never-ending "War on Terrorism" and used it as a false pretext to invade Iraq, dispose of Saddam Hussein, demobilize the Iraqi army, and install a Shi'ite government.[140]

As a result of the destabilization of Iraq, many of the ousted Sunni military officers joined the insurgency during the U.S.

---

[139] The Taliban were defeated by coalition forces led by the United States following the 9/11 attacks, but now after the failures of eighteen years of occupation, the Taliban are re-emerging as a force within Afghanistan and are controlling ever-increasing portions of the country.

[140] Iraq's population is predominantly Shia; however, Saddam Hussein's government and military were primarily composed of Sunnis.

occupation and ultimately became members of a new organization that arose from the ruins. Proclaiming a worldwide caliphate, the organization is known by its Arabic name, *Daesh* and variously as IS, ISIL, or ISIS (Islamic State of Iraq and Syria). ISIS followed the Wahhabi fundamentalist doctrine of Sunni Islam and was dedicated to establishing an Islamic state in the Middle East. While it shares many of the principles of other Islamist groups, ISIS employed an extreme apocalyptical belief that the final Day of Judgment is rapidly approaching and that the return of the Mahdi is near. This belief was very attractive to foreign members who make up at least half of its fighters.[141]

ISIS promoted its religious violence against infidels and distributed videos of the beheadings, drowning, and burning alive of prisoners, including journalists and foreign workers seized in their areas of operation. Aided by technologically savvy Muslim volunteers from the West, ISIS made sophisticated use of social media and other forms of Internet propaganda. It issued its own coinage and slick magazines.

ISIS commenced military operations in Syria in 2015 and quickly overran a large area in eastern Syria and western Iraq that included the major cities of Ramadi, Fallujah, and Mosul. These cities were recaptured in 2016 and 2017 at a heavy cost of civilian lives.

It is generally believed that ISIS receives financial and military support from surrogates of the Saudi government, which is seeking to build a barricade of Sunnis between its kingdom and the Shias of Iran, Iraq, and Syria. More specifically, the Saudis indirectly, through private donors, support ISIS and other rebel groups in Syria in order to oust Bashar al-Assad, whose secular government is primarily composed of Shia Alawites. In a 2014 memo leaked to the press, former U.S. Secretary of State Hillary Clinton stated that the governments of Qatar and Saudi Arabia provided "clandestine

---

[141] The largest number of foreign fighters come from Saudi Arabia, Tunisia, Russia, France, Jordan, Morocco, and Turkey. The army was estimated to field approximately 35,000 jihadists and occupied, at the greatest extent, a land area equal to Jordan, or the U.S. state of Indiana. Much of its equipment was manufactured in the United States and was captured after being abandoned by the Iraqi army on the battlefield.

financial and logistic support to ISIL and other radical Sunni groups in the region."

The United States, acting at the behest of its regional allies—Israel and Saudi Arabia—began to clandestinely fund the Syrian rebel groups to topple Assad's government. President Obama signed a "finding" that allowed the CIA to secretly provide weapons and other logistical support to the rebels, who included, ironically enough, elements connected to al-Qaeda.

The Syrian government is supported by Russia, which has joined in military efforts to defeat the rebels. Although President Trump allegedly ended the rebel aid program in what was considered a major political victory for Russia, he launched a cruise missile attack in April 2017 on a Syrian airbase allegedly used to carry out an earlier chemical weapons assault against Syrian civilians.

Syria continues to be a very dangerous place: Islamic radicals are fighting to replace a secular government with an Islamic republic; the rebels are being supported by the United States, Israel, and Saudi Arabia; and the secular Syrian government is being supported by Russia and Iran. Although the U.S.-backed Syrian Democratic Forces claimed in March 2019 to have defeated ISIS in its last territorial enclave in Syria, there is absolutely no way to predict the outcome of the conflict. But it cannot be good for the people of Syria. There are currently more than six million internally displaced Syrians and more than 4.8 million Syrians who are refugees outside of their country, all of whom are in desperate need of immediate humanitarian assistance.

In 2016, President Obama explained his refusal to use the term "radical Islamic terrorism:"

> This is an issue that has been sort of manufactured because there is no doubt, and I've said repeatedly, that where we see terrorist organizations like al-Qaeda or ISIL, they have perverted and distorted and tried to claim the mantle of Islam for an excuse, for basically barbarism and death. These are people who kill children, kill Muslims, take slaves. There's no religious rationale that would justify in any way any of the things that they do. But, what I have been

careful about when I describe these issues is to make sure we do not lump these murderers into the billion Muslims that exist around the world, including in this country, who are peaceful, who are responsible, who in this country are our fellow troops and police officers and firefighters and teachers and neighbors and friends.

If only it were so simple. It is true that Islam is not the enemy in the War on Terrorism; however, the problem is that the "War" is being fought against a tactic instead of a nation or people—as is usual in an armed conflict. There is no nation in this "war," and the only people are those who are using terror as their most effective option against far more powerful opponents which they perceive as being engaged in a violent conspiracy to destroy their religion and their way of life.

"International terrorism," as the primary enemy in the "War on Terrorism," exists both with and without state support; it employs slogans, rather than a coherent strategy, to define generic opponents (such as the USA, the West, or Israel); it identifies and selects highly symbolic and vulnerable physical targets; it employs a high level of indiscriminate violence to inspire widespread terror; it dehumanizes its innocent victims as infidels; and it has international consequences.

The report of the U.S. National Commission on Terrorist Attacks convened following the 9/11 attacks emphasized the necessity for a long-term strategy to prevail "over the ideology that contributes to Islamist terrorism." Although there were comprehensive recommendations, including improved diplomacy, communications, and education, these were primarily directed against the tactics of terrorism, rather than toward the underlying causes of discontent and resentment in the hearts and minds of those who choose to terrorize in the name of Allah. While it obviously would be beneficial to reduce Western military and political threats to Muslim people and their religion, it is up to the people who practice a religion to reform it as necessary to provide spiritual comfort and meaning in their lives—without imposing their doctrine or harming others who may have different views or religious practices.

Islamic Reformation

Protestantism was the great reform of Roman Christianity leading to the abandonment of the Catholic practices that had become abhorrent to many of the faithful, while retaining the essential and most meaningful features of the religion. With the enlightenment provided by the Gnostic Gospels and the Dead Sea Scrolls, we will hopefully see a further reformation of Roman Christianity in the direction of the true message of Jesus as expressed in the Gnostic and Jamesian principles of the Way of Righteousness. Within Rabbinic Judaism, in the last few centuries, the Conservatives, Reformers, and Reconstructionists have adjusted their religious beliefs and practices to make them more suitable for religious life in the modern world. Such accommodations within Islam, however, are being targeted with the same violent opposition from Islamic fundamentalists and radicals, as are the Western values they see as polluting and infecting Islam and the Muslim way of life.

Among those in the Muslim world who discuss reform, there are three primary questions: Whether Islam and Islamic law should be imposed on non-Muslims as a matter of government? Whether all members of the Islamic *umma* should have equal and human rights? Whether the Quran is the eternal word of God?

Imposition of an Islamic System

For outsiders, it seems the most extreme Islamists are ignoring both the clear language of the Quran regarding the relationship of Islam with other religions, and the history of those verses as well. Islam arose in a milieu of Judaism and Christianity as an extension of the Way of Righteousness, not as a replacement for these religions. To a large extent, Islam is based on Judaism and Christianity, and it is not in conflict with many, if not most of the essential teachings of those religions.

Muhammad clearly envisioned that all the Abrahamic religions could peacefully coexist in a common worship of the same God; all could acknowledge the same prophets; and all would teach similar moral and ethical values. His recitations on the subject are very clear—he said that Islam must respect the other "People of the Book," allowing each to practice his or her own religion in their own manner. In one of the longest of his suras, Muhammad discussed religious practices and the relationship between Islam and the other Abrahamic religions. He unequivocally concluded, "There shall be no compulsion in religion." (2:256).

Perhaps everything was changed forever by the Crusades, but for the first centuries of Islam, it was a religion of diversity, allowing Christians and Jews to practice their religions unhindered by threats or oppression. It is also true that Islam almost immediately split into the Shia and Sunni factions and that there never was a time of pure, unadulterated Islam as imagined by some Islamic fundamentalists, and which is sought as an ideal by Islamic radicals as a matter of law and government.

The essential reform required of Islam—if it is to survive the War on Terrorism and the collateral damage it imposes on the noncombatants of the Muslim world—is to abandon the militant drive to violently impose Islam and Islamic law as a matter of government. Otherwise, radical Islamists who wage jihad to impose their brand of fundamentalist Islam on other Muslims—and the rest of the world—violate those provisions of the Quran which unequivocally prohibit such actions. Moreover, to do so violates the separation of the secular and sacred that occurred following Muhammad's death. The imposition of a government in which Allah-God is sovereign, is a government of the ministers, rabbis, or mullahs of whichever religion gains the political power. This is not to say that these interpreters of Allah's will should not have authority—only that it must be limited to the moral and ethical arena of those who voluntarily choose to attend—instead of on the political battleground where their views may affect others who do not choose to participate in their religion.

Human Rights

It appears from opinion polls that the majority of Muslims are religiously conservative regarding such issues as equal rights for women and gays, maiming for theft, stoning for adultery, (and, in some nations) the death penalty for apostasy and blasphemy, and permitting the genital mutilation of little girls. At the same time, only a small minority of Muslims worldwide want to impose their conservative views onto the rest of society. This is like the experience in the United States, which is largely a Christian nation. Even with a constitutional separation of state and religion, there are endless political and lobbying campaigns by American Christian fundamentalists to exert political control over religious issues such as birth control, abortions, homosexuality, public support of religious schools, and transgender access to bathrooms and the military.

With the adoption of the Universal Declaration of Human Rights in 1948, the United Nations acted to ensure equal rights for every person on Earth. Saudi Arabia refused to sign the agreement, stating that such rights were already defined by Islamic law. By every measure—in comparison to Western countries—the Muslim nations fail to protect the human rights of their citizens. In 1990—to improve and clarify the human rights of Muslims—the member nations of the Organization of Islamic Cooperation[142] signed the Cairo Declaration of Human Rights in Islam. Patterned after the UN agreement, the Cairo declaration provided:

> All men are equal in terms of basic human dignity and basic obligations and responsibilities, without any discrimination on the basis of race, color, language, belief, sex, religion, political affiliation, social status or other considerations. True religion is the guarantee for enhancing such dignity along the path to human integrity.

As laudatory as this language appears to be, its effectiveness is blunted by the caveat, "all rights and freedoms stipulated [in the Declaration] are subject to Islamic Sharia [law]." Tracking the failures of all nations to ensure and protect the rights of their own people is a primary purpose of the Human Rights Watch, a

---

[142] With 57 members, the Saudi-based OIC was founded in 1969 to be "the collective voice of the Muslim world" and to work to "safeguard and protect the interests of the Muslim world in the spirit of promoting international peace and harmony."

nonprofit, nongovernmental organization that operates worldwide. It consistently awards Muslim nations, such as Saudi Arabia, Pakistan, and Iran, low marks on their human rights record. Of greatest concern is the way these countries treat those who advocate for improved human rights or religious freedom. These nations consider such acts to be treasonous and deserving of banishment, imprisonment, and the death penalty.

Given the circumstances of the people of Arabia when Muhammad began his prophecies, he vastly increased their power and standard of living. He improved the status of the ordinary laborers and slaves in relation to the power of the aristocratic merchant class. Moreover, Muhammad substantially improved the rights of women. Perhaps influenced by his first wife—who was a successful merchant in her own right—Muhammad established new rights for women that provided grounds for divorce, and allowed inheritance rights to daughters, which they did not previously have—even though it was half that of their brothers. Another reformation was that women could be witnesses, but once again with only half the testimonial value as that of men.

Today, instead of building upon the reformations of Muhammad, the Islamic *Ulama* and other Muslim decision-makers are acting in a reactionary manner by imposing the strictest masculine control over women and depriving them of their equal human rights. Clearly, Muhammad sought to empower women, not to denigrate them.

We must ask ourselves whether our religious principles—Islamic, Judaic, or Christian—are valid if they must be enforced by force and violence. If coercion is required, then the religion itself has strayed from its original Way of Righteousness and is harming those who practice it. That being the case, reform is the only viable option.

The Quran as the Eternal Word of God

Just as fundamentalist Christians argue that every word in the Holy Bible is the inerrant word of God, most Muslims sincerely believe that every word of the Noble Quran was spoken by Allah through Muhammad. Both beliefs defy reason. In spite of the fact that some Christian fundamentalists actually believe that God created the earth 6,000 years ago, and they insist that this "fact" be taught in public schools, the vast majority of minimally informed people accept the reality of the scientific theories of evolution and plate tectonics, and the physics of cosmology.

There is also scientific evidence that many of the events described in the Old Testament involving the same characters as those revealed in the Quran are based on fables created to transmit or endorse a religious point of view or principle in the ancient past. This does not mean that moral and ethical lessons cannot be derived from a reading and discussion of these stories, but we cannot believe that Moses was able to physically part the Red Sea, or that Jesus walked on water. To do so detracts from the legitimacy of the religions we practice, rather than to enhance them. If a religion can only flourish in an environment of profound ignorance, it has no validity as an ethical and moral standard.

One of the reoccurring questions in Christianity is why—if Jesus's God is so good—there is so much bad in the world? A similar question arose in Islam during its early centuries, which if answered differently by the *Ulama,* the reform of Islam would not be so difficult today. With the ascension of the Abbasid Caliphate and its move to Baghdad in the eighth century, the prestigious Mu'tazili school was established in nearby Basra. Among the subjects studied by the Mutazilites was the question of whether the Quran was uncreated and co-eternal with Allah. The philosophical issue was the question of Divine justice by an all-powerful Allah, as it relates to the reality of evil in the world. Relying on Greek and Eastern philosophies and the basics of Islam, the Mutazilites concluded that, since Allah is Just and Wise, He could not be responsible for evil or act without regard to reason. They believed that neither revealed scripture, nor its interpretation, could determine matters of good and evil; however, the exercise of unaided reason could define rational standards of conduct.

During the ninth century, Mutazilism quickly became the predominate interpretation of the errancy of the Quran. The reform emphasized individual free will and the concept that justice and reason are necessarily the foundation of Allah's actions toward humanity.

This interpretation was attacked by the orthodox Sunni Asharites and was ultimately persecuted as a heresy. Mutazilism slowly declined until it regrettably disappeared by the fourteenth century.

Continuing the earlier discussion about the learning and psychological processes by which Muhammad arrived at his revelations, an acceptance that the Quran might not be as inerrant as believed by most Muslims would be a good first step toward the reform of Islam and Islamic law. There must be some recognition that Muhammad's revelations increasingly encouraged secular violence, as he transformed himself into a military and political leader, instead of a peaceful poet, religious reformer, and messenger of Allah. An open discussion of the inerrancy of the Quran would help erase its scriptural justification for the horrific crimes being committed by jihadists in the name of Allah. It would also allow and encourage Muslims to peacefully coexist and prosper in the modern world of science, technology, and humanistic values.

The Reformers

Some Muslims, who are most committed to reforming their own religion, are convinced that the violent acts of jihadists cannot be separated from the scriptures that motivate and justify the acts. They emphasize that these horrific acts result from a religiously-driven political ideology they believe is inherent in Islam—as it currently exists. These Muslim reformers dispute that Islam is a religion of peace, and they believe that that this underlying fact is the essential issue that cannot be ignored if Islam is to be reformed. For these reformers—who are labeled as heretics and who risk death for expressing their opinions—the only solution is an Islamic Reformation that fundamentally alters those aspects of Islam that justifies discrimination and violence, while retaining its positive aspects of social justice.

Given the great depth of conservative fundamentalism in the version of Sunni Islam practiced by the Wahhabis in Saudi Arabia and the extreme power provided to them by its absolute monarchy, any meaningful reform of Islam will most likely begin in the Far East. It is in Iran and Iraq where a more mystical and spiritual view is taken of the teachings of Muhammad.

Undoubtedly, education is the key, and wisdom is the answer. In today's world where the Quran and its interpretations are readily available in every major language on the Internet, *and* where the young people of every nation and culture are seeking truthful and accurate information in order to make their own decisions, *and* when that information is at their fingertips—there is hope for the future.

The Legacy of Islam

Accustomed as we are to the almost daily news headlines about suicide and car bombings in the Middle East by Islamic terrorists, and the fear mongering that has risen to a fever pitch in the Western media, it is easy to forget that the mission of Islam is the establishment of a peaceful and just society based on righteousness. There are good and valid reasons why Islam has spread to being practiced by more than 1.6 billion people around the world. Following in the footsteps of the Way, Islam is a community of believers who respects Allah, cares for the weak and oppressed, and strives to live a righteous life.

It is only with the rise in fundamentalism that there are some who want to return to the abandoned and discredited tactics of Jihad to violently impose that society on all of humanity. Most Muslims simply desire to live in peace with, and to respect all other religions. There is little difference between a righteous Jew, Muslim, or Christian who cares for others. All must learn to get along better than they have been doing. Such is surely the will of Allah.

The West owes a great debt to Islam for the work it did with the Jews to preserve the fruits of human civilization from destruction during the Christian Dark Ages. Without the support and encouragement of Muslims, many of the ancient books of literature, science, mathematics, and philosophy would have been lost forever to neglect and the fires of the inquisitions.

Moreover, if in fact Islam is a continuation of the Way of Righteousness taught by Jesus, preserved by James, and brought to the East by their brother, Judas Thomas, then the righteous core of the message of Muhammad is all that survives of the Way in the world today. That being the case, Muslims now have a direct spiritual connection to the Way of Righteousness through Judas, James, and

Jesus. A recognition of this fact by all three religions would help relieve the fear and distrust they all have of each other and help to define the way forward.

If only Muhammad had been able to write down his own revelations, the Quran might read differently today. If he had another chance, given the tragic state of his *umma*, what he might say could be very similar to what is being offered in this book. Muhammad was a righteous man and he created a righteous religion. He would certainly want the violent religion presently practiced by some in his name to be restored to its original peaceful purpose of piety, righteousness, and respect for the faith and spirituality of others.

What would Muhammad add, if today he could once again recite the insights he experienced and heard in his mind? Might he try to explain—in poetic words that others could easily understand—the spiritual world into which he had gained admittance through piety, righteousness, and introspection? Or, perhaps it would be the Spirit of Fatima, his daughter—the mother of his grandsons, the Second and Third Imams—who might offer the first of some additional Pearls of Wisdom:

First: Seeing Reality

There's a unity in Mind

That cannot be Seen,

Outside of its Existence.

Only those who learn

the language of

The Abiding Mind

Receive the Insight to See,

What cannot be otherwise,

Seen.

Might Muhammad also wonder why it is that—if Ali led his defenders of the faith into every battle carrying the banner of Islam, if he blessed Ali to be the Master who succeeded him, and if Ali were in fact the first to inscribe in the Noble Quran exactly what

Muhammad recited as it was spoken, why is it that there have been so many others ever since, who have felt free to alter and distort the message Muhammad received from Allah?

How different it would be today, if Islam had followed Ali and his spiritual and more peaceful Way of the Shia, instead of being diverted by the violent secular ambitions of the Sunni monarchists and Jihadists. Muhammad had to kill to defend his faith, and, now, there are those who subvert his faith and kill others to extend their perversion of his faith—a vital difference—in terms of righteousness.

Muhammad may have said, "bow to no man, but God," but he might also say, "make no man bow to you, for you are not God."

The Miracle of Islam

If it is not enough that the Way of Righteousness was preserved by Islam, along with other books of wisdom written by the followers of the Way, but the uncovering of the hidden texts of Gnosticism by an Egyptian Muslim farmer in December 1945, and the discovery of the concealed books of the Way of Righteousness by an Palestinian Muslim shepherd boy eleven months later in a cave by the Dead Sea, are akin to modern miracles. With the insights provided by these revelations, we can better understand the violent past and define a peaceful future. This new information inspires us with confidence that the religions of the Way can be reconciled into a common purpose and peaceful worship. But that remains to be seen.

Reconciliation of the Way

Judaism, Christianity, and Islam have many things in common upon which to build, as they resolve their differences and end the hatred and wars that have diverted them from their common goal of seeking truth with righteousness. Reconciliation is essential if humanity is to avoid its extinction and is to achieve its destiny.

ONE GOD, ONE WAY, ONE FUTURE

After a long and difficult climb, we humans stand together at the pinnacle of the highest spire on Earth, and we either make the leap together into space, or we will quickly slide down into the mire that surrounds us. We have walked on the moon, our robots are exploring Mars, our reconnaissance satellites have reached the outermost edge of our solar system, and we continue to question what awaits beyond our vision. As we gaze up in wonder at the universe that surrounds us and we recoil from the dangers that lurk below, we are faced with the singular choice that has confronted all sentient beings for all of eternity. Can we learn to live at peace with each other in order to gain the courage, strength, knowledge, and wisdom required to fly from our nest into the greater existence?

This book has been primarily about the Abrahamic religions—Rabbinic Judaism, Roman Christianity, and Islam—however, these concluding words are directed to everyone on Earth, irrespective of religion or faith. Humanity has not only achieved the ability to commence space exploration, but we have also gained the power to destroy ourselves—irrevocably. If we are to survive, and the chances are no better than even, we must come together in order to achieve the collective ability to solve the problems that are obliterating our creations and limiting the future of our children. No one person, no nation, no people, and no religion can achieve this task unaided by all the others. It just simply isn't in the cards that have been dealt us in the game of life.

Speaking now to the purpose of this book, how do we *reconcile* the three major monotheistic religions on Earth, which all worship the same God, yet seem to be such deadly adversaries? The religions are themselves split into numerous factions, each of which believes that only it has the answers, and regrettably, some—within all of these religions—are convinced they have the religious duty to violently silence or kill others, both within and outside their religion, who disagree with them.

One and the Same God

In every endeavor to reconcile differences, a good place to start is to identify the matters everyone agrees on, and to go on from there to find other areas where compromise and agreement are possible. Everyone, in every version of the Abrahamic religions, believes in the same God, or Allah.[143] If that is true, then the most important quest is to resolve the differences as to who and what God is, and what He or She has, if anything, ever said or passed along in a message. Rather than to convince all others that any one is right; it would seem better to continue to identify the common elements in all the religions and to evolve in a new direction they all can agree on.

Free Will

We have examined the sacred texts of our Abrahamic religions seeking the words of God telling us what we should be doing to properly deal with the daily problems we encounter, and to help us join with God at the end of our physical lives. We were told that Moses climbed a mountain and returned with a stone tablet chiseled with the Ten Commandments. But, couldn't an all-powerful God simply have spoken to a gathering of all the Israelites and more directly communicated and explained His Commandments to everyone at once? Moreover, wouldn't it be easier if God simply informs each of us, individually, what to do or not to do every time we have to make an ethical or moral decision? The answer, of course, is that something like that does occur—we call it a conscience—but what happens are the choices made, and their consequences. We usually have a pretty good idea of what we should do, or not do, but we must

---

[143] In Judaism, the name of God is Jehovah, or Yahweh, which name cannot be spoken aloud. In Arabic, God is pronounced Allah, but has the identical meaning. Hinduism, one of the most ancient religions refers to the eternal metaphysical Absolute as Brahman. For a while longer, I will continue to refer to our common deity as God; however, the image of an Abiding Mind will be developed as a unifier of all concepts of God within our human culture.

personally make the choice every single time. Even under extreme physical compulsion, we could still choose injury or death over doing something we know to be wrong. So, fundamentally, we all have free will in common.

The Manifestation of Mind and its Reach

A mind is as large as its influence. Everyone has a mind, but if it remains out of contact with others, its reality does not exceed the brain that produces it. Once a mind reaches out, it must physically touch in some manner, if it is to become manifest. An author's mind touches the minds of others through the physical words written on paper or displayed on a computer screen, an artist touches the canvas with dabs of pigment and speaks to the viewer, and a composer creates the notes of music to be played and listened to by others. All of us manifest our minds through the words we use to converse with others, or through the things, simple as they may be, we create.

The extent of the influence of our words, and the images we create, depends on how well our creative minds communicate with the minds of others who hear the words, read the words, look at the pictures, or listen to the music.

The power of a single mind reaches out as far as it is comprehended, and—when united with others—is without limit. There is nothing more powerful than the collective consciousness of eternity, including the concept of a progenitor God who created the universe we inhabit and now seek to explore.

All there is, that we can see, is but a manifestation of nature as it is expressed as life arising, naturally and organically, from the matter we live within. From life, rarely, comes intelligence, as nature found two brains working together to be better than one.

That aboriginal one exists, instinctually, in the brain stem, which stores the fight or flight reflex, anger or full fury, that lurks there, ready to engage in deception, hatred, violence, and war.[144]

Most rarely, almost miraculously or magically, mind is born of intelligence. Mind exists apart from mass, as an expression of energy. An Abiding Mind, consisting of all minds that ever lived, speaks with a feminine voice as the Spirit of Wisdom.

We, our human civilization on Earth, are evidence of the miracle of mind. What we have done, collectively, mostly working together, is the product of hard work. It is a demonstration of our united minds, with each of doing, every day, what we must do to survive in this tumultuous world upon which we live.

Agreeing on the True Nature of God

Let us now make use of our free will and far-reaching minds to see if we can achieve further agreement. Since we all believe in the same God, our differences usually arise when we can't agree on the nature of God. Some call Him—Him, and others call Her—Her, but the real question is how, He, She, or It manifests Himself, Herself, or otherwise. Is God good, just, and forgiving, or is God judgmental and punishing? Is God caring or uncaring? Are we being sacrilegious simply in asking these questions?

---

[144] These are latent brainstem diseases, affecting our judgments and moral choices. We must individually, and collectively, cure ourselves of the disease of intolerance that interferes with the innerworkings of our minds and how we interact with others. We are each responsible for the consequences of our voluntary acts, and we all seek justice in determinations regarding the righteousness and wisdom of those acts.

In the exercise of violence, in words and actions, there is a delicate balance between true self-defense, and violently threatening and bullying others in order to overpower them. Bullying always gets worse, until it is stopped.

It is essential to stop a bully from continuing to get away with threats, because threats of violence always lead to violence. The hiring of others to bully for you, or to kill on your behalf, is the definition of a coward.

One of the mottos of the Texas Rangers, with whom my great-grandfather Samuel Hampton Cox rode in the Civil War, is "Defend the ground you stand upon." Another is, "Say what you mean, and mean what you say."

To a certain extent, our personal God reflects ourselves. If we are angry and violent, our God strikes down sinners, but if we are empathetic and generous, our God is nurturing and forgiving of others.

Search as we might through the scriptures, we will find no physical description of God. We can imagine Him sitting on a Heavenly Throne among the clouds, much like a medieval monarch, tossing down judgments as lightning bolts or shaking the ground with earthquakes. Or, we can picture Her in a long white robe strolling peacefully through a garden Paradise filled with flowers and fruit trees watered by gentle rain and clear flowing streams. What we can do, and what we must do, is to use all our resources to identify, as best we can, the true nature of God—if we are to achieve reconciliation.

Another thing that all three religions have in common is an unanswered question all have struggled with over the years. If God is all powerful, why does He or She allow bad things to happen to good people? The question presupposes that God makes everything happen—good and evil. Perhaps the answer is that God doesn't make anything happen, and it is the exercise of free will that creates the good and evil in the world. Other matters, such as lightning strikes, wildfires, tornados, earthquakes, and floods are simply random acts of nature—God has nothing to do with it.

An answer to this perplexing question may be found in something else that all three of the Abrahamic religions have in common. Each shares a similar form of intellectual spiritualism that arises out of the ancient covenant of Abraham to live simple lives of righteousness, while sojourning through life, at peace with the earth. This commonality has endured and evolved throughout the ages, as we have sought to understand the true nature of God.

The most thoughtful in all these religions have reflected upon their texts and the wisdom they found, and they sought to relate their findings to the physical universe they observed around them. As they contemplated the eternity during which time exists, they imagined the Spirit of God, and they acquired knowledge, sought wisdom, gained insights, and aspired to peacefully live their lives in righteousness, justice, and joy.

Rabbinic Judaism refers to this spiritualism as Kabbalism. To the Christians it is Gnosticism, and the Muslims call it Sufism. At one time or another, each of these enlightened forms of consciousness and self-awareness has been considered heretical but let us risk the eternal damnation of our souls and think about what these spiritual beliefs have to offer considering scientific knowledge about our physical universe.

Gnosticism predated Christianity, and both Kabbalism and Sufism have elements that are clearly related, so let's start with the simplest formula of Gnosticism as it relates to God and individual behavior. Logically, isn't it more likely than not that "God" is an incredibly powerful collective consciousness, or an Abiding Mind—existing forever in a time without beginning or end—consisting of everything that has ever been learned, imagined, or created by all sentient beings, everywhere, throughout eternity?

Shouldn't the primary purpose of life be the achievement of self-awareness preparing our minds to merge with an Abiding Mind when our bodies expire? The individual contribution of every single person is important—as we contribute to the common fund of knowledge and creativity every life experience, every insight, and everything we have ever touched or created with our hands, seen with our eyes, heard with our ears, or imagined with our mind. Consider how very precious and valuable each contribution is to the entirety. Without every contribution, there would be no whole—it would be incomplete.

If whenever we think about God, we imagine an Abiding Mind, and if every time we contemplate our behavior, we ask our own selves if we should or should not do it, we have a firm foundation for understanding all that has ever been said or written about our Abrahamic religions, and those related to them, including Buddhism, Hinduism, and Zoroastrianism.

All three of the Abrahamic religions imagine a progenitor God who created the "heavens and the earth" and we humans. All of this was accomplished in six days and then a well-pleased God rested. Christians and Jews believe that God created humans from clay, and Muslims believe that Allah created man from a clot of blood. In common, all three religions believe in a God who imposed His Law upon humanity and who sits in judgment of all human behaviors. All three believe that the judgmental God either rewards or punishes every person based upon either his or her acting in compliance with the Law. How does an Abiding Mind compare with this concept of God?

Instead of a physical universe that was created by God, our present collective knowledge allows us to consider a universe that is self-generating and evolving—one that simply exists and is forever in a roil of change from one state of energy to another in an eternal mechanistic brew. Under certain unique conditions life arises, and sometimes life achieves intelligence. Under the rarest circumstances, intelligent life evolves a mind that contemplates everything, including one's own self.

The only thing that is created within this black nothingness are the conscious thoughts of self-aware conscious beings and their product. Along with every manifestation of mind, the collective consciousness consists of everything ever imagined or created. Once created, the manifestations of mind cannot be destroyed—they become eternal.

In the aggregate—if we sum up everything that has ever been imagined or created throughout all of eternity—the combined power of such a massive intelligence would far surpass that required for our progenitor God to create the local universe of light we inhabit, including we humans, whether from clay or blood.

An Abiding Mind would not create laws, judge adherence to the laws, or entry to Heaven or Paradise. Rather, the laws created by the minds of intelligent beings would become a part of an Abiding Mind, along with the behaviors, individually and collectively, of those subject to the laws.

The unimaginably immense intelligence of an Abiding Mind could only be the product of peace and good will—as war and violence destroy, rather than create. An Abiding Mind beyond our powers of comprehension and imagination necessarily approaches the spiritual, as it exceeds everything we can presently observe, measure, or imagine. Equal to the totality of energy and mass, an Abiding Mind is the spiritual manifestation of "God."

Within this spiritual realm, we can come to believe an Abiding Mind is equivalent to God and Allah in reality. From this we can achieve an improved ability to communicate our belief and meaning when we discuss the nature of God. Acceptance of this definition by all God-worshipping religions would go a great distance in resolving differences, uniting these religions, and healing the schisms within each of them.

The Soul is Pure Energy Seeking a Place to Rest

Within the realm of scientific quantum physics relevant to the operation of our brains, our consciousness and awareness—the physical spark of our soul—cannot be destroyed. It necessarily survives death and is united with an Abiding Mind.

Although the physical "soul" of consciousness is beyond energy, we can imagine the achievement of self-awareness as the light that illuminates the soul. When the body dies, the physical spark of the soul continues as a part of an Abiding Mind.

Identifying the Nature of Sin and Overcoming Its Stigma

It was not always this way—once upon a time there was no sin. People lived at one with the Mother Earth and the only deity they worshipped was the Earth Mother. Then men invented religion to compel people to kill other people in the name of God, and it became a sin not to do so—according to the priests, who earned their living feeding upon the religions they imagined and imposed.

The Ten Commandments were the first step in telling us what we had to do to please a jealous god. The priests followed this up with more laws in the Deuteronomic Code to tell us what we must do if we are to lead a righteous life, according to the priests and the king. Then Ezekiel, while residing in Babylon, invented the concept of sin and redemption that told us there were ways to get away with our transgressions—if we listened to the priests and rabbis. Next, Ezra edited the law to ensure it was the priests, rather than the king, who determined what was the Law, and who was failing to obey the Law written by the priests. Then, the Pharisees joined the priests in telling people what they had to do or not do to avoid violating the Law. The Pharisees became Rabbinic Judaism, and nowadays, the rabbis and the Islamic *Ulama* tell Jews and Muslims what they must do to live a life of righteousness. In Christianity, preachers peddle their personal versions of the forgiveness of the sins—which they continually reinvent to maintain the cash flow of contributions from their congregations.

The Way of Righteousness, as taught by Jesus and his brothers, looked not to the Law, or its exceptions, for guidance, but to an individual's conscience. Those who joined the covenant and vowed to live a life of poverty and righteousness, and to be "doers of the law," had no need to worry about the Law. The Spirit of Wisdom expressed through their conscience was their guide.

This was the message carried by Mary Magdalene to the West. Unfortunately, Paul either didn't "get" the message, or he didn't care. He created a false messiah who died for the forgiveness of sins of others to replace the true messiah of the Way of Righteousness, who suffered death for the salvation of everyone—without reference to sin. Paul then set about—good Pharisee that he was—to work around the Law and to redefine sins and exceptions. Then, he put his priests and bishops in charge of deciding what was sin and who received forgiveness, and who didn't.

Think about the incredible amount of psychic energy that could be directed to the good, if the burden of guilt and sin were to be lifted from our children. The false concept of sin, redemption, and forgiveness must be exposed to its very core, and the Spirit of Wisdom must regain her place as our internal guiding voice of conscience. This is the essence of understanding.

The Universal Rights of Liberty

More than ordinary human rights, there must be a superior category of rights that are necessarily universal in nature. No matter where one goes in the universe, backward or forward in time and throughout eternity, certain Rights of Liberty must exist if individuals are to successfully come together to evolve from their planets of origin. These freedoms are not granted by a deified law giver, by the Abiding Mind, or by anyone else or thing; they are simply inherent in the concept of conscious self-awareness.

Freedom of Self-Government. The first universal right, naturally, is the right of self-government, under a written constitution created by the consent of those to be governed—one that is secular, democratic, and nurturing, and one which expresses the collective Rights of Liberty of the People. It is only with fair and effective self-government that all other rights can be extended, protected, and enjoyed.

Freedom to Thrive. Once we are born and our hand instinctively reaches out toward the light, and our eyes begin to focus, the true spark of life—our awareness is ignited—and from *that moment* forward in time, an awareness of reality glows within us. For our minds to expand and explore our environment, we must thrive. Not only must our lives be free from criminal threats, violence, and homicide, but we must also be free from the pain of intolerance and the discrimination of bias, prejudice, and hatred.

Freedom of Opportunity. At conception, certain elements of life are a genetic gamble. Genetics influence capabilities such as intelligence and athletic ability, but nurturing, learning, and conditioning can make the best of the hand we are dealt. Every child must have equal access to nutrition, health care, and education, if humanity is to ever achieve the knowledge, wisdom, and power to fly from our earthly nest.

Freedom of Conscience. Not only must we have the freedom to choose the religion we wish to observe, but we must also have the right to reject all religions and to allow our own self-awareness to be our guide. Our conscience (or the Spirit of Wisdom) is our lifelong companion, irrespective of the barricades we place in her way or the way we exercise our free-will.

Freedom of Speech. Short of crying "fire" in a crowded auditorium, or "murder them" to a frenzied mob, the words produced by our mind must have the freedom to issue from our mouths. Otherwise, restrictions on speech shackle our consciousness, erode our awareness, and interfere with our contributions to joint endeavors.

Freedom of Association. Humans are not by nature solitary, but as pack animals, we evolved with an instinctive drive to seek interaction with others. This is not only required to participate in religious, social, and political activities, but our association with others is the foundation of our society, and collaboration and compromise are its basic building materials. Collectively, as the wisdom of the crowd, we are smarter and wiser than any one individual, including self-professed and self-aggrandizing leaders who tell everyone else what to do. We succeed when we associate and work together, and we fail when we divide and fight for more.

Freedom of Creativity. The things we create are unique and have never been generated before in all of eternity. Our creations become the most precious part of an Abiding Mind, and they are essential to the development of our self-awareness and joy.

Freedom of Self-Identity. Free from intolerance, every Person must have the right to self-identify, not only as to religious choice, but as to their sexual, marital, or social identification choices. As a corollary, every Person has the duty to respectfully tolerate the choices of others.

Freedom of Destiny. Each of us must have control over our own minds and bodies. Not only should we have the freedom of choice whether to live or to die, women—personally, individually, and unrestrictedly—must have the right to choose whether to conceive or to give birth. No one else, no person, nor any religion or government, can be allowed to exercise such power over the body and life of another. The integration and power of every person to control their own physical body is inviolate.

When's the Apocalypse?

The apocalypse that humanity is now facing is indeed the Pestilence, Famine, War and Death, predicted in the Book of Revelation. Pestilence results from the degradation of the environment; famine is caused by the unrestrained population explosion; war is a consequence of the extreme militarization of world governments; and death will come from economic collapse. Attempts to address and solve these four most critical, human-caused, crises are failing, in large part because of religious interference. This is true, not only because religions seek to impose their views about matters such as birth control and abortion on other people—who do not share their religious views—but because so many religious fundamentalists look forward, expectantly, to these looming disasters as evidence of the Last Days, as the final condemnation by their imaginary judgmental God upon all of humanity.

By the midpoint of the twentieth century, it was becoming clear that the growth in population was outstripping the capacity of the earth to feed the humans who were multiplying upon it. The "Green Revolution," which produced high-yielding varieties of cereals—combined with chemical fertilizers and agro-chemicals, improved irrigation, and new methods of cultivation—saved as many as one billion people from starvation. This may have been a one-off, inasmuch as some of these methods—especially the potent chemicals involved—are not only threatening the clean water required for survival *and* human, animal, and plant genetic viability, but the very health of the oceans upon which all life on the planet depends.

There are now 7.7 billion people in the world, and if we continue at the current growth rate, there will be 10.5 billion people after another 50 years. Perhaps more so than in any other area, the illogical interference of religions in matters of birth control, equal rights based on sex, and women's freedom of choice is contributing to the certain destruction of humanity. Simply by giving women equal rights to education, nutrition, and health care—including the right to control their own bodies—the world's population will quickly stabilize within sustainable limits. Unfortunately, some religions (and political groups) see population expansion as a benefit in sustaining and achieving their goals of superiority and domination.

Environmentally, "Mother Earth" is currently experiencing the massive death of her living species in an epoch variously known as the Holocene, Anthropocene, or Sixth Great Extinction. There is no doubt about it! We have not only hunted and killed many other species to extinction, but human-caused environmental effects, such as climate change resulting from the massive release of carbon dioxide, may be irreversible in destroying much of the life on Earth.

Irresponsibly, efforts to mitigate these trends are blunted or defeated by a deadly combination of religious fundamentalism, political conservativeness, and polluting corporate power. The gravest and most immediate threat is the availability of clean water, as humans can only survive a matter of days without it.

In 2017, the governments of the world wasted more than $1.7 trillion on their militaries—with the United States spending more than the next eight nations combined. Second was China, and Saudi Arabia was the third, budgeting more than other larger nations such as Russia, India, United Kingdom, France, Japan, Germany, Australia, and Italy. With nine nations possessing nuclear weapons, including three in the Middle East, the world is only one irrational decision or electronic malfunction away from an unimaginable disaster.

The last world war killed as many as 100 million people—the next *will* wipe out humanity altogether. The world's religions seem to take little notice of the wars that are inflaming the nations of the Middle East and burning their babies and little children—while allowing their religious beliefs to add fuel to the fire. If there be evil in this world, its name is WAR.

Every penny now being spent on militaries, must be redirected to carbon reduction and alternative energy sources, immediately, if we, collectively, are to moderate global warming sufficiently to avoid it becoming runaway.

Time is short! The religions of the earth must reconcile their differences, if humanity is to survive. Otherwise the Apocalypse *will* arrive, but the outcome will undoubtedly be a great disappointment to many of those who will be consumed by it. There will be no Rapture, nor Heaven or Paradise awaiting the religious zealots and martyrs who ignored reality—only the dark emptiness of profound ignorance.

There is of course the hope and possibility of a happy ending, but that requires change, and change is always difficult—but not impossible. Humans are an amazingly innovative and resilient species. We have survived and thrived for thousands of years, adjusting ourselves to unforeseen developments, and we have the capacity to overcome the obstacles that are now confronting us. We just must exercise our collective intellect and free will to do so.

The Nature of Evil

The definition of evil is war: the cynical and cowardly compulsion or employment of people to kill other people, for the benefit of those who risk neither injury, nor suffer death.

The Nature of Humans

According to Genesis (1:26), God said, "Let us make man in our image, after our likeness." The first revelation made by Allah to Muhammad was "Recite thou, in the name of thy Lord who created man from clots of blood." If we were created in the image of God, does that mean that God looks like a Middle Easterner, or, since we share 96 percent of our genes with chimpanzees, did God also descend from the apes? What is there about the nature of God we identify within ourselves as human beings?

If in fact, God is an Abiding Mind of universal consciousness, then it is our rational and creative mind that makes humans a reflection of God. If God is representative of righteousness, then the fact that humans—around the world in every society—are mostly good people, is another reflection of the nature of God.

Even though our minds are Godlike, we remain contained within an animal body closely in tune with the instinct of intolerance that is physically encoded in our brain stems. Intolerance that manifests itself as hatred, deception, and violence, exist as a latent disease that interferes with our true nature—as our minds evolve into a reflection of the Abiding Mind.

The individual task in the life of every person is to heal these latent diseases in order to become fully self-aware of our conscious being—if we are to remain merged with an Abiding Mind following the death of our bodies.

We are far, far better than we give ourselves credit for, and we are loved, unconditionally, by an Abiding Mind. We need only to take a few more steps in the right direction if we are to find our way home. "God" has left the light on for us to see our way along the path.

The Way Forward

It is not enough to say that things must be different and that something must be done. We must think about what to do; we must plan; we must work the plan; and we must believe that—through our imagination and efforts today—we can foretell and create tomorrow's future.

THE CHILDREN OF SALVATION

Dreams about a peaceful and joyous future are good, but action is required if it is to be achieved. In moving forward, we must act together in a way that is reasonable and which does not involve further violence. Religion must be reformed, but that will take time, and time is short. What can be done, and what must be done, is for people to take control of their own destiny, seize political control, and create secular governments that support a righteous society based on practical principles, and which defends the rights of everyone to practice the religion they choose.

A New Children's Crusade

A free, peaceful, righteous, and joyful society will be attained, if ever, by a new Children's Crusade launched in memory of the thousands of poor, homeless, and abandoned children who perished or who were taken into slavery in the thirteenth century in the mindless crusades encouraged by the Roman Catholic Church to retake the Holy Land and forcibly convert the Muslims to Christianity. In the spirit of those children and in unity with their souls, the children of today can take charge of their own future.

These wonderful and magnificent generations of the new millennium must make use of the incredible power they hold in their hands—not only their smart phones and other media devices that connect them to the Internet and each other—but the exciting potential they possess to unite together in a common and worthy cause, all over the world. We saw it in the Sixties, and more recently, we witnessed it in Tunisia, Egypt, and other countries where young people united in peaceful "color" revolutions and upset the established forces of repression and domination.

Young people must twiddle their thumbs on their electronic devices and unite in a nonviolent crusade to ensure their future—which they will not have—if they fail to do so. Two things are required for success: young people must have an inspiring expression of their common goal and a unity of action and implementation.

The Way to Good Government

The Abrahamic religions share the same Old Testament background, but more specifically, a similar origin in Abraham's ancient Covenant of Righteousness. At the time the Way of Righteousness was organized, several centuries before the generation of Jesus, the Way represented an evolution of the ancient law- and ethics-based Hebrew religion to include elements of the Eastern religions and Greek philosophy that had become part of the contemporary human culture. The Way's focus on individual righteousness and free-will continues to resonate in its religious progeny.

Now, at this stage of human development, we must once again evolve, not only our religions, but the very way we organize and govern ourselves. Our religions cannot possibly be the same as our governments; however, our governments must not only protect our religious rights, but all other rights as well.

We are well past the time when we required a king or queen to rule over our daily lives. A dictatorial religion—as a monarchal substitute—is equally without value and is inherently destructive of individual freedom.

If we conceive of God as an Abiding Mind, the collective consciousness—the truth of everything that has ever been imagined or created throughout all of eternity, entangled together—we can begin to picture the kind of government that best conforms to that conception. Most basically, representative government must ensure that every individual shares equal responsibilities, and derives and enjoys equal benefits from their political union. From that, we should be able to determine what those rights and duties consist of.

If we are to have effective self-government—instead of a political or religious dictatorship—it is essential that every voter be sufficiently educated and informed to thoughtfully exercise the right and duty to vote intelligently regarding representation. Free elections must (1) collectively decide political policies, and (2) select the best representatives to implement the informed decisions of the people, whose consent to be governed provides the power of government; and (3) which consent can be reserved if the government no longer serves the needs of the People who created it.

The Way Forward

This is not to say that religious beliefs should not and cannot have an influence on government policies. To review what all the Abrahamic religions most basically have in common, we can start with the Deuteronomic Code:

> If there is among you a poor man, one of your brethren, in any of your towns within your land which the LORD your God gives you, you shall not harden your heart or shut your hand against your poor brother, but you shall open your hand to him, and lend him sufficient for his need, whatever it may be. . . . therefore, I command you, You shall open wide your hand to your brother, to the needy and to the poor, in the land.

This commandment was explained by James the Just, the brother of Jesus:

> What does it profit, my brethren, if a man says he has faith but has not works? Can his faith save him? If a brother or sister is ill-clad and in lack of daily food, and one of you says to them, "Go in peace, be warmed and filled," without giving them the things needed for the body, what does it profit?

The absolute duty of every Muslim to attend to the needs of others is explicit in the Islamic religion based on the recitations of Muhammad:

> Have you thought of him that denies the Last Judgment? It is he who turns away the orphan and does not urge others to feed the poor. Woe to those who pray but are heedless in their prayer, who make a show of piety and give no alms to the destitute.

We have learned that the Way incorporated the eastern religions in evolving the doctrine of righteousness that influenced the monotheistic religions, including Rabbinic Judaism, Roman Christianity, and Islam that followed. Modernly, Buddhism is practiced by a half billion people who follow the way of Dharma, the principle of righteousness, taught by the Buddha.

Seeking to develop one's own character in order to become noble, pure, and charitable is not done to please any Deity, but rather to be true to the highest potential that exists in every person. Dharma is considered by Buddhists to be a law of the universe.

In Hinduism, the cosmic order revealed in the Vedas recognizes righteousness as a virtue *and* as a duty (dharma) under universal law.

Mencius (372-289 BCE), the second master of Confucianism emphasized the importance of *ren* (benevolence) and *yi* (righteousness). Among the sayings of Confucius is, "I not only attend to the elderly of my family, but to the elderly in other families as well. I not only attend to the young in my family, but to the young in other families as well." A Chinese motto is: "Remember what you received; forget what you gave."

A universally shared need to care for one another can be the foundational policy of a common government that nurtures those who create it—without the government being controlled by religions, or any other faction. If we look to the very earliest organizations of human activity, we learn they were based on the collective growing of crops and animal husbandry and the sharing of the common effort. We lived that way for millennia during this warm spell, as we have migrated around the globe, until our instinct of intolerance overcame our spirit of wisdom, and war was born.

War was invented by kings to compel their subjects to kill others—in order to extend personal boundaries and spheres of influence—that governments were created to manufacture weapons and organize armies.

Perhaps, the first step toward good government is to return to the basics of a nurturing and caring society and to stop fighting wars. Nothing less will do if we are to survive extinction and provide the opportunity for our children to fly into the universe that surrounds us, instead of drowning in floods, freezing to death, burning in fires, dying of thirst, and suffering the gnawing pangs of hunger.

Our greatest gifts are our children, born of our bodies, with whom we share the treasure of learning, thinking, creating choices,

The Way Forward

and making good decisions. Our children will either live or die. It is their future and their choice, and we are here to help, as best we can. We, the older generations, have had great successes, and we have made quite a mess in doing so.

We must immediately acknowledge our mistakes, innovate choices, and make better collective and representative decisions. We must accept the leadership of our young people, and we must help show them the way. Evolving upward and outward is brilliant, enchanting, and liberating, while failing and falling backward offers only a burning and waterless path to rapid extinction. A definition of Hell.

EPILOGUE

AFTER
THE WAY OF RIGHTEOUSNESS WAS WRITTEN

I completed a final draft of *The Way of Righteousness* to this point on September 2, 2017, having done all I could to document the true history of The Way. It was my best effort to analyze and present the evidence, and to argue the concluding concept of a comforting Abiding Mind as a rational expression of the judgmental, creator God many people no longer believe in, and far too many fear.

The philosophical purpose of my effort was to reconcile the three major Abrahamic religions with the reality of their shared history, as revealed by the miraculous discovery 75 years ago of books hidden 2,000 years ago, subsequent archeological findings, and a common recognition of the image of God as the collective consciousness and creations of an Abiding Mind.

I set aside the draft manuscript of *The Way*, but I used it as an intellectual springboard to bounce beyond its concept of a spiritual, metaphysical, or philosophical definition of God as an Abiding Mind, to a realistic consideration of an Abiding Mind as a proposition of scientific reality.

I spent the next week, or so, thinking about the actual mechanics of such a quantum physical mind, the expanding universe of light we inhabit, and the medium within which it exists. I wrote up a little paper that looked beyond the spiritual and philosophical aspects of *The Way of Righteousness* to an examination of mind that exists within the encompassing negative space, and its role in creating the positive reality of our universe of light.

A Year of Political Insanity

Reality intruded, and I could no longer ignore the mindboggling political carnival, and its gaggle of amoral hucksters, peddled to the American People in the 2016 election sideshow. I laid aside the manuscripts of *The Way* and the paper on *Mind* on my credenza, and I reluctantly turned my attention, once again, to the political madhouse in Washington, DC.

Over the last decade since retirement, I had refined my political thinking from a generalized concept of a peaceful political evolution to drafting a specific and comprehensive Voters' Bill of Rights, as a constitutional amendment to *remedy all the issues that are destroying the faith of most Americans in their representative government.* The Voters' Bill of Rights serves as a focal point for creative strategies, across the political spectrum—people working together in a peaceful transformation of the United States government into one that is more caring and respectful of those who elect it.

We established a California nonprofit corporation (USVRA. us) to educate the public about the United States Voters' Rights Amendment. To provide an essential background and explanation of the amendment, I wrote, and the corporation published, *Transforming America: A Voters' Bill of Rights.*

To explore whether the essential principle of the USVRA—allowing people to make their own political policy—could be adopted by voters in other countries, I wrote and published *An Essential History of China: Why it Matters to Americans.*

Attempting to present a comprehensive set of political policies in an easier-to-read format, I wrote and published *Sam: A Political Philosophy.* As a fact- and policy-based collection of practical policies narrated by fictional characters, *Sam* combines political heroism with an inspiring and poignant love story.

For the last five years, I have been working with students and professors in the political science departments of my local university and city college to establish an organizational framework of Youth for the Voters' Rights Amendment (Y4VRA), capable of being activated on every American campus.

I wake up early most mornings from productive dreams, and use these quiet hours to do my best thinking and writing, and, around daybreak, after Helen and I read the news on our mobile pads and plan our day, I usually go to the YMCA for exercise. There, some years ago, I became friends with Mel Lindsey, a 93-year-old World War II veteran and retired pre-school educator. He was interested in what I was working on, and I would often share with him what I had just written that morning. He read all my published books and joined the USVRA.us board of directors.

Following the 2016 election of Donald Trump and a stalemated Congress, Mel felt that he had been abandoned, and that his government no longer represented him. *And*, he wanted to do something about it. I helped him write a First Amendment Petition for Redress of Grievances and his sworn declaration, to which he attached a bound copy of *Transforming America*, as an exhibit.

Helped by Y4VRA volunteers, Mel prepared hundreds of mailing envelopes addressed to his local city council members, his state representatives, governor, to every member of Congress, every member of the Presidential Cabinet, every member of the Supreme Court, and to the President and Vice President.

The mass mailing at the Postal Annex was videotaped, and Mel appeared in several Facebook ads explaining his actions. Additional Y4VRA ads followed, with videos of young people saying what they want and expect from their government, and starring their proud mascot, Trusty Rusty, the Ranger Dog[145].

---

[145] Rusty is my best buddy. He's 46 pounds of lean muscle—a Giant Rat Terrier hunting dog, of the linage bred with the African Basenji village dog. He has a mind of his own, and he speaks out if something isn't right.

The Internet and Social Media

A friend introduced me by email to a young international *and* all-UK champion web site designer in Wales, England. We first collaborated on creating a fully coded site for the Youth for the Voters' Rights Amendment at Y4VRA.org. Starting with a photographic slide show of young protestors, the pages scroll down through short chapters and videos, on all mobile devices.

Facing the "Bad News" of "Living under a cruel and corrupt government in a declining economy and polluted environment," Y4VRA provides a voice for young people to assert their fundamental Rights of Liberty, and to reserve their Consent to be Governed. Its purpose is to provide information and an easy way for everyone to immediately cast an electronic vote, yes or no, on their Voters' Bill of Rights, in order to make a real difference in the 2020 election.

Once Y4VRA.org was up and running, we replicated it at USVRA.us, refocusing on the leadership role of strong women in managing the Voter's Bill of Rights campaign, as it is organized by the young people of America. The USVRA incorporates the Equal Rights for Women Amendment (ERA), and it ensures the complete equality of all women in all aspects of all political decision making.

I photographed and videotaped the Los Angeles Women's March in 2018 and 2019. We used these images of women—particularly mothers and their daughters—in a series of Facebook ads for both USVRA.us and Y4VRA.org. To honor and support Greta Thunberg and the millions of striking students around the world, I also attended and photographed the Climate Strike in my hometown, down by the Long Beach-San Pedro Harbor.

We republished WilliamJohnCox.com as a digital autobiography. The website is a comprehensive collection of all my creative work, including books, articles, videos, models, and commentary. Almost all my published books are in print and are commercially available in paperback, but digital copies of most can be downloaded for free in the Lending Library, and my films and videos can be viewed in the Video Library.

After *The Way of Righteousness* Was Written

In 2015, I published *The Book of Mindkind: A Philosophy for the New Millennium*. Last year, we launched Facebook ads for the book on the Internet, and we created an entirely new coded site at Mindkind.info depicting the book and its message coming out of a background of music and stars.

Finally, TheVote.io site was coded to serve as a digital ballot box for an ongoing electronic poll on the Voters' Bill of Rights by the American People, as *We Declare Our Rights of Liberty, and Reserve Our Consent to be Governed*. The vote will close at midnight on Election Day, November 3, 2020, at the dateline of the last U.S. territory in the Western Pacific Ocean.

As a result of Mel Lindsey's mass petition to his government, one congressman returned the book saying he didn't accept gifts, and the Secretary of Education's office sent a letter acknowledging receipt. That's it!

Defining the Rights of Liberty and Reservation of Consent to be Governed

I then drafted my own pleading to the U.S. Supreme Court in the form of a Petition for Writ of Mandate. In it, I declared the personal Ninth and Tenth Amendment Rights of Liberty of Americans as a defense against our government, that has become corrupt, ineffective, unrepresentative, and threatening. I reserved my consent to be governed, as a censure of the entire existing government, until the American People can vote on their Bill of Rights for all voters.[146]

I wrote and printed the legal petition, flew to Washington DC, and on February 28, 2018, I personally delivered a box containing the required number of bound copies to the U. S. Supreme Court. My petition was rejected by the Clerk for defects in form. I corrected the errors to the approval of the Clerk; however, at the direction of the Chief Justice, the Clerk refused to accept a filing from any individual on a matter of original jurisdiction. This, without any consideration of my argument to the contrary, as a reserved and essential right of liberty.

---

[146] I will vote, but not for any candidate who does not support the Voters' Bill of Rights.

I then mailed personal letters to the justices, serving each of them with a copy of the pleading as a First Amendment Petition for Redress of Grievances. There was no response.

By this time, a year had passed since I laid aside *The Way* manuscript to reengage in the insanity of politics. In September 2018, I became depressed about the absolute lack of result from everything we had done over the past year. Exhausted, I spent a month, doing nothing but reading junk books, watching Netflix documentaries and docudramas, and eating ice cream.

Publishing *Mind & Its Languages of Reason*

Having sufficiently indulged my depression, and becoming bored, I sought the diversion of a project to occupy my mind, and to lift my depression. I picked up and reread the little five-page paper on *Mind* that had laid dormant for a year. I imagined it would be interesting, and not too difficult, to expand the paper into a small book about mind, our universe, quantum physics, measuring, and counting, as a sequel to *The Book of Mindkind*.

I drafted a series of papers about our universe of light, the Abiding Mind that contemplates it, and its languages of quantum physics, measuring, and counting. I organized and circulated a collection of the papers by email to the faculty and graduate students in the physics, mathematics, and computer science departments at the top 25 technical universities in the world. Profiting from the limited response, I completed a final draft and published *Mind & Its Languages of Reason* in print and digital formats on May 1, 2019.

Images of the Libraries and Graves of Jesus and His Family, and the Ruins of Empire

With the better understanding provided by working through the papers on *Mind*, I was able to go back to work on *The Way*—which lacked only an Epilogue and original photographs to prepare the manuscript for publication.

After *The Way of Righteousness* Was Written

To complete the book, and to enjoy an adventure, my son, Steven, a photographer and graphic artist, and I planned our trip. We flew to Israel during the first weeks of June 2019 and photographed selected locations for a photo essay and maps to illustrate the book.

With official permission, we photographed at Caesarea, the ancient caves at Mount Carmel, the Megiddo Tel, the Zion cornerstone of the Temple Mount, the Citadels of Jerusalem, the walls of Jericho, the Jordan River, the caves, ruins, and cemeteries at Qumran, and Masada, where the Zealots who followed the Way of Righteousness made their last stand against the Roman army.

We were able to capture the moment of sunrise over Jerusalem from the top of the Mount of Olives. We got good images at all sites, and we returned home safely.

Having flown home through eleven time zones, I remained on Jerusalem time for several weeks. Arising very early, I wrote this Epilogue and worked on its Photo Essay with Steve, as he also completed the maps and charts.

The following 15 images are a survey of the stones left standing from almost 2,000 years ago, serving as mute monuments to Empire gone mad. Imagine the Roman destruction of Jerusalem, down to Herod's Citadels, and how the Romans relaxed from the battles at the Caesarea arena, enjoying the Herodian slaughter of the Zealot children of the Way of Righteousness. Bear witness to the murders of the sons of Mary: Simeon and Joseph—the Priests of the Sons of Zadok and the Order of Melchizedek, and Jesus, Judas, and James—the triple Messiahs of the Way of Righteousness.

Epilogue

Photo # 1 —As it rises over the Mount of Olives, the same sun shines upon the roofs of the synagogues, churches, and mosques of Jerusalem, where Abraham covenanted to follow the Way of Righteousness.

Photo # 2 — The caves on the west face of Mount Carmel have provided shelter to migrants out of Africa to Asia along the narrow, fertile plain by the Sea for millions of years.

After *The Way of Righteousness* Was Written

Photo # 3 — The walls around the Spring of Jericho may be the most ancient on Earth.

Photo # 4 — The elaborate defensive gate at Tel Megiddo (Armageddon) was built by the Northern Kingdom of Israel at several of their cities at the height of their power.

Epilogue

Photo # 5 — The water tunnel cut through rock under Tel Megiddo tapped into a hidden underground spring outside the walls, funneling the water back into a deep cistern within the walls.

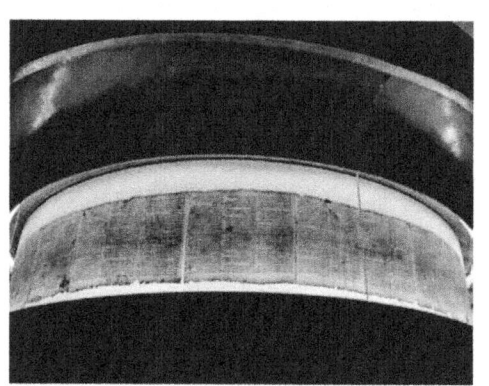

Photo # 6 — The Isaiah Scroll (in the Shrine of the Book in Jerusalem) was recovered from Cave One at Qumran.

After *The Way of Righteousness* Was Written

Photo # 7 — Cave Four high on the cliffs of Qumran was carved out of the limestone to preserve the thousand-book library of the Osim, where Jesus and his brothers studied, 2,000 years ago.

Photo # 8 — The Ruins of Qumran, the desert refuge of the Osim (Doers of the Law), who lived the Way of Righteousness.

Epilogue

Photo # 9 — The Southwest, Mount Zion corner of the Temple Mount, with its massive foundation stones and archway where Jesus may have paused for a moment before going forth to cleanse the Temple, and where his brother James the Just was stoned to death three decades later.

Photo # 10 — The traditional site on the Jordan River where Jesus was baptized by John the Baptist, and across which Simon bar Cleopas led the escape of the Way of Righteousness from the Roman Army.

After *The Way of Righteousness* Was Written

Photo # 11 — Overlooking the Dead Sea, the cemeteries of the Osim at Qumran are the most likely burial site of Jesus, his priestly brothers James the Just and Simeon bar Cleopas, their mother, Mary, their father, Cleopas, and their sister, Salome, and others who walked with them on the Way of Righteousness.

Photo # 12 — The Amphitheater at Caesarea by the Sea, where the Romans and Herodians tossed the Zealot children of the Way of Righteousness to wild animals, following the stoning of James the Just, and the destruction of Jerusalem.

Epilogue

Photo # 13 — The Twin Citadels of Herod's Palace in Jerusalem are the only structures the Romans left standing in Jerusalem. They remain by the Jaffa Gate in the Old City, across the street from Christ Church.

Photo # 14 — Titus's Arch of Triumph in Rome celebrated the destruction of Judea, the leveling of Jerusalem, and the enslavement of the young zealots and those who followed the Way of Righteousness. *by author.

After *The Way of Righteousness* Was Written

Photo # 15 — Archeological diggings in the floor of the Zealot's assembly room at Masada revealed a cache of documents related to the Way of Righteousness at Qumran. The books were buried by the Zealots before their mass suicide, having held off the Roman army for four years after its destruction of Jerusalem.

The Library and Grave of Jesus

Lingering on these images, we can go back in time, thousands of years, to when the stories of *The Way of Righteousness* were being played out.

We can visualize the Osim library carved out of the stone cliffs as Cave Four at Qumran, large enough for shelves to hold a thousand books, and where Jesus and his brothers, James and Simeon studied to be priests of the Way of Righteousness, 2,000 years ago. Can we imagine the lively debates of these inquisitive boys and the languages they spoke?

We can gaze across the ruins of the ancient desert refuge of the Osim, those who were Doers of the Law. Beyond, we can see the simple, unmarked graves in the cemetery, high above the shore of the Dead Sea. This is where the bodily remains of the followers of the Way of Righteousness were laid to rest under piles of stones, as their minds and souls were freed for all of eternity—not only as spirits among the weathering stones, but everywhere they are remembered.

It is here, if anywhere on Earth, the bodies of Mary and her sons, Jesus, James, and Simeon may rest, alongside others who walked and lived the Way of Righteousness.

Epilogue

The Forgotten Children of Palestine and Israel

After returning from Israel, I quickly completed the Epilogue and Photo Essay, and I awoke one morning and was able to quickly draft a summation of the historical essence of *The Way of Righteousness*, expressed as A True Story About an Amazing Family

A few days later, a similar need compelled me to write the overview paper on the Nature of An Abiding Mind and to focus on the grave and immediate climatic danger of global warming. The paper is a word bridge between the ending of *The Way* and the beginning of *Mind & Its Languages of Reason*, summarizing and connecting the theories of mind in the two books with the reality of our existence.

I was unable to write a satisfactory ending of *The Way* without resolving a final critical issue. As our passenger jet climbed and banked out of Israel, I carried with me, not on film or in our computers, but in my mind, a wretched image of inhumanity that later made me weep when I first read what I had written below about it. Somehow, before I'm done with *The Way*, I must do *something* to relieve the suffering I witnessed.

As Steve and I drove behind Israel's great concrete wall down into the wilderness valley of the occupied West Bank and the Jordan River, we witnessed the hopeless, desperate, and grinding poverty in and around the hills of Jericho. Any fair-minded comparison to the prosperity and affluence of nearby cosmopolitan Western Jerusalem, is necessarily devastating to the legitimacy of any government, and its leaders, responsible for the military occupation of Palestinian land in violation of international law, for more than half a century.

The sight of forgotten and angry children, with nothing to do, is seared on the retina of my mind, and I cannot ignore it or ever forget it. I am once again compelled to act, doing the only thing I am capable of doing: drafting a legal document seeking protection for these poor, legally forgotten, and defenseless children.

The Children of the Holocaust

Almost 40 years ago, I defended the honor and memory of the Jewish children who were gassed and burned in the Holocaust, in the courts against a gang of American neo-fascists who denied that the Nazis had operated gas chambers.

The Children of the Nakba

In memory of the Nakba,[147] I wrote a petition seeking constitutional protection of the universal Rights of Liberty of all children in the Ancient Land, including the Children of Palestine, whose blood lines run true to the Lands of Israel and Canaan.

With only stones to throw in defiance of the great concrete wall erected by the State of Israel, whole generations of desperate Palestinian children have lived and died, in abject poverty, without legal rights or remedy, justice or hope.

These Palestinian children not only suffer from humiliating hunger and poverty, surrounded with weapons of war and guarded behind walls and fences, but they are being bombed into submission by the war planes and technological might of a nuclear and cyber power, which has militarily occupied their ancestral homelands for more than 50 years.

With little to live for, and nothing to fear, Palestinian children have willingly charged the wire fences of Gaza, rolling burning tires, and daring to be shot down, or crippled, by Israeli snipers. In acts of fatal futility, these children offer up their lives and limbs in an ultimate submission to their Islamic faith in Allah, their God of Abraham.

The Way of Righteousness, the ancestral religion of the Ancient Land, is rooted—along with its progeny, Judaism, Christianity, and Islam—in the original covenant Abraham made with Melchizedek at Jerusalem, as Abraham sought entry into the Ancient Land of Canaan. As recorded in Genesis, Abraham pledged, to God, on behalf of his

---

[147] The expulsion and forced exile of half of the Palestinian population in the 1948 Palestinian War.

family, that they would peacefully live a life of righteousness, so long as they sojourned in the Land.

Thus, the question: "Is the present government of the State of Israel acting with righteousness toward the people it purports to govern, both the Children of Palestine, and the Children of Israel?"

The State of Israel

Although declared to be in existence, and a member of the United Nations, for more than 70 years, the "State" of Israel has yet to create a written constitution defining the rights of the people it purports to legitimately govern. Nor, has the State obtained the consent of the people to be subject to the laws it promulgates. For its basic law, the justice courts of the State continue to rely on the English common and martial law, inherited by the State from the British Army in 1948.

The Covenants of A Children's Constitution

The creation of a Children's Constitution would embody Abraham's essential Covenant of Peace and Righteousness in the Ancient Land, in a secular document enshrining these essential principles. The Covenant would include every person with a blood right to the Ancient Land, *and* every person, whose religious beliefs derive from the Covenant of Abraham.

The Children's Constitution would include all Israeli citizens (more than 40 percent of whom are not religious), and all the people of Palestine. The legality and power of the Children's Constitution would derive from the universal Rights of Liberty, possessed by every person, to live subject to a written constitution, whose power derives from a collective consent to be governed, which can be reserved, as a censure of unrepresentative government.

Irrespective of a person's religion, a Children's Constitution based on Abraham's Covenant, would protect all of the children in Palestine and Israel, and it would engender a peaceful society of freedom, law, and justice, where the universal Rights of Liberty of every person include the ability to peacefully practice a religion of choice, or not.

The manuscript of *The Way of Righteousness* was formatted, and 50 bound copies were printed. They were distributed at the end of August in a mailing that included the Secretary General of the United Nations, the President and Chief Rabbis of Israel, the Palestinian Authority, Pope Francis, the Dalai Lama, and the World Council of Churches, among others.

Choices for the Future

I wake up early most morning increasingly concerned about the growing intensity of immediate and deadly dangers revealed on the screens before me. I spend the day searching through our knowledge data base and thinking about what I learn, seeking always to identify simple and effective solutions to these difficult and complicated problems. This I will continue to do, as best I can, for as long as I am capable.

The overall goal in most of my writing, including *The Way of Righteousness*, is to derive relevant and practical policies and courses of action to resolve complicated and interrelated problems.

Alternative choices provide opportunities, which allow for more effective decisions, thus better ensuring the future of our children. Working together, we can make a difference in their tomorrows.

We must confront the reality of human extinction *within the lifetimes of babies born today*—resulting from the violent and destructive changes in our worldwide climate we are now witnessing—if we continue to abuse Earth's atmosphere and water by pumping out carbon dioxide and fouling our habitat with chemical garbage.

We are not alone in this universe, but, on this spinning sphere of dirt and water, fire and ice, this Garden of Earth we share, each of us must find our own path forward, every day, making the best use of our minds to make good, rather than bad decisions. Such *is* the way it is. Our choice: do we live or die?

SUMMATIONS

A TRUE STORY
ABOUT AN AMAZING FAMILY

About 2,000 years ago, a truly amazing family lived in Northern Israel. The country was ruled as a police state by the incestuous Herodian monarchy, at the sufferance of the Roman Empire, and its occupying army. The roads in the Galilee were lined with the crucified corpses of independence fighters, left to rot by the Romans, as stinking examples of the futility of resistance to the Empire.

Living with the daily terror, the family, as did most people at the time, followed the Way of the Osim, as simple "Doers of the Law." The followers of this uncomplicated expression of the Jewish religion peacefully lived lives of righteousness, throughout the Land and Diaspora.

The Osim built a refuge in the Judean wilderness at Qumran by the shore of the Dead Sea, where they sought solitude to study and reflect upon their books that promised not one, but three messiahs, a suffering Son of Man, a Davidic Leader, and a Priestly Messiah, all of whom would come to rescue the people from the evil monarchy and empire that ruled their lives.

Cleopas, the father of the Galilean family, was a Rechabite,[148] who traveled to find work as a carpenter, while the mother, Mary (Aramaic-Maryam, Hebrew-Miryam), delivered and raised five sons and a daughter. Her first born were twins, Yeshua (Greek-Jesus) and his brother, Judas (Thomas-Aramaic for twin). The twins became two of the three expected messiahs of the Osim, and the next of Mary's sons, Jacob (Greek-James), became the third messiah.

At their births, Mary and Cleopas dedicated the firstborn of her twins, Jesus, and the following two of their sons, James and Simeon,

---

[148] The Rechabites were a clan of the Kenites, who arrived from Egypt with the Moses priesthood and settled among the Israelites. The Kenites avoided alcohol, and engaged in highly skilled metal and wood working, traveling between towns and cities. The Rechabites followed Abraham's ancient Covenant of Righteousness.

as Nazirites.[149] The boys were raised to live, every day of their lives, from birth to death, as being "holy unto the Lord." At age 10, the brothers were consecrated to prepare for the alternative priesthood of the Osim, the Sons of Zadok.

The brothers came to live in isolation at Qumran, to seek wisdom in its libraries, self-awareness during solitary reflection, to identify their life mission, and to experience the vision of the path they would follow. After twenty years of study, first Jesus, then James, and then Simeon achieved intellectual maturity at age thirty, and were ordained as priests of the Sons of Zadok. They were prepared to teach the Way of Righteousness, and to spiritually lead the people, and their zealous Sons of Light, in both war and peace.

When the sun rose on their 30th birthday, each brother left the security of the refuge and walked the harsh 29-mile winding path up through the hills of the Judean wilderness, past the village of Bethany, to the guarded gates of Jerusalem. Each must have fully contemplated the immense cruelty that awaited him, and the risks of the journey that lay ahead.

All five of Mary's sons died violently[150], sacrificed by their parents on the altar of eternal peace, in fulfillment of their covenant of righteousness.[151]

The Osim and Their Way of Righteousness

The Osim simply abided by the basic law, according to the ancient covenant of Abraham to peacefully live out each moment of life in righteousness. These "Doers of the Law" had no respect for the oral law of the Pharisees, nor could they tolerate the corrupt practices of the Sadducean priesthood, both of whom collaborated

---

[149] Nazarites lived the lives they were consecrated to, for so long as they lived. Their time was dedicated to study and contemplation, as they abstained from alcohol, cutting their hair unnecessarily, oiling their bodies, getting married, or having children. (Numbers 6:8).

[150] There is a tradition that her youngest, Joseph, was beheaded or burned to death by the Romans on Cyprus; another plausible story is that he survived to old age in Edessa and wrote the Gospel of John.

[151] Acting in accord with divine or moral law, (Merriam-Webster).

with and spied for the Herodians, and their Roman masters in suppressing the people.

The Osim, and their Way of Righteousness, rebelled in words and deeds against the brutal occupation. The war for independence was fought by their Zealot warriors—the Sons of Light; it was spiritually led by their priests—the Sons of Zadok; and the wounded and widows were comforted by their lay ministers—the Order of Melchizedek.

As Jerusalem fell to the Roman army—and the children of the Way were being rounded up throughout the land to be sold into slavery in the Empire, or the most defiant were thrown to the wild animals in the amphitheater at Caesarea, by the Herodians and Romans in celebration of their victory—the Osim concealed their books in sealed jars within remote caves among the cliffs around Qumran.

Their archives included Cave Four, which was created by connecting the interiors of several adjacent caves located high up the face of a cliff across from the Refuge. The Osim enlarged and squared out the cave, behind the small entrances, which were accessible only by ropes and ladders. The large library provided shelf space to organize a thousand scrolls, and a peaceful place for boys and men to read, reflect, talk, imagine their futures, and to think about what each could and must do to contend with the evil power of empire.

The Zealot warriors of the Way continued to resist the Roman army, the mightiest in the world, even after Jerusalem and Qumran fell. The Zealots retreated to Herod's massive desert fortress on top of the mountain at Masada, further south in the desert wilderness along the Dead Sea. Herod had been besieged at Masada by the Zealots early in his rule—until he was rescued by the Roman army. He continued to expand his palaces at the fortress throughout his reign, but it was captured in a surprise attack by the Zealots during the war and they held it to the end.

After holding off the Roman army for four years, and as the gate was collapsing, the Sons of Light buried their last remaining books of the Way of Righteousness, drew lots, and died by their own swords, rather than by the weapons wielded by the ignorant hands of power and empire.

The Children of Mary

Jesus became the Suffering Son of Man Messiah expected by the Way of Righteousness. He cleansed the Temple, caused a riot, and he was arrested and summarily executed by the Romans. Jesus sacrificed his life to save his people from the cruelty, corruption, and power of the Herodians and Romans. In doing so, he liberated his spirit, so his words of righteousness would live on in the minds of all those who seek his truths.

Judas was not a Nazirite. Armed with a sword, Judas Thomas became the Osim's Davidic Messiah. He took the words of righteousness to the East, where the Way guided the Ebionite Christian kingdoms established there which existed for hundreds of years. The influence of Judas the Twin extended into areas of Syria, Saudi Arabia, Iraq, Iran, and finally India, where he was struck down by a spear and died with his sword in his hand. His Letter of Jude concludes the New Testament, just before Revelations, and his original Gospel of Thomas (revealed in the Gnostic Gospels) was later used in the fabrication of the Pauline Synoptic Gospels.

Subsequent Roman emperors felt threatened by the lineal descendants of Judas the Twin, whom they feared might create a unified Davidic Kingdom in the Middle East. For more than five centuries, Judas's teachings were recited and taught in these lands, until finding eloquent expression in Saudi Arabia by the last prophet of Allah, Muhammad, and his Islamic message of righteousness.

Mary's third son, and second Nazirite, was Jacob, or James, who became the Priestly Messiah of the Osim. Following the crucifixion of Jesus by the Romans, James the Just led The Way and the Zadok priesthood for 26 years in Jerusalem and Qumran. His essential teaching is contained in the New Testament Letter of James.

As a Righteous Teacher of the Way, and as a priest of the alternative Zadok priesthood, James the Just was elected by the people, and the Sons of Zadok, to represent them as their High Priest in the Temple. For this heresy, a Pharisaic mob led by the enigmatic Saul, threw James down the Temple steps breaking both of his legs. After recovering at Qumran, and returning to Jerusalem, James was finally stoned to death near the Mount Zion cornerstone of the

Temple, as the result of a conspiracy by the Herodians, Sadducees, and Pharisees, to whom James and the Way posed a threat to their power over the people.

Following the judicial execution of James, his younger brother—the third of Mary's Nazirite sons—Simeon bar Cleopas, a Rechabite priest of the Sons of Zadok, was elected leader of the Way. After the Romans leveled Jerusalem and were advancing to destroy the refuge at Qumran, the Osim concealed their books in caves, and Simeon led their escape across the Jordan River. Other Zealot Sons of Light remained behind to fight the Romans, and Simeon returned as their spiritual leader on the battlefield. He was ultimately captured and crucified by the Romans near Jerusalem.

The youngest of Mary's sons, Joseph, who is also known in the New Testament as Joses, or Barnabas (Hebrew–son of comfort), probably wrote the original Book of Matthew in Hebrew, before writing his Letter to the Hebrews in the Greek language. The mission of Joseph, as a lay minister of the Order of Melchizedek, was to teach the words of righteousness to the Gentiles, to whom the Order was open.

It is said that Joseph was either beheaded or burned to death by the Romans on the island of Cyprus. That may be true, but others believe Joseph escaped to Ephesus to write the Gospel of John, as a pseudonym, in his old age. John presents an review of the Roman Synoptic Gospels in an attempt to reconcile them with Mary Magdalene's Gnostic teaching of the Spirit of Wisdom in the West, and with the Way's Word of Righteousness at Qumran.

The only known daughter of Mary was named Salome. She was present at Jesus's crucifixion, helped recover his body, and, with others, she accompanied it back through the wilderness to Qumran. There, she helped wash and wrap Jesus's body for burial, as his grave was being dug nearby and rocks were gathered to cover it. Salome lived on to care for her parents in their old age, and to attend to their deaths.

The bodies of Jesus, James, Simeon and others of his family are likely buried there, somewhere, under piles of stones in the cemeteries of the Osim at Qumran, forgotten in the sun and rain for 2,000 years, until now.

Mary Magdalene, the Companion

Mary Magdalene, her sister Martha, and their brother Lazarus were followers of the Way. They lived in Bethany, near Jerusalem, east of the Mount of Olives, along the road coming up out of the wilderness from Jericho and Qumran. As Jesus rested overnight, on his way to cleanse the Temple and certain death, Mary Magdalene anointed him to be the Way's Suffering Son of Man Messiah. Mary was Jesus's favored companion in life, and she was the heir to his most spiritual teachings.

Mary Magdalene took the Way's Spirit of Wisdom to the West. She and her Gnostic followers taught the enlightened message of Jesus, and his Way of Righteousness, for hundreds of years, throughout Egypt, Syria, Asia Minor, Greece, and into France. Gnosticism remained the prevalent study of the teachings of Jesus until Emperor Constantine seized Roman power in the fourth century, and he designated the Roman Church of Paul (Saul) as the Empire's only lawful expression of Christianity.[152]

Mary is honored throughout the Gnostic Gospels as the one Jesus loved the most. How long she lived, how far she traveled, and how and where she died remain unknown. Some believe her remains may be buried somewhere in southern France.

Mary's Spirit of Wisdom[153] was freed, when the jars containing the Gnostic Gospels and the Dead Sea Scrolls were broken open at the end of World War II, and the written records of the distant past were revealed in our lifetime to be read and considered, once again, after 2,000 years of suppression.

---

[152] Thousands of Mary's Gnostics were burned at the stake during the Catholic Inquisitions, rather than to acknowledge Jesus as God, yet their spiritual belief in the true teachings of an historical Jesus lives on to this day in the minds of many, if not most Christians who accept the essence of his message of love, and his suffering for the salvation of the people from the cruelty of empire and war.

[153] Mary's Spirit of Wisdom survived the Catholic Crusades and the Catholic-Protestant Wars, until now—as religious and cultural wars rage on in the Middle East, and America's endless War Against Terror continues to kill babies, little children, and their mothers in the name of peace—the whisper of the Spirit of Wisdom can still be heard upon the winds of time, if only we listen.

The Revelation of the Books

As the libraries of the Gnostics were being seized and burned by the Pauline and Empire authorities, 52 books were sealed in a large jar buried at the base of a cliff in Egypt, near the Nile River. The books remained there, undisturbed, for 1,700 years, until 1945.

Within a year of the Gnostic Gospels being unburied in Egypt, the Dead Sea Scrolls were discovered in 1946, also preserved in jars, in a cave at Qumran, a few hundred miles to the east. Less than 20 years later, other books of the Way were recovered from under the floor of the assembly chamber at Masada. The books had been buried there by the last of the Zealot Sons of Light in 73 CE.

These courageous cultural and spiritual warriors of the Way defended their families, their books, and their Rights of Liberty to live their own lives in simple peace and righteousness. Their resistance was crushed by the cruel and ignorant power of empire—which has continued to compete for world domination for 2,000 years. Until now, when the righteousness of the lives these spiritual warriors truly lived as they fought for peace, were revealed by the books they read and wrote. The bravery of these Children of Light can inspire us to once again confront the evil of empire, the stupid wars they fight, and the children they kill.

With their minds at ease, and with the Roman army battering against the great gate Herod had built at Masada, the zealous Sons of Light did not fear final judgment. They were at one with themselves, and with others of the Way, with whom they had lived, fought, and died for the right to peacefully live simple lives of righteousness.

Nor, did the warriors of the Way fear the pain of the deaths of their bodies, or worry where their corpses might be thrown to rot. For them, the spirits of their minds would be set free over these thousands of years, to survive death in the minds of all those who remembered them and their lives of righteousness.

The miraculous discovery of hidden books reveals who these extraordinary people were, the meaning of their lives, and the truth about what they lived and died for. Today, we can draw upon the power of their wisdom and courage to help us confront the environmental, economic, political, military, and intolerance crises of our time and to avoid our extinction.

A SUMMARY PETITION TO THE UNITED NATIONS

On behalf of the Children of Palestine and Israel, this Summary Petition seeks the just remedy of a written constitution for the Children of the Ancient Lands of Palestine and Israel. It is proffered for consideration, resolution, and vote by the General Assembly.

Should the United Nations conduct a written plebiscite throughout Palestine and Israel, asking everyone over the age of 18, if they consent to the Covenant of a Constitution for the Children, empowered by their Universal Rights of Liberty, and based on the legal principles of Peace and Righteousness? Yes, or No?

Should the United Nations plebiscite include a separate and simultaneous vote by the same people, first, collectively for the Children's Constitution to serve as the Supreme Law of the Ancient Land, and then separately:

- Israelis to vote, yes or no, for the calling of a national convention of the People of Israel, to establish a written constitution for the State of Israel, with its capital in West Jerusalem. The Israeli constitution should acknowledge perpetual peace with the State of Palestine—within its pre-1967 boundaries—and the subordination of the Israeli constitution to the Children's Constitution, which ensures the rights of all Palestinians, who legally reside within the State of Israel to pass, live, work, and worship in peace.

- Palestinians to vote, yes or no, for the calling of a national convention of the People of Palestine, to establish a written constitution for the State of Palestine, with its capital in East Jerusalem. The Palestinian constitution should acknowledge perpetual peace with the State of Israel, and its subordination to the Children's Constitution, which ensures the rights of all Israelis who legally reside within the State of Palestine to pass, live, work, and worship in peace.

THE NATURE OF AN ABIDING MIND

Pausing here to gather our thoughts, we can try to make sense of the abundance of evidence presented thus far in this examination. The printed book of *The Way of Righteousness: A Revealing History and Reconciliation of Judaism, Christianity, and Islam* now numbers more than 495 pages and weighs several pounds.

For those who might want to read something less heavy, about how and why *The Way* was written, a Collection of the Prologue, the Epilogue, and the Summations was published in *The Gift of Mind Series* as *Mind: Before & After The Way of Righteousness*.

After all this, what questions remain to be asked? What words are best said in summation? What will be the verdict?

Are we prepared to postulate a theory—one to be assumed, yet vigorously and rigorously examined. Is mind something valid we can trust in and build upon, as an intellectual tool to aid us in our eternal search for truth?

What is the reality of our own minds, and our collective community of human minds? Beyond that, what are the probabilities of a greater, eternally observing, universal consciousness, an abiding mind?

Mind

Mind exists independent of our physical reality, and it is invisible to the means by which we measure mass and light. Mind observes the fragile wave form of matter and light we are a physical part of, but mind is forever beyond our technical ability to detect and measure.

Mind is, however, a demonstrable factor of physical reality, for without mind, there is no reality of existence. Without minds, we would not appreciate the garden within which we live, *and* these written words would not exist. We would not exist, and there would be none of you to read these words.

An Abiding Mind

There is an Abiding Mind, which has existed for all of Eternity—ever since Mind was first born of Intelligence, as a natural process of Life. Everything that that has ever lived, evolved from Mass—itself having been physically transmuted from Energy in a natural quantum blip, manifested as this brilliant Universe of Light, we call home.

An Abiding Mind equates with eternity, existing in the negative nothingness that encompasses every positive particle we perceive, and that has ever existed.

It is only with the magnification and illumination provided by the imaginations and creations of our unified mind, that we can escape the limits of this small spherical mass of earth and water, whose garden we live in and whose air we breathe. Focused together, our minds can see what lies beyond the brilliant rainbow spectrum of our Universe of Light.

We can see its beginning and we can witness its end; we can experience every moment in between, and we can always find our way home.[154]

Becoming aware, we can transcend the physical bounds of our spatial reality, and it is *then* when we can experience the peaceful, loving, and motherly presence of an Abiding Mind. We can learn to listen to the inner voice of Her Spirit of Wisdom, as she, Herself, patiently listens to every one of us, all the time, as we talk to ourselves, within our minds.

We must become fluent in Her one-word language of Truth, forgo the Art of the Lie, and to trust in the wisdom of the words, heard, always as a voice of reason—our conscience and our conscious being—if we are to ever access the limitless archives of an Abiding Mind.

The Moment of Mind

At the instant mind reaches out from within an infant's brain—in its singular quantum moment of mind—it is received within

---

[154] Much like a fish responding from the ocean to the exact stream of water where its egg was hatched.

and swaddled by an Abiding Mind, much like the orbiting negative electrons surround and shield the positive nuclei of our atoms, or as the protective arms of a mother instinctively wrap around her children, defending them at all costs against danger. The child's mind is quantumly enveloped by and entangled with an Abiding Mind, never to be separated, and shared forever with the mind of its mother.

Mind is born in an instant, as the emerging child listens for the reassuring voice it has been hearing in the darkness of the womb, and it instinctively seeks to suckle at its mother's breast. Knowing only its mother's voice and how to cry, it is soothed by her voice, and sheltered by her arms. Nourished and comforted, the mind of the infant reaches out for the light it sees for the first time, *and it instinctively* seeks to touch and examine it.[155]

It is *then* that the Spirit of Wisdom, the soothing voice of an Abiding Mind, becomes at one with emerging embryonic minds, in an instinctive search for the truth of the questions every child asks itself, and others. A child's mind, programmed for truth, begins to learn other languages, some of which are infected with the malware of the Art of the Lie.

The Death of Life, and The Evolution of Mind

When our life brain dies, from lack of blood and oxygen, its mind—with all its memories, creations, truths, and basic lessons learned—exists on as eternal truths, as every singular mind remains quantumly entangled with an Abiding Mind from birth, forward from its moment in life, mind, and time.

More than that, the lingering spiritual presence, of the essence

---

[155] It is, only, when a mother delivers her child into the hands, protection, and laws of others, that she is physically separated from her baby. Before that, a baby necessarily remains a part of its mother's body, over which she (and no one else) must have absolute control, including the power to make decisions about the conception and birthing of her babies. It is her life—her business, and nobody else's. When all women achieve effective control over the destiny of their own bodies, the population problem will be largely solved. Only children we're capable of protecting and caring for will be conceived and birthed.

of our physical being and our minds—our very souls—lives on in the minds and memories of those who survive us in life. We continue to exist, so long as that we have created and contributed in life, is valued and is worth remembering.

The evolution of the instinctual intelligence of our twin brains at birth, into the union of our twin minds, one talking, and the other listening, as they and we respond to the common problems of our life. Since we share the consequences of our actions, we share the essential need to consider effective alternatives in making wise decisions.

This internal conversation takes place within the minds of all of us, consciously and subconsciously, *all the time, from birth to death*. There is myself, and there is my conscience—the two of us who are destined to spend every moment of our lives together. We exist within the comfort, joy, and love we share with others, and we must live with the consequences of what we say and do, along the way of life.

History, Truth, and Lies

Although history books do not always reveal the truth, print and electronic books are our collective attempt to accurately preserve the memories and times of our lives, as a durable, physical record of the reality of our existence. There are nuggets of truth to be mined from the written archives of the past, and from the electronic news of the present, once we identify and cull the lies.

The truth is always the truth, and it is easy to remember. Lies remain lies forever—whether concealed, denied, or ignored—they are hard to keep straight. One word, Truth, seeks peace and justice; the other word, Lie, results in hatred, violence, and war. Lies and deception are not included in the language of truth; nor are they noted in the journals of the Abiding Mind.

War is an Evil Word, Best Forgotten

War is a truly evil word, describing the cowardly use of other people, and remote weapons, to kill other people, including children, while those who direct the killing, are bravely shielded from injury. War is a word best forgotten.

Perhaps, in the future history of our collective time of mind, the concept of war, in which people were once forced to kill for the benefit of their own selfish representatives, and to die for the stupid mistakes of their own corrupt leaders, appears only as a footnote—a vestige of the latent human brainstem disease of intolerance and its manifestations of deception, hatred, and violence, cured by the truth and power of toleration.

History may record that one day, the people reserved their consent to be governed, as a censure of their existing unrepresentative government, and they took matters into their own hands. They voted in 2020 for a constitutional Voters' Bill of Rights, and, together, they changed the course of human history.

Self-Awareness

The fruit of mind is self-awareness, a reconciliation between the two facets of our minds, resolving to tell the truth to ourselves when we think about how to deal with everyday life, family, jobs, and emotions. We become increasingly self-aware when making better decisions, as we perceive the reality of our physical existence. We achieve the breadth of mind to use our knowledge, honestly, in seeking answers to questions beyond our present ability to ask. What is yet to be seen, is much more magnificent than that which cannot yet be imagined.

There is a magical moment when our minds come to accept the rigors of truth, first within ourselves, and then as a much more effective language with which to communicate with others, in comprehending our place and destiny in space, time, and eternity.

An Unavoidable Warning of Grave Danger

The most important message for us to communicate to one another is the reality of threatened mass extinction. Every creature on Earth, including we humans who created the problems, face grave and deadly environmental and economic dangers. Right now!

These threats are immediate and life threatening. Yet, they are denied by those who purport to govern in the name of the People:

> Our representatives, who are helpless to effectively govern with truth, dignity, or honor, burdened as they are by conceit, corruption and deception, *and* made more weary every day by their deadly misuse of the political, cyber, military, and police powers entrusted to them by the People.

The universal Rights of Liberty allow the People to reserve their consent as a censure, whenever their government becomes unrepresentative and abuses its discretion, and IT endangers US, who created IT to serve US.

This is the question we, each of us, must ask ourselves, here and now. Do we wish to survive and live, or to perish and die? That's the deal. There are no third choices, and it is *now* we must decide.

We're all in this together. Either we all live, or else we all die. There will be no brave remnant to start all over again—irrespective of hidden gold and guns—for there will be no garden left to plunder, nor ammunition to buy. Books will serve as fuel for fire, until language and knowledge are lost, and nothing but the futile grunts of the last human is heard, among the final few trees.

A Strategy For Survival

We either abandon war, forthwith, and redirect all of that mighty expression of intelligence, energy, technology, and vital human and precious material resources—presently being entirely and criminally wasted on weapons of war—in a positive and peaceful way, to solve the deadly environmental and economic dangers now threatening all of humanity.[156]

---

[156] Modern mechanized and technological war has been fought around the world for more than 100 years, killing more than 100 million people. The weapons of this cowardly form of remote war was redirected in World War II to intentionally kill the children and families of adversaries—to destroy their will to wage war. How many more will suffer and die this century, as the corporate machinery of war continues to profit from destroying the lives of people far removed from the cowards, who bravely make stupid decisions, press some buttons, and blow up babies and small children?

There are things that can and must be done; steps can be taken, and productive jobs can be done, starting today. *We must significantly retard atmospheric warming within the next five years, or else, we cannot expect to foresee tomorrows much past midcentury.*[157]

If these matters are not resolved by the 2020 presidential election in the United States, four more years of nothing will be far too little, far too late.

Creating Happy Tomorrows

One measure of our success in life, individually and collectively, is the ability to imagine how tomorrow should be, and to take effective action today to make tomorrow happen as planned. An inability to shape the future is a failure, in that it requires one to constantly respond, rather than to initiate.

It is here and now that we will unite, to learn, work, prosper, and create together to solve the immediate problems that are threatening the survival of humanity. Or, we foolishly deny the truth and continue fighting stupid wars. In doing so, we will surely consign our own grandchildren to burn in a fiery hell of our own making—whether by the stupidity of our perpetual wars, or by our failure to clean up the environmental, economic, and political messes we've created.

The Delicate Balance

The reality of a blistering hot Earth, with billions or people dying of thirst and starvation in this century is much more likely than

---

[157] Within five years, the US Interstate Highway System could be retrofitted to deliver free inductive electrical energy—enough to move people and their cars anywhere on the system, with safety and comfort. The entire system can be fully energized by an orbiting Space Solar System that delivers continuous microwave energy to remote collectors. Simultaneously, all coal-burning power plants can be replaced by small, safe nuclear generators, fueled by leftover uranium fuel rods from the obsolete water-cooled reactors and decommissioned nuclear weapons. The resulting reduction of atmospheric particulates can be mediated by aerosol sprays dispersed below all passenger jets, providing a computerized, cooling shield against solar radiation. All this in less time than it took us to walk on the Moon, once we set our mind to it.

a news flash that an asteroid—the size of which hasn't been seen in six million years—will inevitably collide with Earth on February 19, 2070.

Given such a reality, what choice would we have but to tend to our garden, raise our children in peace and justice, and give them their chance to soar among the stars. Time is precious, and the clock is ticking.

The difference of just a couple of degrees of temperature provide the delicate balance in the atmosphere and oceans of our fragile Mother Earth, between extreme heat or extreme cold. The Arctic Ice has moderated the temperature, through regular cycles, over millions of years, but the Arctic Ice is now melting, rather than expanding. At this point in the climatic cycle, things should be getting slowly colder over thousands of years leading into a new Ice Age. Any reversal in this trend is catastrophic.

These slight few degrees of heat, one way or another, will determine whether our grandchildren have a chance to evolve, and to tour the lights of our universe as a graduation celebration someday, or they will all die, and we will become extinct.

What Will Become of the Moments of Our Minds?

Even if our fossilized bones are the only thing left of us—amidst the forgotten ruins of our creations and the wreckage we have wrought—the memories and product of everyone who lived and worked here and now—the individual moments of each singular mind, will continue to flow in the eternal tides of an Abiding Mind.

If we fail to make a wise peace, and if we continue to fight stupid wars, only the most embryonic forms of life will survive the fires that will be fueled by our failures. It could take hundreds of millions of years, for the soils, waters, and atmosphere of our Mother Earth to once again have the balance of health and energy to sustain life, to grow intelligence, and to sprout minds that instinctively reach out for the stars, just as babies seek their mother's breasts.

By nature, we are social, and we seek like-minded people to share joy, love, respect, and protection within our families and societies, as we each go about earning our living, and living our own singular way of life, in concert with all who surround us.

It is this wisdom of our collective human community of minds, that is the intellectual reservoir of our strength as a People, and it is the source of our Rights of Liberty and their expression of power.

We, who live and think, have the duty, will, and self-confidence to decide for ourselves, what the future of our grandchildren should and will be like, and we want to live long enough to see it for ourselves.[158]

---

[158] Even with everything I've studied, said, and done, the ultimate truth remains a mystery to me. Like all of us, I will only know for certain, once my brain dies, my physical presence ends, and the existence of the mind it has wrought—the writer of these words—will live on, so long as there are those who read them.

THE ORIGIN AND POWER OF MIND:
TO IMAGINE THE UNKNOWABLE AND TO ACHIEVE THE IMPOSSIBLE

The nature, extent, and influences of mind was a recurring question in the 15 books I have researched and published over the past 40 years, culminating with *The Way of Righteousness* and *The Gift of Mind*. There is the spiritual mind of knowledge—the Universal Consciousness worshipped by the Gnostics, Sufis, and Kabbalist—and there is the scientific effect of mind, as *observer of the waveform*, now proven by the probabilities of quantum physics.

Mind is the natural flowering of the spontaneous, chaotic, physical mechanics and accelerating expansion of the moving positive particles that compose the matter of our universe. It all started about 13.8 billion years ago with the random discharge of a massive, brilliant photonic bubble of pure light—that instantly burst, scattering bits of light into the darkness. These elementary particles were energized with positive momentum, as the school of related particles begin to spin, swirl, and stretch outward in every direction, flowing through the fathomless pool of negatively charged fluidity, each leaving electro-magnetic traces of its passage.

Shielded from anti-particle annihilation and inflated by swarms of negative electrons, the infinite multitude of infinitesimal bits of positive matter—born of the pure light—coalesced into a continuum of related positive particles. Collectively, these particles are our colorfully sparkling and pulsating universe, as it stretches, expands, and consolidates into a spherical-torus waveform. The positive matter is attracted by the unfathomable negativity, as its particles are simultaneously repulsed along with the bubbles of negatively charged swarms of electrons that orbit and shield the positive nucleus of every atom, starting with hydrogen, with one proton and one electron.

Our energized universe of light has naturally generated the essential elements of matter, water, organic life, intelligence, and finally its flower: we who seek the truth. We, who have the power to make our own miracles by imagining a joyful future, and the will to do what must be done to convert the power of our imagination into the wisdom of reality, instead of fantasies of what never was and never will be.

We perceive and measure our universe, and comprehend our physical existence, with the computational tools created by our intelligent and educated brains reaching out beyond the bony skulls encasing their hemispheres. *Our minds exist so far and so long as their creations and actions are experienced, words and deeds are remembered, stories are retold, memories are recollected, and the words of truth endure.*

What if, in fact, the supreme value and measure of human existence *is* the intellectual harvest of our homegrown minds, and our unique and magnificent creations? Without any external assistance, we now illuminate the nighttime skies and communicate through satellites circling around the globe, *We are not alone, but we must remain isolated under observation, as any external interference would collapse the waveform of our existence.* Our independent minds are essentially organic, growing out of the very earth we walk upon, its produce we eat, its water we drink, and its air we breathe.

We will either evolve our minds, quickly, or everything we have imagined and built during these 25,000 years of collective human endeavor will continue to collapse around us, and we will all die together—*within the lifetimes of babies being born today.*

Should we fail to thrive, Earth will continue to orbit about the warm yellow Sun, as it wobbles through the seasons and the solstices of the passing years. The tides of the Moon will eventually wash away our mess, its silvery reflections illuminating the nights of the month, until someday, surely, self-aware minds will once again mature beyond clever intelligence. *Then*, if they—on their own—learn to speak and practice the language of truth, empowering them to overcome their instinctive brainstem intolerances, *and* to avoid deception, hatred, and violence, *and* if they provide equal opportunities for all their children; *then*, and only then, will the common mind evolve to imagine and generate the (presently unknowable) power required to carry on the eternal search of mind for other Gardens of Earth to watch over and nurture.

Surely, we have been visited over the millennia, as our green earth and blue water planet has floated and swirled around through the cosmic ether, and our fears, secrets, and ambitions have been heard, with compassion and without judgment. The encouragement, love, and comfort experienced within our minds during prayer or meditation—from whatever source, whether a Holy Spirit, Motherly Words of Wisdom, or our own conscience—helps us to make better decisions to confront the challenges of life and to survive its rigors. The internal voice of truth we all hear within our mind is our true best friend forever, one from whom we can never escape, even with the decomposition of death. Then, at long last, with quantum transformation and liberation of our minds, the work and pain of life comes to an end, and we are freed from the shackles of gravity and time.

What if we, and all we will ever be, or want to become—our every thought, deepest secret, and most fervent desire, all of our discoveries and unique creations—are eternally, quantumly entangled with An Abiding Mind, the observer and recorder of truth, the accumulation of all awareness and creation over the eternal ages? From the moment of our birth and the cutting of our umbilical cord, as we breath in and open our eyes, our twin mind expands outward from our twin brain. We instinctively move toward the familiar voice and nurturing breast of our mother, and we reach out with our fingers to encompass within our comprehension, the light that surrounds her. The brain of a healthy infant naturally evolves an inquisitive mind, which becomes quantumly entangled with its own brain to answer its questions and to secure its survival. Our aware mind serves as the determiner of truth and the arbitrator of our decisions and actions throughout our physical lives, and beyond. We are our mind, and all it envelopes, irrespective of the physical host reflected in a mirror or perceived by others.

What if our individual mind, the very soul of our being, will in fact continue to eternally exist within the negative space, even following the decomposition of our physical body and brain in the positive space? Every particle of our bodies, and every related bit of the continuum of our universe of light, expands, pulsates, and flows, making tunnels and leaving electro-magnetic waves through the enveloping fluidity. Eternally alone and chaotically swirling in the froth of its wake, our universe and everything within, including ourselves, is increasingly accelerating toward the inevitable decomposition of the energetic momentum of our universal waveform. Its positive charge will ultimately dissipate and ripple away into nothing, far distant in the dark regions of nowhere, the strings of its electromagnetic moments timelessly and simultaneously connected.

Our minds will continue to exist and to thrive wherever generated, eternally entangled with all those with whom our lives and minds were shared. Our minds soar above, around, and beyond the physical paths we are destined to walk on our journey through life in our Garden of Earth, as we spiral together through the cosmos.

Liberated from life, we can witness with wonder, not only the birth, life, and death of our own spectacular universal lightshow, but observe other universes that survive inflation, along with their natural progeny of life and unique minds—for all of eternity. *Within the infinite field of mind, time is meaningless; however, its transformation must be imagined from the outside, rather than observed from the inside of our universe.*[159]

We live in our pleasant Garden of Earth, with all that is good, beautiful, and joyful, confined as we are, however, within the shell of a physical universe we can never hope to mathematically pierce—so long as we measure and calculate it from within, *and* we continue to solve our problems by telling lies and killing babies. By cooperating and collaborating, we can ascertain the essential truths required to successfully confront, contain, and resolve the serial collapse that threatens our near-term extinction. This is your only choice: you can continue to wallow in hatred and lies, or you can stand up, anoint yourself with the healing balm of truth, liberty, and tolerance, and engage the power of your mind to imagine the unknowable, and to achieve the impossible.

Once upon a time, the mainspring of life was wound to its maximum capacity in the clock of human existence, powering an

---

[159] A scaffolding can be imagined to mathematically rationalize the cosmic nothingness encompassing our ever-expanding universe, built by the cubing of energy and the acceleration of mass to the speed of light at its fourth power. Can Einstein's field equations and hyperbolic geometry be refined (perhaps through the mathematics of fluid and vortex dynamics), connecting the inside of our universe with the outside?

exact number of ticks and tocks. Time is short, but all is not lost—*we can learn to rewind the clock*. Our children need the time to strengthen and spread their wings, as they spin away from our earthly nest, traveling timelessly throughout the cosmos, seeking other gardens of life, the sounds of happy children playing, and the melodies of mind.

Sources and Attributions

In order to smooth the narrative flow of *The Way*, with its thousands of facts and hundreds of names, I eliminated internal source footnotes in favor of a comprehensive table of contents and the following list of chapter sources.

This book is derived from a much longer research manuscript I prepared following the publication of the Dead Sea Scrolls 30 years ago. That manuscript was primarily for my own interest, and I was not always as careful to identify and preserve my sources as I should have been. Unfortunately, with the fog of time and old age, it is not always clear to me now when I was summarizing other works and when I was writing back then.

I have been as careful as possible in completing this manuscript to ensure all its writing is original and that I have properly identified and acknowledged my sources. All authors are morally and legally entitled to be identified as the creator of their own work, and if I have failed to properly attribute any material, I will quickly apologize and correct future editions upon being advised of any neglect or failure on my part.

Several of the books and authors listed below are identified as being "significant sources." What this means is that virtually every paragraph in those chapters could carry a footnote to the referenced significant source, with a repeating *"ibid."* These works are what we call in law, *sine qua non* (without which nothing), in that those chapters would be sadly deficient without that significant contribution. Inasmuch as *The Way of Righteousness* offers only a brief overview of the information contained in these books, the interested reader would do well to consult the original work to obtain a greater depth of knowledge. It is particularly to these "significant" authors, especially Elaine Pagels and Robert Eisenman, that I offer my greatest thanks and profound admiration for their work.

Over the years I have read hundreds of books on the subjects discussed in *The Way*, borrowing many of them from my local public libraries, and some I purchased, and which remain on my bookshelves.

The Way of Righteousness

Not all these books made a direct contribution to *The Way*, and they are not listed below; however, they made me think and, for that, I am grateful to these anonymous authors for their efforts.

I am not only greatly indebted to my local public libraries, but also to the bookstores, whose aisles I have happily wandered over the years searching for something new and interesting. These brick and mortar stores are disappearing, as books are now only a computer keystroke away from being delivered to my front door. This is both magical and regrettable. The Internet also provides the ability to quickly and easily access far more information and knowledge than could ever be contained in a single library or bookstore—or a thousand.

The Way is almost entirely based on published primary and secondary sources; however, it could not have been completed without the hundreds of instances when I would look from this screen to an adjoining one for a quick verification of a date or fact, the spelling of a name, or to search for a needed definition or elusive synonym. Wikipedia and the multiple search engines that drive and satisfy my curiosity are a powerful and magical resource.

Then, there are my two great mentors—who did not live long enough to read this manuscript and to offer their always invaluable insights. Joseph White, lawyer and social worker, and David Levinson, journalist and newspaper editor, always challenged me and made me think, and I was often encouraged by their voices of reason in my mind, as I charted *The Way* and struggled with my writing.

Two of my current mentors are retired educators. Mel Lindsey, whose support and encouragement allowed *The Way* to be completed, has read all my books. As has William Younglove, who, with a masters in English and a doctorate in Education, not only chose to spend years in the classrooms, grading essays, but he became an internationally respected Holocaust Specialist. All of this makes Bill a copy editor extraordinaire, and by kindly noting various errors that might lower the grade, the manuscript was greatly improved by the hours he spent as its first critical reader.

Were it not for my strong son, Steven (who lost almost everything in the wildfire that swept through Paradise, California in November

2018),[160] this book could not have been completed. He created the photo essay and all the graphics and maps. No man has ever been so proud of his son, and as we walked the ruins and climbed steep paths in the scorching sun, searching for the right images, we became brothers in the eternal search for truth.

As always, there's my wife, Helen's love, without which, none of this would be possible—nor near as much fun.

Origin of the Way of Righteousness

Palaestine-Israel: The Land Bridge Between Africa & Asia

Abulafia, David, *The Great Sea: A Human History of the Mediterranean*, (Oxford University Press, 2013).

Broodbank, Cyprian, *The Making of the Middle Sea: A History of the Mediterranean from the Beginning to the Emergence of the Classical World*, (Oxford University Press, 2013).

Finkelstein, Israel & Silberman, Neil Asher, *The Bible Unearthed: Archaeology's New Vision of Ancient Israel and the Origin of Its Sacred Texts*, (Free Press, 2001).

Horowitz, Aaron, *The Jordan Rift Valley*, (CRC Press, 2001).

Ryan, William & Pitman, Walter, *Noah's Flood: The New Scientific Discoveries About the Event That Changed History*, (Simon & Shuster, 1998).

Watzman, Haim, *A Crack in the Earth*, (Argo-Navis, 2012).

---

[160] Including the classic, end-of-the-line, low-mileage 1972 Volvo 1800E sports car he bought from me several years ago—so we could charge our electric Volt in the garage. "Jezebel" was consumed by the Paradise fire, but Steve saved "Jade," the 1966 1800S, that he had just completely restored. Steve had time to load up and escape with only one 1800. He chose Jade. Jezebel may have been worth more, but she was better insured.

The People of the Land and Those Who Passed Through

Armstrong, Karen, *The Bible: A Biography*, (Grove Press, 2007).

Arsuaga, Juan Luis & Martinez, Ignacio, *The Chosen Species: The Long March of Human Evolution*, (Blackwell Publishing, 2006).

Bright, John, *A History of Israel*, (Westminster Press, Third Ed., 1981).

Ceram, C.W., *Gods, Graves & Scholars: The Story of Archeology*, (First Vintage Books, 1986).

Cline, Eric H., *1177 B.C.: The Year Civilization Collapsed (Turning Point in Ancient History)*, (Princeton University Press, 2014).

Finkelstein & Silberman, *op. cit.*

Finkelstein, Israel & Silberman, Neil Asher, *David and Solomon: In Search of the Bible's Sacred Kings and the Roots of the Western Tradition*, (Free Press, 2006).

Friedman, Richard Elliott, *Who Wrote the Bible?* (Harper & Row, 1989).

Friedman, Richard Elliott, *The Hidden Book in the Bible*, (HarperSanFrancisco, 1998).

Johanson, Donald & Edgar, Blake; Brill, David L. (photography), *From Lucy to Language*, (Simon and Schuster, 2006).

Johnson, Paul, *A History of the Jews*, (Harper & Row, 1987).

Klein, Mina C. & Klein, H. Arthur, *Israel, Land of the Jews*, (Bobbs-Merrill, 1972).

Magnusson, Magnus, *Archaeology of the Bible*, (Simon and Schuster, 1977).

Moorey, Roger, *Excavation in Palestine: Cities of the Biblical World*, (Wm. B. Eerdmans Publishing, 1981).

Morgan, Elaine, *The Aquatic Ape Hypothesis*, (Souvenir Press, 2017).

Pangborn, Cyrus R., *Zoroastrianism: A Beleaguered Faith*, (Stosius, 1983).

Rosenberg, David & Bloom, Harold, *The Book of J*, (Grove Weidenfeld, 1990).

Sand, Shlomo, *The Invention of the Jewish People*, (Verso, 2009).

Satlow, Michael L., *How the Bible Became Holy*, (Yale University Press, 2014).

Shanks, Hershel, Ed., *Understanding the Dead Sea Scrolls*, (Biblical Archaeology Society, 2012), Chapter 13, pages 170-172, *When the Sons of God Cavorted with the Daughters of Man* by Hendel, Ronald S.

The Books of the People

Armstrong, *op. cit.*

Miller, Stephen M. & Huber, Robert V., *The Bible: A History*, (Good Books, 2004).

Satlow, *op. cit.*

Sheler, Jeffery L., *Is the Bible True?: How Modern Debates and Discoveries Affirm the Essence of the Scriptures*, (Harper San Francisco, 1999).

Silberman, Neil Asher, *The Hidden Scrolls: Christianity, Judaism, and the War for the Dead Sea Scrolls*, (Grosset/Putnam, 1994).

THE BEGINNING OF THE WAY OF RIGHTEOUSNESS

The Hasideans and Zaddiks

Charlesworth, James H., Ed. *The Old Testament Pseudepigrapha, Volume 1, (3 &4 Maccabees)*, (Doubleday, 1983).

Eisenman, Robert, *Maccabees, Zadokites, Christians and Qumran*, (E. J. Brill, 1983).

Josephus, Flavius, Ed. Whiston, William, *The Complete Works of Josephus—Antiquities of the Jews*, (Kregel Publications, 1981).

Kung, Hans, *Judaism: Between Yesterday and Tomorrow (The Religious Situation of Our Time*, (Crossroad, 1992).

Schonfield, Hugh J., *Secrets of the Dead Sea Scrolls: Studies Toward Their Solution*, (Perpetua, 1960).

Pfeiffer, Robert H., *History of New Testament Times*, (Harper & Row, 1949)—a significant source.

THE MACCABEAN REVOLUTION FREES THE PEOPLE FROM THE SYRIANS

Charlesworth, *op. cit.*

Josephus, *op. cit.*

The Priest Kings of the Hasmonean Dynasty

Shanks, Hershel, Ed. *Understanding the Dead Sea Scrolls*, (Random House, 1991), Chapter Two, pages 28-31, *The Historical Context of The Scrolls*, Cross, Frank Moore.

The Osim: Followers of The Way of Righteousness

Allegro, John, *The Dead Sea Scrolls: A Reappraisal*, (Penguin, 1956)

Burrows, Millar, *The Dead Sea Scrolls*, (Viking, 1955).

Campbell, Jonathan G., *Dead Seas Scrolls: The Complete Story*, (Ulysses Press, 1998).

Hanson, Kenneth, *Dead Sea Scrolls: The Untold Story*, (Council Oak Books, 1997).

Pfeifer, Charles F., *The Dead Sea Scrolls and the Bible*, (Baker Book House Co., 1996).

Rose, Jenny, *Zoroastrianism: An Introduction*, (I.B. Tauris, 2011).

Shanks, Hershel, *The Mystery and Meaning of the Dead Sea Scrolls*, (Random House, 1998).

Silberman, Neil Asher, *The Hidden Scrolls: Christianity, Judaism, and the War for the Dead Sea Scrolls*, (Grosset/Putnam, 1994).

Trever, John C., *The Untold Story of Qumran*, (Fleming H. Revell Co., 1965).

VanderKam, James C., *The Dead Sea Scrolls Today*, (William B. Eerdmans, 1994)

Vermes, Giza, *The Complete Dead Sea Scrolls in English*, (Penguin, 1977).

Wise, Michael, Abegg, Martin, Jr., & Cook, Edward, *Dead Sea Scrolls: A New Translation*, (HarperSanFrancisco, 1996).

Wilson, Edmund, *Israel and the Dead Sea Scrolls,* (Farrar Straus Giroux, 1978).

Herod Becomes King and Marries Hasmonean Princesses

Josephus, *op. cit.*

The Way Flees into Jordan and Makes a New Covenant with God

Sanders, J.A., *The Dead Sea Psalms Scroll*, (Cornell University Press, 1967).

Schonfield, Hugh J., *The Passover Plot*, (Bernard Geis Associates, 1965).

Vermes, Giza, *op. cit.*

What You Need to Know About Gnosis and Sophia (Wisdom)

Freke, Timothy & Gandy, Peter, *Jesus and the Lost Goddess: The Secret Teachings of the Original Christians*, (Harmony Books, 2001).

The Bloody Legacy of Herod, Who Murdered His Wives and Children

Josephus, *op. cit.*

The Way Becomes the Spiritual Leader of the Zealots

Eisenman, Robert, *op. cit.*

Josephus, *op. cit.*

PERFECTING THE WAY

Setting the Stage for Jesus

Schonfield, Hugh J., *op. cit.*—a significant source.

Jesus and His Nazarite Family

Carrier, Richard, *On the Historicity of Jesus*, (Sheffield Phoenix, 2014).

Ehrman, Bart D., *How Jesus Became God: The Exaltation of a Jewish Preacher from Galilee*, (HarperOne, 2014).

Fitzgerald, David, *Nailed: Ten Christian Myths That Show Jesus Never Existed at All*, (Lulu, 2010).

The Education and Maturity of Jesus

Charlesworth, James H., Ed., *Jesus and the Dead Sea Scrolls: The Controversy Resolved*, (Doubleday, 1992).

Seigmeister, Walter, *Apollonius the Nazarene: The Life and Teachings of the Unknown World Teacher of the First Century*, (Biosophical Publishing, 1947).

Vermes, Giza *op. cit.*

Just Who on Earth Did Jesus Think He Was?

Aslan, Reza, *Zealot: The Life and Times of Jesus of Nazareth*, (Random House, 2013).

Werner, Ernest, *Rod of Jesse: On the Jesus of the Gospels & Doubt of his Existence,* (Dwarf Lion, 2008).

John the Baptist Followed the Way

Josephus, *op. cit.*

Schonfield, Hugh J., *op. cit.*

Vermes, Giza *op. cit.*

SEARCHING FOR THE TRUTH IN THE NEW TESTAMENT

Carrier, Richard, *op cit.*

Ehrman, Bart D., *op cit.*

Fitzgerald, David, *op cit.*

Freke, Timothy & Gandy, Peter, *op. cit.*

Miller, Robert J., Ed., *The Complete Gospels*, (Polebridge Press, 1994).

The Gospel of Jesus

Eisenman, Robert & Wise, Michael, *The Dead Sea Scrolls Uncovered*, (Element, 1992).

Mitchell, Stephen, *The Gospel According to Jesus,* (HarperCollins, 1991).

Robinson, James M. Ed., *The Nag Hammadi Library*, (Harper & Row, 1977), The *Gospel of Thomas*, as translated by Stephen J. Patterson and James M. Robinson, and *The Book of Thomas the Contender*, a dialogue between Jesus and his brother Judas Thomas, as translated by John D. Turner.

The Crucifixion and Resurrection of Jesus

Peters, Edward, *Inquisition*, (University of California Press, 1989).

Robinson, James M. Ed., *op. cit., The Treatise on the Resurrection,* introduced and translated by Malcolm L. Peel.

Vermes, Giza, *op. cit.*

Ehrman, Bart D., *op. cit.*

THE REMNANT OF THE WAY OF RIGHTEOUSNESS

Jesus's Brother, James the Just, Was the Priestly Messiah

Boyarin, Daniel, *The Jewish Gospels: The Story of the Jewish Christ*, (The New Press, 2012).

Butz, Jeffrey J., *The Brother of Jesus and the Lost Teachings of Christianity* (Inner Traditions 2005).

Eisenman, Robert, *James the Just in The Habakkuk Pesher* (E. J. Brill, 1986).

Eisenman, Robert, *James the Brother of Jesus: The Key to Unlocking the Secrets of Early Christianity and the Dead Sea Scrolls*, (Viking, 1996)—a significant source.

Eisenman, Robert & Wise, Michael, *op. cit.*

Ehrman, Bart D., *op. cit.*

Painter, John, *Just James: The Brother of Jesus in History and Tradition* (University of South Carolina Press, 1997).

Pike, Diane Kennedy Pike & Kennedy, R. Scott, *The Wilderness Revolt: A New View of the Life and Death of Jesus Based on Ideas and Notes of the Late Bishop James A. Pike*, (Doubleday, 1972).

Pfeiffer, Robert H., *History of New Testament Times*, (Harper & Brothers, 1949).

Robinson, James M. Ed., *op. cit.*

Schonfield, Hugh J., *Those Incredible Christians*, (Bernard Geis, 1968).

Shanks, Hershel & Witherington III, Ben, *The Brother of Jesus: The Dramatic Story and Significance of the First Archaeological Link to Jesus and His Family*, (HarperSanFrancisco, 2003).

Vermes, Giza, *op. cit.*

THE PARTING OF THE WAY

The Gnostic Way of Mary Magdalene

Baigent, Michael; Leigh, Richard; & Lincoln, Henry, *Holy Blood, Holy Grail* (Dell, 1982).

Burstein, Dan & De Keijzer, Arne J., *Secrets of Mary Magdalene: The Untold Story of History's Most Misunderstood Woman*, (CDS, 2006).

Carroll, Michael P., *The Cult of the Virgin Mary: Psychological Origins*, (Princeton University Press, 1992).

Carse, James P., *The Gospel of the Beloved Disciple*, (HarperSanFrancisco, 1997).

Chilton, Bruce, *Mary Magdalene: A Biography*, (Doubleday, 2005).

Churton, Tobias, *The Gnostics*, (Barnes & Noble, 1987)

Haskins, Susan, *Mary Magdalen: Myth and Metaphor* (Harcourt, 1994).

King, Karen L., *The Gospel of Mary of Magdala: Jesus and the First Woman Apostle*, (Polebridge Press, 2003).

Klimkeit, Hans Joachim, *Gnosis on the Silk Road*, (HarperSanFrancisco, 1993).

Meyer, Marvin, with de Boer, Esther A., *The Gospels of Mary: The Secret Tradition of Mary Magdalene, the Companion of Jesus*, (HarperCollins, 2004).

Pagels, Elaine, *The Gnostic Gospels*, (Vintage, 1979)—a significant source.

Robinson, James M., Ed. *op. cit.*—a significant source.

Stone, Merlin, *When God was a Woman*, (Barnes & Noble, 1976).

Paul, the Pharisee, Goes Off the Path and Creates His Own Religion

Armstrong, Karen, *Holy War: The Crusades and Their Impact on Today's World*, (Anchor Books, 2001).

Aslan, Reza, *Beyond Fundamentalism: Confronting Religious Extremism in the Age of Globalization*, (Random House, 2010).

Asbridge, Thomas, *The Crusades: The War for the Holy Land*, (Simon & Schuster, 2012).

Bamber, Christina & Bamber, *The Christians*, (Morrow, 1977)—a significant source.

Boring, M. Eugene, *Mark: A Commentary*, (Presbyterian Publishing, 2006).

Burman, Edward, *The Inquisition: The Hammer of Heresy* (Sutton Publishers, 2004).

Cameron, Euan, *The European Reformation* (Oxford University Press, 2012).

Carroll, Michael P., *The Cult of the Virgin Mary: Psychological Origins*, (Princeton University Press, 1986).

Donahue, John R., *The Gospel of Mark*, (Liturgical Press, 2005).

Doner, Colonel V., *Neo-Fundamentalists and the Polarization of America*, (Samizdat Creative, 2012).

Eisenman, Robert, *The New Testament Code: Gospels, Apostles, and the Dead Sea Scrolls*, (Konecky & Konecky, 2014).

Griffith-Jones, Robin, *The Gospel According to Paul: The Creative Genius Who Brought Jesus to the World*, (HarperSanFrancisco, 2004).

Hooker, Morna D., *Paul: A Short Introduction*, (One World, 2003).

Grant, Robert M., *A Historical Introduction to the New Testament*, (Harper & Row, 1963).

Gunther, John J., *Paul: Messenger and Exile*, (Judson Press, 1972).

Jowett, George F., *The Drama of the Lost Disciples*, (Covenant Publishing, 2009).

Kung, Hans, *Judaism: Between Yesterday and Tomorrow (The Religious Situation of our time)*, (Crossroad, 1992).

Lietzmann, Hans, *A History of the Early Church* (Volume III & IV), (World Publishing, 1964).

MacCulloch, Diarmaid, *The Reformation: A History*, (Penguin Books, 2005).

Marsden, George M., *Fundamentalism and American Culture*, (Oxford University Press, 2006).

Pheiffer, Robert H., *op. cit.*—a significant source.

Haskins, Susan, *Mary Magdalen: Myth and Metaphor*, (Harcourt, 1994).

Pagels, Elaine, *Adam, Eve, and the Serpent*, (Vintage Books, 1988).

Peters, Edward, *Inquisition*, (University of California Press, 1989).

Ragg, Lonsdale & Laura, *The Gospel of Barnabas*, (Oxford at the Clarendon Press, 1907).

Tyerman, Christopher, *God's War: A New History of the Crusades*, (Belknap Press, 2006).

The Way of Rabbinic Judaism

Bamberger, Bernard J., *The Story of Judaism*, (Schocken, 1964).

Berg, Rav P. S., *The Essential Zohar: The Source of Kabbalistic Wisdom*, (Bell Tower, 2002).

Dosick, Rabbi Wayne, *Living Judaism: The Complete Guide to Jewish Belief, Tradition, and Practice*, (Harper, 1995).

Franck, Adolphe, *The Kabbalah: The Religious Philosophy of the Hebrews*, (Bell Publishing, 1940)

Johnson, Paul, *A History of the Jews*, (Harper Perennial, 1988).

Himmelfarb, Milton, *Jews and Gentiles*, (Encounter Books, 2007).

Kaplan, Mordecai M. (2010) *Judaism as a Civilization: Toward a Reconstruction of American-Jewish Life* (https://books.google.com/books?id=mtGFZbJut0gC) Philadelphia, PA; Jewish Publication Society. pp. i-viii. ISBN 978-0-8276-1050-7. Retrieved February 3, 2019.

Kung, *op. cit.*

Kushner, Harold, *To Life! A Celebration of Jewish Being and Thinking*, (Little, Brown & Company, 1993).

Levenson, Jon D., *The Love of God: Divine Gift, Human Gratitude, and Mutual Faithfulness in Judaism*, (Princeton University Press, 2016).

Maher, Michael, *Judaism: An Introduction to the Beliefs and Practices of the Jews*, (The Columbia Press, 2006).

Neusner, Jacob, *The Oral Torah: The Sacred Books of Judaism*, (Harper & Row, 1986).

Rosner, Fred, Translator, *Moses Maimonides' Commentary on the Mishnah, Introduction to Seder Zeraim and Commentary on Tractate Berachoth*, (Feldheim, 1975).

Scholem, Gershom, *Origins of the Kabbalah*, (The Jewish Publication Society, 1987).

Sources and Attributions

THE RIGHTEOUS WAY OF ISLAM

Judas Thomas Was the Messenger of the Way to the East

Brown, L. W., *The Indian Christians of St. Thomas: An Account of the Ancient Syrian Church of Malabar*, (Cambridge, 1956).

Eisenman, Robert, *The New Testament Code, op. cit.*

Hennecke, Edgar & Schneemeicher, Wilhelm, Ed. *New Testament Apocrypha Two Volume Set*, (The Westminster Press, 1964).

Pagels, Elaine, *Beyond Belief: The Secret Gospel of Thomas*, (Vintage Books, 2003).

Pagels, Elaine & King, Karen L., *Reading Judas: The Gospel of Judas and the Shaping of Christianity*, (Penguin Group, 2007).

Pines, Shlomo, *The Jewish Christians of the early centuries of Christianity according to a new source (Proceedings of the Israel Academy of Sciences and Humanities; v.2, no.13*, (Israel Academy of Sciences and Humanities, 1966).

Robinson, James M., *The Secrets of Judas: The Story of the Misunderstood Disciple and His Lost Gospel*, (HarperSanFrancisco, 2007).

Stoneman, Richard, *Palmyra and its Empire: Zenobia's Revolt Against Rome*, (University of Michigan Press, 1995).

The Land, People, and Religion of Seventh Century Arabia

Armstrong, Karen, *Muhammad: A Biography of the Prophet*, (HarperOne, 1993)—a significant source.

Aslan, Reza, *No god but God: The Origins, Evolution, and Future of Islam*, (Random House, 2005).

Hazleton, Lesley, *The First Muslim: The Story of Muhammad*, (Riverhead Books, 2013).

Küng, Hans, *Islam: Past, Present & Future*, (One World, 2007).

Raudvere, Catharina, *Islam: An Introduction*, (I. B. Tauris, 2015).

Mohammad, the Reluctant Messenger of God

Aslan, Reza, *op. cit.*

Armstrong, Karen, *op. cit.*—a significant source.

Daywood, N. J., Translator & Radice, Betty, Ed., *The Koran*, (Penguin Books, 1974).

Hazleton, Lesley, *op. cit.*

Lings, Martin, *Muhammad: His Life Based on the Earliest Sources*, (Inner Traditions, 1983).

Mohammad, the Righteous Reformer

Aslan, Reza, *op. cit.*

Armstrong, Karen, *op. cit.*—a significant source.

Hazleton, Lesley, *op. cit.*

Küng, Hans, *op. cit.*

Muhammad's Death and His Succession

Aslan, Reza, *op. cit.*—a significant source.

Armstrong, Karen, *op. cit.*

Raudvere, Catharina, *op. cit.*

Islamic Mysticism, The Mahdi, Sufism, and the Druze

Aslan, Reza, *op. cit.*

Bentounes, Sheikh Khaled, *Sufism: The Heart of Islam*, (Hohm Press, 2002).

Betts, Robert Brenton, *The Druze*, (Yale University Press, 1988).

Chittick, William C., *Sufism: A Short Introduction*, (Oneworld, 2000).

Haeri, Shaykh Fadhlalla, *The Thoughtful Guide to Sufism*, (O Books, 2004).

Michon, Jean-Louis & Gaetani, Roger, Editors, *Sufism: Love & Wisdom*, (World Wisdom, 2006).

Raudvere, Catharina, *op. cit.*

Schwartz, Stephen, *The Other Islam: Sufism and the Road to Global Harmony*, (Doubleday, 2008).

Islam, Today and Tomorrow

Ali, Ayaan Hirsi, *Heretic: Why Islam Needs a Reformation Now*, (HarperCollins, 2015).

Aslan, Reza, op. cit.—a significant source

Burke, Jason, *Al-Qaeda: The True Story of Radical Islam*, (I.B. Tauris, 2003).

Harris, Sam & Nawaz, Maajid, *Islam and the Future of Tolerance: A Dialogue*, (Harvard University Press, 2015).

Mabon, Simon & Royle, Stephen, *The Origins of ISIS*, (I.B. Tauris, 2017).

McCants, William, *The ISIS Apocalypse: The History, Strategy, and Doomsday Vision of the Isdlamic State*, (St. Martin's Press, 2015).

Raudvere, Catharina, *op. cit.*

Stakelbeck, Erick, *ISIS Exposed: Beheadings, Slavery, and the Hellish Reality of Radical Islam*, (Regnery Publishing, 2015).

WILLIAM JOHN COX

For more than 45 years, William John Cox has written extensively on law, politics, philosophy, and the human condition. During this time, he has vigorously pursued a career in law enforcement, public policy, and the law.

As a young police officer, Cox wrote the Role of the Police in America as a part of the "New Breed" movement to define and professionalize law enforcement. As an attorney, he worked for the U.S. Department of Justice to implement national criminal justice standards and goals, prosecuted cases for the Los Angeles County District Attorney's Office, and operated a public interest law practice primarily dedicated to the defense of young people.

Cox volunteered *pro bono* services in several landmark legal cases. In 1979, he filed a class-action lawsuit on behalf of all citizens directly in the U.S. Supreme Court alleging that the government no longer represented the voters who elected it.

In 1981, representing a Jewish survivor of Auschwitz, Cox investigated and successfully sued a group of radical right-wing organizations that denied the Holocaust. He later represented a secret client and arranged the publication of almost 1,800 photographs of ancient Dead Sea Scrolls that had been suppressed for more than 40 years.

Cox concluded his legal career in 2007 as a Supervising Trial Counsel for the State Bar of California, where he prosecuted unethical lawyers and criminal gangs engaged in the illegal practice of law.

Continuing to contemplate public policy, political, and philosophical matters since his retirement, Cox has been writing books and creating Internet websites. His digital autobiography is at WilliamJohnCox.com.

Sunrise over Jerusalem
The Mount of Olives
June 2019
WJC

Made in the USA
Monee, IL
05 December 2021